ERIC WILLIAMS

& the Making of the Modern Caribbean

COLIN A. PALMER

The University of North Carolina Press ♦ Chapel Hill

WILLIAMS

& the Making of the Modern Caribbean

Publication of this book was assisted by a grant from
Princeton University.

Designed by Eric M. Brooks
Set in Quadraat & Othello by Keystone Typesetting, Inc.
Manufactured in the United States of America

The paper in this book meets the guidelines
for permanence and durability of the Committee
on Production Guidelines for Book Longevity
of the Council on Library Resources.

Library of Congress Cataloging-in-Publication Data
Palmer, Colin A., 1942–
Eric Williams and the making of the modern Caribbean /
Colin A. Palmer.
     p. cm.
Includes bibliographical references and index.
ISBN-10: 0-8078-2987-0 (cloth: alk. paper)
1. Williams, Eric Eustace, 1911– 2. Trinidad and
Tobago—Politics and government—20th century.
3. West Indies, British—Politics and government—
20th century. I. Title.
F2122.W5P35   2006
972.98304'092—dc22   2005022334

10 09 08 07 06   5 4 3 2 1

To the

ERIC WILLIAMS

MEMORIAL COLLECTION

and the

PEOPLES OF

TRINIDAD AND TOBAGO

CONTENTS

ILLUSTRATIONS

ACKNOWLEDGMENTS

♦ ♦ ♦ ♦ ♦ My scholarly interest in Eric Williams began in 1994, when the University of North Carolina Press invited me to write a new introduction to *Capitalism and Slavery* on the occasion of its republication. In subsequent years I conducted research in the Public Record Office in London, the Eric Williams Memorial Collection (EWMC) in St. Augustine, Trinidad, and the National Archives in College Park, Maryland. Erica Williams Connel must be commended for establishing the EWMC and for working indefatigably to make it a model for similar archival collections in the Caribbean. It is a national treasure. I owe a special debt of gratitude to the staff of these fine archives, especially Dr. Glenroy Taitt, Kathleen Helenese-Paul, and Sylvie Pollard of the EWMC and Walter Hill of the National Archives. During my frequent visits to these collections I enjoyed the hospitality of various individuals and wish to thank them all, especially Keith Benjamin in London.

The Research Foundation of the City University of New York and Princeton University provided very generous financial assistance for the research and writing of the manuscript. I tender my sincere thanks to these fine academic institutions.

I also appreciate the invaluable help I received in preparing the manuscript from a number of other persons. Jean Washington had the unenviable task of typing the first draft of the manuscript and deciphering my handwriting, doing so with commendable ingenuity. Naela El-Hinnawy typed subsequent drafts with considerable speed, efficiency, and good humor. Gen Gillespie, Azaria Mbughuni, and Allison Palmer provided technical assistance at important moments in the manuscript's evolution.

A number of colleagues and friends read the manuscript, including Bridget Brereton, Selwyn Carrington, Sean Greene, Franklin Knight, Robert Tignor, and Maurice St. Pierre. In addition, the class of 2003–4 of The Scholars in Residence Program at the Schomburg Center for Research in Black Culture, as well as Miriam Jimenez Morán, then assistant director of the program, read two chapters of the manuscript. I thank all of these selfless individuals for their careful reading of my work, their valuable criticisms, and their identification of the errors that it contained. Needless to say, I am entirely responsible for the final product. The manuscript also profited from the comments of the two scholars who read it for the University of North Carolina Press, and I thank them for their role in making this a better book.

ERIC WILLIAMS

& the Making of the Modern Caribbean

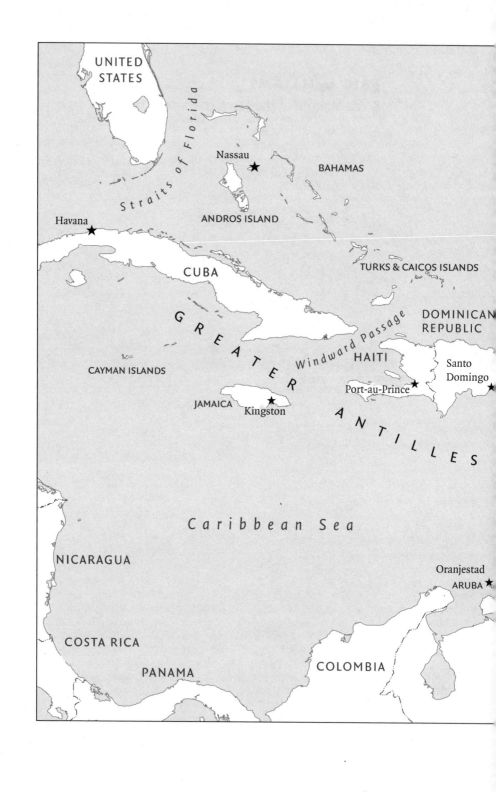

Atlantic

Ocean

L E E W A R D   I S L A N D S

Canal de la Mona

San Juan ★

VIRGIN ISLANDS

ANGUILLA

BARBUDA

PUERTO
RICO

SAINT KITTS-NEVIS

ANTIGUA
★ St. Johns

MONTSERRAT

GUADELOUPE

Basse-Terre ★

L E S S E R   A N T I L L E S

DOMINICA

Roseau ★

Fort-de-France ★ MARTINIQUE

W I N D W A R D   I S L A N D S

Castries ★ SAINT LUCIA

SAINT VINCENT
Kingstown ★

BARBADOS
★ Bridgetown

CURAÇAO
★ BONAIRE
Willemstad

St. George's ★ GRENADA

Caracas
★

Port of Spain
★ TRINIDAD & TOBAGO

VENEZUELA

INTRODUCTION

♦ ♦ ♦ ♦ ♦ "The circumstances of my birth were quite unremarkable," Eric Eustace Williams wrote in the unpublished version of his memoir. "They," asserted Williams, "in no way differed from those of other West Indian children of the lower middle class." The year was 1911, the month was September. Delivered with the assistance of a midwife, Eric was the first child of his parents. His birth was not reported immediately because it "coincided with a smallpox epidemic and stern government measures to enforce vaccination." Since he was "supposed to be quite ill" when he was born, Williams surmised that "no doubt there was a desire to spare me the pain of vaccination until it was absolutely necessary." Consequently, his birth was not registered until October 12, eighteen days after he was delivered.[1]

The child of economically challenged parents, Williams was born in a small house on Oxford Street in Port of Spain, Trinidad. He recalled that the house "reminds one of a square wooden box placed right on the street pavement." His father—thirty-three years old at Williams's birth—was "a strong, silent man, reserved except in the company of close friends, somewhat inclined to asceticism." He was "a son of his class, partial to a good Sunday table and the usual delicacies at Christmas and other festive seasons." His mother, ten years younger than his father, "was much lighter in color than he was." She had a French name, "of which both she and my father were quite proud."[2]

Williams's father, by dint of his class background, received only a primary school education. He entered the civil service as a junior clerk at age seventeen. As Williams would later observe, "My father was a superior soul, a superior soul was he, cut out to play a superior role in the god damn bourgeoisie." But "the only difficulties were that the bourgeoisie wouldn't allow him . . . because he lacked social qualifications. The necessary social qualifications in Trinidad were colour, money and education, in that order of importance. My father lacked all three."[3]

Trapped in a low-paying job with a family that increased in size every two years, his economic situation was precarious. As Williams expressed it, "The family followed the basic West Indian pattern, a growing disproportion between population and resources, between birth rate and purchasing power." He thought that his father's "reputation for independence of outlook and speaking his own mind" was a disadvantage in dealing with his white superiors and impeded his chances for promotion. His father "found himself passed over in favour of men who were younger, more pliant, more malleable." The inevitable consequence of his economic plight was "the increasing load of debt and judgment summonses, which afforded the authorities the excuse they needed for bypassing my father." In the twenty years before Williams left Trinidad for England, his family had changed houses "no fewer than eight times."[4]

Having won a scholarship at age eleven, young Eric entered Queens Royal College, in Port of Spain, "an imposing structure" designed "to produce coloured Englishmen in the West Indies."[5] A disciplined and outstanding student, he eventually won the prestigious Island Scholarship in 1931. Over his father's objections, he eschewed medicine in favor of reading for a degree in history at Oxford University.

The Trinidad and Tobago into which Eric Williams was born was a colonial society par excellence. The two islands, of some 1,980 square miles, had a population of about three hundred thousand. A majority of the residents were of African descent, their ancestors having been brought there as slaves. Indians, who were imported as indentured servants after slavery ended, constituted a smaller but growing minority. Individuals of European descent—the English, the French, the Spanish, and the Portuguese—made up a third group. Because of their racial ancestry, the latter exercised economic, social, and political power disproportionate to their numbers. As in other West Indian communities, whites occupied the pinnacle of the racial hierarchy, setting social standards and behaving as if it was their divine right to rule the islands to serve their own interests. This society made no pretense about being egalitarian. It was never based on the consent of the governed, and its survival depended on various coercive mechanisms. The Habitual Idlers Ordinance, for example, allowed the authorities to require those who could not prove they had a job to work on private estates.[6]

Eric Williams's childhood coincided with the development of a nascent black working-class consciousness in Trinidad and Tobago. In 1914 Marcus Garvey founded the Universal Negro Improvement Association (UNIA) in Jamaica, promoting an aggressive black nationalism. Embracing a "race first" ideology, the UNIA had an impact on the racial consciousness of Trinidadians as it did elsewhere in the diaspora. Soldiers who served in the British West Indies Regiment during World War I returned home full of complaints about racial mistreatment and unwilling to accept the status quo. Although their demand for the same compensation as their English counterparts was rejected, it was an indication of changing times. More ominous were the strikes—particularly by dockworkers—that occurred in 1919 and 1920. These were clear signs of a working-class consciousness that threatened the colonial elite.

Young Eric would have been aware of these stirrings by the working class, even if he did not yet understand their significance. An avid reader, he would have seen reports of the strikes in the newspapers his father purchased or more frequently obtained from friends and neighbors. His godfather was T. Albert Marryshow, a noted Grenadian politician and one of the acknowledged fathers of the West Indies Federation. It may be surmised that the boy would have listened intently to Marryshow's discussion of the issues of the moment when he came to visit. He recalled that "T. A. as he was affectionately called by my father" was "addicted" to "high flown phrases and literary allusions."[7]

The beginnings of a working-class consciousness were accompanied by new demands for constitutional reform, articulated primarily by the middle class. Not only were West Indians aware of the principles of national self-determination that helped to animate World War I, but a growing middle class and the presence of a group of intellectuals ensured that demands for representative government would acquire some urgency. As a student at Queens Royal College, Williams must have followed the debates on constitutional reform in the press. But clearly, he spent his formative years in a colonial society where the subordinate groups were beginning to imagine a new definition of themselves, portending a different future.

During the years 1931–48 Williams lived outside of Trinidad and Tobago. Between 1931 and 1938 he completed his undergraduate and postgraduate studies at Oxford, and between 1939 and 1948 he served on the faculty of Howard University in Washington, D.C. After 1942 he also was employed by

Eric Williams on receiving the bachelor's degree at Oxford University, 1935. Photograph courtesy of Eric Williams Memorial Collection, University of the West Indies (Trinidad and Tobago). © Eric Williams Memorial Collection and used by permission.

the Anglo-American Caribbean Commission and its successor, the Caribbean Commission, both created to develop and implement economic and social programs in the Caribbean. In 1948 Williams became deputy chairman of the Caribbean Commission, a position he held until 1955. Although the job involved a good deal of travel, Trinidad was his base.

The years spanning the thirties and fifties were significant ones in the social and political life of the Caribbean. Beginning in 1934, some territories, including Puerto Rico, St. Vincent, St. Kitts, and British Honduras, experienced labor unrest as employees demanded improvements in their working conditions. Led by Grenadian-born Tubal Uriah Butler, Trinidad's oil field workers struck in 1937, an act that became the catalyst for other strikes and serious industrial disputes. Jamaican dockworkers and workers in the sugar industry, led by Alexander Bustamante, walked off their jobs the following year. In the wake of these disturbances, labor unions and political parties emerged throughout the region.

In response to the social unrest, rising nationalism, and political demands, colonial authorities modified the Crown colony system and introduced universal adult suffrage in the 1940s. Recognizing that colonialism was being assaulted everywhere, the United Kingdom began to prepare the larger territories for internal self-government. In addition, in 1947 it sponsored a conference in Montego Bay to explore the potential creation of a West Indies Federation.

Eric Williams's entry into politics was hardly a surprising development after his ties with the Caribbean Commission were severed in June 1955. In the previous year he had begun to give a series of lectures at the Trinidad Public Library in Port of Spain to educate the people about their history and to promote a sense of West Indian nationalism. He continued his lectures in 1955 on a range of subjects—among them, "The Educational Problems of the Caribbean in Historical Perspective," "The British West Indian Federation," "Lands, Peoples, Problems," "John Locke," and "The Democratic Tradition in Western Civilization and Its Relevance for the West Indies."[8] The scholar dazzled his listeners with the depth of his learning and his oratory, while simultaneously building up a reservoir of respect and goodwill, particularly among African Trinidadians.

Williams did not restrict his scholarly expositions to the literati who flocked to hear him at the public library. To reach a larger audience, he renamed Woodford Square in Port of Spain the University of Woodford Square, creating a large open-air lecture room for the "students" who came in the thousands to hear him speak. Explaining the rationale for the "university," Williams stated: "Somebody once said that all that was needed for a university was a book and the branch of a tree; someone else went further and said that a university should be a university in overalls. With a bandstand, a microphone, a large audience and slacks and hot shirts, a topical subject for discussion, the open air and a beautiful tropical night, we have all the essentials of a university."[9] This was an extraordinary experiment in public education. Williams's mission was to create a citizenry that was well informed about its history, conversant with topical matters, and politically conscious. He never avoided complex issues but spoke from the perspective of a West Indian nationalist who was seeking to destroy all vestiges of colonialism. Under his tutelage, the citizens of Trinidad and Tobago became, arguably, the most politically sophisticated in the Anglophone Caribbean.

Recognizing that Trinidad and Tobago was not then blessed with an abundance of leadership talent, Williams saw his opportunity and took it. On January 15, 1956, he and his supporters formally established the People's National Movement (PNM) in preparation for the general elections scheduled for later that year. The party's leaders were primarily middle-class professional men. Most of them were African Trinidadians, although there was a sprinkling of Indo-Trinidadians, chiefly Muslims and Christians. The Hindus, suspicious of black leadership, generally stood apart until they eventually found a home in the Democratic Labour Party (DLP), which later became the principal opposition to the PNM.

The PNM was Trinidad and Tobago's first modern political party. Modeled somewhat after Norman Manley's People's National Party in Jamaica, it was highly structured. At the base was the party group, which could consist of as few as twenty members. The constituency group, comprised of two representatives from each party group, coordinated all of the party's activities at that level. At the apex of the structure was the General Council, composed of a variety of party elected officials. The PNM's leader was chosen every five years at an islandwide convention.

Although the founders of the PNM employed a stridently nationalist rhetoric, the party was reformist in its animating ideology. It adopted a firm anticolonial stance, supported a Federation of the West Indies, a reorganization of the territory's economy with special emphasis on the development of agriculture, and industrialization. Its vision was that of a harmonious multiracial society. Eschewing socialism, the party also avoided any formal association with trade unions, unlike the British Labour Party and the People's National Party in Jamaica. Running on this platform, and led by Eric Williams, the PNM candidates won thirteen of twenty-five seats in the general election held on September 24, 1956. Coming less than a year after the PNM's formation, this was a remarkable achievement. The governor of Trinidad and Tobago, Edward B. Beetham, invited Williams to form a government the following day, and he was sworn in as chief minister on October 26 after some constitutional issues had been resolved.

For the next twenty-five years Eric Williams dominated the PNM and the political life of Trinidad and Tobago. His control of the party was almost absolute, but he commanded the loyalty and adulation of thousands of people. On the other hand, Williams displayed an incapacity to deal with dissent in the PNM, removing those who had fallen out of favor without a backward glance.[10] His relationships with other Caribbean leaders were frequently rocky, but none doubted his considerable intellectual gifts. In 1961 the U.S. consul general, Edwin Moline, described Williams's role and standing in his party:

> He is the subject of adoration in photos, articles, letters, studding the pages of The Nation. He is a member of every important committee in the upper reaches of the party, and no one wants to make a decision without direct or indirect evidence of his approval. The rank and file look to him for education, inspiration, and authority. He formed the party, led it to un-expected victory in its first political effort, and speaks for it in government and in international affairs. More effectively than any other single member he articulates its tactics and strategy, its practical objectives and its philos-ophy. As a professional historian he gives the members an understanding of their origins and a view of their future. He is their Leader and he can tell them almost anything he wants them to hear. He can scold, exalt, lead marches, burn documents, turn himself around 180 degrees. In the view of the rank and file there is almost only one thing even Williams cannot do: he cannot do wrong. There is no one in the party with this mystique, charisma, or image. Without him, the party would break into a number of pieces; Williams knows it, the lesser lights know it.[11]

An indefatigable worker, Williams brought much energy and passion to contemporary issues, sometimes arrogating too much responsibility to him-self. In 1970, for example, he would head four ministries in addition to serving as prime minister. Sir Stephen Luke, the British official who led the committee responsible for handling matters relating to the inauguration of the West Indies Federation scheduled for 1958, observed in January 1957 that Williams had "extraordinary personal qualities." His energy "is inex-haustible; he is one of the most remarkable public speakers I have ever heard; he is, of course, exceptionally intelligent." Luke "clearly perceived why the PNM is a movement and not a party, why so many people feel, since the [1956] general election, some sense of national revival." He had de-tected "none of the weaknesses and prejudices" for which Williams "has been criticized."[12]

Williams's critics accused him of harboring dictatorial tendencies, but he was, for the most part, committed to democratic principles. Reviewing Williams's early months as chief minister, Stephen Luke observed that his "special concern is to keep the Governor, his Ministers, the Legislative Council and his party and the public generally fully in the picture. In his dealings with me, he has been consistently courteous, accessible, ready to accept advice, willing to consider suggestions, and anxious for help."[13] This favorable assessment of the young chief minister was not shared by the opposition and by colonial officials as the years wore on. Williams, British high commissioner Richard C. C. Hunt reported in 1970, was fortified "in the belief that he is indispensable, his answer to difficulties is to try to do even more himself and immure himself in his office behind a mounting pile of files, creating the material for a new and updated history of Trinidad and Tobago."[14]

Williams was an ardent foe of colonialism, a political stance that drove his historical scholarship and political behavior. Maintaining that colonialism was the source of the Caribbean's problems, he used all the rhetorical power at his command to assault its historical, contemporary, and systemic expressions. Convinced that the islands were individually too small and impoverished to transform their condition and to play significant international roles, Williams was an articulate and persistent advocate of their political federation and economic integration. His vision of a political and economic union of the region was sufficiently elastic to include some of the non-English–speaking territories. None of this could be accomplished, however, without the willingness of the other territories to abandon their endemic insularity for a collective good.

♦ ♦ ♦ ♦ ♦ This study is not intended to be a full-scale biography of Eric Williams. It does have biographical attributes, however, since I address crucial moments in Williams's life up to 1970, when the February Revolution threatened his continuation in office and marked a watershed in his political career. At another level, this work is a political history because it examines Williams's role in shaping the political development of the Anglophone Caribbean between 1956, when he became the chief minister of Trinidad and Tobago, and 1970, when he fell on difficult times. Williams was at the center of most of the conflicts, struggles, and challenges that defined the Anglophone Caribbean during those fourteen years. Finally, the book is also conceived as an intellectual history. More than any other British West Indian politician of his times, Williams was committed to the life of the mind and the world of books. A prolific scholar, he wrote seven books, edited an eighth, and coedited a ninth. His most distinguished work, *Capitalism and Slavery* (1944), helped to shape and redefine the historiography of the Caribbean. Williams's intellectual positions were not divorced from the real world of politics. In fact, the ideas he espoused in *Capitalism and Slavery* and in his other works informed his practice of the art of politics, not always with satisfactory consequences.

This work, I should emphasize, is not a history of Trinidad and Tobago between the years 1956 and 1970, narrowly conceived. Selwyn Ryan has already written an admirable book on aspects of those years.[15] I am primarily interested in elucidating Williams's activities on the larger Caribbean stage and the dialectical relationship between the domestic imperatives in Trinidad and Tobago and Williams's positions vis-à-vis the region as a whole. Chapter 8, "The Economics and Politics of Race," may be somewhat of an exception, but Williams was so proud of the racial diversity of his nation that its internal dynamics command attention. The developing racial cancer in Trinidad in the 1950s and 1960s, however, had threatening implications for the body politic in Jamaica and British Guiana (later Guyana), among other countries. Chapter 8 is not so much a history of the 1970 racially inspired revolt against Williams as it is an examination of the seeds of the crisis and Williams's management of it.

In writing this book, I made the decision to avoid interviews with Williams's contemporaries. He remains such a dominant, haunting, and polarizing presence in the life of Trinidad and Tobago that my search for the proverbial "truth" would have been made much more difficult by highly partisan accounts of his career. Consequently, I relied almost entirely on archival sources and on the voices of the major political actors of the period. Because Williams is, and was, a controversial figure, I tried to document my conclusions as carefully as I could, perhaps overburdening the reader with lengthy quotations. But this needed to be done since, in many respects, this is a pioneering work. I had few road maps to follow.

The book begins with an analysis of Williams's ideas on colonialism. Chapter 1 sets the context for understanding Williams's positions and actions regarding the West Indies Federation (Chapter 2), the Chaguaramas dispute (Chapter 3), and the imbroglio with the United Kingdom over the "golden handshake"—that is, the parting gift on the occasion of the nation's independence (Chapter 4). The fourth chapter also discusses Eric Williams the human being and enters the partisan debate on the ingredients of his personality, an intriguing issue that a scholar could hardly avoid. I decided to discuss Eric Williams the man in the middle of the book, rather than earlier, so as not to prejudice the readers' perceptions of and responses to him. It is my hope that by Chapter 4 readers will have been exposed to enough information about Williams to form an independent judgment of his personality and how it may have shaped his worldview and his statecraft.

Chapters 5 and 6 observe Williams as he undertakes the futile tasks of integrating Grenada into a unitary statehood with Trinidad and Tobago and mediating the racially inspired internecine warfare in British Guiana. Chapter 7 places him on an even broader stage as it examines his attitudes toward Africa and Africans and the place he ascribed to the peoples of that continent in the construction of a West Indian identity. Finally, Chapter 8 addresses the racial question in Trinidad and Tobago and shows how the language of race became a metaphor for the society's ills.

For the sake of convenience, the designation "Trinidad" refers to "Trinidad and Tobago." Similarly, "African Trinidadian" and "African Guianese" are used interchangeably with "black Trinidadian" and "black Guianese." The nomenclatures "Indo-Trinidadian" and "Indo-Guianese" are also used interchangeably with Indians in both the Trinidadian and Guianese contexts. Although I am aware that many scientists now maintain that "race" is a social construct and that it lacks any biological basis, I use the term in the way in which it would have been understood in the Caribbean and elsewhere during the period covered by this book.

My study ends in 1970, with the suppression of the Black Power–inspired February Revolution. A chastened Eric Williams promised to implement reforms and sacked some of his ministers. But this was a horrible personal and political crisis for him, and he seems never to have regained his confident stride, at least not entirely. In 1973, after seventeen years in office, Williams announced his resignation as political leader of the PNM and hence as prime minister. The party and a large number of his supporters persuaded him to withdraw this act of self-abnegation. His best years behind him, Williams would remain head of the government until his death in 1981.

♦ ♦

CHAPTER 1

INTELLECTUAL
DECOLONIZATION

♦ ♦ ♦ ♦ ♦ ♦ "The history of our West Indian islands can be expressed in two simple words: Columbus and Sugar," Eric Williams proclaimed in a lecture he delivered at the Trinidad Public Library on April 19, 1944. As he awaited the publication of *Capitalism and Slavery* later that year, the young historian was preparing the ground for the reception of its bitter assault on colonialism. His audience on that April day was comprised mainly of the local intelligentsia, many of whom were English and therefore white. Entitled "The British West Indies in World History," the talk must have made some of his listeners uncomfortable as Williams underscored many unpleasant truths about the region's history. "The West Indian islands were discovered," he said, "to assist in the solution of Europe's problems. Thus they were from the very beginning, an extension of Europe overseas."[1]

In this speech Williams was focusing on the themes that he had addressed on previous occasions and that would be the signifiers of his career. His preoccupation with colonialism—its impact on the colonizers and the colonized—was not an empty intellectual exercise to advance his reputation or to score academic points. Rather, it was a consequence of his familiarity with imperial power as a citizen of colonial Trinidad and Tobago, his racially unpalatable experiences in England as a student, his deep understanding of the nature of colonialism, and his vision of a world free from the excesses of the past. Williams's condemnation of colonialism was not restricted to its expression in the Caribbean. He was consistent in his criticism of colonial rule in Asia and Africa. The colonized peoples, regardless of their ethnicity or location, were his brethren, his partners in suffering, and brothers and sisters in the struggle for justice and independence.

Eric Williams was born and came to maturity at a time when Liberia, Ethiopia, and Haiti were the only predominantly black African and Caribbean nations free from colonial rule. He was knowledgeable about the invasion of Ethiopia by Benito Mussolini in the 1930s, the occupation of Haiti by the Americans, and the denigration of peoples of African descent everywhere. Years later, Williams recalled the ways in which he and his contemporaries were socialized as colonial subjects. "The intellectual equipment with which I was endowed by The Trinidad school system," Williams wrote in his autobiography, "had two principal characteristics—quantitatively it was rich; qualitatively, it was British. 'Be British' was the slogan not only of the Legislature but also of the school."[2]

Williams was harshly critical of the other deleterious effects of the colonial education he received. He considered his schooling "un-West Indian." "My training," he added, "was divorced from any thing remotely suggestive of Trinidad and the West Indies." Only the academically weaker students were expected to study West Indian history. "What the school disparaged," Williams wrote, "the society despised."[3]

Having won a highly coveted island scholarship, Williams left for Oxford University in 1932 to read for a degree in history. Specializing in British colonial history, he confessed that he took "a very independent line" with his tutor, R. Trevor Davies.[4] Williams distinguished himself academically and was awarded the Doctor of Philosophy degree in 1939; his dissertation was entitled "The Economic Aspect of the Abolition of the West Indian Slave Trade and Slavery." This work was later revised and published as *Capitalism and Slavery* (1944). Williams's confrontation in England with a crude British racism left an indelible impression on him. White students doubted his intellectual capacity and some even ridiculed him. Williams believed that his race also placed him at a disadvantage when he applied for a fellowship at All Souls College, Oxford, in 1935.[5]

Although he had a profound appreciation for the achievements of the English over time, Williams rejected the racism that characterized their relationship with the black and brown peoples they colonized. Thus, his unrelenting assault on colonialism had multifaceted underpinnings. As a historian, he was deeply cognizant of the ways in which colonialism was justified intellectually by metropolitan scholars and of the necessity for the colonized to confront and undermine such claims. As a scholar, he understood the structural relationship between the imperial powers and their colonies and the ways in which colonialism fostered the exploitation of its victims. As a child of colonialism, Williams knew firsthand the psychological damage experienced by colonized peoples, forcing him to assume the burden of helping to make the people of Trinidad and Tobago whole again. As a politician, his mission was to free his society from all vestiges of colonial rule.

Williams was highly conversant with the works of such imperial scholars and writers as Thomas Carlyle, Edward Long, Lord Macaulay, Reginald Coupland, and Arnold Toynbee. None of these intellectuals doubted the essential superiority of Europeans, although twentieth-century writers like Coupland and Toynbee never defended slavery or supported its reintroduction. But their descriptions of African peoples were suffused with a distressing cultural chauvinism at best and a barely disguised racism at its worst. To Toynbee, Africans arrived in the Americas "spiritually as well as physically naked" but possessing a "childlike spiritual intuition." Coupland extolled the virtues of British colonial rule and praised the humanitarian impulses of the British, especially in regard to the emancipation of enslaved people.[6] Such nationally self-serving scholarship led Williams to observe that "the British historians wrote almost as if Britain had introduced Negro slavery solely for the satisfaction of abolishing it."[7]

As a descendant of enslaved Africans and as a scholar, Williams was on secure ground when he claimed that "the most offensive statements ever made in terms of the capacity or the incapacity of certain peoples have been made by historians in the universities." "Imperialist historians," he argued, "openly set out to despise the West Indian capacity, and today you are independent."[8] The influence of these scholars, he maintained, permeated all sectors of British society, affecting attitudes and governmental policies. Referring to historians at universities, Williams charged: "It is they who[,] in the British circles in particular, were able to penetrate the ranks of the people who became the members of Parliament, the members of the Cabinet running the government, the members of Parliament making the laws for the colonies, the administrators and governors governing the colonies, creating a climate in the public mind which is responsible for the attitude . . . to West Indian areas and West Indian people today.[9]

Familiar with the disparaging ways in which colonized people had been depicted by imperial scholars, Williams called upon them to reject the histories written by those who "sought only to justify the indefensible and to seek support for preconceived and outmoded prejudices."[10] To him, the newly independent people of Trinidad and Tobago must reject "the intellectual concepts and attitudes worked out by metropolitan scholars in the age of colonialism." He proclaimed the "old intellectual world" dead, "strangled by the noose that it put around its own neck."[11]

The men who inhabited that old intellectual world had a particular penchant for denigrating those upon whose backs British power partially rested. Thomas Carlyle dismissed the notion that blacks had any rights, ranked "the Demarara Nigger" just ahead of horses, and doubted the wisdom of emancipation in the West Indies. Slavery's demise, he said, had reduced blacks to a state of idleness, "each one carrying a rum bottle in his hand, no breeches on his body, pumpkin at discretion, and the fruitful region of the earth going back to jungle round him."[12]

Although Carlyle was especially vituperative in his assault on blacks, his ideas were broadly representative of British intellectual opinion on peoples of African descent and their capacities. Their pernicious assertions about these peoples undoubtedly reflected and shaped British popular opinion. Williams described such ideas and representations of West Indians as "the great lie of history," adding: "It is being exposed with all the ruthlessness that it deserves."[13] He had dedicated his life "to the exposure of this lie, to the repudiation of the many calumnies and detractions with which we have been afflicted and to the filling of the gap caused by our long period of amnesia."[14] But Williams did not see himself fighting this battle alone. Such calumnies, he contended, should be addressed by universities in newly independent countries. It was their task "to challenge, deliberately, all that has been written in respect of the national history. I mean the West Indies, Africa, Ghana, Tanganyika, etc., all that has been written in the imperialist period."[15]

Aware that the colonial experience shaped the colonized in psychologically damaging ways, Williams knew that the task of intellectual decolonization would be difficult to accomplish. "It is one thing to get rid of colonialism," he said. "There will be joy before the angels of heaven for every imperialist sinner that repents but if you colonial nationalists think that it is as easy as that, I am afraid they have another thought coming to them. I go a little further than that. A lot of the colonial attitudes are not dead at all."[16]

In the context of mental decolonization, Williams emphasized the need for writing national histories. To him, the imperial powers had treated the West Indian islands as producers of sugar, ignoring them once that economic need became less compelling. The West Indies now formed in the popular imagination "a picture of fun-loving people, West Indians have been responsible for this picture, a place for tourists, a place where you could leave the United States with several inches of snow in the month of February or March, and get down and walk half-naked on the beaches, a place where you do nothing but drink rum punches and forget."[17] To counteract this frivolous image, the islands needed to have their own national histories. It was "nonsense," however, to think that only West Indians could write their history, since "some of the most reactionary people in respect of colonialism . . . are West Indians themselves."[18] The colonial experience had left its imprint on these people, and embracing a different construction of themselves would be a slow, arduous process.

♦ ♦ ♦ ♦ ♦ Ideas such as these were staples of Williams's rhetoric as scholar, teacher, and politician. The political education of the citizens of Trinidad and Tobago, and by extension those of the West Indies as a whole, became his passion. An orator of considerable gifts and one given to a brilliant turn of the phrase, Williams used these talents to educate, cajole, chastise, and challenge his people. Employing all of his oratorical and intellectual gifts, Williams delivered his most famous and contentious speech on intellectual decolonization at the University of Woodford Square on March 22, 1961. Strident and combative in tone, brimming with the insight of the trained historian, Williams used the occasion to explain to his listeners why they had to destroy the shackles of the colonial past and command their future.

Williams's "Massa Day Done" speech, as this particular oration came to be known, was delivered at a time when nationalist movements were growing in strength in the colonial societies of Africa and Asia. India had won its independence in 1947 after a protracted struggle with the British. Ghana received its independence in 1957, thereby energizing nationalist movements in other parts of Africa. The Algerians contested French colonial authority by employing violence, and so did the Kenyans against the British. Although there was some nationalist fervor in the West Indies, it never attained the passion that characterized its counterpart in many African and Asian societies. The style of nationalist expression was more genteel, more muted, less confrontational, and less vituperative.

Williams was certainly aware of these nationalist sentiments in the Caribbean region; indeed, he had played a part in creating and shaping them. His first book, The Negro in the Caribbean (1942), was an overt assault on colonial rule in the Caribbean as a whole. His second book, *Capitalism and Slavery* (1944), provided the historical roots for his arguments and was a sustained attack on the extant scholarship on slavery's role in the construction of the British economy and on the humanitarian impulse in the abolition of slavery.

Williams, who had accepted a post with the British- and American-financed and controlled Anglo-American Caribbean Commission in 1945, had an uneasy and acrimonious relationship with his superiors. Emotionally committed to improving the condition of the Caribbean peoples, sensitive to their need to assume responsibility for their own destiny, and conscious of his intellectual superiority over his white bosses, Williams refused to be silenced or to modify his critique of colonial rule in accordance with their wishes. His personality prevented him from a supine acceptance of their orders and his high degree of political consciousness made such a response wholly impossible. When his superiors suggested that he withdraw an article that he had submitted for publication on race relations in Puerto Rico and the Virgin Islands on the ground that "the timing was not right," Williams declined: "It struck me that if West Indians are to think only when Britain and the United States consider it is the right time for them to do so, we will never think at all. . . . I consider that each and every moment of each day and every day is a fit and proper time to attack racial discrimination and I said so."[19]

Williams was equally adamant in defending his *Negro in the Caribbean* from its detractors. Standing up to one of his superiors who thought that the book was not "objective,"[20] and who implied that he should repudiate it to save the Caribbean Commission embarrassment, Williams was "prepared to give no quarter and ask for none. I knew that if I yielded, they would wipe the floor with me forever after that."[21] Williams, who prided himself on his historical skills to a fault, would brook no criticism of his work and certainly not from those who were the acknowledged defenders of the horrendous status quo. As he declared: "I was not prepared to listen to any criticism about my vested interests in the West Indies. I would not capitulate for one moment to those interests. No question of unfavorable reaction to my book could be maintained."[22]

Eric Williams was relieved of his duties with the Commission in June 1955, his political and intellectual stands having become increasingly unpalatable to his superiors. As he explained, "I endured tortures at the Caribbean Commission, where I had to tolerate all sorts of metropolitan upstarts who thought my ideas for the future of the West Indies too extreme. Everywhere I went I met suppression." To Williams, the issues that led to his dismissal were "not personal but political; they involve not a single individual but the West Indian people."[23] This assertion, made within four hours of his dismissal to an audience of about twenty thousand people in Port of Spain, was not rhetorically empty, as subsequent developments would amply demonstrate. Williams was consciously seeking to depersonalize his conflict with the Caribbean Commission and to make it into a cause with which all colonized West Indians could identify. He was the black and gifted colonial whose efforts to enhance the lives of his people had been stymied at every turn. He had been crucified on the altar of colonial interests by men who defended an unjust status quo and who were the enemies of the people, inasmuch as they were his. By dismissing him so callously, the Commission had unintentionally liberated Williams to find his own voice and to put his talents at the disposal of the people of Trinidad and Tobago and their brethren elsewhere. "I was born here," Williams told his audience on that warm June night, "and here I stay with the people of Trinidad, who educated me free of charge for nine years at Queens Royal College, who have made me whatever I am, and who might be at any time the victims of the very pressures I have been fighting against for twelve years."[24] In language reminiscent of that used by Booker T. Washington in his speech at the Cotton States and International Exposition held in Atlanta in 1895, Williams vowed "to let down my bucket where I am, now, right here with you in the British West Indies."[25]

The animating ideological thrust of Williams's vow was, to be sure, quite different from the one that guided Booker T. Washington. In his so-called Atlanta Compromise, Washington had urged blacks in the American South to accept racial segregation, cooperate with whites, and use their energies to build a prosperous region. Williams, on the other hand, was not interested in any compromise with the status quo in the West Indies. His pledge "to let down my bucket" in the West Indies, as his audience that night undoubtedly understood, was fraught with tantalizing implications. Williams's experiences with the Caribbean Commission had enhanced his political consciousness, pushed him in the direction of a more overtly political career, and in time gave him a larger stage to test and implement his ideas, for good or for ill.

Not everyone who heard it was impressed by Williams's speech. U.S.

consul general William P. Maddox felt that Williams was seeking to exploit his dismissal "to his own personal, and political advantage." According to Maddox, Williams displayed an "inordinate vanity, delusions of intellectual superiority, and acute sense of racialism." His "racialism," charged Maddox, "turns into vindictiveness against the representatives of the metropolitan governments which form the Commission, and establishes him in the eyes of his public as a champion of the Negro masses of the West Indies." Williams had said nothing that night that deserved such a harsh condemnation, but Maddox was right in noting his appeal to people of African descent as a whole, not just the "masses." "It is a safe guess that he has launched a new phase of his political career in Trinidad and the British West Indies," Maddox concluded.[26]

It is in the context of Williams's developing political consciousness, his understanding of the deleterious effects of colonialism on the West Indies, and his unhappy experiences with the Caribbean Commission that his "Massa Day Done" speech of March 1961 should be placed. He delivered it approximately four years after he had become chief minister of Trinidad and Tobago. As head of government, he experienced firsthand how the colonial system operated and how the structural mechanisms it created impeded change. Williams gave the speech in the midst of a difficult battle with the United States over the return of the land on which the Chaguaramas Naval Station had been constructed to the people of Trinidad and Tobago. He was also troubled by the fact that many of his fellow citizens did not share his view of colonial rule on the one hand or understood the consequences of its demise on the other. In response to a recent story in the *Trinidad Guardian*, a frequently harsh critic of the chief minister, Williams had publicly chastised the newspaper on December 22, 1960, when he first declared that "Massa Day Done." This emotionally charged pronouncement was inflammatory and abusive, but Williams wanted to hit his target with all the rhetorical venom he could muster.

As the politically astute Eric Williams must have expected, some people greeted his pejorative "Massa Day Done" with approval while others were outraged. Calling Williams's use of the expression "wicked," the opposition Democratic Labour Party formally asked him on March 5, 1961, to apologize for his intemperate language. Not one to be silenced, especially when he knew that history was on his side, Williams used the imbroglio to give his compatriots another history lesson on March 22 and embarrass his critics in the process.

The March 22 "Massa Day Done" speech will go down in the historical annals as one of the strongest indictments of the psychological impact of colonial rule made by a head of government anywhere. Williams began his extraordinary address by assaulting his critics in the opposition party with unusual vehemence, even for him: "I accuse the DLP of deliberately being the stooge of the Massas who still exist in our society. I accuse the DLP of deliberately trying to keep back social progress. I accuse the DLP of wanting to bring back Massa Day. . . . I say Massa Day Done."[27]

Such strong criticism of the DLP membership was, of course, rhetorically excessive. Williams had gone too far in accusing the party of "wanting to bring back Massa Day." But the DLP, whose members were primarily Indo-Trinidadian, had committed a serious misjudgment by demanding that the chief minister—who was on solid intellectual ground in his use of the appellation "Massa"—retract it. The party leaders may have been unfamiliar with the historical trajectory of the term and its continuing symbolic and pejorative meanings in the West Indies, particularly for peoples of African descent. Williams seized upon this apparent historical gaffe, claiming: "They have not the slightest idea as to the constituents of progress in our society and the elements of our historical evolution. All that they can see in the slogan, Massa Day Done, is racial antagonism. This [is] characteristically stupid. Massa is not a racial term. Massa is the symbol of a bygone age. Massa Day is a social phenomenon. Massa Day Done connotes a political awakening and a social revolution."[28]

Williams clearly relished the opportunity to denounce his opponents before a friendly audience in Woodford Square. He dismissed them as "this pack of benighted idiots, this band of obscurantist politicians, this unholy alliance of egregious individualists who have nothing constructive to say."[29] To some extent, this was good theater in a political culture where rhetorical abuse had an honored place, and Williams was its best practitioner. Still, there was much to be gained politically by linking the DLP to an ignoble past and accusing it of intellectual bankruptcy.

In explaining what the term "Massa" connoted, Williams described a West Indian past dominated by whites who exploited enslaved blacks and contract workers from Portugal, India, and China for their own advantage.

Living in opulence, usually in England, Massa monopolized political power as well. "Massa," Williams declared, "constituted the most backward ruling class history has ever known." Massa's rule had outlived the emancipation of slaves: "The period of Massa's ascendancy, the period of Massa'a domination over workers who had no rights under the law, the period of Massa's enforcement of a barbarous code of industrial relations long after it was repudiated by the conscience of the civilized world, lasted in our society for almost 300 years."[30]

Massa's domination of West Indian society produced a slavish mentality that Williams said had ended. "Massa Day Done, Sahib Day Done, yes suh Boss Day Done," he proclaimed. Massa still lived, however, "with his backward ideas of the aristocracy of the skin." Speaking of his opponents in Trinidad and Tobago, Williams observed that "Massa still has his stooges, who prefer to crawl on their bellies to Massa, absentee or resident, Massa this, Massa that, Massa the other, instead of holding their heads high and erect."[31] By asking him to repudiate the term "Massa," Williams charged, the DLP was "telling the people of the West Indies, that they want Massa to continue the social control, monopolizing the political power, stultifying economic development, disciplining the workers. They are in fact telling us that they are as much the stooges of the Massa of the 20th century as the house slaves were of Massa's eighteenth century counterpart."[32]

To innoculate himself against charges that his speech would exacerbate racial tensions, Williams was careful to underscore the point that "if Massa was generally White . . . not all Whites were Massa, at the same time not all Massas were white."[33] The chief minister was reminding his audience that "Massa" represented a class of persons, an orientation that transcended phenotype or ethnicity. He used the speech to affirm the People's National Movement's embrace "of all races and colors and from all walks of life . . . dedicated to the pursuit of national ends, without any special privilege being granted to race, color, class, creed, national origin."[34]

The U.S. consul general doubted Williams's claim that his use of "Massa" was not intended to exacerbate racial tensions: "To conclude that there is not a strain of racialism, in the 'Massa Day Done' expression would be as naïve as to assume that there is no feeling on this issue in the heart of almost every non-white." On the other hand, he found Williams's "theory of peaceful social revolution" a more satisfactory description of contemporary developments than the conclusion that his statements were deliberately "wicked" and "provocatively anti-white."[35]

Williams's speech demolished the arguments of his detractors and silenced them. But silence did not mean a universal acceptance of his line of reasoning, since many European creoles felt that the pejorative comments were directed specifically at them. There could not be, however, a persuasive critique of his historical analysis of the prototypical Massa and the economic and political system that he had created and shaped. Once again, Williams's historical training had served him well, giving him the opportunity to provide an intellectually unassailable perspective to contemporary debates. The University of Woodford Square was the forum for these exercises in political education and theater. No other politician of his times had such a stage in the Caribbean, and none employed the lessons of history to serve contemporary needs as effectively as did Eric Williams.

♦ ♦ ♦ ♦ ♦ Williams, of course, was not the only West Indian leader or intellectual to adopt an anticolonial stance. George Padmore, his compatriot, had already articulated his criticisms, and C. L. R. James, another son of Trinidad and Tobago, was renowned for championing the cause of colonial peoples. Jamaican barrister and politician Norman Manley was also a leading critic of colonialism, as were Cheddi Jagan and Forbes Burnham of British Guiana. But not every West Indian politician advocated self-government. Alexander Bustamante, the Jamaican trade unionist and politician, once said that "self-government means slavery," though he later changed his position and led Jamaica to political independence in 1962.[36]

Eric Williams never publicly acknowledged the influence of his contemporaries on the evolution of his political consciousness. In any event, the nature and extent of such influence are always difficult to identify, measure, and assess. Williams was most famously an independent thinker, and his chronic intellectual arrogance would not have permitted him to identify any ideological godfathers. Still, he grew to adulthood at a time of enormous intellectual ferment in the Caribbean and elsewhere in the colonial world. He was also the son of a society with a proud tradition of producing gifted, noisy, and pugnacious intellectuals, including J. J. Thomas, a nineteenth-century nationalist; Henry Sylvester Williams, an ardent twentieth-century pan-Africanist; George Padmore, another anticolonialist and pan-Africanist; and

C. L. R. James, Williams's high school teacher and later his mentor. James was also an outstanding political theorist, indefatigable writer, and formidable intellectual. Although Williams became a member of this extraordinary pantheon of intellectuals, he stood apart from them in the sense that he was the only one who achieved significant success in electoral politics.

As a student in England during the 1930s, Williams would have heard the anticolonial sentiments being voiced by Africans, Asians, and West Indians. Whether he participated in the activities organized by the emerging anticolonial and nationalist organizations in England, such as the West African Students' Union and the League of Coloured Peoples, is uncertain. Nevertheless, it can be argued that Williams's ferocious anticolonialism was honed during his sojourn in the metropolitan country.

When he accepted a teaching position at Washington, D.C.'s Howard University in 1939, Williams joined a very distinguished faculty; many of its members were prominent leaders of the African American struggle for social justice. Alain Locke, a philosopher and a major figure in the Harlem Renaissance, was a close associate. In his foreword to Williams's first book, The Negro in the Caribbean, Locke described the author as "a citizen of the Americas in the larger sense."[37] Williams's other colleagues at Howard included Charles S. Johnson, a prominent sociologist; Ralph Bunche, a political scientist who later won the Nobel Prize; and E. Franklin Frazier, another sociologist and outstanding scholar. Williams also had some interaction with W. E. B. Du Bois, the distinguished intellectual and activist, as well as with Rayford Logan, a highly respected historian. The young Trinidadian historian would have been profoundly influenced by the ideas of these and other associates, as much as by the arguments that legitimized the developing assaults on racism in the United States. Williams distanced himself from any overt political activity in his host country, however. He recalled that he "concentrated on my work, and I soon came to be regarded as a worker doing his own work and minding his own business."[38]

Williams, on the other hand, did not manifest such ostrichlike disinterest in political activity on his return to Trinidad and Tobago. There he led the charge against colonialism with an energy and a pugnacity that the territory had never before witnessed. But although he proclaimed Massa Day Done, this was more a rhetorical flourish than an accurate representation of the moment. Williams had denounced those in Trinidad and Tobago who clung to colonial habits of thought and behavior, but he knew that the attitudes of those who occupied the centers of colonial power either in Trinidad and Tobago or in London could not be so easily exorcised. The officials in London were, for the most part, men given to extreme condescension in their relationship with the political leaders in the colonies and independent nations. They had come of age at a time when nationalist stirrings in the colonies had begun to challenge the foundations of the British Empire, and metropolitan responses were, at first, oppositional, confused, and contradictory. As colonial officials struggled to accept an emerging new order, they also had to adjust to the personalities of the leaders and the frequently strident language of nationalism. Williams, a brash and impatient intellectual, had the unsettling capacity to rankle these officials in a way that at times could be counterproductive.

♦ ♦ ♦ ♦ ♦ Williams's verbal assaults on colonialism were bitingly effective, but his scholarship was even more significant. *The Negro in the Caribbean*, a penetrating examination of contemporary conditions of the region's inhabitants, was the culmination of a study supported by a fellowship from the Julius Rosenwald Fund. To complete the work, Williams spent two years visiting the islands. In his foreword to the book, Alain Locke observed: "It is hoped that this study will furnish a closer and sounder bond of understanding between the Negro-American and his brother West Indian, known all too limitedly merely as a migrant rather than with regard either to his home background or with reference to our common racial history and problems."[39]

Divided into nine brief chapters, the book provides a survey of the history of the islands, their economic structures, the life of contemporary inhabitants, and a vision for the future. Williams identifies foreign domination as the principal villain; it is primarily responsible for the appalling social conditions of the majority of the people, the inequality of incomes, and the political weakness of the masses. He concludes that "the Caribbean lives under a government of sugar, for sugar, by sugar," an assessment that won him no friends among the colonial elites. Moreover, he asserts, "the Negro's right to decide his own affairs and own life is not a question for argument." The author proposes that the various territories comprising the region should form a political and economic federation, a development that made "common sense."[40] To Williams, the islands had "a common heritage of slavery, a labor base essentially the same." They were "burdened by the same curse, sugar, the dynamics of the different areas are the same, and it is time to pay more heed to the fundamental identities than to the incidental differences."[41]

This somber analysis of the Caribbean region provided the necessary ammunition for those who would contest colonial rule. Its publication preceded by a mere two years the appearance of *Capitalism and Slavery*, which represented a watershed in the historiography of slavery. This work attempts "to place in historical perspective the relationships between early capitalism as exemplified by Great Britain, and the Negro slave trade, Negro slavery and the general colonial trade of the seventeenth and eighteenth centuries."[42] Williams did not conceive the book as "a study of the institution of slavery" but as an analysis "of the contribution of slavery to the development of British capitalism."[43] His book, he asserted, was an investigation "of the role of Negro slavery and the slave trade in providing the capital which financed the Industrial Revolution in England and of mature industrial capitalism in destroying the slave system."[44]

This was a strikingly original thesis—bold, imaginative, and certain to be controversial. Williams had set himself the task of challenging assumptions and conclusions that had been the staples of British historians whose focus was slavery and emancipation. By examining a great deal of evidence and using the optic of a talented product of the colonies, Williams turned some of the accepted conclusions on their head. He demonstrated the organic relationship between the slave trade, the manufacturing industries in England, the plantation system in the West Indies, and the growth of British capitalism during the eighteenth century. As he expressed it, "The commercial capitalism of the eighteenth century developed the wealth of Europe by means of slavery and monopoly."[45] This finding, based as it was on much statistical evidence, emphasized the centrality of African slaves to the economic development of England and by extension continental Europe. British historians, some of whose works were marred by racist assumptions, had been more concerned with telling the story of British emancipation and less with the ramifications of the human commerce and the institution of slavery for the economies of the imperial nations.

Taking issue with the conclusions of British scholars like Reginald Coupland, Williams maintained that emancipation was driven primarily by economic considerations.[46] Although he believed that "the humanitarians were the spearhead of the onslaught which destroyed the West Indian system and freed the Negro," he nevertheless felt that their role had been "grossly exaggerated by men who have sacrificed scholarship to sentimentality."[47] When slavery in the West Indies began its economic decline in the aftermath of the American War of Independence, according to Williams, British capitalists were prepared to abandon the institution. Thus "the Capitalists had first encouraged West Indian slavery and then helped to destroy it. When British capitalism depended on the West Indies, they ignored slavery or defended it. When British capitalism found the West Indian monopoly a nuisance, they destroyed West Indian slavery as the first step in the destruction of West Indian monopoly."[48]

Moreover, slavery could not coexist with the industrial capitalism of the nineteenth century that it had created. The institution had become anachronistic in an economic world where machines were being given pride of place in contradistinction to coerced black labor. Williams's argument complicated the reasons for emancipation, showing that economic self-interest trumped the humanitarian impulse as the motive force for liberation.

Capitalism and Slavery, although a work of serious scholarship, was suffused with an angry, condemnatory tone. The British were clearly in the wrong on the slavery question, and Williams said so repeatedly. He could not be neutral on such a moral issue. Nor could he, as a descendant of enslaved people, distance himself from their history and adopt a pose of lofty dispassion. Imperial historians whose conclusions Williams contested were certainly not neutral in their discussions of slavery and emancipation or even, in some instances, of the rights of peoples of African descent in society. Williams candidly admitted: "I have taken a political line in the book, which West Indians more than anyone else need to understand."[49]

When it was published, *Capitalism and Slavery* received much more attention than did *The Negro in the Caribbean*. This was understandable given the highly controversial issues it addressed and conclusions it reached. By underscoring the centrality of black slavery to the European economies, Williams had hit an imperial nerve, opening historical and historiographical wounds that still show no signs of healing. Some imperial historians were quite dismissive of the book, preferring to attack the presumed motives of the author rather than engaging his arguments seriously. D. A. Farnie, a prominent British economic historian, charged that *Capitalism and Slavery* presented Williams's "own community with the sustaining myth that 'capitalism' was responsible for their condition[,] a view that has not found favor in Western Europe, where history has been separated from its tap-root in myth, but has been found highly acceptable to the educated elites of Africa and Asia."[50] Noted American historian Frank Tannenbaum described the book as being tarnished by "a strongly flavored faith in the economic inter-pretation of history, given strident enthusiasm by a visible notion of Negro Nationalism."[51]

Reviewers of African descent were uniformly favorable in their assess-ment of *Capitalism and Slavery*. Located mostly in the historically black univer-sities in the United States, they greeted the work as a major achievement by a black scholar. The book, to be sure, was not a study of slavery, as Williams himself stated, but it did address the role of black labor in the construction of the European economies. The study of the black presence in the Americas was still in its historiographical infancy, and African American scholars welcomed any addition to the literature, particularly one as erudite as Wil-liams's work. Carter J. Woodson, a pioneering black historian, thought that the book represented "the beginning of the scientific study of slavery from the international point of view."[52] Lorenzo Greene, another distinguished scholar, observed that "a work of this kind has been long overdue and Dr. Williams has filled the need in brilliant fashion."[53]

Capitalism and Slavery has become a classic, joining *The Black Jacobins* (1938), the major study of the St. Domingue slave revolution by C. L. R. James, as one of the two best-known works by a West Indian–born histo-rian. The book remains at the core of scholarly disputations on the two central issues it addresses. It is a measure of the author's accomplishment that *Capitalism and Slavery* continues to generate such debates more than half a century after its appearance. In light of the enormous amount of research on slavery, the slave trade, and the European economies since 1944, it is not surprising that some of Williams's conclusions have been refined.[54] But his signal achievement resides in his having understood that British capitalism was inextricably bound to African labor and that the nature of the imperial connection with the West Indies had to be rescued from the nationalist excesses of British historians.

Capitalism and Slavery was Williams's most important and enduring his-torical work. He would return to its thesis in later volumes such as his *History of the Peoples of Trinidad and Tobago* (1962) and *From Columbus to Castro: The His-tory of the Caribbean, 1492–1969* (1970). More importantly, perhaps, Williams had used the argument that Britain had exploited black labor and despoiled the West Indies to promote its own economic well-being as a weapon to demand more British aid when he became prime minister of Trinidad and Tobago. Colonial officials found this formulation of the problem deeply irritating, although they lacked the intellectual equipment to refute this charge. Williams the politician thus used the lessons of history, as he saw them, to redress contemporary wrongs in the new West Indian nations that he was helping to create.

◆ ◆ ◆ ◆ ◆ Eric Williams, who visited eleven African countries in 1964, always stressed the similarities in the colonial experiences of Africans and West Indians. Breaking with the view of some of his contemporaries, he saw this connection as being primarily an economic one. The trade in African slaves established the link and the European partitioning of Africa at the Conference of Berlin, held between November 1884 and February 1885, and gave legitimacy to the scramble for African soil. As Williams told students at the University of the West Indies, St. Augustine, Trinidad and Tobago, in 1964: "The European countries sat down just 80 years ago at the Conference in Berlin and carved up Africa as if it was an African chicken and they were at their Sunday dinner, and this one would take that, and that one would take that etc."[55]

Although Williams emphasized the economic relationship between Africa and the West Indies, it did not mean that he was blind to its racial dimensions. Rather, he thought that if he framed the nature of the association in economic terms, emphasizing its unquestionably exploitative character, he could use it more effectively to denounce the imperial villains. "The connection is principally an economic one, taking the form, fairly well established at the time, of compulsory labour, slavery," he said. Returning in 1964 to the argument that he first advanced in *Capitalism and Slavery*, Williams stressed that that connection promoted "a tremendous capital accumulation that went to build up the industrial revolution in Britain, in France, parts of Holland, the Eastern Seaboard of the United States of America."[56]

According to Williams, "West African labour and West Indian soil and climate were very largely responsible for the fact that country X, or country Y, or country Z in the world is to be regarded as developed." Accordingly, there was a "community of interest between Africa and the Caribbean on this question of anti colonialism."[57] The West Indies, Williams repeated over and over again, existed to meet the needs of the imperial countries. As the major

A rare photograph of Eric Williams wearing clear eyeglasses, rather than his customary dark-tinted ones, and his ever-present hearing aid. Date unknown. Photograph courtesy of Eric Williams Memorial Collection, University of the West Indies (Trinidad and Tobago). © Eric Williams Memorial Collection and used by permission.

producers of sugar, the islands were led to believe that they were important. That view had continued to prevail in the West Indies, but, in his opinion, the contemporary West Indies formed "the most insignificant of all the regions of the world. The West Indies has to fight a persistent and desperate battle for recognition in the world."[58]

He warned that colonialism was being replaced by "neo-colonialism," a concept to which he had been introduced on his African trip, especially in Ghana. He condemned the unequal nature of the trading relationships between the developed and the developing countries. He was also highly critical of economic assistance whereby the recipient was required to use the funds to purchase goods only from the grantor. As he noted: "There is a lot of economic aid going on in the world over the years but it has not been—contrary to what people say—economic aid from developed countries to developing countries, it is the developing countries that have been giving substantial economic aid to the developed countries by providing a market for their capital goods and so on."[59]

"Tremendous and gigantic projects" like Russian aid to Egypt for the Aswan Dam could be defended, but "in respect of minor projects and minor countries . . . it is a rope around your neck."[60] Williams's forceful articulation of this point would earn him much disfavor from British officials in particular.

Williams was acutely aware of the challenges that new nations faced in order to break with "the old procedures inherited from the old world."[61] To him, "decolonization was not only economic and political, it is not only an attack on the economics of neo-colonialism and an attack on colonialism and getting rid of colonies in Africa, it is also an intellectual process." He added: "Imperialism has produced over generations a cultural imperialism which continues to dominate, which persists long after the political and economic conditions which gave rise to it have disappeared."[62]

The independent countries, then, had to assert their cultural autonomy, drawing on their indigenous heritage. They had to develop new educational strategies to cleanse themselves of old habits of thinking born of the colonial experience. Consequently, as Williams wrote in his third book, Education in the British West Indies (1950), the educational system should play the role "of a midwife to the emerging social order."[63] History should be the start of this intellectual exorcism. Its teaching "should not, as heretofore, present the British West Indies through British spectacles as so many annexations and by-products of European power politics. Rather, it should emphasize the history and development of the islands and people themselves."[64] At every level of the educational process, Williams emphasized, the content of the instruction should be related to the lived experiences of the students.

Under the circumstances, Williams urged the abolition of the colonial practice of external examinations for students in the secondary schools.

Since these examinations were prepared in England, "their content determines automatically the curricula of the British West Indian schools."[65] The external examinations "reflect the interests, environment and knowledge of the examiners." He ridiculed, for example, a test question that asked students in the tropical West Indies to write an essay on "a day in winter."[66]

A strong advocate of a state-controlled university, Williams maintained that such an institution "should constitute a source of inspiration that will contribute to the well being of a people as a whole, and to the material welfare of individuals of every calling, employment and occupation."[67] The university should reflect local conditions and "take into account the social and economic needs of the islands." But he saw another imperative for the creation of a British West Indian university: "An independent university will give the people of the British West Indies a confidence in themselves, their own roots, and their own potentialities. It will be a symbol of their aspirations to nationhood, in harmony with their current demands for self-government, and concrete testimony of the growth of independence in intellectual as well as in other fields."[68]

The British West Indian university that Williams envisaged had opened its doors in 1948, not as an independent institution, but as a college of London University. Its curriculum was, for the most part, determined by London University, although in time it became more sensitive to the needs of the Caribbean region by introducing courses with that emphasis. The University College of the West Indies, at it was called, was located in Jamaica, as Williams had suggested in *Education in the British West Indies*; later sister campuses were established in Trinidad and Tobago and in Barbados.

Eric Williams, understandably, took a great deal of interest in the curriculum of the University College. As the elected head of government of Trinidad and Tobago, he sat on the Council, the institution's governing body, which included representatives from all the islands that were supporting it. Still a practicing scholar, Williams could not resist the opportunity to help shape the fledgling college in accordance with the ideas he had advanced in his book. The faculty sometimes resented his interference, but Williams was undoubtedly responsible for the requirement that all students take courses in the history and culture of the Caribbean. As he explained in a 1964 address at Howard University: "Our first job is to see today that whilst we need agronomists and whilst we need teachers and whilst we need all these people, we don't give them the training that they would have got in the nineteenth century in Europe or in America, we don't divorce their training from the culture of their country. We don't divorce it from the people they are called upon to serve; we link from the start with the nationalist and independence movement, which has put them in the University in the first place. The colonial regime never put them in the university."[69]

Williams was very proud of his position as pro chancellor of the newly autonomous University of the West Indies during 1963–71. This gave him a stronger voice in its academic affairs, something he had always desired. In 1961, seemingly acting on his own volition, he asked the government of India to endow a chair in "Indian Culture and Civilization," to be located in the College of Arts and Sciences at the Trinidad and Tobago campus. The Indians accepted the request "in principle" and agreed to donate a representative collection of books on India and Indian culture to the campus library.[70] The endowment eventually materialized. Williams's request for the academic chair demonstrated his keen sensitivity to its intellectual, racial, and political ramifications in Trinidad and Tobago. Indo-Trinidadians, in particular, welcomed its establishment, which enhanced the university's prestige as well.

Inasmuch as Williams was thoroughly committed to the intellectual decolonization of the Caribbean region, he was a child of the times. He challenged the assumptions that permeated the colonial educational system as vigorously as he could, but he was never able to completely exorcise those colonial demons from his soul. Williams was psychologically tied to the British, though much less so than many of his contemporaries, to be sure, but at times those chains were very discernible. Perhaps it is fairer to say that he had ambivalent feelings about the former mother country and the British Commonwealth. In October 1964, for example, he observed—probably in a fit of anger—that "the truth is there is really no such thing as the Commonwealth: it is largely sentimental."[71] Barely a month later, Williams wrote to Prime Minister Harold Wilson proposing "a strengthening as early as possible [of] the Commonwealth presence in the Caribbean."[72]

His letter to Wilson was an open invitation to Britain to enhance its influence in the Caribbean, especially in intellectual circles. Williams maintained that an increased British presence would "serve as a sort of insurance against Western hemispheric pressures and the Organization of American States in particular." This was a veiled reference to the expanding role of the United States in the Caribbean region. He told Prime Minister Wilson that he had "been giving serious thought to the problem imposed by this presence in the University field, where the almost total lack of Commonwealth and particularly British interest in exposing us to the attentions of such agencies as the Ford Foundation, with the infiltration of influences and practices that I am not too happy about."[73]

Williams did not identify the "influences and practices" that troubled him, but clearly he preferred to embrace the British he knew over the Americans for whom he had an abiding distrust. To counteract these U.S. influences, he proposed to visit several universities in the United Kingdom to establish contacts between them and the University of the West Indies. Specifically, he wanted to promote faculty exchanges involving a senior "Britisher" in exchange for a junior West Indian. He also hoped to study the structure of British universities such as Oxford and Cambridge in order to see whether they were applicable to the University of the West Indies and its three campuses. He had a special interest in the degree of autonomy that the Constituent Colleges of the United Kingdom's universities possessed at the undergraduate level and whether these could serve as a guide to the University of the West Indies and the "impending revision of the statutes of the university." Further, the West Indian prime minister wanted to discuss a proposal he had previously made that the University of the West Indies should be selected as a Commonwealth training center principally for African students. The program would be supported by an expanded Commonwealth technical assistance scheme.

Williams would later report to the legislature in Trinidad and Tobago that one of the aims of his mission was to explore the feasibility of joint research projects in specific fields between the University of the West Indies, British universities, and Commonwealth universities in Canada, Africa, Asia, Australia, and New Zealand. The projects that he proposed for collaborative research reflected his own priorities; if adopted, their findings would have enormous implications for the relationships between the developed and developing members of the Commonwealth. Williams thought that such projects should undertake a critical evaluation of economic aid by developed countries to developing countries, as well as an appraisal of the development plans of the developing countries including planning techniques and organization. He also wanted a study of the comparative costs of production in the sugar industry and a critical survey of the nature of trade in the Commonwealth. This was an exercise in wishful thinking, since such a politically driven research agenda would probably have met with little enthusiasm from British politicians and scholars.

Williams sought to reassure Harold Wilson that his university mission did not necessarily carry a price tag. He was interested in "giving life and vitality to our Commonwealth relationship." He elaborated: "What we are so concerned with is that in many respects the Commonwealth does not necessarily, and in some cases does not immediately involve, any question of money. It is a question of attitude and approach and frank discussion, about all of which we have had many and serious grounds for complaint in past years. It is in this new spirit that I have raised the question of collaboration and consultation at university level."[74]

In the summer of 1965 Williams, accompanied by Philip Sherlock, vice chancellor of the University of the West Indies, visited a dozen British universities. Their mission, although well received by the host institutions, commanded little attention in the Caribbean. Nothing of major significance came of it in terms of sustained collaborative efforts with the universities, but the idea was unquestionably a good one. Ironically, Williams had sought the help of those whom he had denounced as intellectual colonizers, demonstrating the tenacity of the colonial past and a present that was still bound to it. Williams realized the strength of these umbilical ties all too well, and he anticipated the tensions that would arise once the colonial child became an adult and therefore independent.

♦ ♦ ♦ ♦ ♦ Shortly after Trinidad and Tobago became self-governing in 1962, Williams told British high commissioner Norman Costar that some things had changed in his country's relationship with Britain. To begin with, Trinidad would no longer put up with interference from any outside power. This did not mean that his government wanted Britain to decrease its interest in Trinidad and Tobago, though Costar would undoubtedly find that Williams would be giving Britain a few "knocks" from time to time. According to Costar, the new prime minister feared that Britain would abandon Trinidad and Tobago to the Americans, either politically or economically. Were this to occur, Williams could not tolerate any U.S. attempt to interfere in his nation's affairs. He wanted a British presence as a counterpoise to U.S. efforts to dominate the islands, which, wrote Costar, Williams "professes to fear."[75] In light of these statements, Williams's letter to Harold Wilson seems perfectly understandable, if not predictable.

Eric Williams demonstrated a similar ambivalence in the economic poli-cies he pursued. Short of investment capital yet committed to a bold and costly economic development program, he sought outside sources of sup-port to achieve his objectives. Costar reported that Williams also told him that Britain's help was essential for his nation's economic growth. Indepen-dence, he said, was the time for more, not less, investment and loans. He needed the money to give his nation a good start to self-determination.[76] Thus, while on the one hand the author of *Capitalism and Slavery* denounced neocolonialism, on the other hand he was forced by financial exigencies to provide a hospitable environment for foreign capital. This dilemma was never resolved, and in 1970 Prime Minister Williams would face a dramatic revolt against his policies. The inevitable tensions between political ideology and the realities of government came into sharp relief.

But there were other uncomfortable realities as well. Williams and the other leaders of predominantly black countries operated in a Common-wealth that was not particularly friendly to their aspirations. South Africa practiced a vicious form of racial segregation, and both Canada and Aus-tralia had instituted racially restrictive immigration policies. Prime Minister R. G. Menzies of Australia, for one, was unhappy with the increasing num-ber of Commonwealth members from black countries, "some of whom have no real independence except political, and quite a few of them are strangers to our notions of self government and civilized administration." Many of his colleagues, he asserted, had "great anxiety about the Commonwealth and the disappearance of so many of its old characteristics," an unmistakable allusion to the presence of the African countries. Menzies was saddened by the fact that the Commonwealth "has nothing like the appeal for us that the old one had." He despaired of the "benefit" that was derived from "having a somewhat tenuous association with a cluster of Republics, some of which like Ghana are more spiritually akin to Moscow than to London."[77] Such attitudes, by no means unique, made the work of the leaders of the newly independent countries more difficult. Not only did they have to confront the consequences of economic neglect and the challenge of redefining them-selves, but they had to deal with the sneers and sometimes the obstruction-ism of those who wished to maintain or return to the old order.

"When Dr. Williams speaks of West Indian nationalism, independence, it comes from the very roots of his being," wrote the editor of the *Nation*, C. L. R. James, in 1960.[78] This was not an exaggeration, and it captured the essence of the man and his commitment to ending colonialism. Williams did not have to engage in a war to advance that cause in Trinidad and Tobago, as some other leaders in Africa had to do. His weapons were his pen and his acerbic rhetoric. But as Williams understood only too well, political independence invited more battles. An intellectual and mental decolonization had to follow in its wake, and the newly independent nation had to guard against the demon of neocolonialism. Williams discovered that the old order could not and would not be easily vanquished. As he put it in 1962, "The power and influence of colonialism were never greater than on its death bed."[79] Here Williams was referring to the psychological chains that bound former colonists to the colonizers. Although his comment was an exaggeration, he would confront elements of this harsh truth in his capacity as head of the government of Trinidad and Tobago.

◆ ◆

CHAPTER 2

THE CHALLENGE OF POLITICAL AND ECONOMIC INTEGRATION

◆ ◆ ◆ ◆ ◆ Norman Manley, the premier of Jamaica, delivered a major broadcast to the people of Trinidad and Tobago on June 17, 1960. The newly inaugurated West Indies Federation was experiencing difficult times, and Manley was assuring his audience and the rest of the region that the federation would prevail and that it was in the best interest of the islands to remain united. "Each of us alone is small in the world today," Manley said. "Because we are small, it is the simple truth that for us unity is strength," he added. "The West Indian nation has a manifest duty to go forth as a free people, as an example of unity accomplished, of prejudice overcome, of brotherhood realized."[1]

Manley's call for unity among the Anglophone islands was the political mantra of many leaders, particularly in the Eastern Caribbean after World War I. Among the most prominent advocates of the Federal idea were T. Albert Marryshow of Grenada, Arthur A. Cipriani of Trinidad, Grantley Adams of Barbados, and Norman Manley of Jamaica. Arguing that the small size of the islands imposed limits on their potential for economic development and their international stature, these and other leaders promoted federation as the panacea. Concerned about the future of these colonies, and increasingly anxious to abandon them, the British government also strongly encouraged federation.

The first major step toward the creation of the West Indies Federation occurred in September 1947, when, at the invitation of Arthur Creech Jones, the secretary of state for the colonies, all of the West Indian governments, including British Guiana, met in Montego Bay to lay the foundation for a federation. There was considerable enthusiasm for such a gathering, and the delegates approached their task with seriousness. Delegate Alexander Bustamante, the chief minister of Jamaica, was the most skeptical about the creation of a viable federation. Bustamante admitted, however, that he could see no reason "why one day, whether that day is tomorrow, or next year, or another year, there should not be federation of all the British West Indies." He acknowledged that "the time has come not just for Federation but for self government." Still, he doubted whether a federation could succeed because the islands were at different stages in their constitutional development. As the chief minister said in his colorful metaphorical style: "Jamaica can walk, Trinidad is creeping. Barbados and British Guiana are right behind Trinidad or almost the same. St. Kitts and St. Vincent are attempting to creep and only attempting. Antigua is creeping, and of all the other small islands, some can barely creep on the palm of their hands, and others on hands and feet, and others not at all, yet you say to us 'We want you to federate.' How can the walking and the creeping and the babe who has not begun to creep yet, how can they walk on the same avenue?"

These were politically ominous observations. The "pauperized" state of most of the islands also worried Bustamante. "I have never heard," he said, "that in joining with bankrupts one can become successful or prosperous." Bustamante was fearful that Jamaica would have to spend its resources to support the proposed federation: "Whilst we want to be very liberal to our brothers and sisters across the sea and take them out of their difficulties, whether it be Grenada, St. Kitts, or another, whilst we want to be very generous to them and whilst some people say we of the West Indies are all alike, to me Jamaica and Jamaica's interests come first. It must be so."

Norman Manley, the leader of the People's National Party in Jamaica, contested Bustamante's arguments. Manley was not a member of the legislature but attended the 1947 conference in Montego Bay as a representative of the Caribbean Commission. In a direct response to Bustamante's use of the "creeping" analogy, Manley observed: "When people talk about the unseemly and slow process that is involved in creeping, I can't help but feel that, slow it may be, you may get somewhere by creeping if you know where you wish to go."

Manley rejected Bustamante's concerns about the economic condition of the potential federation. He believed that "so far from feeling that we would be financially weaker, we should realize that there would be a gain in our credit potentiality and our ability to organize our whole financial machinery if we are united together." Whereas Bustamante was more focused on the practical aspects of federation, Manley expressed a larger vision. He passionately believed that "our areas are destined for nationhood and destined to make a real contribution to the civilization of the world." Manley was certain that "if we won't leave our little boat and get into that larger vessel which is able to carry us to the goal of our ambitions, then . . . we are doomed and purblind and history will condemn us."[2]

Bustamante's concerns notwithstanding, the conferees made some important decisions. Perhaps the most significant was the creation of a committee—the Standing Closer Association Committee—to write a Federal constitution. The delegates urged constitutional changes in the territories that lagged behind Jamaica, Barbados, Trinidad, and British Guiana. It also authorized studies on issues crucial to the operation of the proposed federation. These included the implications of introducing a Federal civil service and a customs union. Bustamante echoed the concluding spirit of the meeting when he declared before its adjournment: "Everyone realizes that there are obstacles in the way of our final goal, . . . we should be big enough to blast away the obstacles."[3]

The planning for federation continued over the next decade. Bustamante became an advocate, insisting in 1954 that "we must federate and we are going to federate."[4] Additional conferences held in London in 1953 and 1956 hammered out the terms of the union as well as the level of Britain's financial support. The 1956 conference, in particular, revealed disagreements over the structure of the federation, the site of the Federal capital, a customs union, internal free trade, and the powers of the central government. Eric Williams was not present at these meetings since he held no elected or legislative position. But his role in the politics of federation would change with his assumption of the post of chief minister of Trinidad and Tobago in October 1956.

Williams was an early and committed federalist. In a lecture at Howard University, Washington, D.C., in May 1940, he endorsed the idea of federation in the West Indies. The following year he predicted that "with true democracy and internal self-government these British islands could set about abolishing the present absurdity of a congeries of tiny isolated governments duplicating each other at tremendous cost. . . . Some form of a federation is demanded at least by common sense." Williams developed this argument in his first book, The Negro in the Caribbean (1942). He advocated "a political federation of the various units according to nationality," as well as "an economic federation of all the Caribbean areas." As someone who had become thoroughly familiar with the problems of the region by virtue of his scholarly training and travels, Williams was thinking in Pan-Caribbean terms, especially in relationship to economic integration and development.

Williams repeated these ideas with admirable consistency. In 1943 he maintained: "We who have the interests of the West Indies at heart must therefore realise that in the world of the future, the West Indian islands, if they are to play any part, must cease to think of themselves as island units and must begin to think and plan in terms of a federated West Indian group. Jamaica, by itself, Trinidad by itself, Barbados by itself, and I may say Cuba and Puerto Rico by themselves, will always be entirely at the economic mercy of the more advanced and more powerful countries of the world."[5]

Williams probably never guessed that he would play a central role in the construction of the federation and its brief history. During his tenure at the Caribbean Commission, he declined to comment on specific proposals for federation advanced by the Caribbean governments because they "were associated with the work of the Commission."[6] Freed of those constraints in 1955, when he left the Commission, and in his new post as chief minister of Trinidad and Tobago in 1956, Williams was finally in a position to help shape the federation he had promoted in his speeches and writings.

Although a strong advocate of federation, Williams was a severe critic of the structure that had been proposed at various times since the 1947 conference in Montego Bay. Outlining his own vision of a West Indies Federation in February 1955, he asserted that "the hope of economic advantage from federation comes first, followed by the desire to be independent of foreign control." He believed that "military insecurity" was "relatively unimportant" because of "our strategic position in respect of the Panama Canal." The separation of the islands by sea weakened "the factor of geographical neighborhood" but strengthened the case for "co-ordinate government."

Williams supported the transfer "of the power of borrowing" from the state governments to the Federal government, thereby reducing the competition among them for loans. In view of what he saw as a "growing duplication" in the islands in the area of economic development, he wondered whether the Federal government should not have the power to integrate territorial development plans. Similarly, he questioned whether the financial needs of the central government might not require the transfer of the income tax from territorial to Federal control. Although Williams did not answer these two questions at the time, subsequent developments would show that he supported a strong Federal center with the ability to impose taxes and regulate economic development in the territorial units.

Given his antipathy to colonialism, it is not surprising that Williams advocated immediate dominion status for the federation. He welcomed "an autonomous British Caribbean community equal in status to the other members of the British Commonwealth, in no way subordinate to any of the others in any aspect of its domestic or external affairs." On the other hand, he strongly endorsed substantial British economic assistance: "The British Caribbean Federation has a claim on the United Kingdom government, which no other part of the British Empire has. That is that the very presence of the two largest racial stocks, the African and the Indian, is the result of deliberate British policies designed to produce sugar and other products in the West Indies to meet British needs. . . . We can get grants from Britain for past services rendered which need not be regarded as charity or need not afford a basis for continued political control."

To Williams, the political and economic imperatives suggested that "what we need in the British Caribbean is Federation, any federation, and . . . the cardinal mistake made in this whole business was made years ago by the British government which should have written a federal constitution and simply put it into effect. When we were all crown colonies or even in 1947, that would have been progress." Williams noted that the United Kingdom had imposed a confederation on the Canadians, so there was a precedent for such imperial action. There is no doubt, however, that Williams would have criticized the British most severely had they done what he was proposing in 1955.[7]

Williams attended his first official meeting concerned with federation in January 1957. The 1956 London conference had created a Standing Federation Committee (SFC) to plan and oversee the transition to Federal status. Consisting of sixteen individuals chosen from the federating territories, the SFC was chaired by Sir Stephen Luke, a respected British civil servant. The London conference had also authorized the formation of a Federal Capital Commission to study and recommend a site for the Federal capital. Led by Sir Francis Mudie, this commission was asked to submit a list of three sites in ranked order. Its report, commonly known as the "Mudie Report," would be considered at the January 1957 meeting of the SFC, scheduled to take place in Jamaica.

In making its recommendation, the Federal Capital Commission con-

Eric Williams (first row at far right), other Caribbean leaders, and the West Indies Standing Federation Committee, Senate House, University College of the West Indies, 1957. Photograph courtesy of Eric Williams Memorial Collection, University of the West Indies (Trinidad and Tobago). © Eric Williams Memorial Collection and used by permission.

sidered several factors: "the political and social sentiment throughout the area," the "convenience of the site in relation to the Federal area," and the "availability of land both for immediate buildings and for future expansion." In addition, it examined the "suitability of communications by sea, air, cable, telephones and road," as well as the availability of support services such as hotels, educational facilities, and water supplies. Based on these criteria, the commission selected Barbados as the preferred site, followed by Jamaica and Trinidad. Its reasons for ranking Trinidad third were particularly scathing. The commission was troubled by "the instability of that island's politics and the low standard accepted in its public life." It found credible "the widespread reports of corruption in the public life of Trinidad" and that "these practices appear to be tolerated." Such tolerance "would be a disquieting augury for the future of a capital located there." Furthermore, the Indians in Trinidad allegedly "have ideals and loyalties differing from those to be found elsewhere in the Federation and they exercise a disruptive influence on the social and political life in Trinidad which would vitiate the social and political life of the capital if it were placed on that island."[8]

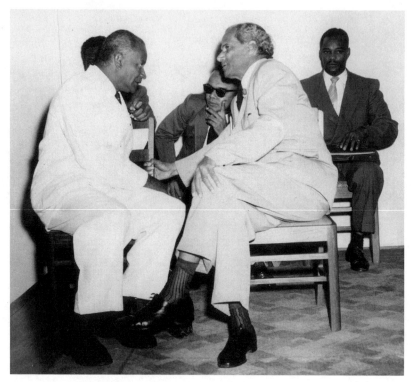

From left to right, Sir Grantley Adams of Barbados, Eric Williams of Trinidad and Tobago, and Norman Manley of Jamaica, ca. 1957. Photograph courtesy of Eric Williams Memorial Collection, University of the West Indies (Trinidad and Tobago). © Eric Williams Memorial Collection and used by permission.

These pejorative comments about Trinidad and Tobago understandably pleased no one, least of all Chief Minister Eric Williams. Rejecting the commission's recommendations and succumbing to intense lobbying, the SFC voted to award the capital site to Trinidad. Williams was undoubtedly pleased by having won a highly coveted trophy. No one who supported Trinidad on the fateful day of the vote could have predicted the terrible problems that would ensue when the SFC chose the American-leased Chaguaramas Naval Station as the specific site of the capital.

Williams did not stand for election to the Federal Parliament, although the People's National Movement became an "associate" of the West Indies Federal Labour Party (WIFLP). Led by Norman Manley, the WIFLP proclaimed itself socialist, a self-identification that prevented the "nationalist"

PNM from becoming a formal member. With Manley also deciding not to enter Federal politics, Grantley Adams of Barbados became the obvious choice for prime minister when the WIFLP won the election in March 1958. It did not bode well for the future of the federation that there was no love lost between Adams and Eric Williams. Nor did Adams have better relations with Alexander Bustamante, who would become a virtual thorn in his side. A few days before Adams took the oath of office, Bustamante attacked him mercilessly: "Adams has ruled over abject poverty for long years in Barbados, without visible improvement. How can this insular Adams who lacks sufficient imagination, do any good for the ten federated states, having ruled over pauperized Barbados for so long, obviously without realizing the state of poverty there?"[9]

♦ ♦ ♦ ♦ ♦ Eric Williams began to play a very active role in the life of the federation by virtue of Trinidad's selection as its capital. When the SFC chose the Chaguaramas Naval Station as the site of the capital in Trinidad, Williams, after some initial reluctance, undertook an aggressive campaign to oust the Americans, who held a ninety-nine-year lease that they had signed with the British in 1941. On becoming prime minister in May 1958, Adams looked askance at Williams's aggressive involvement in a matter that he thought fell under the jurisdiction of the Federal government, namely relations with a foreign power. Williams was angered by what he perceived as the Federal government's passivity in the struggle for Chaguaramas and was deeply offended when Adams, without consulting him, accepted an Anglo-American proposal to review the lease agreement in ten years.

The tensions between some of the top leaders of the region exacerbated the problems confronted by the infant federation, including the islands' small size, their physical separation from one another, and their economic deprivation. In 1953 these islands had a total population of 2.8 million. Jamaica, the largest island, had about 1.5 million inhabitants, whereas Montserrat had only 13,000 (less than 1 percent of Jamaica's population). In terms of land area, the ten islands comprised approximately 8,000 square miles, of which 4,700 were in Jamaica, 2,000 in Trinidad, and 1,300 divided among the other eight territories. To make matters worse, miles of sea separated them. Situated in the west, Jamaica was about 1,000 miles from the nearest island located in the east.

The ten federating territories were also characterized by their poverty. In

1953 their gross national product amounted to £230 million, with Jamaica making up about 50 percent of it. The average per capita income of the islands was £69. Trinidad, the richest island, had a per capita income of £121, Barbados £79, Jamaica £73, and the remaining islands less than £50. In contrast, the United Kingdom had a per capita income of £312 and the United States £846. Excluding grants, the total revenue of the ten islands amounted to £30 million in 1953. Trinidad and Jamaica accounted for £25 million of this amount. The Federal government was not much better funded, starting out with an annual budget of only £2 million. The problems created by insularity, distance, and poverty required imaginative leadership to confront and resolve them. Grantley Adams, by most accounts, was not up to the task. The bickering between some of the island leaders on the one hand, and with Adams on the other, only made matters worse.

Adams commanded much respect and even affection in his native Barbados, but his standing elsewhere was considerably less favorable. As the prime minister of the West Indies Federation, he quickly developed a reputation for making political gaffes and for incompetence. Lord Hailes, the governor general of the federation, confided to Alan Lennox-Boyd, the secretary of state for the colonies, that "Adams is not quite a big enough man for the job, apart from his laziness and lack of drive and leadership. There is a considerable amount of vanity."[10]

This unflattering assessment was amplified in a memorandum that the Colonial Office prepared for Lennox-Boyd a few months later. It asserted that Adams "has completely failed to arouse the necessary degree of positive or enthusiastic response to the federal experiment or show the dynamic leadership required to enable the newly formed Federation to rise to its possibilities." The memorandum accused Adams of "antagonizing many of the leaders of the units." The prime minister had also angered his ministers by "his high handedness and discourtesy" to them. These failings had not "been counterbalanced by any real ability or grasp of problems." The only "merit" detected in Adams was "his moderating influence on the more hot headed of his team." His shortcomings could be "partly due to failing health, and his mental powers certainly appear to have deteriorated."

According to the memorandum, Adams's ministers were "not a very impressive collection," either. The only exception was the finance minister, Robert Bradshaw: "Though formerly a well known rabble rouser and anti-

European[,] he has proved a fearless and (within limits set by inexperience) a competent Minister of Finance and has shed much of his earlier extremism. He is the only Federal Minister who has gained the confidence and affection of the officials and were it not for his arrogant, tactless behavior, [which] has alienated many small island politicians[,] he might otherwise have been acceptable as a successor to Sir Grantley."

On the other hand, Deputy Prime Minister Dr. Carl LaCorbiniere "has not been a success." The memorandum also accused him of disclosing government secrets to the press and of engaging in "underhand intrigues." Minister of Communications and Works Andrew Rose had "ability," but "as a Trinidadian has been the Trojan Horse of Dr. Williams in the Federal Council of State and reports all Council of State Secrets to Dr. Williams." Minister of Labour and Social Affairs Phyllis Allfrey, the lone white and only female in the Cabinet, was "an artistic Fabian intellectual with a fey Kittenish manner and a good heart but she does not seem to have a very clear idea of what she is about." Concluding its assessment, the memorandum declared that the minister of agriculture and national resources, Frank Ricketts, and the five ministers without portfolio "are nonentities."[11]

Statements such as these reveal the Colonial Office's contemptuous and patronizing attitude toward the leaders of the federation. But however negative and harsh the appraisal was, it contained elements of truth. Many of the most experienced and competent politicians in the territories had chosen not to seek Federal office. Others had been defeated at the polls. Using an analogy borrowed from the game of cricket, Sir Kenneth Blackburne, the governor of Jamaica, thought that "the politicians decided (probably wrongly) to put their 2nd xi in to bat."[12]

The Daily Gleaner echoed Blackburne's conclusions. It noted that Jamaica had "sent on the majority side both as senators and as members, a most unimpressive and inconsequential set of representatives. So Jamaica became something of a laughing stock in Port of Spain. Small wonder that Sir Grantley Adams, never methodical, never an administrator, sniggered and snapped his fingers at Jamaica and did what he liked with the Council of State."[13]

Grantley Adams, it must be said, manifested few of the leadership qualities required in a prime minister of a fledgling political federation. Adams, as Lord Hailes suggested, by temperament and political style, was given to lethargy. The British high commissioner in Canada found him to be "surprisingly complacent" about the "prospects for the future." Hailes also thought that Adams was not up to the job physically. In November 1959, for example, Hailes wrote that Adams "strikes me as far from well and I am not at all sure how long he can last either politically or physically." The governor of Jamaica similarly concluded that the federation "has not been given the needed leadership by its Prime Minister."[14]

Writing in October 1959, Philip Rogers of the Colonial Office also attributed the federation's problems to the "inefficiency of the Federal Government" and the "appalling inadequacy of Sir Grantley Adams." He maintained that "the relative weakness of the administrative machine of the Federal Government" was another problem. This was due to Adams's "lack of leadership" and to "certain weaknesses" among the civil servants. He singled out the Federal secretary, John Mordecai, for particular blame: Mordecai was not "a clear headed or incisive administrator." The financial secretary, Blache Fraser, was "a more marked weakness." Under the circumstances, Rogers wondered whether the governor general might not wish to seek a dissolution of the Parliament, thereby forcing new elections. Nothing came of this suggestion.[15]

If British officials showed little respect for Grantley Adams as a person, they demonstrated even less regard for the office he held. When Adams was planning to make an official visit to London in April 1959, J. O. Moreton of the Colonial Office wrote to Prime Minister Harold MacMillan's office to arrange a meeting with him. "The Colonial Secretary," Moreton wrote, "thought the Prime Minister might find it worthwhile to see him for ten minutes or so." In a similar vein, when Adams visited the United Kingdom two years later, the colonial secretary sent a profile of Adams to MacMillan reminding him that he had agreed to meet with Adams "as a sop for our having (a second time) refused to support the West Indies suggestion that he should attend the Commonwealth Prime Minister's Conference." Adams was denied admission to the conferences because the West Indies Federation was not yet independent, and the gathering was restricted to nations that enjoyed that status.[16]

The cavalier way in which the Colonial Office treated these visits by Adams to London is simply astonishing. That the British prime minister was asked to grant the prime minister of the West Indies an audience of ten minutes, or to meet with him as a "sop," was a clear indication of the way in which Adams was perceived as well as the people he represented. Eric Williams's constant complaint was that Britain saw the West Indies as insignificant, since the islands had outlasted their value to the United Kingdom. His rhetoric may have been harsh, but the truth of his accusations was undeniable.

The profile of Adams that the Colonial Office prepared for his meeting with MacMillan in 1961 was interesting for its negative portrait of the visiting leader. The assessment of Adams was important since the perception of him helped to shape Colonial Office policy for his administration. Adams's position, the profile began, was "not wholly secure." Personally, he "has a somewhat sleepy exterior and is in fact lazy, though he has an agile mind particularly in a political tight corner." He also had a reputation for "polished urbanity and a rather old-world charm." After he had received the red-carpet treatment in Canada, "there have been reports of [his] growing irritability, swollen-headedness and a readiness to take offense."[17]

The Jamaican *Daily Gleaner*, never an admirer of Adams, was also unhappy with his leadership. Unlike the British officials, however, the paper believed that Governor General Hailes also displayed mediocre leadership qualities: "Federation, as is, has sunk to depressing and (to patriots) nauseating levels of desuetude, decadence, and leadership. The joint career at the top of Lord Hailes and Sir Grantley Adams, despite their personal charm and pleasant intentions, will go down in history as a regime so dopey that it were better had it truly slept."[18]

Adams bristled at the criticism of his leadership that came from his colleagues. Unsparing in his rhetoric, Alexander Bustamante delighted in taunting the prime minister about his failure to eliminate poverty in Barbados. As he charged: "From Jamaica's point of view the only supposed cause for our entering into Federation is that we would become a nation by joining the other West Indian islands, most of them impoverished including Barbados, a country with fine people but poor, with nothing much to show from the regime of Adams for near upon 30 years—the same 'genius' who may now guide us to ruin."[19]

The two men had little to do with another, preferring to engage in a war of words from a distance. Adams's relationship with Norman Manley and Eric Williams was frigid at best. He harbored a deep suspicion that both leaders were conspiring to remove him from office. Adams never felt secure in his position as prime minister and worried that Manley had enough support among the other leaders to replace him at any time. Manley never disabused him of this notion. When Adams wrote Manley on September 14, 1960, that he could not pretend "that I am not convinced that there is a movement a foot—conspiracy is not too strong a word if you consider how it is being done to get me to resign or to oust me from the Prime Minister-ship," Manley did little to reassure him. He merely told Adams that when new Federal elections were held, "there will be a completely new situation and what happened then would be worked out in the light of the results of the election under normal Parliamentary and Party procedures."[20]

Manley never plotted to remove Adams, but as he was the most distinguished and popular statesman in the West Indies at the time, the job of prime minister was his for the taking. The Colonial Office was deeply disappointed when the highly respected Manley declined to run for Federal office, believing that he had the requisite stature, vision, and experience to lead the new federation. Less than a year after the federation was inaugurated, Philip Rogers of the Colonial Office admitted: "Two years ago I felt that the failure of Mr. Manley to become Federal Prime Minister had ruined the prospect of the Federation being effective in its early years, and conceivably ruining its prospects for surviving. Events since then have certainly borne out that view."[21]

Rogers made his comments at a time when the future of the federation was in great doubt. The Jamaican government, led by Manley, had begun to entertain the prospect of withdrawing from the alliance if certain constitutional changes were not implemented. In October 1958 Prime Minister Grantley Adams had threatened to impose an income tax retroactively on the ten federating states, a most politically injudicious declaration that generated a firestorm of protest in Jamaica. It embarrassed Manley and gave Bustamante an opportunity to remind Jamaicans that the federation was not in their best interest: "There are already tears in the eyes of some over Federation. I say if Federation continues under the existing terms, one day not only will most of us mourn, but the day will come when our children's children will curse those who thoughtlessly embroiled us in it."[22] On the other hand, the prime minister's comments pleased Eric Williams, the fervent advocate of a strong Federal government. In a dramatic gesture of support, he was at the airport to greet Adams on his return to Port of Spain.[23]

Williams, however, was not so delighted with Adams's position on Jamaica's decision to build an oil refinery. Although Norman Manley strongly supported internal free trade, he opposed the immediate introduction of a customs union. Manley appeared to be contradicting himself on the principle of free trade when he decided to build an oil refinery in Jamaica, granting the Esso Oil Company tax incentives and protection against competition. As the chief minister of oil-producing Trinidad and Tobago, Williams regarded this move as contrary to the economic interest of his country, and it soured his relationship with the Jamaican premier. When Grantley Adams did not denounce Manley's behavior in strong terms and when his government ultimately approved the construction of the refinery, Williams was furious. Recognizing that Jamaica's refinery would mean a loss to Trinidad of its sister island as a market for its petroleum products, Williams accused the Federal government of deliberately endorsing "a policy which it ought to recognize as leading to the Federation's destruction."[24]

The issue that ultimately produced the most difficulty for Williams, Manley, and Adams was the degree of power that the Federal government should exercise over the individual territories. Under Manley, who took office in 1955, Jamaica had experienced remarkable economic growth. Consequently, he opposed any interference, or any appearance of interference, by the Federal government in Jamaica's right to pursue its own economic path, including its industrial developmental program. Manley was adamant in his rejection of a strong Federal government. Eric Williams, on the other hand, was equally insistent on the opposite approach.

Williams articulated his position on the power of the Federal government in a pamphlet entitled The Economics of Nationhood, published in the fall of 1959. He advocated a strong Federal center, with the West Indies Federation possessing—among other powers—sole control of external affairs, defense, immigration and emigration, customs, the raising of loans, and exchange control.

The federation should be empowered to set income tax rates and impose excise duties, death duties, and so on. As he explained in The Economics of Nationhood:

These islands have a long history of insularity, even of isolation, rooted in the historical development of their economy and trade and the difficulties of communication for centuries. No amount of subjective, that is to say historical, cultural or other activity of the time can be expected to overcome this heritage. Only a powerful and centrally directed economic coordination and interdependence can create the true foundations of a nation. Barbados will not unify with St. Kitts, or Trinidad with British Guiana, or Jamaica with Antigua. They will be knit together only through their common allegiance to a Central Government. Anything else will discredit the conception of Federation, and in the end leave the islands more divided than before.[25]

The Federal government, however, would share with the units the responsibility for industrial development and economic planning. Overall, a strong Federal center meant a diminution in the power of the individual territories and their leaders. *The Economics of Nationhood* further proposed that the federation become independent on April 22, 1960.

♦ ♦ ♦ ♦ ♦ Capitalizing on the differences between the views of the two leaders and seeking to undermine local support for Manley, Bustamante raised the specter of Jamaica's secession from the federation if three demands were not met. First, the constitution should be changed to divest the Federal government of any right to tax the individual federating units; second, representation in the Federal Parliament should be proportional to the population of each unit; and third, any customs union should contain protections for Jamaica's economy and its workers.[26] The politically pragmatic Manley embraced all three positions.

The issue of representation by population was the easiest to resolve. Bustamante's proposal made sense theoretically, but it ignited fears in the rest of the Caribbean that it was a ploy to dominate the federation. Manley supported the proposal, however, and vigorously fought for its approval at an Inter-Governmental Conference held in 1959. Williams was not enthusiastic about this idea, but, if it were accepted, he wanted representation linked to per capita contribution to the federation as well. Trinidad, as the wealthiest of the ten islands, contributed the most to the federation on a per capita basis. "If we are to count heads," Williams opined, "I see no reason why we can't count pockets as well." Then he added, tongue in cheek: "I suppose we will have to count flying fish in Barbados."[27] In the long run, however, Williams did not press his point, and a formula was agreed upon that increased the number of seats in the Federal House of Representatives from 45 to 64. The formula allocated one basic seat to each unit and additional seats for each 55,000 residents. As a result, Jamaica obtained 48.5 percent of the seats, a sizable increase from the 37.8 percent that it had previously enjoyed.[28] The twin issues of Federal power to tax the territories and the creation of a customs union proved more contentious and would remain divisive throughout the brief life of the federation.

Through his impassioned advocacy of representation by population and other issues, the wily Bustamante assumed the upper hand in dictating federation policy that coincided with his Jamaican policies, outwitting Manley time and time again. Taking advantage of the ambivalence of many Jamaicans to the federation, Bustamante played on their fears and forced Manley to assume positions on Federal issues to which he was evidently not passionately committed. The two men had their optic on the pulse of the electorate, manipulating Federal difficulties to suit their domestic political imperatives.

Although Manley fully understood the federation's long-term advantages to Jamaica's future, the same could not be said about Bustamante. He never embraced the principle of the economies of scale, at least not at the Federal level, preferring to regard the union as a drain on Jamaica's resources. On the other hand, Bustamante correctly insisted that the federation needed substantial economic assistance from the United Kingdom if it were to succeed, a position from which he never wavered. His description of the other islands and their leaders was often pejorative and insulting. For example, he disagreed with Eric Williams's positions on the federation and thus dismissed him as an "intellectual fool."[29]

Bustamante was never entirely consistent in his attitude toward the West Indies Federation either in his public or private statements. Theodore Sealey, editor of the *Daily Gleaner*, the lone morning newspaper, informed Lord Hailes in January 1959 that Bustamante had confided to him that if Jamaica seceded from the federation and tried to go it alone, the island would have a dictatorship in a decade. Evidently, he viewed the alliance as a safety valve against such an eventuality. But Bustamante confused his colleagues with his shifting positions. Donald Sangster, his competent, respected, and trusted deputy, told Governor Blackburne a few months later that "you never know when Bustamante will get out of bed in the morning and say either that Federation is dead or that Federation is a good thing." Hailes, who called upon the aging Bustamante at his residence in November 1959, noted that he expressed guarded support for the federation. "During our 1½ hours of champagne conversation," the governor general reported, "he interrupted the story of his life more than once to revert to the topic of Federation, each time ending up by saying, 'It may work now' in 'serious tones.' "[30]

Neither Bustamante nor his Jamaica Labour Party (JLP) offered a coherent plan for the future of the federation. On June 4, 1960, he and six senior members of the JLP met with the secretary of state for the colonies to share their views with him. Bustamante repeated his claims that the economic condition of the islands was the federation's major problem and that "Jamaica and Trinidad, already poor, could not finance the development of the smaller islands." According to the minutes of the meeting, when the secretary of state asked whether the JLP would support the federation "politically" if sufficient funds were available, "Sir Alexander and Mr. [Robert] Lightbourne, in consultation and after some hesitation, said that their thought on this was not settled; but that the availability of the funds might affect their view." This was an extraordinary admission, coming two years after the federation had been inaugurated. It showed that the JLP's hardening approach to the Federal union was based less on principle and careful analysis and more on the exigencies of Jamaican domestic politics.[31]

As premier, Norman Manley was never able to deal effectively with the twists and turns of the JLP's Federal policy. On October 25, 1959, he declared that "all the Jamaica Labour Party had was great irresponsibility which masquerades as policy." He accused the party of endorsing a bipartisan policy on federation and of taking part in Federal conferences and agreeing with the decisions, only to renounce them later. "What a pity," Manley proclaimed, "that we have such a contemptible opposition. What a blessing it would be for Jamaica if we had an Opposition that knew where to draw the line between national interest and political nastiness." In a clear allusion to Grantley Adams and his unpopularity in Jamaica, Manley cautioned: "Well, men come and men go. And to argue that federation is wrong because the leadership is misguided is to put the cart before the horse. If the horse won't pull, don't throw away the cart."[32]

The *Daily Gleaner* also noticed the sharp inconsistencies in Bustamante's position. Referring to his anti-Federal stance, it chastised him in late 1960 as a "quick-silver politician" who was blaming the "federal decline" on Manley and his party. Consequently, "we have the strange anancy spectacle of the man who first put Jamaica into Federation, now on the outside, a leader for secession."[33]

Colonial authorities were irritated by the divisions among the four leaders, but they were also unhappy with the white elite of some islands that opposed federation. Governor Blackburne of Jamaica, for example, reported that Manley agreed with him that "the more prosperous members of the community" rejected federation not only because they feared higher taxes but also because of "a desire to retain the present position in Jamaica with internal self government under the umbrella of the U.K. rather than to see Jamaica as part of a completely self governing Federation subject only to control by West Indian politicians." Blackburne admitted that he was very familiar with such people, having encountered them in the Leeward Islands, where he had served as governor.

Seeking to temper the opposition of these citizens, the Colonial Office considered strategies to win their support. Philip Rogers recommended that Neville Ashenheim, a wealthy businessman in Kingston and chairman of the board of the Gleaner Company, be targeted for special attention. Ashenheim, a close adviser of Alexander Bustamante, was "the real villain," since he was one of the leaders of the Kingston group of merchants "who look at their narrow interests and think that they are best served by Jamaican isolation." Rogers suggested that Ashenheim be shown that if the federation obtained concessions in foreign markets for the rum and cigars that he produced, it would redound to his economic benefit. He needed to be educated on "which side his rum and cigars were buttered on." Similarly, Rogers believed that if Bustamante visited the United Kingdom, "it is just possible that we might get Members of Parliament of both parties to urge on him a change in his political line, and to work on his vanity for that purpose."[34]

Governor General Lord Hailes doubted whether such blandishments would serve their purpose and thought that it would be politically injudicious for London to be involved in such lobbying. "I do not think these operations by remote control mostly by expatriates will bear good fruit," he ventured. In his opinion, West Indians were "too far advanced to be greatly influenced in the last resort by outside advice." Sensing the mood of the people, Hailes stressed that it was West Indians alone "who will make or mar Federation and their future."[35]

♦ ♦ ♦ ♦ ♦ Unlike Bustamante, Eric Williams was never ambivalent about the necessity for a Federal union. His active involvement in the politics of the West Indies Federation began with his assumption of the office of chief minister of Trinidad and Tobago in October 1956. Adams, Manley, and Bustamante could all claim a Federal record that spanned a decade or more. Fresh from his victory in the elections, and fortified by an astonishing understanding of the history of federations around the world, Williams began to energetically promote the Federal idea. Less politically experienced than the other men, he wanted to move more quickly in resolving the terms of the union. It was his naive belief that his colleagues would be guided by the vision of a stronger, more economically viable, and politically influential West Indies and would be willing to make short-term sacrifices for the future greater good.

As early as 1955 the committed anticolonialist advocated that the federation start with full dominion status. Speaking in Jamaica, Williams maintained that Governor General Lord Hailes should hold reserved powers only in areas of defense and external affairs, and only for a five-year period. He adamantly opposed any appointees of the British government sitting in the Executive Council, as that was "totally incompatible with the ideas I have for the development of the West Indies." Williams repeated his demand for dominion status with regularity, and in 1957 the PNM unilaterally set the date for West Indian independence as April 22, 1960, at 11:00 A.M.[36]

Williams encountered criticisms from colleagues regarding his haste to independence. In 1959 he answered such objections by saying that "every hour, every minute that we delay, we are giving play to [the] disintegrating forces and ideas that should have been put in their place long ago." But, he assured his critics, "we are not nationalists for the sake of being nationalists, though nationalism is no crime. We are not for independence for the sake of independence, though independence *per se* is worth having." Then the West Indian nationalist contended: "Our militant nationalism, our determination to establish immediate independence, our search to develop self-government in every shape and form, have their roots in our need to establish nationhood, to take our place in the world, and to lay the foundations of a national economy in which all our potentialities and aspirations can be realized. The problem is not that we may go too fast, but that we have been moving too slowly."[37]

Grantley Adams, in contrast to Williams, was never an advocate of early independence. In April 1959 he told the secretary of state for the colonies that there was entirely too much talk about that prospect. He preferred to discuss the criteria for independence, rather than setting a date. Accordingly, Adams was never in the forefront of the demand for independence. His seeming indifference to its timing led the Colonial Office to observe in March 1961 that "Adams's principal purpose these days appears to be to delay [independence] largely because he fears this will bring closer the point when he will be dropped" as prime minister.[38]

Williams's strident advocacy of his positions—whether on Chaguaramas, dominion status, or a strong Federal center—prompted some West Indian leaders to question his motives. Governor Blackburne reported that Norman Manley "intimated to me, though it was a somewhat unworthy thought, he was forced to conclude that Williams was now engaged in paving the way for succession to the post of prime minister so he could run both the Federation and also Trinidad."[39] Williams never acknowledged that ambition, but given his strong federalist stance and his Pan-Caribbean visions, he would have welcomed a larger political stage than Trinidad afforded.

Yet, in moments of disappointment and pique, Williams harbored thoughts of secession from the alliance. Worried that his ideas on the structure of the West Indies Federation would not prevail at the intergovernmental conference scheduled for September 1959, he told British attaché Douglas Williams that if his proposal was not adopted he would "quickly" lead Trinidad out of the federation and request independence. But he was concerned about whether the British government would permit such a course of action. So frustrated had Williams become with Manley on Federal issues that he informed Lord Hailes in August 1959 that his party was considering a revocation of its associate status with the WIFLP. Such an action, had it occurred, would have jeopardized the survival of the Adams administration. His threat not withstanding, Williams assured Hailes that he would do nothing to damage the federation, though he would not allow Jamaica to have its own way. Williams said that "he will make certain that any blame for the failure of the Federation, if this were to come to pass, will be laid squarely at Manley's door."[40]

Williams, according to Hailes, accused Manley and Adams of being unprepared to subordinate their territorial interests to those of the federation. This charge was justified, but Williams was himself a Trinidadian nationalist and his optic was focused squarely and unapologetically on his country's best interests. It was to his advantage that a weak and divided opposition in Trinidad and Tobago was not snapping so fiercely and persistently at his heels on Federal issues as Bustamante and his party were doing to Manley in

Jamaica. A befuddled Adams tried, within his limitations, to balance the competing interests of the islands and seemed not to unduly privilege one above the others.

As Bustamante continued his assaults on federation and tensions with Trinidad grew, a beleaguered Manley visited London from January 9 to 16, 1960, to discuss with the secretary of state for the colonies the conditions under which Jamaica would remain in the West Indies Federation. Manley's minister of finance, Vernon Arnett, and a number of civil servants accompanied him. The delegation asked the secretary of state to answer two questions. First, what were "the minimum powers and capabilities which the Federal Government of the West Indies should have in order to satisfy the requirements of effective sovereignty and achieve membership in the Commonwealth"? And second, what would be Britain's attitude if Jamaica "decided to leave the federation and seek separate independence"?

In response to the first question, the secretary of state outlined the minimum conditions necessary for the federation to achieve independence. These included the possession of a defense force capable of maintaining the peace and deterring "any minor incursion by an outside aggressor," a diplomatic organization to conduct the federation's external relations, an effective central administration capable of executing the government's policies, and adequate financial resources to underwrite its responsibilities. In addition, the federation would need to ensure that inhabitants of one unit-territory were free to move to any other unit (that is, to immigrate within the federation's boundaries), central control of the currency, the initiation of a customs union, and the constitutional right and ability to negotiate and implement international treaties.

In answer to the second question, whose implications were more threatening, the secretary of state said that Jamaica's secession would be a disappointment to those who had hoped that the federation would survive, achieve independence, and assume its place as a member of the Commonwealth. In a guarded statement, he assured the delegation that Jamaica was in a "marginal position" for sovereignty in terms of its size, population, and resources. On returning home, Manley interpreted this to mean that "Britain will not attempt to force Jamaica to remain in the Federation against her will."[41]

The conference and the implied permission given to Jamaica to secede and proceed to independence if the circumstances warranted it represented a new stage in the Federal odyssey. Manley, in principle, could now use the threat of secession to obtain the concessions Jamaica needed, but this maneuver alienated the other federated islands and generated further suspicions as to Jamaica's real intentions. Ironically, the results of the conference energized Alexander Bustamante, because the way was now cleared for him to demand Jamaica's secession since Britain would not stand in the way of independence for the island. Manley won a pyrrhic victory, for he could claim that the conference gave him options insofar as Jamaica's future was concerned. But, on the other hand, Manley was riding the proverbial horse going simultaneously in two directions. Hamlet-like, his rhetoric was both federalist and sympathetic to Jamaican independence. Manley's failure to take a position and articulate it vigorously was a major source of weakness for the Federal cause in Jamaica.

Seizing the initiative once again, Bustamante declined in May 1961 to have his party contest a by-election to fill a vacant Federal seat. Realizing that this was a frontal assault on Jamaica's remaining in the federation, Manley decided to take the issue directly to the people. He announced that he would hold a referendum on Jamaica's future in the federation, confident that the country would vote to remain a part of the union. The election would not take place for another sixteen months, giving the protagonists ample time to take their message to the voters. Manley had not consulted the Colonial Office or Grantley Adams before he announced his decision, but the secretary of state for the colonies lent his support when he learned about it. Adams, however, was critical of the move, prompting an angry and pointed letter from Manley: "I cannot pretend to be surprised . . . because I have given up hoping that anybody in the Federal Government will try to understand the realities of my position or will appreciate the fight I am making to save Federation. . . . Bustamante has made a challenge which had to be accepted. . . . I have done it and it is an irrevocable act. . . . I beg you to keep your hands and the hands of your colleagues off this matter."[42]

With a referendum in Jamaica imminent, Williams, Manley, and Adams all realized that Jamaica and Trinidad had to resolve their differences if the federation were to survive. As the largest territories, they had to reach a modus vivendi and make the requisite compromises in their positions. Recognizing the precarious state of the federation, Williams took the initiative to resolve their differences by inviting Manley to participate in informal talks. The two men held three such meetings, two in Port of Spain in February and May 1960, and a third in Antigua the following September. A fourth discussion, which took place in June 1960, was also attended by the colonial secretary, Iain McLeod.

These meetings were important exercises in statesmanship. Much depended on the ability of the two leaders to transcend their differences and temper their mutual distrust. Almost twenty years his junior, Eric Williams had a deep respect for Norman Manley and had sought his advice on his professional options in the early 1950s. Although their relationship had been strained by their disagreements over the structure of the federation, their official lines of communication had not been severed.

The last meeting, in Antigua, was the longest and most important of the four. Before it occurred, Williams held out an olive branch to Manley: "My Government has given careful consideration to all possible permutations and combinations in the event of changes in the composition of the Federation and has come to the firm conclusion that the only Federation worth pursuing was that established by agreement between representatives of the units in 1956."[43] This was, by any measure, a stunning retreat by Williams from his advocacy of a strong Federal center. With Williams disposed to make significant concessions to Jamaica in order to save the federation, the future seemed promising.

According to one account of the secret meeting in Antigua, Williams and Manley reached substantial agreement on the issues that would be the temporary preserve of the units but that would eventually become a Federal responsibility "either exclusively or concurrently." These issues were placed on what was called the "Third List"; those that were exclusively the preserve of the Federal government were placed on the "Federal List." Although this was later to be a source of contention between the two leaders, Williams agreed with Manley's proposal that an item could not be transferred from the Third List to the Federal List unless it had "the support of unit territories having not less than two-thirds of the population of the Federal area." Since Jamaica claimed approximately 50 percent of the Federal population, this amounted, essentially, to a veto power. In a quid pro quo, Manley was willing to support a five-year delay in the implementation of freedom of movement within the federation, an issue of critical importance to Williams, who feared an influx of inhabitants of the smaller islands to Trinidad. The two leaders also agreed to modifications in the Federal government's ability to coordinate the economic development of the islands and to limitations on its authority to impose a customs union. In explaining these and other concessions to Jamaica, Williams would later say: "We could see no other way of saving the Federation, because we were convinced that to insist on our conception would break up the Federation. We disagree with Jamaica's thinking. . . . We believe Jamaica's fears exaggerated. But, if to save the Federation it was necessary to respect these fears, to respect apprehensions, which would, at worst, drive Jamaica out of the Federation . . . then we of Trinidad and Tobago decided that Jamaica was not to be pushed to the wall." Unfortunately, the "agreement" was stillborn, as Williams and Manley had different recollections of the understanding on Jamaica's veto power. In any event, Williams's ministers never formally endorsed it, and without their approval, voluntary or coerced, his hands were tied.[44]

Over the next several months the various unit politicians continued their bickering over the Antigua pact, groping for agreement and direction. Manley and Williams related to one another uneasily at these meetings, and Adams began to curry favor with the leaders of the Leeward and Windward Islands. Williams rejected any proposal that would grant Jamaica the veto power it sought but remained disposed to having a Federal center weaker than the one that he had advocated so vigorously. Manley reaffirmed his support for a delay in the implementation of freedom of movement, and the politicians from the smaller islands endorsed one proposal or another based on an assessment of their future interests.

Eric Williams, the committed federalist, began to contemplate his nation's withdrawal from the federation if Manley lost the impending referendum. On May 15, 1961, at an intergovernmental conference in Trinidad, he said that if Manley lost, "Trinidad would consider the 1956 contract to have been broken and the Federation automatically dissolved. Jamaica and Trinidad combined contributed 81.7% of Federal revenues. Under various proposals, these combined contributions would range between 80% and 85%. Trinidad could not be expected to carry the financial and economic burden of the Federation without the assistance of Jamaica."[45] It is doubtful whether anyone who heard these words understood their full import.

♦ ♦ ♦ ♦ ♦ After ironing out some of their disagreements but with many yet to be settled, the West Indians met at Lancaster House, London, on May 31, 1961, to begin crafting their independence constitution. The conference would test the political ingenuity of everyone present and their will to keep the Federal union alive. At first the delegates were guardedly optimistic that they would be able to resolve their differences, but they soon began to behave in their customary insular and quarrelsome fashion. The two burning issues that seemed to elude solution were the Jamaican veto power and freedom of movement within the federation. Fearing that he might lose the referendum if Jamaica were not granted the veto power he wanted, Manley was not open to compromise.

The delegates spent days wrangling on the issue before they finally accepted a compromise proposed by the secretary of state for the colonies. In effect, it placed an income tax and industrial development on what was called the "concurrent list." This meant that the unit territories had the primary but not the exclusive legislative responsibility for them. The compromise gave what amounted to a veto power to each unit if it opposed the Federal government's attempt to pass legislation on either one of the issues in question. The provision read: "Any proposal that the Federal Government should assume powers to legislate on the subjects 'Development of Industries' and 'Taxes on Income and Profits' will not come into force until the proposal has been approved by a majority of each House of the Federal Legislature and by an absolute majority of the Representative House of each Unit Legislature." This measure would considerably weaken the Federal center, and a seething Eric Williams refused to support it. He had been prepared, albeit reluctantly, to grant Jamaica a veto power, reversing his earlier stand, but he could not endorse its extension to all of the units. In a later explanation of his position, Williams said that the compromise "transferred the veto power from Jamaica, which Trinidad and Tobago considered offensive to any single territory thereby compounding the offense. It effectively suppressed any prospect of the emergence of a movement in Jamaica itself to bring Jamaica more in line with the thinking in other parts of the Federal area."[46]

The proposal for freedom of movement within the federation was equally contentious. The smaller islands were strongly in favor of it, but Williams was firm in his opposition. He argued that the population pressures in these islands should not be managed by facilitating immigration, but by improving their economic conditions so that the inhabitants would be disinclined to move. Williams feared, with good reason, that immigrants would flood Trinidad if freedom of movement were implemented before the economic conditions of the smaller islands improved. He did not want the new constitution to set a time for its implementation, preferring to leave it open-ended or indeterminate. Deserting Williams on this issue, Manley joined the majority of the delegates in supporting the proposal that freedom of movement should be introduced within nine years of the achievement of independence.

From the perspective of his own country, Williams's positions had much to recommend them. In the years 1958, 1959, and 1960, the nearby island of Grenada had sent 6,046 people to Trinidad and Tobago and 3,083 to the United Kingdom. During the same period St. Vincent dispatched 4,106 inhabitants to Trinidad and 1,452 to the United Kingdom. Overall, Williams estimated that Trinidad admitted 7,500 other West Indians annually in the years immediately preceding 1960. If such a movement to Trinidad continued, not only would it exacerbate population pressures on the island, Williams maintained, but also the cost of placing migrants in jobs would amount to about $422 million in ten years. Over the same period, the cost of providing modest housing for them would be $70 million, a water supply $11 million, and education approximately $25 million.

In addition, there was much statistical support for Williams's argument that the islands were neglected by the mother country. The best way to keep the migrants at home, he said, was to increase capital expenditures, thereby making more jobs available. The United Kingdom was extremely parsimonious in its capital grants to their economies. According to Williams, the islands received the following capital grants in 1960:

Antigua	$657,000
Dominica	1,100,000
Grenada	241,000
Montserrat	388,000
St. Kitts	1,100,000
St. Lucia	172,000

Such dramatically spartan financial assistance from the imperial country prompted Williams to declare: "Development is absolutely unthinkable in such terms, and migration is inevitable . . . the only answer is economic aid for development."[47]

With Manley's support for the freedom of movement proposal, his long-standing tensions with Williams became an open breach. The two old friends left the meeting without saying good-bye, and their wounds bled for years. Williams found the delegates' decisions on the two divisive issues so repugnant that he disassociated his country from them. So ended another unhappy chapter in the history of the West Indies Federation. It was the last time that representatives of all ten islands met on the Federal question.

Norman Manley got his way at the Lancaster House Conference but at the expense of much goodwill from the other islands. Francis Galbraith of the U.S. Embassy confessed that "it would take more insight and expertise than is possible to bear here into the personalities, personal jealousies, ambitions, inter-island rivalries and political intrigues in the West Indies to adequately assess [its] outcome." Few observers argued with this assessment. Colonial officials, according to Galbraith, proclaimed the conference "a success only in that it was not a failure." They thought that Norman Manley had played "a stellar role in helping the conference over the various impasses." Eric Williams was, by contrast, "negative and antagonistic in his manner and actions." Grantley Adams was also "less than helpful and encouraged Barbadian recalcitrance, among other things."[48]

A jubilant Norman Manley returned home to the cheers of his worshipful supporters. Eric Williams, smarting from his reverses, maintained a gloomy silence and left for South Asia. Trinidad's Governor Solomon Hochoy admitted that he and Ellis Clarke, a trusted Williams associate and later ambassador to the United Nations, worked to calm his leader's anger. In a handwritten letter to Hugh Fraser, under secretary of state for the colonies, Hochoy noted: "At first Dr. Eric was inclined to give a very full account of the London talks to the House adding his disappointments etc. Indeed, his report would have done everything which you and I feared. He would have added fuel to the fire. . . . I was able with Ellis Clarke's help, to steer him off that."

Adhering to a gallant and statesmanlike silence, Williams declined to make any critical comment on the conference until long after Manley lost the referendum in September. Privately, however, he confided to William Christensen, the deputy chief of the U.S. Mission, that once the conference was over "he was determined then that he would not attempt to take Trinidad into Federation." He said that it "was most fortunate that the Jamaica referendum had failed," and that it would have been a "tragedy" if Manley had prevailed.[49]

Williams broke his public silence on the Lancaster House Conference on November 4. In an interview that he gave to C. S. Espinet, the managing editor of the *Trinidad Guardian*, he said that his policy up to the time of the meeting was to make "every conceivable effort" to "accommodate the difficulties that had been raised by Jamaica." But to him, the conference repre-sented "a total sellout to Jamaica, the price paid being the antagonizing of Trinidad and Tobago"; he was not prepared to go "along with the Lancaster House mess." The decisions it reached "violated every concept of Federa-tion. They would have been totally disadvantageous to Trinidad and Tobago and they would have made the West Indies Federation the laughing stock of the entire world." Williams admitted that he had intended to take the whole matter to the people, with a recommendation that they reject the Lancaster House decisions. If the people failed to accept his recommendation, he would "sever his connections with Trinidad and Tobago and retire into obscurity from which I would plan never to emerge. I did not intend to be a part to any bastardization of Federation."[50]

Williams continued his assault on the conference in an address to the Trinidad Legislature in January 1962. He told the lawmakers that the meeting "marked the disintegration of the Federation," and he condemned "the total absurdity of the decisions" that were made there. "We consider," Williams said, "that the Jamaica Referendum merely dotted the 'I's' and crossed the 'T's' of what would ultimately have been inevitable, if not with Jamaica with some other territory." Williams may have spoken more in sorrow than in anger given his strong commitment to the Federal concept. It could hardly have been easy to witness the demise of a union that he had tried, in his own way, to save. Lionel Seukeran of the Democratic Labour Party (DLP) was not at all sympathetic to the premier's position. "The man that killed federation sits before me," he said. "I charge Dr. Williams as being the destroyer of federation," Seukeran added.[51]

Still, Jamaica's decision to secede did not automatically sound the death knell for federation. Despite his bellicose comments about the Lancaster House decision, Williams had not made up his mind regarding Trinidad and Tobago's political future. His comments on November 4 suggest that he had been so displeased by the conference that he was going to lead a secessionist movement in his homeland. This could have been an exercise in hyperbole or the ill-considered remarks of a man still seething from his disappoint-ments at Lancaster House.

♦ ♦ ♦ ♦ ♦ Eric Williams did not make his country's future an issue in the general elections scheduled for December 1961. The opposition DLP de-clared its support for Trinidad remaining in the federation, provided that it received substantial external aid, increased quotas for immigration to the United States and Canada, and guarantees that its products would have markets in the United Kingdom, the United States, and Canada, among other conditions. The DLP called Williams's decision not to make the federation an issue in the election campaign "undemocratic, dictatorial, and a direct negation of democracy."[52]

As he contemplated the direction in which he would take the country, Williams received the advice of Professor Arthur Lewis, a distinguished economist and vice chancellor of the University of the West Indies. Lewis was on a leave of absence from the university to help the remaining nine units develop a strategy for the survival of the West Indies Federation. Williams had indicated on several occasions that Trinidad was unprepared to undertake the financial burdens of the federation if Jamaica seceded; if Jamaica did so, Trinidad would follow suit. This threat was not taken very seriously, and there was still hope in London and in the Windward and Leeward Islands that Williams could be persuaded to keep Trinidad and Tobago in the union. Grantley Adams was ambivalent, however. He and Williams were not on speaking terms, and he would have been pleased if Williams followed Jamaica's lead. On the other hand, Adams knew that Trinidad's inclusion was crucial to the federation's preservation.

Williams had three options: first, he could keep Trinidad in the federation and become its dominant leader; second, he could ask for political independence as Jamaica had; or third, he could invite the eight smaller islands or, at least some of them, to join Trinidad in a unitary statehood. Each option had its own appeal. Federation would enhance Williams's stature in the Eastern Caribbean, and his country would be the first among equals. But, as Williams was acutely aware, Trinidad would pay dearly for the privilege. Independence, though also costly, meant that Trinidad could begin to chart its own destiny, unfettered by any obligations to the smaller islands. With unitary statehood, Trinidad's size and independence would be enhanced by the absorption of its neighbors, but it would inherit their economic problems as well.

Arthur Lewis, when he met with Williams in the fall of 1961, found him attracted to the idea of unitary statehood with the other islands. Williams had probably not given much attention to its implications since he was in the throes of a general election campaign. But the prospect of increasing the size and stature of Trinidad—and his own power and influence in the Caribbean—must have been rather tantalizing. There were, however, practical issues that stood in the path of this dream becoming a reality. First, the Indian population in Trinidad would not have welcomed it, as it feared domination by what would have been a permanent black majority. Second, the smaller islands and their leaders looked askance at what they called "Trinidadian imperialism" and were not likely to agree to give up their identity for a union with their larger sister island. There was also the added complication that Williams would not have won a popularity contest in any of those territories, and his relationship with their leaders was consistently rocky.

Williams's impressive victory in the December 1961 elections, with his party winning twenty of the thirty seats, strengthened his hand immeasurably. His triumph was an endorsement of his accomplishments in office since 1956, and his country's future was his to shape. Williams held the trump card, and he knew it. He teased and titillated his citizenry during and after the election campaign as to his preferred course of action. Arthur Lewis was no more successful in getting Williams to declare his intentions. The mystery ended on January 14, 1962, when the General Council of the PNM— under Williams's direction—voted to withdraw from the federation and to seek independence for Trinidad and Tobago. The resolution left the door open "to the future incorporation in the unitary state of Trinidad and Tobago of any Territory of the Eastern Caribbean whose people may so desire, and, on terms to be mutually agreed or to the future establishment of a Common Economic Community embracing the entire Caribbean area."[53]

This dramatic decision signaled the end of any hopes to salvage a smaller West Indies Federation. The pro-federation politicians in the Windward and Leeward Islands received the news sadly, recognizing that federation had received a deathblow. For Eric Williams, the decision represented a repudiation of his long-held dream of a political union of the Anglophone Caribbean. His critics would later accuse him of destroying the federation, but the issue was not that simple. In an effort to keep Jamaica in the union, and hence save it, Williams had compromised his position on the need for a strong Federal center, as he had outlined in his *Economics of Nationhood*. The Lancaster House Conference, and the decisions it had made, led Williams to reassess his commitment to federation and ultimately made his decision to opt for independence easier. Had Norman Manley won the referendum,

Williams would have undoubtedly remained committed to federation, swallowing his disagreements for the larger good.

The survival of federation with the nine remaining units posed another problem for Williams. An Eastern Caribbean Federation led by Trinidad was certainly a tempting morsel. The leaders were willing to accept a strong Federal center, endorsing the principles enshrined in the *Economics of Nationhood*. But Williams would not enter into such a union if it imposed a crippling economic burden on his own country. Without the commitment of significant external economic aid, federation lost its appeal. As an ardent nationalist, Williams's first loyalty was to Trinidad and Tobago, even if the Federal pull and promise never died.

Although the political union was dissolved, Williams's commitment to the economic integration of the Caribbean never waned. In fact, a few months after Trinidad opted for independence, he told a meeting of the British Caribbean Association in London that his nation planned to work "towards the undertaking of some form of Caribbean Economic Community, with powers within the economic sphere which might ultimately extend to political spheres."[54] Such an economic entity, Williams contended, would establish a relationship with the European Economic Community (EEC), which had just recently been created. And he did not rule out the prospect of another political union. In August 1962 he told an interviewer of the British Broadcasting Corporation: "I don't see any future for the West Indian area that excludes planning in that direction. In so far as we in Trinidad and Tobago, with independence and a large population majority can influence things, we have been moving in that direction, not limiting ourselves to our former colleagues in the Federation, we have begun discussions with Guiana, that are going on now."[55]

Having just led the fight against federation, Alexander Bustamante's JLP government had no stomach for such talk. It recognized, however, that if the United Kingdom joined the European community, Jamaica would lose the preferential treatment that some of its products enjoyed in British markets. Consequently, it would be to the nation's advantage to have an alliance with the EEC in order to protect those concessions. The issue was stillborn, however, as France vetoed Britain's application for admission to the EEC in 1963. This setback notwithstanding, Williams floated the idea of a loose association of the Anglophone islands patterned after the Organization of African Unity. It would also include other countries in the region with the exception of Cuba, Haiti, and the Dominican Republic, whose antidemocratic forms of government Williams found abhorrent. He would later soften his stance on the inclusion of these three nations in any potential union.

Jamaica was sympathetic to periodic meetings of the heads of government of the independent and self-governing Anglophone countries, but not to the presence of non-British territories at these gatherings. The first such meeting with the leaders of Trinidad, Jamaica, Barbados, and British Guiana took place in Port of Spain in 1963, and additional ones were convened in 1964 and 1965. These conferences, particularly the first two, addressed questions of regional cooperation, but they resolved nothing of significance. Frigid relations between Williams and the Jamaican leaders, especially in 1964, made the prospect of cooperation between the units more difficult.

Williams's ideas on a closer economic association in the Caribbean area found concrete expression in a series of discussions that he held with the secretary of state for the colonies and with the heads of government of Puerto Rico and the Netherlands Antilles in the summer of 1964. In his meeting with Secretary of State Nigel Fisher on July 21, Williams proposed the creation of a new Caribbean union that would be initiated by a customs union but that would eventually include a regional airline and a shipping service. The union would consist of Trinidad, Puerto Rico, Suriname, the Netherlands Antilles, the French islands, British Guiana, Jamaica, Haiti, and the Dominican Republic. Williams noted that such a union would be incomplete without Cuba, but because of its Marxist regime that prospect "was out of the question for the present." Fisher later noted that his meeting with Williams was "friendly," and that he had provided "enough ideas to keep officials busy for a long time to come."[56]

This latter observation notwithstanding, colonial officials were not enthusiastic about Williams's proposals. One internal analysis doubted whether a customs union would provide "equal advantages" to "countries at widely different stages of industrial development and with widely different development potential." Since "nearly all the countries of the region are members of trading groups wider than the Caribbean," the analysis noted, "the establishment of a customs union would be inconsistent with at least some of these arrangements." Puerto Rico, it speculated, would not join a Caribbean customs union since it already enjoyed a special trading relationship with the United States, which purchased 97 percent of Puerto Rico's exports. "It seems improbable," according to the analysis, "that Puerto Rico would be prepared to lose free entry for her products [into the United States] in exchange for free entry into the far smaller Caribbean market." It predicted that without Puerto Rico's support, Eric Williams "may be unable to proceed further."

Similarly, colonial officials expressed doubts about the feasibility of a regional airline. The "political and commercial obstacles" were "likely to be insurmountable" inasmuch as the other countries were not expected "to be willing to merge their national airlines." Their analysis was no more optimistic about a regional shipping service, since the existing one—a holdover from the defunct West Indies Federation—operated at a deficit.[57]

Williams was most likely unaware of the misgivings of the colonial authorities. A week after his conversation with Nigel Fisher, he met with Governor Luis Muñoz Marín of Puerto Rico to confer about the possibility of cooperation with the other Caribbean territories in such areas as shipping, aviation, and tourism. The two leaders agreed to create a number of joint study groups to consider these issues as well as the feasibility of a regional development bank, an investment company, and a scheme for hurricane insurance. Williams also visited Paris to discuss with the French foreign minister, M. Couve de Murville, matters related to the economic integration of the Caribbean and specifically the inclusion of the French dependencies of Martinique and Guadalupe in such a union.

Williams also had a series of candid talks with Efraim Jonckheer, minister-president of the Netherlands Antilles, who visited Trinidad in early August 1964. Williams later told Norman Costar that "these people certainly mean business." Costar was less impressed, reporting to his supervisors in London that it was difficult to see any "positive outcome" in the "commercial and economic field." But Williams's "new scheme," as Costar described it, was based on a closer economic relationship between Trinidad, Puerto Rico, and the Netherlands Antilles in the first instance.[58]

Nothing tangible resulted from these Williams-inspired initiatives. The prospect of Caribbean economic integration was not enhanced by Williams's stormy relationships with other Anglophone Caribbean leaders. In 1964 he was hardly on speaking terms with Alexander Bustamante of Jamaica or his deputy, Donald Sangster. When Norman Costar advised him in July 1964 that he should discuss with Jamaica the question of a regional shipping service for the islands, he, according to Costar, "replied heatedly that I knew very well that he had no lines with Jamaica." The leaders of the smaller islands distrusted his motives, describing him as "the threat from the South." Aware of these attitudes, David Rose, the administrator of Antigua, reminded Williams that he could not expect "post Federation bitterness" to abate quickly and the policies for which he wanted the support of those islands frequently became known to them through the newspapers. Williams could not, Rose told him, "be altogether surprised if his good intentions were sometimes misconstrued in these islands." Although Costar admired some of Williams's ideas on economic integration, he thought they were "fraught with practical difficulties and it may be doubted, given his personality, whether he is the man to bring them to fruition." He considered it "a pity" that "a useful movement to reverse the fragmentation of the Caribbean area is likely to suffer from the personality of the man who is inspiring it." Williams's "abrasive personality (to use the phrase of a *Trinidad Guardian* editorial)" Costar asserted, "is calculated ultimately to antagonize the very people on whose cooperation the success of his ideas most depend."[59]

There was a thaw in the relationship between Jamaica and Trinidad in the summer of 1965, although one British functionary in Jamaica reported that Donald Sangster's "feeling of distrust and dislike of Williams had clearly not abated." Norman Costar believed that Williams was feeling isolated because he "rotates his friendships and his enmities and at the moment is on poor terms with most of his neighbours, Commonwealth and Foreign, in the Eastern Caribbean." Consequently, "it is natural . . . for him to look to the fence at the Jamaican end of the garden, and in recent weeks Dr. Williams has said nothing nasty about Jamaica, which for Dr. Williams is almost a mark of favour."[60]

Such unflattering observations about Williams's personality and moods notwithstanding, his human weaknesses cannot fully explain why his ideas had little resonance in the islands. Coming so soon after the collapse of the West Indies Federation, the disposition among several Anglophone leaders to pursue new avenues of cooperation was either absent at worst or tepid at best. They were skilled practitioners of the politics of suspicion, and any new initiative—particularly one associated with Eric Williams—invited skepticism, a crippling form of second-guessing, and ultimate death through inertia. Williams's Pan-Caribbean vision, however, had much to recommend it given the region's common history of European exploitation, colonialism,

and economic deprivation. But it could not, at the time, vanquish the coun-
tervailing pulls of insularity, mediocre leadership in some cases, and competing imperial loyalties. The French, the Dutch, the English, and the Span-
iards had imprinted their territories in significant ways, and a few farsighted
leaders like Williams tried to transcend their fratricidal tendencies and forge
a common purpose, albeit with little success.

Disappointed with the failure of any movement toward economic integration, Williams observed in 1965 that "more than three years after the enunci-
ation of our goal of Caribbean Economic Community, PNM's policy has
been conspicuous by its lack of success."[61] The first tangible step in the
direction of economic integration in the region occurred when Barbados,
Antigua, and British Guiana signed a free trade agreement in 1965. Williams
was never involved in the negotiations and reacted with indifference to its
creation. Although the agreement was not implemented, it laid the foundation for the larger Caribbean Free Trade Association (CARIFTA) that was
established in 1968. Its members would eventually include all the former
members of the defunct federation as well as Guyana and the Bahamas.

♦ ♦ ♦ ♦ ♦ Throughout his career, Eric Williams never wavered from his
vision of a politically and economically integrated Anglophone Caribbean.
He imagined a closer association with other countries in the Caribbean but
felt that ideally such arrangements would be restricted to those nations that
embraced democratic ideals. In the early 1960s Williams was deeply suspicious of Fidel Castro's motives in the region and had little contact with
him or his government. He enjoyed warm relations with the leaders of
Puerto Rico but had no affection for those in Haiti and the Dominican
Republic. Still, by 1964 he was willing to accept Cuba, Haiti, and the Dominican Republic into the larger Caribbean economic union that he was con-
templating. Williams envisaged a Caribbean region free from colonial rule,
responsible for its own destiny, and integrated, if not politically, at least
economically. Small and economically disadvantaged, each island would be
considered insignificant and irrelevant on the international stage, but their
impact would be enhanced if they spoke with one voice.

Williams had articulated the need for a West Indies Federation with greater
passion than any of his contemporaries. Irritated by his criticisms of the
fledgling union and its slow pace toward dominion status, Grantley Adams in
March 1960 bluntly reminded him:

Those who have studied the politics of the West Indies during our lifetime know that the Premier is not the only person who has fought for the idea of Federation. I know that people in the West Indies have not forgotten the work of some of the real federalists like the late Captain Cipriani and T. Albert Marryshow who were in the forefront of the effort to build up a strong labour and nationalist movement when Dr. Williams was still a schoolboy. . . . The post war efforts of the political leaders of the West Indies from Montego Bay to Lancaster House to achieve self government and independence were made without any assistance from the Premier of Trinidad and Tobago, whose desire to interfere has now become greater than his desire to help.[62]

Eric Williams possessed the energy and the impatience of one who was new to the political fray. His elders—Adams, Manley, and Bustamante— viewed him as an iconoclastic upstart who declined to follow their lead. But Williams also had the distressing tendency to alienate his colleagues with his sharp tongue, his difficulty in absorbing criticism or dealing with opposing points of view, and his marked intellectual arrogance. Given his undisputed brilliance and the fact that he presided over the largest and wealthiest territory, his leadership of the Eastern Caribbean would have been his for the taking, had it not been for his human limitations.

In the end, the political integration of the West Indies eluded Williams, although he had long fervently championed its cause. Jamaica's secession from the federation gave the coup de grace to such plans, and an angry and disappointed Williams ultimately expressed disinterest in leading a smaller, poorer Eastern Caribbean federation. Williams, however, had a lingering affection for the Federal idea and continued to provide intellectual leadership for the principles of free trade and the economic integration of the region. These efforts, in time, achieved some success, but the centralized planning he wished for the area, and worked to achieve, remained unrealized.

◆ ◆

CHAPTER 3

THE STRUGGLE FOR
CHAGUARAMAS

◆ ◆ ◆ ◆ ◆ Nothing could temper the enthusiasm and determination of the crowd, not even the torrential showers that drenched it on that warm April morning in 1960. Some sixty thousand strong, it was the largest march that Trinidad and Tobago had ever seen. The banners held high by some told the entire story: "Dignity Is Incompatible with Colonialism," read one. "Road to Independence Passes through Chaguaramas," proclaimed a second, and "We Want Chaguaramas . . . Not Grapefruit" demanded a third. Led by Chief Minister Eric Williams, the "March for Freedom" began at Woodford Square and, as it passed Queens Park on its way to the U.S. consulate, a group of young men broke into a "calypso trot." "Uncle Sam, we want back we lan," they rhymed.[1]

The proceedings started on April 22 at 11:00 A.M., the day and hour that Eric Williams had unilaterally set to proclaim the independence of the British West Indies. The crowd went wild as Williams hoisted the flags of Trinidad and the West Indies, an act that symbolized "freedom in fact, if not in law," he said. Addressing the crowd, the chief minister declared: "We have beaten our heads against the forces and agents of colonialism, against the unswerving and often discourteous hostility of the British and American governments, on the one hand, and on the other, against the servile mentality and inferiority complex bred among some West Indians by centuries of colonial rule." But this had been to no avail. "Thus it is," he regretted, "we find ourselves today, on what should have been our historic Independence Day, cheated of our rights and frustrated in our aspirations."

The dramatic high point came when Williams identified seven "deadly sins with which we have been afflicted" and consigned them to the flames. He identified these sins as the constitutions of Trinidad and the West Indies, the Mudie Report on the site of the Federal capital, the telephone ordinance of 1939, the U.K.-U.S. Chaguaramas Agreement of 1941, a recent statement on race made in the Trinidad Legislative Council by the DPL, and a copy of his persistent foreign-owned critic, the *Trinidad Guardian*. As Williams threw each offending item into the flames, he intoned, "We consign it to the flames . . . to hell with it."[2]

The nationalist fervor of the crowd was high and the speakers rose to the occasion. Patrick Solomon, Williams's principal lieutenant, read a memorial condemning colonialism and affirming the West Indies' right to independence: "In the world of 1960 colonialism had [*sic*] no place. The political oppression, economic exploitation, social degradation, cultural inferiority which it brings in its train have been universally repudiated." The memorial characterized the British West Indies as "the last remnants and tatters of the colonialism from which the world has steadily liberated itself." The West Indies Federation was "a glorified crown colony, a 19th century anachronism." The American base at Chaguaramas constituted "the most deadly menace that has yet appeared to our national interests and our social and political aspirations," the memorial maintained. It ended on a defiant note:

We demand an independent Federation.

We demand full internal self-government for Trinidad and Tobago.

We demand the revision of the 1941 agreement between the United Kingdom and the United States of America in a conference in which Trinidad and Tobago enjoys direct, separate, equal and independent representation.

We demand the return of Chaguaramas and other leased areas ceded without our consent and against our will.

We demand the right, the inalienable and imprescriptible right to decide our own destiny.

Long live the independence of the West Indies!

This anticolonial rhetoric had no precedent in the British West Indian islands. It was one measure of Eric Williams's role in shaping the nationalist mood of his nation as well as an indication of changing times in the Caribbean. As Williams told his listeners on that April morning: "Our march in Port of Spain is the symbol of our march throughout the West Indies. We march legally and constitutionally in a grand political demonstration—without liquor, without jumping up, without calypsoes, without disturbance, without molestation of onlookers, or spectators . . . we march with disci-

Eric Williams speaking at the University of Woodford Square at the start of the famous "march in the rain" during the fight for Chaguaramas, April 22, 1960. A sign stating, "Uncle Sam, we want back we land," is displayed. Photograph courtesy of Eric Williams Memorial Collection, University of the West Indies (Trinidad and Tobago). © Eric Williams Memorial Collection and used by permission.

pline, dignity and decorum, as befit the citizens of a country who have publicly declared our intention of independence."[3]

In the days preceding the march, local U.S. and U.K. officials worried that it would become violent. Writing to Williams on April 9, Governor Edward B. Beetham suggested that the demonstration be confined to Woodford Square in Port of Spain and warned that it could make the resolution of the Chaguaramas dispute more difficult. Outraged by this message, Williams, in one of his signature letters, told Beetham that "on this matter of Chaguaramas you and I, Governor and Premier, are on opposite sides." He castigated Beetham for appearing to be "ranged against the Government and People of Trinidad and Tobago on issues which we expected that you above all were in a position to understand and appreciate our policy." Williams reminded him that "we have had for nearly three years to fight tooth and nail, every inch of the way, against American intransigence, British hostility, and Trinidadian treachery" to obtain separate representation for his government at the conference to review the U.K.–U.S. Chaguaramas Agreement. In his report to the Colonial Office, Beetham stated that Williams reacted "violently" and "hysterically" to his letter, indicating that he did not take the chief minister's observations seriously.[4]

The fears expressed by the expatriate officials were misguided. But they had consistently underestimated the nationalist passions that drove the people on the related questions of Chaguaramas and political independence. By 1960, Eric Williams had made Chaguaramas the single most contentious issue of his then brief tenure as head of government. In the process he simultaneously alienated the Americans and to some extent the British, enhanced the nationalist fervor of a large number of his countrymen, and led others to connive with the Americans against him. The dispute placed on full display the ugly side of the domestic politics of Trinidad and Tobago, the haughtiness and intransigence of the Americans in their dealings with a small country, Williams's considerable strengths as a leader, and the myopia of some of his opponents.

The controversy over the presence of the U.S. military base at Chaguaramas had its origins in the selection of Trinidad as the site of the Federal capital in 1957. The other main contenders for that honor had been Jamaica and Barbados. Trinidad had won primarily because of its proximity to the other Eastern Caribbean islands, an advantage where travel between them was concerned. Jamaica had lost mainly because of its distance from the other units, and Barbados never really had strong support from its sister islands. Eric Williams was delighted with the choice of Trinidad, but little did he realize that its selection would involve him in one of the most acrimonious disputes of his political career.

The capital having been chosen, it became the responsibility of the Standing Federation Committee (SFC)—the body entrusted with the task of planning for the inauguration of the federation—to select a location in Trinidad. On May 8, 1957, the SFC announced that it had chosen a site on Trinidad's northwestern peninsula, an area that formed a part of the land that the United Kingdom had leased to the United States in 1941 for the construction of the Chaguaramas Naval Station. The site was only seven miles from Port of Spain on one of the most picturesque parts of the island. The problem with the choice was that the United States had no wish to surrender Chaguaramas or any part of it to the Federal government. When the U.S. State

Department heard that Chaguaramas had been selected as the site for the federation, it indicated that it was willing to surrender Waller Field as an alternative location. Waller Field was a deactivated base in the north central portion of the island that had been released to the local government under an agricultural utilization agreement. According to the terms of this agreement, the United States could demand its return if it were needed in an emergency.

In a discussion with the British colonial attaché in Washington, State Department officials emphasized that they had sent word to the SFC that the United States would never surrender Chaguaramas. As the attaché reported, the U.S. State Department "was inclined to take the view that the choice of [the] North Western Peninsula was somewhat provocative, paid little regard to their role in the defense of the Caribbean area, and did not augur well for future relations with the West Indian Federation. They stated Chaguaramas was a key point in the defense of the whole Caribbean area, and they saw no possibility of their being able to find similar facilities elsewhere."[5]

The U.S. Departments of State and Defense would cling to this position for the next several years. Concerned about a potential dispute, the secretary of state for the colonies informed the governor of Trinidad and the colonial attaché in Washington on May 13 that it would be unfortunate if the Chaguaramas issue were to damage the new federation's relationship with Washington at the outset. He said that his government believed "that American goodwill may well prove to be worth more to the new Federation than the North West peninsula of Trinidad." Under the circumstances, he wanted the governor to ask the SFC to review its decision "in the light of the State Departments' views . . . and accept Waller Field, but telling them that Waller Field is *probable* and by no means certain." Should the committee decline to review its recommendation, Her Majesty's government "would almost certainly find it most difficult to support a request for a release of the whole of Chaguaramas." He speculated, however, that some part of it might be a subject for negotiation.[6]

It is interesting that within days of the selection of Chaguaramas as the capital site, the United Kingdom and the United States had taken positions from which they would not readily budge. The SFC members knew that they held the weaker hand, but they refused to be bullied. On May 11 they assured Governor Beetham that it was not their intention to adopt a "provocative or unfriendly" stance toward the United States. Nevertheless, they "expressed strong resentment at the indefinite perpetuation, whether in Trinidad or elsewhere, of the arrangements made by the United Kingdom and United States Governments in which West Indies [sic] themselves had had no voice."[7]

To resolve these differences, the SFC requested meetings in London and Washington with the two governments. Beetham, sensitive to West Indian nationalism, endorsed this request, suggesting that the U.S. Department of Defense should be represented in the discussions. But there were signs that the issue was becoming more complicated. As early as March 25, Eric Williams had told Douglas Jenkins Jr., the U.S. consul general in Port of Spain, that the SFC "favored" the naval station at Chaguaramas over other sites but that it had also been impressed "with the possibilities of the Waller Field area." Williams admitted that "he was not particularly taken with Chaguaramas as a site." He preferred Waller Field and thought that the Americans were more likely to release it if they were assured that an alternative airfield could be provided in the event of a military emergency.[8]

Even at this early stage, Eric Williams had good reasons for his lukewarm reception to the potential selection of Chaguaramas as the capital site. He knew that the Americans occupied the area as a result of the 1941 agreement with Britain, and that this could not be violated. In fact, during the election campaign that brought him to office in 1956, the manifesto of the People's National Movement (PNM) pledged to respect "all international obligations, financial, economic and military, with special reference to the Agreement on the United States Bases." Williams gave a similar assurance to the U.S. envoy to Trinidad and Tobago after the selection of Chaguaramas was announced, a decision that pleased the Americans enormously. The Colonial Office, gratified by the chief minister's position, believed that it reflected "his desire to be scrupulously correct about international agreements."[9]

Understandably, Williams's colleagues in the West Indies were not pleased by his position. Some grumbled that he wanted the Americans to remain at Chaguaramas because the naval station employed about eight hundred to one thousand Trinidadians. When the SFC debated whether to ask the Americans to release Chaguaramas, Williams and the other delegate from Trinidad and Tobago abstained from voting. Williams was also unwilling to serve as a member of the delegation to London to settle the problem, since his government wanted no part of the plan to seek the release of the naval base. He would attend the London meeting only as an observer and would participate in the discussion only if the 1941 agreement were to be revised or if a new one were to be agreed upon.[10]

Members of the SFC were aghast, believing that Williams's attitude would "fatally prejudice the delegation's chance of success." According to the U.S. consul general, Premier Grantley Adams of Barbados engaged in a "heated exchange with Williams"; he and others "forcefully argued" that "Williams had a responsibility to the SFC as well as to Trinidad, and that as a member of the SFC he was in duty bound to accept the verdict of the majority and to work for its achievement, rather than acting like a spoiled child and refusing to play." Williams promised to reconsider his position.[11]

Williams kept his promise, and on May 22 Governor Beetham was able to tell the secretary of state for the colonies that the chief minister had decided to join the delegation. Williams, however, did not want the U.S. authorities to interpret his participation as a retreat from his election pledge on the sanctity of international agreements. The next day Beetham reported that the U.S. State Department had no objection to Williams serving as a delegate and welcomed his stance on the Chaguaramas issue. Obviously hoping that Williams's position would prevail in London, the State Department felt that further discussion without Trinidad's participation would be "impracticable."[12]

With the conference scheduled to begin on July 16, the parties involved started to plan their negotiating strategies. The West Indians were naively confident that sentiment would prevail and that the Americans would release Chaguaramas as an expression of goodwill to the new federation. The Americans were not so disposed and seemed to view the conference as an exercise in public relations and as a sop to the West Indians. U.S. Department of Defense representatives were not anxious to discuss the issue with the West Indians and threatened to boycott the talks if the United Kingdom did not reveal its position to them.[13] The U.S. State Department also sought to know the line that the British would be taking with the West Indians so that it could plan its strategy accordingly. In effect, the American officials wanted the two nations to act in concert against the West Indians, an approach that the United Kingdom resisted, albeit weakly.

To bolster their case at the forthcoming conference, American officials sent a memorandum to the British on June 13 outlining their position. The eight-page document asserted that the Chaguaramas base "is designed to be the key to United States defense planning for the entire Caribbean and South

Atlantic area." Without it, "anti-submarine warfare would be dependent upon long-range aircraft and surface units whose availability, mobility and striking power would be seriously limited." If the base were abandoned, "no effective defense against submarines in the area could be mounted." The memorandum stressed that even if a suitable base were identified elsewhere, the cost of relocation would run in excess of $100 million. It also rejected as impractical the partitioning of the base. "It is felt that our long-term relations with the Federation," the memorandum stated, "which are of high importance to the United States, would suffer less from a complete rejection of the request for release than would be the case were we to attempt to mollify West Indian sentiment by agreeing to partial release."[14]

The United Kingdom was also interested in determining the importance of Chaguaramas for the defense of the Western Hemisphere and commissioned the Air Ministry to undertake such a study. Based on its findings, the Air Council of the Air Ministry concluded that the facilities at Chaguaramas "could be of significance only during the post-nuclear phase of a global war." Moreover, "so far as the air component of such facilities is concerned, and in relation solely to the defense of the United Kingdom and of the West Indies, the Air Council feel that the disappearance of the United States base from Trinidad would not be a serious loss." In the council's opinion, "the problem should be regarded as purely a political conflict between the wishes of the United States Government, and the aspirations of the countries of the proposed Caribbean Federation."[15]

The two governments thus reached quite different conclusions on the importance of Chaguaramas for the defense of the hemisphere. But the British were not prepared to take the side of the West Indians against their North American ally. Although U.K. officials maintained that they were going to adopt a neutral stance in the conference, this was disingenuous. Prior to the start of the meeting, they briefed the Americans on how to deal with the West Indians, advising them to stress the strategic reasons for the retention of Chaguaramas.[16]

The U.S. strategy as it evolved was largely an exercise in deception. On July 13 the American ambassador to the United Kingdom, John Whitney, cabled the U.S. secretary of state to explain the strategy that the American delegates would adopt at the conference. Whitney said that from the outset the Americans would place the onus on the West Indians to defend their selection of Chaguaramas and their desire to force the United States to spend large sums of money to relocate. Since he believed that the West Indians would "obviously require something to go home with," he hoped that he would be authorized to offer them "grant assistance in construction elsewhere" at an "appropriate juncture" in the talks. He would only make the offer of assistance in the most general terms and probably outside of regular meetings "unless there appears to be some softening of [the] West Indies position." Ambassador Whitney emphasized that although the U.S. delegates would not depart from their "basic position," "we must maintain [the] impression of having [an] open mind." He indicated that the Americans planned to assure the West Indians at the end of the conference that they would "further study" the issue.[17] The United States was clearly just going through the motions and had no intention of changing its position. It was a tactic that was unworthy of a powerful nation dealing with a group of small, relatively weak, and impoverished islands.

When the conference opened on July 16, Norman Manley of Jamaica rose to present the West Indian case. He emphasized that the decision to select Trinidad as the Federal capital "was basic and irrevocable." Chaguaramas was an excellent site because it was close to Port of Spain, thereby saving the federation the cost of building a new town, as some countries such as Australia had been forced to do. Unaware that the Americans had come to the conference with their minds already made up, Manley urged them "to look at the matter in a broad and generous spirit." He asked them "to consider that the good relations between them and the West Indies . . . is of supreme importance that . . . [they] should be preserved and enhanced in the future."[18]

In his reply, Ambassador Whitney emphasized that Chaguaramas was the only viable site for the U.S. naval base and stressed its importance for the defense of the Western Hemisphere. He said that the United States appreciated the position of the West Indians and supported their journey to statehood. Whitney thought that the whole issue could be reduced to a contest between the political aspirations of the West Indians and the military imperatives of the United States.

As the discussions continued, there was no indication that either side would retreat from its position. The British urged the West Indians to abandon their request for Chaguaramas and accept an alternative site in Trinidad. But the delegates stood firm, showing no divisions in their ranks. Probably sensing that the West Indians were basing their claims on principle, Ambassador Whitney did not attempt to mollify them by raising the question of economic aid as a quid pro quo.

Eric Williams was, at best, a less-than-enthusiastic member of the West Indian delegation. He was, after all, at odds with the other delegates on the location of the capital site, but his opinion could not be ignored since he was the chief minister of the territory in question. Before his departure for England, Williams had asked to see the still-classified documents relating to the circumstances under which the 1941 Leased Bases Agreement had been signed, though he evidently had no time to read them until after his arrival. The historian-turned-politician immersed himself in these records and additional ones he received in London, experiencing an epiphany in the process. On July 17, the second day of the conference, Williams dramatically reversed his position and announced that he could no longer endorse the 1941 agreement. He now supported the complete evacuation of Chaguaramas by the Americans, but he left the door open for negotiating an alternative site on the island. In any event, if the United States declined to accept his request, the matter would have to be addressed by his party and his government.[19]

This wholly unexpected development must have delighted the West Indian delegates as much as it confused their counterparts from the United States and the United Kingdom. Two days after Williams dropped his bombshell, Alan Lennox-Boyd, the secretary of state for the colonies, told Philip Rogers of the Colonial Office that his "instinct is that Williams's speech jolted them [the Americans] into recognizing the inherent dangers of adopting a purely negative attitude." Nevertheless, Ambassador Whitney maintained that "we can get away with this without a real battle."[20]

Williams explained his new position to the delegates in a lengthy memorandum. He expressed his "wholehearted support" for his colleagues' stand on the question of Chaguaramas and gave them a history lesson on why he felt compelled to seek an abrogation of the 1941 agreement, quoting at length from the correspondence of Sir Hubert Young, governor of Trinidad and Tobago at the time the agreement was consummated. Not only had Young strenuously opposed the selection of Chaguaramas as the site of the U.S. naval base, but he also had believed that the needs of the people should be paramount in any such decision. In a letter of October 22, 1940, to the secretary of state for the colonies, Young wrote that he hoped "that it might be found possible to combine the provision of the necessary facilities for the United States forces with at least some of the requirements of the Colony in which they were to be our welcome guests for such a long time. . . . It was in my opinion essential that these arrangements should contain no germs of future friendship or hostility."

Governor Young had been concerned that if Chaguaramas were leased to the Americans, Trinidadians would be denied access to one of the most cherished parts of their island:

> I am informed that for the past hundred years this particular area has been the recognized holiday area not only for all those who have not the opportunity of going elsewhere but for every class of the community. There is no other place in the Colony in which anything approaching the same amenities and facilities could be provided and I should be quite unable to agree to this suggestion unless it were proved that the requirements of the naval and military situations could be met in no other way. . . . The cutting off of these amenities from the people who at present enjoy them and from the increasing number who might potentially enjoy them in future . . . would cause friction which it was desirable to avoid.

Young wanted to see the Americans confined to one area of the island "and not dotted about in different localities." He suggested that the Caroni swamp, if reclaimed, would be a suitable site for the naval base. The Americans summarily rejected that suggestion, and when Young visited Washington to press his case, he found no support for it. This proposal having failed, the governor advocated the appointment of a Joint Commission to study the issue further, since Chaguaramas had been selected after only a ten-day exploratory tour of the island. Young argued: "It seems hardly reasonable for a foreign power to expect to find a suitable site for the 99 years lease . . . in a closely populated island like this in ten days."

He thought that the undue haste in the selection of a site was due to the fact that the Americans "did not regard the object of the Mission as the quest of a naval and air base for the United States in a part of the British Empire, for the security of which the British was and would remain responsible, so much as that of a naval, military and air base in an outlying island of the South American continent, for the defense of which the United States Government would assume responsibility, and which was to serve if necessary as a jumping-off ground for operations by the United States Army in South America."

Governor Young was correct. Unable to obtain a location in South America, the Americans turned to the British, who were only too willing to make their colonial territory available. As the British ambassador to Washington told Young: "It is practically impossible for the United States to get any equivalent facilities in Venezuela or other parts of the north of South America because of the sensitiveness of all South American Republics to give the United States permanent facilities on their own territory. That is why [the] United States Government is so concerned that the work at Trinidad should be begun and completed as soon as possible."

The British continued to brush aside all of the concerns raised by the governor and his Executive Council. Young felt that the British government needed to be sensitive to the fact that the constitutional status of Trinidad and Tobago could change over the ninety-nine-year period of the lease, thereby threatening the legitimacy of any agreement. He wrote that "in making arrangements which were to hold good for a century[,] it would be prudent to bear in mind the degree of self-government that might be attained by the people of the colony before the end of that long period." In addition, the governor insisted that any agreement with the Americans should be made with the consent of the legislature.

It seemed to Eric Williams that there was much similarity between the arguments in these letters and the Americans' present insistence that Chaguaramas could not be released. The chief minister mockingly observed: "It is impossible to give up Chaguaramas because of its deep-water harbor. It is impossible to find another base. It is impossible to move from Chaguaramas because it is too costly. It is impossible to surrender Tucker Valley, which has a beach house, golf course, plantation, hospital, radio station etc. One is tempted to ask after reading the document, what is possible? The document disregards entirely the only thing that is really impossible—that is to ask Trinidad people in 1957 to put the seal of approval on what was done in 1940 in defiance of the Governor's views."

Williams noted that the United States claimed that it would cost $100 million to abandon Chaguaramas for another site. By his calculation, that sum amounted to thirty-four cents a year per head for the 3.5 million people of the federation for the unexpired portion of the lease, or eighty-three years. Williams thought that was "a small price to pay for West Indian goodwill and the avoidance of friction." But, he added, "no amount of money would be able to buy that goodwill if the West Indian people learn how the rights of Trinidad were trampled upon in 1940."

The chief minister predicted an intensification of friction between the Americans and the people of Trinidad and Tobago. "What appears to the Americans as only a base, what the SFC sees as the only capital, I see as an explosion of the first order," he warned. Williams was proposing that the Americans leave Chaguaramas and that the United States, Trinidad, and the United Kingdom reach "an amicable agreement" on "a footing of equality" regarding an alternative site for a U.S. base on the island. Although there was no time for this in 1940, he said, "we have the necessary time in 1957."

Some delegates must have been surprised at the strident tone of Williams's memorandum. The chief minister had embraced a profoundly nationalist stance on the issue and was going out on a limb from which he could not possibly retreat. The dye was cast:

> The other representatives of SFC are dealing with the question of a site for the Federal Capital. In my position as representative of Trinidad and Tobago on the SFC, I am also dealing with the same thing. But I am also concerned with another question which does not concern them, at least not directly, and that is the question of the disposition of Trinidad's territory . . . as the Chief minister . . . I could not possibly put myself in a position in 1957 of being less concerned and less vigilant in defense of the fundamental interests of the people of Trinidad than a British Colonial Governor and the Executive Council of the period of 1941. To do so would not only be a gross betrayal of the confidence which the people of Trinidad have so generously placed in me, my Party and my Government. It would also be political suicide. I intend neither betrayal nor self-destruction.[21]

Williams's memorandum provided an accurate description of Sir Hubert Young's very real concerns in 1940–41. But he was probably unaware of Britain's unhappiness with U.S. behavior in the Caribbean even before the agreement was signed. On December 24, 1940, a Colonial Office memorandum prepared by the secretary of state complained about the incessant American demands for more land in the Caribbean and their implications for British sovereignty in the area. The secretary of state for the colonies acknowledged that "I am gravely disturbed at the apparent implications of some of these demands, and I feel that my colleagues should be aware of the dilemma which seems about to face us, either of being false on the one hand to the reiterated pledges given both to the West Indian Colonies as well as to the public in this country relative to the maintenance of full British sovereignty in the Islands, or on the other hand of imperiling our good relations with the United States." Furthermore, West Indians were becoming concerned that the establishment of the bases "will affect British sovereignty in these ancient Colonies and derogate from their cherished British nationality." Black West Indians feared "that American treatment of the Negro and coloured population will follow the lines notorious in the Southern United States."

The Colonial Office was disturbed that the Americans had sent an unauthorized "Economic Mission" to the colonies, an act that violated British sovereignty. British officials were also bothered by the fact that the United States had offered the use of the West Indian bases to other American republics without seeking their approval. In addition, the United Kingdom was not amused when U.S. ships and aircraft visited its colonies without permission; these were "high handed acts," the 1940 memorandum charged. Nor were British officials pleased when the United States declined to send representatives to London to complete the final arrangements for the Lease Bases Agreement, demanding instead that the British officials go to Washington. This conduct was "in keeping with the attitude adopted generally by United States representatives in discussions with the colonial governments over the sites based in the West Indies; in some cases local objections to the United States demands were brushed aside as unworthy even of consideration."[22]

American "high handed" behavior notwithstanding, the United Kingdom agreed to all of the U.S. requests for land in Trinidad and the other islands. In the case of Trinidad, the Foreign Office telegraphed the British ambassador in Washington on January 2, 1941, that all the "United States needs in matters of site to be leased" had been met. The ambassador was authorized to tell the U.S. government that the lease agreement "involves the people of Trinidad in great sacrifices and is taken in many respects contrary to the views of the local Government. In these circumstances His Majesty's Government hope that for their part the United States authorities will reciprocate our generosity by doing everything in their power to minimize the disturbance which is bound to be created by granting to them such extensive concessions."[23]

These documents, along with the ones that Williams cited in his memorandum, supported his contention that the people of Trinidad and Tobago had no voice in the appropriation of their land. To give teeth to his claims, Williams prepared a draft of Trinidad's proposal on Chaguaramas and presented it to the conferees. The document urged an immediate evacuation of those areas of Chaguaramas "least essential to existing operations" and recommended the creation of a Joint Commission to find "an alternative site in Trinidad for a combined base embracing naval, air and such military installations as may be necessary in the event of war." If that proved unfeasible, the commission should seek a site on a "nearby" island. It should also make an "economic appraisal" of the cost of a new base. Williams wanted the commission to include technical and military representatives of Trinidad, the United States, the United Kingdom, and the s f c. Its report should be submitted by the end of January 1958 at a conference of the aforementioned countries to be held in Trinidad.[24]

Williams was easily the dominant personage at the conference. His insistence that the Americans should begin the process of withdrawing from Chaguaramas had dramatically altered the tenor of the discussions. His strong support for Chaguaramas as the capital of the West Indies Federation clearly strengthened the s f c's case. By the time the conference ended on July 23, 1957, the delegates had accepted his proposal to create a Joint Commission "composed of representative technical experts [from the United States, the United Kingdom, Trinidad, and the s f c] to investigate all aspects of the British West Indies request to make Chaguaramas available, taking into full account military and economic considerations."

The conference on Chaguaramas had failed to resolve the issue, but the creation of the Joint Commission was an acceptable compromise. All of the delegates had agreed on the need for a U.S. naval base in the Eastern Caribbean, but the West Indians and the Americans disagreed on whether Chaguaramas represented the only suitable site for it. Significantly, the Americans did not promise to accept the decision of the Joint Commission if it went against them. However, the American ambassador to the United Kingdom, who led the U.S. delegation, observed: "It is the basic policy of the United States never to force ourselves into a place where we are not wanted nor to remain in a place where we are not welcome."[25]

On returning home, Williams delivered an oral report on the conference to the Trinidad Legislative Council. In his speech, he reviewed the circumstances that led to his volte-face on the question of the Chaguaramas site, the memorandum that he had delivered to the conferees, and his proposal for the immediate evacuation of the unused portions of the base. Williams stressed that "the real issue involved . . . was the question of self government for Trinidad and Tobago as well as for the Federation." He thought that the point was best made by a remark at the meeting "that instead of the West Indies behaving like people who hope to get independence after five years, they behaved as if they were already independent." Williams felt that "no apology is necessary for this." As the West Indies was moving toward dominion status, Williams advised that "we have to start now doing for ourselves what was formerly done for us by others."

Knowing that his critics regarded his reversal on Chaguaramas as an expression of anti-Americanism, the chief minister assured the legislators that in the discussions at the conference there was never "any suggestion of hostility to the U.S.A. or of a desire to exclude the U.S.A. from the Federal area either by the Federal Delegation or myself." Williams skillfully used his report to the legislature to remind Americans about their own history as opponents of colonialism. He linked Trinidad's contemporary struggle with those waged by America against Europe. Invoking the name of former secretary of state and later president John Quincy Adams, Williams noted that in 1819 Adams had characterized the presence of European colonies in the Americas as "a physical, moral, and political absurdity." The historian-scholar went on to acknowledge U.S. Secretary of State Richard Olney's assertion that any permanent political union between a European and an American state was unnatural and inexpedient. These and similar anticolonialism statements by Presidents Grover Cleveland and Theodore Roosevelt led Williams to conclude that the United States was unique in its possession of "so profound and powerful a tradition, among people and government alike, of opposition to colonialism and sympathy—more often than not, practical, for the aspirations of colonial peoples."

His attempt to link Trinidad's present situation with America's anticolonial history was an appeal to sentiment as much as it was an indictment of that nation's seemingly hypocritical stance on Chaguaramas. He reported that his West Indian colleagues at the London conference had "stressed the difficulty inherent in the inheritance for a further period of 83 years of an international agreement to which the Federation . . . was not and is not a party." Williams pointed out that Thomas Jefferson was one of the earliest advocates of a federated West Indies, calling it "an enrapturing prospect into futurity." He predicted that an "amicable solution" would be found, thereby "laying the foundation of a firm and lasting concord between the great federation of the north and the infant Federation which will soon be born on its doorstep."[26]

For the most part, Williams's report to the council was conciliatory in tone and optimistic in its expectation of a satisfactory solution to the issue. He was careful to emphasize that if the Americans vacated the naval base and demanded compensation, Trinidad would not be responsible for paying it "directly or indirectly."[27]

The expectation that the Americans would participate in the work of a Joint Commission in a spirit of openness and goodwill was soon seriously undermined. Barely three weeks after the London conference ended, it was reported that the Americans were beginning to install a guided missile tracking station at Chaguaramas that they said was part of a network of such facilities that extended from Patrick Air Base in Florida to Ascension Island in the South Atlantic Ocean. When he got wind of the construction, Norman Manley was outraged. He and the other West Indian leaders thought that if the Americans intended to take the commission's work seriously, they would not be undertaking new construction before the matter was settled. Manley said that such activity by the Americans "looks as if they regard the setting up of a commission as a farce . . . and I think the whole attitude . . . is insultive." He added:

> If it is true that they are planning to put more facilities at the Base at a time when we are about to appoint a Joint Commission to consider it then I regard that as a positive breach of faith. I am certain America could not think of doing anything like that except to a colonial territory that it believes is helpless to protect itself and in that case I hope they will remember that we will not always be a colonial territory and that it is our territory. The fact of the matter is that in my opinion if things go on like this, the thing is going to take on a very bitter character and the friendly atmosphere that has prevailed so far is going to disappear.[28]

Eric Williams was also incensed by the news about the tracking station. His government immediately issued a statement claiming that the new construction constituted:

1. A complete disregard of all that is implied in the agreement to appoint the Joint Commission;
2. Substantial prejudice to the efforts of the commission to find a fair and just solution of the problem referred to it;
3. In the minds of the public, an indication of a thorough lack of

sympathetic understanding on the part of the U.S. government of the West Indian request for the release of Chaguaramas as the capital of the West Indies;

4. Reasonable ground for public resentment of what is generally interpreted as an attitude of domination to a small, friendly neighbor.[29]

Shortly thereafter, a Trinidadian delegation presented a memorandum to the newly formed Joint Commission that registered, according to F. J. Leishman of the British Embassy in Washington, the government's "strong protest against continuation of the work" on the station. Faced with such protests, the U.S. consul general requested British help to calm local opinion "on the issue of the missile tracking station and to remove it as an issue from the Commission's deliberations."[30]

Norman Manley correctly predicted that the tone of the discussions on the capital site would change; the missile tracking station issue was the first indication that that would occur. The U.S. Department of State was not pleased with Manley's comments. In a statement that it sent to the American consul general in Kingston for dissemination, it explained that the decision to construct the tracking station had been made in January 1957 and the contract to build it had been finalized in April. To suspend the construction on the basis of the London discussions would have been costly and, the statement added gratuitously, "would have deprived a substantial number of Trinidad workmen of gainful employment." The U.S. government assured the public that it was not "attempting to prejudice the findings" of the Joint Commission.[31]

But the damage was already done and the credibility of the United States had been harmed. The new construction intensified West Indian suspicions of American intentions, and Williams was one of the principal critics. The West Indians questioned the timing and political intent of the construction while the Joint Commission was being formed. Williams also seethed over related matters. When the new U.S. consul general, Walter Orebaugh, called on him on October 8, 1957 Williams did not greet him "with the normal exchange of pleasantries"; instead, "in [a] piquant tone" he drew attention to the harsh line that the American press was using in its discussion of Chaguaramas. If that continued, he would be forced to make public the documents that revealed America's "high handed tactics" in the 1940–41 negotiations. According to Orebaugh, Williams said that Trinidad would leave the West Indies Federation if it were to lose the capital because Chaguaramas was not available as the site. He predicted that the federation would fail if another island were chosen as the capital, and the Americans would be blamed for that disaster. Had Chaguaramas been a British base, Williams boasted, he would have evicted its personnel "in a week."[32]

Williams's strong endorsement of Trinidad as the capital site contradicted his earlier position. For instance, in late 1954, in a paper entitled "My Federal Record," Williams stated that he was "frankly not interested" in the issue. As he explained: "It could be Carriacou, for all I care, so long as it is in the British West Indies and not in London, Timbuktu or Tierra del Fuego. One thing I do know, however. The jealousy between large cities in other federations has resulted in the selection of the smaller and less important centres as the capital. . . . The importance of Trinidad would, to my mind, in the light of the historical record, be in itself a powerful reason for rejecting it as the Federal capital of the British West Indies."[33] Times, of course, had changed. Williams was now the chief minister of Trinidad and committed to protecting its interests.

Realizing that his Chaguaramas stance had struck a responsive chord in many of his countrymen, Williams launched a sustained verbal campaign against the continued U.S. presence at the site. He depicted a mistreated colonial Trinidad that had had no say in the alienation of its soil by an imperial country that showed scant regard for the opinions and desires of the colonized. Britain had acted insensitively, imperiously, and improperly in 1940–41, and an aggrieved Trinidad on the verge of independence needed to reclaim its soil and its self-respect. The Americans, accordingly, had no moral right to remain in Chaguaramas in light of changing times and circumstances. The demand for their evacuation, Williams asserted, was not driven by anti-American sentiment—hence his willingness to provide an alternative site for the U.S. base on Trinidad's soil. Rather, it was based on a people's right to control their own destinies and their national soil.

♦ ♦ ♦ ♦ ♦ Williams's position on Chaguaramas was controversial in Trinidad and elsewhere in the West Indies. Trinidadian Solomon Hochoy, then the acting governor, told the U.S. consul general on August 14, 1957, that the view that Chaguaramas was the only satisfactory location for the capital was "pure political froth." Hochoy said that he told Williams that Waller Field was a better site and would contribute much to the development of the northeastern section of the island. He also reported to the consul general that Williams's ministers were divided on the issue, and that opposition in their ranks would increase if he continued on his present course. Gerard Montano, the minister of labor, had expressed the strongest opposition to Williams's position. Hochoy promised, according to the consul general, "to urge upon the wavering members of the Executive Council, the dangers of the present course, the absurdity of the claim that Chaguaramas is the only possible site, and the advantages of Waller Field." The American envoy was pleased that Hochoy gave his assurance that he would be "working behind the scenes" to promote Waller Field or some other areas as the capital site.[34]

The Democratic Labour Party (DLP), the principal opposition party, did not share the chief minister's nationalist fervor and worried about the implications for future relations between the United States, Trinidad, and the West Indies Federation. The DLP sensed, as Williams and the PNM did, that the Chaguaramas issue could be exploited to partisan advantage. According to the U.S. consul general, Bhadase Maraj, then leader of the DLP, and Albert Gomes, a prominent member, viewed Williams's position as a function of "personal antipathy to the United States resulting from his Caribbean Commission experience and a marital problem which was keeping him from going to the United States." Thus, Williams's political stance was disparaged as stemming from nothing more than personal pique. The DLP assured the consul general that the Chaguaramas issue would be used against Williams in the forthcoming Federal elections.[35] As the debate intensified, it revealed serious divisions in Trinidadian society. The issue became racialized as people of African descent generally supported Williams, whereas Indians and those of European descent tended to endorse the position of the DLP.

Albert Gomes was notably harsh in his condemnation of Eric Williams, Grantley Adams, and Norman Manley for their stand on Chaguaramas and for embroiling "the West Indies in a senseless struggle with the Americans." Singling out Manley for special abuse, he declared that "he must not be surprised to discover . . . that the line he is now pursuing in the Chaguaramas affair differs in no way from that which a good Communist would adopt in the same circumstances. This is very bad for the West Indies." Manley's sin was his fervent West Indian nationalism, a position that matched the spirit of the times. Ghana had become independent in 1957, and national liberation movements existed all over Africa. By linking Manley—and by extension

Williams and Adams—to communism because of their pro–West Indian stance, Gomes's was the voice of a discredited past.[36]

Several political leaders in the other islands were also not enthusiastic about a potential American release of Chaguaramas. Their primary concern was that Williams's behavior would endanger good relations with the United States, with negative economic consequences for a largely impoverished region. The Jamaica Labour Party, the opposition party in Jamaica, was not particularly troubled by the presence of the U.S. base on its sister island. Edwin Allen, one of the party's deputy leaders, told the American consul general in Kingston that the West Indies Federation should not attempt to contest any serious U.S. opposition to releasing the site. In an interesting aside, the consul general said that he was surprised to find Allen, a graduate of London University, "shrewd and surprisingly articulate," a judgment that certainly smacked of racial condescension. He described the prominent Jamaican legislator as "a very dark, squat, unimpressive-looking individual with a harsh, guttural voice (reminiscent of Louis Armstrong)." Despite these alleged defects, the consul general took Allen seriously and quoted him as saying that American goodwill should not be forfeited over a relatively trivial matter. In view of the fact that the United States was committed to the defense of the West Indies, its refusal to leave Chaguaramas would produce no significant reaction, Allen predicted. Should the federation be required to find a new capital, financial support from the United States to construct it would, however, be welcomed, he added.[37]

Some Caribbean leaders were also concerned that Williams was exploiting the Chaguaramas issue to enhance his own political standing, with the objective of eventually becoming prime minister of the federation. Others accused him of anti-Americanism, even though he made a distinction between an assertive West Indian nationalism and anti-Americanism. His critics invariably conflated the two questions. Unaccustomed to dealing with the nationalist aspirations of colonized peoples and insensitive to their struggles, the Americans also equated the request for the release of Chaguaramas with anti-Americanism. Prior to Eric Williams's volte-face on the issue at the London conference, U.S. officials had never felt threatened by him. The *Trinidad Guardian*, the largest circulating daily newspaper, had been the most persistent advocate of the American release of the base, but Williams's change of heart had altered the political climate. By August 1958 the U.S. consul general in Port of Spain had begun to fear the emergence of a "Yankee, Go Home" movement fanned by Williams. Although the consul general observed that Williams was "circumspect in language and has emphasized that a spirit of goodwill and friendship existed at the London conference," the official organ of the P N M, the *Nation*, led by its editor C. L. R. James, "has been beating the drum in a series of front page editorials, each more violent than its predecessor."

The consul general found it hard to believe that "seasoned campaigners as Manley and Adams would be prepared to stick with Williams on the Chaguaramas issue to the point of going along with him in stirring up a hornet's nest of anti-Americanism throughout the West Indies and inviting the inevitable backfire." That being the case, the U.S. State Department should emphasize to Manley and Adams that if the West Indians persisted in demanding the release of Chaguaramas in the face of its acknowledged centrality to the defense of the hemisphere, they would alienate the American public. If that occurred, they "must expect to find themselves without the pale of American financial assistance and technical aid." In addition, "present arrangements such as that providing for the importation of West Indian agricultural labor into the United States might be endangered." The two leaders should be assured that if the West Indians succeeded in getting Chaguaramas, they would inherit only "a shell"; the U.S. Navy "for economy reasons would salvage and remove everything of value even down to the water mains and electricity lines."[38]

U.S. officials had good reason to believe that the issue could be resolved by threats of economic reprisal. Their experience with some other poor and developing nations must have fortified the view that principles were inconsequential in the face of economic need. Ironically, Sir Grantley Adams, as one of the chief spokespersons for the West Indians, lent his support to such a contention. After meeting with Adams in August 1957, the American consul general in Barbados informed the U.S. State Department that "the Premier was very frank in stating that behind the West Indies' request for the relinquishment of Chaguaramas was the question of money. In his view, the West Indies being poor in resources could ill-afford to build a new town for its capital—the United States being rich could afford to write off the construction costs of the Naval Base as an expended weapon of war and build another base in some other part of the West Indies."[39] If Adams's assertions are given any credence, it is clear that the request for Chaguaramas was not inspired by anti-Americanism, at least from his perspective. Had he known of this conversation at the time, Williams would have contested Adams's claims, invoking the imperatives of anticolonialism. As the controversy developed, however, the Americans had difficulty distinguishing between nationalist claims and anti-American rhetoric.

Statements like the one made by Adams fed American suspicions that economic aid would supersede any larger principles involved in the Chaguaramas dispute. This was certainly not the view of Eric Williams at the time; he insisted that "I want everybody to know that the government of the PNM . . . is not at anytime to be bought . . . the issues involved are far more serious."[40] At one level, such suspicions by the Americans diminished the principles that legitimized Williams's request for the release of Chaguaramas. On another level, they suggested with a degree of validity that some West Indians were willing to sacrifice their national self-respect on the altar of economic aid. The Massa who Williams would eventually denounce in 1961 was still very much alive in the imagination and behavior of many. But there is also a third conclusion that can be drawn from such assertions that privileged economic aid over principles. They gave comfort to the United States that disputes with poor and developing nations could be neutralized by the offer of financial assistance.

In the months preceding and after the start of the deliberations by the Joint Commission, Williams began to educate his countrymen on the issues involved in the dispute. He was energized by the challenge and obviously enjoyed the intellectual aspects of the combat. But it was also an opportunity for him to reach a larger international audience, especially colonial societies that were struggling to contest the might of imperial countries or those that would be their successors. His language was not always temperate, something his critics thought was hurting the cause as well as the image of the West Indies.

The Americans were never certain that Eric Williams spoke for the majority of his countrymen on the Chaguaramas issue. When Consul General Walter Orebaugh met with him on October 10, 1959, the chief minister warned that if the Americans were seen as successors to British colonial rule in the West Indies, their presence would be opposed by a majority of Trinidadians. Probably in response to this statement, Orebaugh began a survey of "public and official opinion in Trinidad concerning the Chaguaramas capital site issue." Three months later, he reported that among the working classes who held any opinion on Chaguaramas, the majority wished the Americans to remain in possession of it. Many of these residents were either current or former employees of one of the U.S. military establishments. The Indians were "probably" more favorable to the American presence than were people of African descent.

Orebaugh's canvassing of public sentiment further revealed that there was "a numerous element among the middle and upper-class Negroes (the creoles) who would like to see the Americans shown who is 'boss' in Trinidad." The consul general attributed this feeling to "envy" of the United States that was "compounded with a retaliatory instinct for the widely-held opinion that the Americans generally regard the negroes as an inferior race." Another ingredient, he said, was "an overzealousness to rid Trinidad of the attributes of 'colonialism' with which our possession of Chaguaramas is associated." The "less well educated class" also feared that the U.S. presence would invite "enemy attack in case of hostilities." According to Orebaugh, intellectuals, politically sophisticated "whites," and influential members of the PNM believed that the Americans would not have agreed to "negotiate" the base issue unless it had already decided to make substantial concessions. Still, "the politically sophisticated" believed that the West Indian strategy was injudicious, since it endangered U.S. economic and technical support for the West Indies Federation.

Following in the footsteps of many other observers, Orebaugh was interested in the psychological makeup of Eric Williams as a way to predict his behavior on the Chaguaramas issue. He described Williams as an "obdurate person" who was "especially disinclined to change his mind in dealing with 'whites.'" Williams "has little love for the United States and Americans." Orebaugh reported that "on several occasions during the past three months" he "has been surly, captious and less courteous than ordinary good breeding dictates when prominent Americans have called on him to pay their respects." During a recent visit from Senator George Aiken of Maine, Williams "managed barely to be civil[,] showing transparently that he is inclined to carry chips on both shoulders when Americans are about."

Orebaugh observed that "numerous Trinidadians" thought that it was "sheer madness" for the Americans to "yield" on Chaguaramas. Orebaugh agreed, believing that the United States would "suffer a disastrous loss of prestige with little, if any, compensating credit for being magnanimous and generous." If Chaguaramas were yielded, "it would only be a matter of days or weeks before the West Indies Federation . . . would be rapping at our door for further economic assistance."[41]

The relatively new chief minister of Trinidad and Tobago was sensitive to fiscal issues and the need for continued American benevolence. The personnel at the Chaguaramas base contributed an estimated US$250,000 to the economy of the host island, a considerable sum at the time. If the base were vacated and an alternative site could not be found in Trinidad, the island would suffer economic consequences, to say nothing of 800–1,000 base-related jobs. At the time, Williams was also seeking U.S. economic aid to help finance his five-year development plan. Thus, the chief minister was walking a very tight rope by promoting the evacuation of Chaguaramas on the one hand and requesting American financial assistance on the other. The main distinction between Williams and his opponents/critics at this stage was that Williams saw no contradiction between the assertion of a virulent Trinidadian and West Indian nationalism vis-à-vis the United States and the simultaneous expectation of U.S. economic aid. The chief minister knew that the two countries needed each other: Trinidad needed economic help, and the Americans needed a base on the island. But this was not a simple quid pro quo. The American Goliath would be cut down to size, humiliated, and forced to acquiesce to the rules laid down by the West Indian David. This was realpolitik Caribbean style, the methodology of which Williams had undoubtedly learned from his study of European statecraft and of such masters of the art as C. von Metternich of Austria and Otto von Bismarck of Germany.

♦ ♦ ♦ ♦ ♦ The planning for the Joint Commission's work continued despite the debate generated by the Chaguaramas issue. By December 1957 all of its members had been named. The chairman was Sir Charles Arden Clarke, a distinguished Englishman and former governor general of Ghana. Having worked throughout the winter, the commission was ready to submit its report by early spring. The West Indian leaders were optimistic that it would endorse their choice of Chaguaramas as the capital of the West Indies Federation. British colonial officials were extremely nervous that if the commission found against the West Indians, the result would be increased tensions with the Americans.

The Americans, on their part, were not overly concerned about the commission's findings and participated in its work simply for public relations purposes. The installation of the missile tracking station at Chaguaramas starting in August 1957 was one indication of this, and the U.S. Navy's announcement in April 1958 that a new South Atlantic Command would be created and also headquartered at Chaguaramas was another. According to Admiral Gerald Wright, the commander in chief of the U.S. Atlantic Fleet, the new command would execute American responsibility for antisubmarine defense, the protection of shipping, and other missions. Wright promised that "this force will strengthen our bonds of friendship between United States and those countries in South America and Africa bordering the Atlantic command area." The message he conveyed was that, regardless of the conclusions of the Joint Commission, U.S. forces would remain at Chaguaramas. R. W. Jackling of the British Embassy in Washington, found the announcement "inexcusable" and questioned its timing just before the release of the commission's report.[42]

Although the British wanted to appear impartial in the Chaguaramas dispute, they almost always tilted on the side of the Americans. The two countries did not try to influence the deliberations of the Joint Commission directly, but they exchanged notes and their respective envoys had conversations on how to handle the West Indian politicians, especially Williams. The Americans insisted that the British, in the words of H. A. A. Hankey of the Foreign Office, "tranquilize opinion in the West Indies in order to provide a suitable atmosphere in which the Commission would conduct its work." They were incensed when Eric Williams lodged a protest with the commission against the installation of the tracking station, since they had already given the assurance that their representatives on that body would not be influenced by the fact that the work was in progress. Hankey observed, accurately, that "the West Indian politicians have not co-operated very willingly in refraining from public discussion of the capital site issue during the work of the commission." On the other hand, the Americans were "disingenuous in misrepresenting the significance of the exact site inside the base of the tracking station, and the extent of land which it would cover."

The imminent release of the commission's report, with its expected rejection of the West Indian position, created great apprehension in both London and Washington. British officials feared that there might be an explosion of anti-Americanism as well as disruptions of the events associated with the inauguration of the West Indies Federation scheduled to begin on April 22,

1958. The Colonial Office believed that it was obligated to persuade the West Indians to accept the report, to seek another site in Trinidad, and to avoid reopening the question of which island should have the capital. If the latter occurred, the future of the federation would be endangered. If the report were unfavorable to the West Indies, Hankey noted on March 17, the British would try to contain hostile reactions and to dispel the U.S. State Department's "illusions" that Britain had not done enough to prevent the hostility. Hankey cautioned, however, that "by over-playing our hand now with the West Indian politicians we might, by appearing to range ourselves too firmly on the American side, undermine our power to influence them in the right direction when the crucial moment arrives."[43]

This view appeared in a letter from the Foreign Office to Sir Harold Caccia, the British ambassador to the United States, on March 21. The Foreign Office asked Caccia to assure the U.S. State Department that the British were doing everything possible to stifle hostile opinion in Trinidad, but that "it is no more possible for the Governor to muzzle the press in Trinidad than it would be for the Administration to do so in the United States." The office expressed surprise at receiving an aide-mémoire from the U.S. secretary of state, Christian Herter, declaring that his country would not vacate Chaguaramas irrespective of the Joint Commission's recommendations. Consequently, the Foreign Office stressed that "the most critical moment" for British support of the Americans "will presumably come . . . when it becomes clear that whatever the nature of the report the Americans intend to remain inflexible." The Americans could help the British in "our task," the Foreign Office continued, by making "some economic concessions which would be valuable to the Federation and to the Trinidad government." These might include foregoing some of their duty-free rights and publicizing locally an offer of economic aid. The latter should be done carefully "in order to avoid the impression that a bribe was being offered." In addition, the Americans should accept the suggestion to send warships more frequently to Chaguaramas to show that the naval station was "in serious use."

The British, the Foreign Office continued, would accede to the U.S. request that the United Kingdom not propose a partitioning of the Chaguaramas base as a solution. The State Department needed to be assured that British officials "have acted in accordance with our degree of responsibility for keeping the agitation within manageable proportions if possible, and that they can count on us not to let them down over the defense aspect of the problem." To the secretary of state for the colonies, it seemed that "the Americans want it both ways, in both encouraging anti-colonialism of all kinds and then lecturing us for not behaving as colonialists."[44]

The Americans did not immediately reject the suggestion regarding economic concessions to the West Indies, but they were fearful that its acceptance and implementation would establish a precedent for other overseas bases.[45] They took some false comfort, however, in the fact that Williams's party, the PNM, had suffered a defeat in the recently held federal elections, winning only four of the ten seats at stake. Although the election was in some respects a referendum on the PNM's stewardship in office, the opposition DLP supported the Americans on Chaguaramas. The opposition party in Jamaica, the Jamaica Labour Party, also defeated Norman Manley's People's National Party, winning twelve of the seventeen contested seats. Pleased by these results, American officials saw them as evidence that there was little popular support for a U.S. evacuation of Chaguaramas. This was, of course, a self-serving misreading of the election results, particularly those in Trinidad and Tobago.[46]

The Americans were relieved when they were given advanced word that the Joint Commission had upheld their position on Chaguaramas. Emboldened by this information, Walworth Barbour of the American Embassy in London wrote Selwyn Lloyd, the British secretary of state for foreign affairs, that his government hoped that the interest of all concerned parties would be best served "by firm, polite advice from Her Majesty's Government to the West Indies to the effect that in the light of the Commission's report Her Majesty's Government is not in a position to request the United States Government to release all or part of Chaguaramas and that the request of the Standing Federation Committee of the West Indies to that end should be withdrawn."[47] Irritated by this imperious request, P. Dean of the Foreign Office observed that "the truth is that the Americans have been pretty tiresome over all this and their suggestion that we should send 'firm, polite advice' to the West Indians is really unnecessary."[48] Lloyd was also not amused by this request. He told the American ambassador, John Jay Whitney, that "the West Indian governments have achieved a degree of independence which demands the utmost discretion in the manner in which a delicate subject of this kind is handled."[49]

The chairman of the Joint Commission, Sir Charles Arden-Clarke, submitted his report to the four governments on March 25, but its contents were not released to the public until May 15 after the inaugural festivities of the West Indies Federation had been completed. The 36-page report was endorsed unanimously by all of the commission members. According to the report, the commission functioned "as a fact-finding body of technical experts."[50] After examining a massive amount of data, it supported the claim that "the best location for a base in the Eastern Caribbean is actually on the Gulf of Paria." Trinidad's location on the main sea-lane between the east coast ports of North and South America, and at the eastern end of the Caribbean with the Panama Canal at its western end, made it an ideal location for a naval base. In fact, Trinidad could be fairly described as "The Gibraltar of the Caribbean."[51] Similarly, the Chaguaramas base met all of "the strategic and military" requirements for a naval base in the Eastern Caribbean.[52] To partition the base was "not practicable," and there was "no significant portion of useable area within the Chaguaramas Naval Base that is not essential to the Base's mission."[53]

Unquestionably, the report constituted a major victory for the United States. It upheld all of the American claims, and its legitimacy was enhanced because there were no dissenters. After consultation, the British and the Americans issued separate statements welcoming the report's conclusions. The Americans hoped that the issue was now permanently settled, and the British urged the West Indians to withdraw their request for the release of Chaguaramas.[54] Understandably, West Indian leaders were not pleased. Federal prime minister Grantley Adams rejected the "view" expressed by the Americans and the British in their respective statements and called for an early conference of the parties involved to consider the commission's conclusions. An angry Norman Manley condemned the United Kingdom for conniving with the United States and for publishing a "one-sided statement" designed "to prejudice" and prevent further discussion of the matter in the West Indies. Such behavior was an "insult and an outrage to the people of the West Indies and their Federal Government."[55]

Manley complained that the unilateral statement by the British violated the understanding reached at the London conference that the four parties would consider the Joint Commission's report at a later meeting. The behavior of the British, Manley said on May 26, "is not only an insult, but a flagrant, naked breach of what we had agreed to do. . . . England deliberately intervened for the purpose of making it more easy for America to withstand any further pressure. I am absolutely satisfied that England and America got together behind the backs of the other parties to the roundtable conference for that purpose." On the other hand, an obviously delighted Sir Alexander Bustamante praised the United States for "having shown great dignity and having demonstrated a high sense of moral democracy" in agreeing to have the matter considered by the Joint Commission. "It serves the West Indies right not to get Chaguaramas as site for Federation's capital," he said.[56]

Colonial officials were sympathetic to the difficulties the Joint Commission's report created for Prime Minister Grantley Adams. His party held a small and thus precarious majority in the Federal Parliament, and the report did nothing to strengthen his political position. Wanting to exploit the situation, the opposition DLP hastily introduced a motion of no confidence in the government. Fearing that the young government might be defeated and thereby forced to resign, the Colonial Office extracted a promise from the U.S. State Department to review the Chaguaramas issue in ten years. The news served its purpose, and the Adams government survived. Eric Williams, however, was not placated by this gesture of compromise and demanded a conference of the four governments involved to discuss the Joint Commission's report and to reopen the question.

British officials wavered on the issue of a new conference, eventually arriving at a consensus that one was necessary but without separate representation for Trinidad and Tobago. This decision to hold a new conference was never conveyed to the West Indians, at least not for another fifteen months. In the interim, British officials tried, with varying degrees of enthusiasm, to persuade the Americans to accede to the West Indian requests. Secretary of State John Foster Dulles was a major obstacle to any such accommodation with the West Indies. In fact, on June 14, 1958, he told Selwyn Lloyd that the United States was "not prepared to deal direct with the West Indians on this [Chaguaramas] issue."[57] This posture of lofty intransigence would remain the hallmark of U.S. policy until officials, in light of changing circumstances, could no longer justify it to themselves, much less to the other interested parties. When the Americans agreed in October 1958 to hold a conference in ten years to review the issue, the Colonial Office maintained: "While we were glad to learn that the Americans have agreed that the review of the Chaguaramas question in ten years' time should be accompanied by a conference, we would prefer not to pass this on to the West Indies [Federal government] or to Trinidad at present. It would, we feel, be undesirable to let them know the news at present since Williams might well conclude that the Americans were weakening and step up his campaign for a Chaguaramas conference as soon as possible."[58]

If British and American officials nourished the hope that the Joint Commission's report would temper Eric Williams's position on Chaguaramas, they were seriously mistaken. In fact, the report strengthened his nationalist fervor, leading him to launch an even more vigorous campaign to force an American withdrawal, the likes of which the Anglophone Caribbean had never experienced. The campaign infuriated the Americans, alarmed the British, and annoyed many citizens of Trinidad and the West Indies in general. None of this deterred Williams; he seemed to thrive on the passions he had unleashed. It was a struggle rich in drama, one that simultaneously captured the spirit of anticolonial struggles and revealed the compromises that their leaders sometimes had to make, as their pragmatism tempered their idealism.

Williams's first major salvo after the report's release was to make a motion in the Legislative Council on June 6 that the legislators endorse the request of the West Indies Federal government for an early conference of representatives of the four governments to consider the document. Such a meeting, he added, should be held in Trinidad. In a lengthy speech, Williams reviewed the history of the problem and condemned the unilateral statements that Britain and the United States had issued in their acceptance of the report. These statements slammed the door "in the face of the people of the West Indies and their representatives."[59] By presenting his motion he wanted to "claim the right of the people of the West Indies and the right of the people of Trinidad and Tobago to be heard in their own cause." Accordingly, his government "repudiates the unilateral statements" of the two governments in question. Williams was outraged by the 1941 agreement whereby Trinidadians were "sold for scrap" and insisted that in 1958 "nobody is going to give away or surrender one iota of Trinidad's soil without reference to the elected government of the people." Under the circumstances, he said, "We demand the right to be heard." Referring to the Joint Commission's report, the chief minister wryly observed: "One gets the impression that the only reason for Trinidad's existence on this earth is that a naval base had to be located somewhere."[60]

Williams rejected the report's claim that it would be too costly to relocate the Chaguaramas base and questioned the conclusion that it was crucial for the security of the region. "If it were" crucial, he argued, "then . . . it should not have been neglected as it obviously has been." Citing the agreements that the United States had signed with other countries for bases since 1941, Williams pointed out that none was for longer than twenty years, in contrast to the ninety-nine-year lease at Chaguaramas. "Must we have a treaty in the West Indies for 99 years as against 20?" he asked. He also wanted the agreement revised "to bring it more in line with treaties elsewhere, to bring it more in line with the new spirit that has spread all over the world in the opposition to bases by Mr. Nehru, the opposition in Ceylon, the struggle in Cyprus, the opposition in Latin America."[61]

Alluding to the struggle ahead, Williams observed that "the discussions which some are now trying to close are only now beginning." He assured the legislators that the governing body of the PNM supported his stance. Its "line" was: "Go ahead, do not back down; you have a case, a strong moral case; put it before the eyes of the world. Above all, if your Federation backs down now, your Federation is going to be kicked about from pillar to post until the end of time."[62] In responding to criticisms of the opposition at the close of the debate, Williams condemned some of the speakers for being "the mouthpieces of a foreign power"; indeed, he accused one of them of quoting from a "secret" U.S. document that he, Williams, had in his possession.[63]

The speech set the tone of the campaign that Williams would wage for the return of Chaguaramas over the next several years. Filled with historical allusions and statistics, it was at once combative, defiant, and conciliatory. Two weeks later the chief minister returned to the Chaguaramas problem. In a statement he read to the Legislative Council, he complicated the issue by questioning whether the council had actually ratified the 1941 agreement. Consequently, "Is the lease valid?" he inquired. Williams pointed out that the "supplementary areas" acquired by the United States since 1941 had not been "signed, executed, or registered." These areas included Tucker Valley, Flagstaff Hill, La Lune, Blanchissense, Green Hill, Carlsen Field, Monos, Huevos, Chacachacare, Arima, Verdant Vale Quarry, and Manzanilla.[64]

Williams argued that the Land Regulations of Trinidad and Tobago allowed the governor to grant leases for a term not exceeding thirty years. The government "has not yet been able to identify any authority for the disposal of Crown Lands in 1941 for 99 years in excess of the term prescribed by the Land Regulations." Moreover, the rent-free provisions of the 1941 agreement also violated Trinidadian law, which provided for the payment of rent for the leasing of Crown lands.[65]

In light of these discoveries, the chief minister wondered whether a lease in fact existed. "Has the United Kingdom, Parliament, or the Sovereign in effect exercised the right to dispense with or suspend the laws of Trinidad and Tobago relating to the duration of leases of Crown Lands?" he asked. The answers to the questions he raised "are basic to the self government of Trinidad and Tobago. The questions involve the legality, the validity of the United States occupation of the Leased Areas. They ultimately pose the problem—can the United Kingdom by treaty with a foreign power bind Trinidad and Tobago, even in the days of Crown Colony Government, to obligations, commitments and concessions unknown to or inconsistent with Trinidad laws duly assented to by the Governor and not disallowed by the Secretary of State for the Colonies?"[66]

To resolve this legal uncertainty, Williams announced the appointment of a commission consisting of "legal experts" to "inquire into and report upon the legal basis of (a) the occupation by the United States of areas of Trinidad and Tobago from 1941 to the present day, and (b) the terms and conditions thereto."[67]

These questions threw a significant wrench into the dispute. Taken by surprise and chagrined that Williams had challenged the legitimacy of the 1941 agreement, British colonial officials took immediate steps to assert their political supremacy. In a telegram to Governor Beetham, the Colonial Office expressed its intention to "scotch the idea that by disclosing legislative anomalies and flaws in leases, Trinidad Government can cast doubt on the right of United State Government to retain bases. Our lawyers regard this as self evident absurdity." The office pointed out that as a colony Trinidad lacked "sovereignty," and in any event the governor's reserve powers sufficed in the context of the 1941 agreement. In addition, the Foreign Office contended that the responsibility for the external relations of Trinidad and Tobago resided with Her Majesty's government and that the governor retained the power to act without the consent of the Legislative Council.

It is unclear whether the contents of this and similar letters were ever communicated to Williams, since the governor's deputy in Trinidad cautioned that such legal arguments could be seen as an attempt to influence the findings of Williams's Legal Commission. He thought that any reference to the governor's reserve powers should be avoided.[68] In its internal discussions, however, the Foreign Office was far from convinced that Williams's claims had no legal merit. On August 25, D. H. T. Hildyard of that office admitted that "Dr. Williams has a strong card, in that the Trinidad Government have omitted to enact a certain amount of legislation necessary to give effect to the 1941 agreement . . . and the legal position in the Chaguaramas base is therefore far from satisfactory."[69]

♦ ♦ ♦ ♦ ♦ Eric Williams's relentless assaults on the Leased Bases Agreement greatly unnerved and annoyed colonial officials. But they never conceded publicly that the agreement was of questionable legality because it had not been ratified by the local legislature. Nor had the imperial government validated it by exercising its reserve power. To innoculate themselves against having to concede the validity of Williams's arguments, the Colonial Office concocted a fraudulent scheme to thwart and nullify them. At first, the officials discussed whether to ask the newly inaugurated Williams government to introduce legislation to ratify the agreement retroactively. Governor Beetham warned against such a course, as he considered it "inadvisable and undesirable for any attempt to be made to press Government to introduce the necessary legislation at this juncture." He reported that Solomon Hochoy, the Trinidadian-born colonial secretary, had expressed the view that "no new government could be expected to embark upon controversial legislation which would appear, not only [to] be a curtailment of the rights and privileges of its own people, but also to confer greater privileges on foreigners vis-à-vis its own people, when it had not yet had the time nor the opportunity to implement to any material extent promises made to the country."[70]

Beetham thought that he had a better idea. Realizing that the issue of the agreement's legality would not disappear, he asked the Colonial Office to send him a fraudulent dispatch, which could be later dated and numbered as required, to demonstrate that the authorities had left it to the Trinidadian government to validate the agreement when the necessity arose, even to be retroactive. There was, obviously, no statute of limitations on its implementation. "Would it not be provident for me," Beetham inquired in February 1958, "to have an unnumbered and undated dispatch now so that when the moment arrives I could telegraph for the number and date which I would fill in?"[71]

The Colonial Office agreed to participate in this deception and sent the following undated "dispatch" to Beetham, even including references to a fictitious 1954 savingram:

TRINIDAD

NO.

Sir,

1. I have the honour to refer to correspondence ending with your savingram No. 2/54 of the 2nd January, 1954, regarding the desirability of introducing comprehensive legislation to implement the Leased Based Agreement of the 27th March, 1941.

2. I know of course that power exists under the Leased Bases (Temporary Provisions) Ordinance, 1941, to make Regulations, if necessary with retrospective effect, to implement that Agreement; and I recognise that it may be possible to give effect to certain of its terms by means of administrative direction. While it has been the view of Her Majesty's Government that such temporary expedients should be replaced by comprehensive legislation at the first convenient opportunity, it is recognised that the Government of Trinidad will wish to consider when it would be appropriate to do so. In the meantime, Her Majesty's Government assume[s] that all the powers and privileges conferred by the Leased Bases Agreement will be made available as and when necessary either by administrative direction or by Regulations under the Leased Bases (Temporary Provisions) Ordinance; and that; should an incident occur in which failure to give local effect to the Agreement is, or is likely to become, an issue, the Trinidad Government will take steps to correct the position, e.g. by exercising the power to make Regulations with retrospective effect. It is, however, considered particularly inappropriate that matters of jurisdiction should be dealt with by retrospective legislation.

3. I therefore hope that, if it is still considered inexpedient to introduce comprehensive legislation, an assurance in the above sense can readily be given.

I have the honour to be,

Sir,

Your most obedient

humble servant,

ALAN LENNOX BOYD

GOVERNOR,

SIR EDWARD BEETHAM, K.C.M.G., C.V.O., O.B.E.,

etc.,   etc.,   etc.[72]

Colonial officials, however, were concerned that this deception could be discovered and alerted Beetham to some of the potential difficulties:

SECRET & PERSONAL   22nd February, 1958.
As you will see from the enclosure to this letter, we have accepted the suggestion in your telegram Personal No. 11 that you should have an unnumbered and undated dispatch on the subject of U.S. Bases legislation ready to be numbered and dated when a suitable time arrives to produce it.

This course however is not without difficulties. It would be easy enough to backdate the dispatch so as to allow a sufficient interval between the apparent dates of issue and receipt. It would not however be so easy to allot a number consonant with the date since all such numbers would already have been used before we received your telegram. Another snag might arise if the Secretary of State were out of the U.K. at the selected date since the dispatch would then bear the wrong signature.

These are not perhaps very material difficulties, but because of them it would be better, if time allows, for us to send another original of the dispatch through the usual channels if you can give us sufficient notice (say ten days) of the date on which you wish to produce it. But if the favourable moment arrives so suddenly that this is not possible, we agree that you should produce the enclosed copy and we will do our best to overcome the difficulties I have mentioned.

        (W. I. J. WALLACE)
        Sir Edward Beetham, K.C.M.G., C.V.O., O.B.E.,
        Government House
        Port-of-Spain
        TRINIDAD.[73]

It is not known if Beetham ever issued the "dispatch." He had not done so by June 1958, leading one colonial official to observe that it "lies unnumbered and undated in Sir E. Beetham's safe." Still, the official added: "With all the advantages of hindsight it seems to me rather a pity that we did not take this bull by the horns before. However, there is at least this advantage, that Dr. Williams seems to be giving himself a considerable length of rope so that if we do have to twitch the noose rather sharply by reminding him of the existence of reserve powers it will be against a background that it is he rather than we who are manifestly being unreasonable."[74] The official was not troubled by the morality of the deception, of which he was manifestly a part.

The record is silent on whether Beetham conveyed the fraudulent contents of the dispatch to Williams. Since the Legal Commission appointed by the chief minister never submitted a report, it is conceivable that its members knew of its existence and accepted its "authenticity." The Colonial Office had pulled the legal rug from under Williams, denying him a trump card. It was unquestionably a low point in the behavior of the imperial authorities, a crass exercise of Machiavellian-like deception and ruthlessness. Eric Williams, as we shall see in Chapter 4, was always accused of being "paranoid." In light of the Colonial Office's behavior in this instance and in others, the chief minister's moods and distrust of the London officials were at times entirely understandable.

♦ ♦ ♦ ♦ ♦ Williams did not confine his campaign to speeches in the Legislative Council, official statements, and legal contestations. Not surprisingly, he also took his case directly to the people. In a press conference on July 12, 1958, he observed that even if Chaguaramas were not required for the Federal capital, it could meet other needs, such as "tourist development." But, he added, "there need be no problem if some of the Trinidad population stopped conducting themselves in the eyes of the world like stooges."[75] This statement reflected a shift in the chief minister's thinking. He now wanted the land back whether or not it was to be used as the capital site.

Williams's insistence on the right of his small island to have a voice in who occupied its soil and on what terms continued to irritate the Americans, particularly those officials who were assigned to Port of Spain. They had to listen to his persistent denunciation of the U.S. presence in his speeches and press conferences, and the Nation published similar assaults with distressing frequency. Unable to control Williams or at least to silence him, the American consul general in March 1958 thought that the time had come for the United States to take some action against him. Walter Orebaugh wrote the U.S. secretary of state that "I am firmly convinced we cannot attack [the] problem on a piece meal basis. We must review our position, assess our strength in area, decide upon a plan of action, and then proceed [with] implementation. . . . We must disengage with Williams and work for his ultimate demise."

Orebaugh did not elaborate on what he meant by Williams's "demise." He may have meant that the State Department should support the chief minister's opponents, with the intention of defeating him in the next election. Conceivably, he could also have meant a military coup or his assassination. Orebaugh urged the State Department to convene a small group of representatives from "appropriate agencies" to meet in ten days "to produce a coordinated plan of action." Any plan that emerged should be given the stamp of "highest Departmental approval." The consul general offered to send his deputy to Washington to participate in the conspiracy.[76] The available evidence does not indicate whether anything came of this proposal.

In July 1959 Consul General Orebaugh returned to the question of Williams's removal from office. In a letter to four State Department officials, he noted that since there "seems to be more or less agreement that Williams cannot, or at any rate will not be handled, it is . . . I believe timely to consider . . . what we can do about Williams." Although "the man is riding high," he could run afoul of his colleagues. But, Orebaugh cautioned, "we cannot, of course, get into a program to 'get' Williams without getting into local affairs to a far greater degree than anything we have done heretofore." Once again, the consul general was tantalizingly vague about the proposed modus operandi, and it is not clear whether his proposal was considered in Washington.[77]

Forgetting the nationalism that animated the historical experiences of their own country, before and after the Revolutionary War, U.S. officials dismissed such sentiments in the West Indies with the most pejorative language. Still, they felt that American interests in the area would be threatened in the long run if these nationalist stirrings were not contained and if the United States, in the words of Walter Orebaugh, did not take the necessary steps "to increase the palatability of a US base system in the West Indies." Orebaugh also believed the American presence would be endangered when the islands attained dominion status unless the United States took care to develop West Indian cooperation. According to Orebaugh, American prospects "are likely to be worsened by the degree to which Eric Williams is able to expand his future political role." To Orebaugh, "rabid nationalists like Williams" could "arouse a sense of frustration in the public to keep the Chaguaramas pot boiling." In addition, the diplomat observed, "there is an intellectual and political current among certain leaders that feeds on racial and anti-colonial bitterness."[78]

Walter Orebaugh showed no deep understanding of the wellsprings of Trinidadian nationalism. In October 1959 he reported that Eric Williams was so preoccupied with the Chaguaramas issue that it "border[s] on mania."

The consul general saw the impasse principally in racial terms, describing it "as an emotional issue . . . rooted in Williams's mind as part of a struggle against colonialism, and a cause in which the 'colored' can show their new strength in the face of the 'whites.' " To this racial factor "can be added the known, and heretofore somewhat latent, anti-Americanism which is part of Williams' background." Williams was using Chaguaramas to divert attention from domestic problems such as taxes and unemployment. Orebaugh speculated that he was going to "pitch his allegations, inferences, and even untruths in such a way as to emotionalize the issue." Williams would seek to internationalize it as well, Orebaugh lamented.

Under the circumstances, the consul general saw little hope of achieving a compromise with Williams: "The nature of his demands, his personality and ambitions, his motivating force, and the long-run danger he poses for United States interests in the Caribbean, all add up to the conclusion that the United States cannot deal reasonably with the man, either now or in the future. To the maximum effect feasible, and within the means, which can be developed, we should work for the weakening of Williams' political position in Trinidad and his eventual replacement by more rational elements."

This was not a call to remove Williams from office by force. But it had ominous undertones. Orebaugh thought that the United States should provide aid to the West Indian Federal government to maximize its political and economic viability, thereby reducing Trinidad's influence. "Federation and Federal leaders can be used to counteract Dr. Williams," he suggested. In addition, the United Kingdom as the imperial power should be urged to "use its full influence to contain Williams."[79]

The American officials in both Port of Spain and Washington, D.C., had little if any experience in negotiating with West Indians or having to pay them serious attention. They were, after all, colonials, and the United Kingdom handled their relationships with foreign powers, as it had done in the 1941 agreement. Moreover, at the time of the Chaguaramas dispute de jure segregation still existed in the United States, and African Americans were being denied their constitutional rights in the South. If white Americans, particularly southerners, did not accord black people due respect in their native land, it was doubtful that West Indians who were not white would be treated much differently. Their views, even those on the disposal of their own land, hardly carried any weight. The State Department's refusal to deal with the West Indians directly did not rest entirely on the legal ground that the

United Kingdom was responsible for their foreign affairs. The fact that the color of their skin was black or brown was a major consideration given the racial climate of that period.

Orebaugh's recommendation that the Americans intervene directly in the political life of Trinidad and Tobago had precedents in other societies. The United States had already been implicated in the overthrow of heads of state in Guatemala and Iran. Consul General Orebaugh seems to have been proposing a similar fate for Eric Williams. Williams's crime was that he was fiercely critical of the U.S. presence at Chaguaramas. His departure from office would have probably gratified some of his domestic opponents, but few would have endorsed the means that Orebaugh seemed to recommend. Had Orebaugh's proposal come to light at the time, it would have seriously hurt the American cause, enhanced Williams's popularity, and invited almost universal condemnation.

Walter Orebaugh was singularly inept as consul general, and his deputy, Philip Habib, was hardly more competent. Douglas Williams, the British colonial attaché in Washington, who spent two weeks in Trinidad in late July and early August 1958, was "frankly appalled at the way the Americans are mishandling the situation locally." He was convinced that "the fault lies . . . in the joint firm of Messers Orebaugh and Habib." Orebaugh's "whole background and approach to problems make him quite unfit for the present situation in Trinidad," the British envoy asserted. The consul general, he reported, had spent World War II on "special operations" in Italy and later worked for the U.S. Central Intelligence Agency. Thus:

He has a mentality adapted to that sort of approach and I think in his heart of hearts really sees the situation in those terms. If he could take to the hills and organise an anti P N M movement with Mr. Habib stowed away in some bazaar in Port of Spain as his local intelligence agent, he would be perfectly happy and would do a thoroughly good job. What he lacks is any idea of how to employ diplomacy, tact, and patience in a situation where those are the only qualities which are even likely to get him anywhere. He keeps on harping on the fact that "somebody must do something." He is not prepared to leave the situation to time and the influence of good personal relations and good sense. He thinks of it entirely in terms of fostering countermovements and of somehow trying to buy off the agitation. The effect of his efforts is in consequence always the very opposite of what he intends them to be, and the mistrust of him and of the whole American consulate in Port of Spain is very considerable.

Douglas Williams proposed to convey his misgivings to his "contacts" in the U.S. State Department. "It now seems to me that Orebaugh's personal approach to the local situation in Trinidad is colouring the whole of the American attitude over Chaguaramas, with results which could be unfortunate for all of us," he concluded.[80] Orebaugh was later quietly recalled to Washington after being accused of interfering in local politics.

◆ ◆ ◆ ◆ ◆ In addition to American hostility, Eric Williams faced significant domestic opposition as his campaign intensified. His opponents hurried to the U.S. consulate to record their fears and to enjoin the Americans to resist his demands. Feeling that they were powerless to thwart the chief minister and despairing that the United Kingdom was unlikely to take their side, these Trinidadians viewed the Americans as their only hope. Although the Chaguaramas issue was the one that angered them most, they voiced a catalog of other complaints. The U.S. officials gave them a polite hearing and reported the sense of these conversations to their superiors in Washington.

The practice of colonized peoples seeking the ear of the metropolitan power to advance one cause or another was well known. In this instance, such prominent leaders as Victor Bryan, an African Trinidadian and opposition member of the Federal Parliament, as well as Rudranath Capildeo and Ashford Sinanan, two distinguished Indo-Trinidadians and leaders of the DLP, bared their souls and shared their political strategies and ambitions with the Americans. Williams was not averse to talking to the diplomats, but he was more reticent about his political plans when he met with them, particularly the Americans. This is hardly surprising since he was the head of government and was usually an antagonist of the British and the Americans; thus he could neither run to them for political help or advice nor discuss his modus operandi with them.

Sir Joseph Mathieu-Perez was one of the first prominent citizens of Trinidad and Tobago to call on U.S. officials to express opposition to Williams's Chaguaramas policy. Mathieu-Perez, a former chief justice, told the Americans on October 29, 1958, that he opposed the four-power conference that Williams was demanding. According to Consul General Orebaugh, he said that if the Americans agreed to hold such a conference, "their influence and prestige would decline to the vanishing point." U.S. policy should be one of "reasonableness but firmness." Mathieu-Perez repeated the point that under no circumstances should the Americans agree to confer with Williams.[81]

DLP officials, too, were not reluctant to take their complaints to the Americans, usually to assure them of their opposition to the release of Chaguaramas. On July 10, 1959, for example, in a meeting with Philip Habib, now the acting U.S. consul general, Ashford Sinanan, the leader of the opposition in the Federal Parliament, and Simbhoonath Capildeo, a DLP member of the Legislative Council of Trinidad and Tobago, charged that British colonial officials were enhancing Williams's "power and prestige" in "such a manner as to be criminal." Sinanan wondered whether the Americans also intended to "appease" Williams on the Chaguaramas issue. He insisted that Chaguaramas was more properly the responsibility of the Federal government than of Trinidad. He warned that Williams was intent on embarrassing the Americans and whipping up anti-American sentiment. Furthermore, the two visitors told Habib, Williams was jeopardizing U.S.–West Indian relations and Williams and his "arch-conspirator, the communist C. L. R. James," were planning to introduce "totalitarianism" into the West Indies. Sinanan reminded Habib that the DLP was willing to continue supporting the Americans despite the PNM's accusation that they were tools of the United States. His party was committed to fighting what he called Williams's anti-Americanism. Ten days later Werner J. Boos, the acting chief secretary of Trinidad and Tobago, also visited Habib to express his disenchantment with Williams's Chaguaramas policy.[82]

Williams's demands regarding Chaguaramas and his insistence that Trinidad and Tobago should have independent representation at any conference to resolve the issue of the use of Trinidad's soil also ran afoul of the Federal government. Prime Minister Grantley Adams and his ministers believed that Williams was encroaching on the Federal preserve, since the conduct of foreign affairs was its responsibility and not that of any unit of the West Indies Federation. This was constitutionally accurate, but the federation had not yet achieved dominion status so foreign affairs remained in the hands of the United Kingdom.

Williams dismissed such political sensibilities, seeing himself as the only authentic spokesperson for the peoples of Trinidad and Tobago. When Robert Bradshaw, the Federal minister of finance, told a public meeting in St. Kitts in June 1960 that "Chaguaramas is a Federal problem," Williams responded characteristically: "Federal problem, my foot. Chaguaramas is no longer a federal problem—it is a problem for Trinidad and Tobago. Chaguaramas is Trinidad property and the Americans are camping on Trinidad soil. When they get off, it will be taken over by the Government of Trinidad and Tobago. If the Federal Government still wants to come and talk to us about using it for a federal capital, they can come in and we'll sit down with them and bargain about it."[83]

It was widely suspected that Adams did not want the Chaguaramas problem resolved in Williams's favor, because he hoped that the Federal capital would be relocated in Barbados. Williams, on the other hand, was not expected to accept such a development. There was even speculation that he would lead Trinidad and Tobago out of the federation if Trinidad lost the capital. Matters took an ugly turn in March 1960, when the two leaders exchanged accusations in a public brawl. Expressing some frustration with the Federal government on a number of issues, Williams told a press conference that "Trinidad and Tobago is not going to support any West Indian Federal Government which starts off by being the stooge of the Colonial Office." Stung by this criticism, Adams said that it was "beneath contempt."[84]

Williams minced no words in condemning his opponents, but one speech that he delivered at San Fernando on May 30, 1960, was particularly vitriolic. No opposition exists, he said, that "can present to the national community an alternative program for the advancement of our national aims. Opposition there is, opposition galore, but it is opposition for so. It is the opposition of old talk, the opposition of bacchanal, the opposition of a caste of unregenerate diehards in its death throes, the opposition which seeks to perpetuate colonialism."[85]

By the end of 1959, however, there were signs that U.S. officials had begun to develop a more mature understanding of the roots of the crisis, seen through the optic of Eric Williams and his supporters. This emerging perspective appears in a lengthy memorandum that the new and more sensitive consul general, Edwin Moline, sent to Washington on December 23. Moline was, in a sense, establishing the context for the forthcoming conference to discuss revision of the 1941 Leased Bases Agreement. He explained that he was interested in providing "a preview of West Indian views" to "facilitate the obvious U.S. task of limiting [their] demands" in the upcoming negotiations. This was to be done "in the interest of protecting essential U.S. requirements." The consul general emphasized that "what originated as a specific request for a particular piece of ground has now burgeoned into a wide desire among the responsible leaders of the West Indies for a review and readjustment of U.S. base rights." He insisted that the West Indian demands were driven by a strong sense of nationalism. Ignoring the contrary views of politicians like Albert Gomes, Ashford Sinanan, and Alexander Bustamante, Moline opined, "the West Indian nationalist, and all politicians are nationalist in the West Indies, cannot accept that standards applicable in other parts of the world are not acceptable in his bailiwick." Moline was, of course, alluding to the terms of the U.S. base agreements with Libya, Iceland, and the Philippines.

The new consul general noted that it was no longer possible to speak of "the localization of West Indian attitudes." He thought that "the intransigence and the extremism of Dr. Williams on the base issue . . . while still not approved by the majority of political leadership in the West Indies, has nevertheless had an impact on West Indian thinking on the issue." The solution "of the bases problem in the West Indies will have to be applicable equally throughout the Federation" since the same standards had to apply in all of the territories. Moline advised the State Department to acknowledge the West Indians' sovereignty over their land in view of the forthcoming changes in their constitutional status, asserting that "expression of this fact will have considerable meaning to West Indian leaders."

Moline also suggested that the length of the lease period be reduced, since "ninety nine years has the appearance of perpetuity." Furthermore, deactivated areas of the U.S. bases in Trinidad, St. Lucia, Antigua, and Jamaica should be released. Chaguaramas, however, would remain a problem because the demand for it included "elements of fetishism, or elements of pride, or elements contrary to past commitment." As the West Indians were almost certain to demand compensation for base rights, the U.S. negotiators should be prepared to confront that question. Such compensation "would be of major value in Trinidad in enabling Williams to minimize or abandon claims to the Naval Station." Moline admitted that this amounted to "buying the right to stay." He predicted that the West Indians would seek other revisions in the treaty on issues such as the right of access to the bases, the U.S. military use of local public services, custom privileges, and so on.

The consul general reminded his superiors that "without any doubt, the status quo, in so far as U.S. bases in the West Indies are concerned, can no longer be realistically expected to hold. We cannot expect merely to maintain rights granted under war conditions, 18 years ago, for which West Indians do not now recognize as an immediate and pressing need." This was a remarkable and important shift in American thinking, a development that was in large measure the result of the pressure that Eric Williams had applied on intransigent American authorities.[86]

To keep the Chaguaramas dispute alive, Williams used a variety of tactics. Among them, in the aftermath of the Joint Commission's report, was a campaign to harass the Americans at Chaguaramas. His list of U.S. abuses was lengthy. For example, Williams accused the Americans of violating the terms of the 1941 Leased Bases Agreement, which allowed them to avoid paying customs duties on their imports. It was common knowledge on the islands that some of these goods found their way into the hands of citizens of Trinidad and Tobago. "Chaguaramas is the greatest source today of smuggling in Trinidad and Tobago," Williams alleged. "You have these violations of the custom law of Trinidad and Tobago, almost daily."

Williams also denounced the Americans for landing military planes at Piarco Airport in contravention of the agreement. Such activity, he claimed, had damaged the airport because it was unsuited for such heavy aircraft. He calculated that since that practice began, Trinidad had lost US$250,000 in landing fees; moreover, the physical damage to the airport amounted to US$1 million. Williams was incensed that the Americans were also violating Trinidad's immigration laws, as his government had no record of who went to the bases, crossed the border, and moved around the islands. He was not pleased that U.S. troops were "walking around Trinidad and Tobago, at Piarco [Airport], with guns. We want to know why they should do that. Our police don't carry any guns," he asserted.

Williams created a minicrisis when he took umbrage at the Americans selling their surplus citrus fruits to Trinidadians. Trade with Trinidadians was prohibited by the 1941 agreement, so this commercial relationship was clearly a violation. Previous governments of Trinidad and Tobago had permitted the Americans to engage in this trade, but Williams was not so disposed when he became aware of it. He ordered the appropriate government department not to process the necessary papers so that the Americans could receive payment for the citrus they had sold, thereby producing prolonged and mutual recriminations. The chief minister also complained that Americans had brought their racial virus to Chaguaramas and mistreated citizens of Trinidad and Tobago.[87]

These complaints about U.S. behavior and petty acts of governmental harassment were designed to make life for the Americans intolerable and hasten the resolution of the conflict. One issue, perhaps more than any other, was particularly serious and played a major role in exacerbating tensions between Trinidad, the United Kingdom, and the United States. On June 9, 1959, Chief Minister Williams told the Executive Council that he had reports of a "reliable nature" that radiation leaks were occurring within the Chaguaramas base. Sensing the politically explosive nature of this information, Williams immediately asked the United Kingdom to investigate. Four days later, he dispatched two of his ministers, Patrick Solomon and John O'Halloran, to London to make urgent representations to the British government to act and to "allay mounting tension and alarm locally."

In responding to these concerns, the United States assured officials of the United Kingdom and Trinidad that the only kinds of radiation at the base were the standard types resulting from domestic and hospital equipment. Trinidadian officials were suspicious of such claims, and rumors began to circulate on the island, exacerbating fears about the impact of the radiation on the health of its citizenry. Acting on a proposal from the Colonial Office, the U.S. State Department agreed to allow a British technical expert to visit the base and determine whether any radiation hazards existed. The individual selected was D. R. Evans, the principal scientific officer of the Ministry of Supply. Evans was scheduled to arrive in Trinidad on July 10, but his visit was postponed when the Americans announced that the station would be operating on reduced power between July 11 and 14 and would cease operating altogether from July 15 to August 15 owing to construction. The news of this delay produced considerable apprehension in Trinidad and rumors that these delays were intended to give the Americans time to either conceal the problem or remove the offending equipment.

When public outcry about the delays did not abate, the Colonial Office agreed to send Evans to Trinidad on August 21 once the Americans confirmed that low-power operation at the station would resume on August 25. Chief Minister Williams was, as to be expected, quite animated on the subject and gave a lengthy speech at Woodford Square on July 3. Obviously bent on using the radiation issue to berate the Americans and heighten nationalist fervor, Williams walked a precarious political tightrope. Although he had no firm evidence about the veracity of the charges leveled against the Americans, he had to speak in such a way as to give the impression that he did.

"There is evidence to suggest that there is some danger to the population," Williams said, "but the important thing is we don't know . . . there is some danger, we don't know what. It is a question of sheer self defense."[88]

Trinidad's minister of health, Dr. Winston Mahabir, once thought by British and American officials to oppose Williams's stand on Chaguaramas, gave his chief minister strong internal support on the radiation issue. In mid-July, after a trip to the United Kingdom, Mahabir informed the Cabinet that he was firmly convinced that the presence of a U.S. base in Trinidad "involved our population in hazards over which a Minister of Health has no control." He thought that the presence of a U.S. base "exposes us to liquidation" instead of "protecting us from danger." The minister, according to a British Intelligence report, stated that it was his "inescapable conclusion" that "we must oppose the existence of ANY foreign base on our territory, and offer no alternative accommodation to the Americans, if and when this question arises." Mahabir offered to "suppress this point of view for the moment" but emphasized that it was "neither frivolously conceived nor lightly held."[89]

The health minister's position on bases went far beyond anything Williams had advocated. Williams had never said that the Americans should not be offered an alternative site for a base. Mahabir's astonishing observations showed the degree to which some Trinidadian officials had seemingly become radicalized on the question of Chaguaramas. In an act of acute political amnesia, Mahabir would later write in his memoirs that the radiation issue constituted an "immaculate deception" by Williams. He assured his readers that what he was about to relate about the dispute "will read like an anancy story," brazenly ignoring his earlier strong private support of his chief minister.[90]

Williams, in retrospect, was not crying wolf about the radiation threat. In a secret letter to Ambassador D. A. Logan in Washington, the Foreign Office admitted that it had "very little idea as to the power or effect of stations of this kind and practically no technical details when we actually gave our agreement to the installation in Trinidad." The office was "very much in the dark," although the Americans had given their assurance that "the base was strictly conventional." But the British officials had now learned that "the Trinidad Station was one of the largest radar installations in existence, and that US technicians had been talking freely of the hazards from radiation."

That being said, the Foreign Office believed that "we are all in for a very difficult time with Dr. Williams; and we count on the State Department to help us to handle him, particularly since they are very likely to have to do so on their own before long."

Realizing that it had a public relations disaster on its hands, the Foreign Office feared the worst. It also chafed under the oft-repeated American criticism that the British were not doing enough to control the West Indians, dismissing them as having a "totally unrealistic attitude." The two governments knew that the radiation issue provided Williams with additional ammunition with which to chastise the Americans and demand the evacuation of Chaguaramas. The British, however, had come to understand, and to some extent sympathize with, the nationalistic wellsprings that fertilized the dispute.

Concerned that the United States would dismiss the radiation allegations, and irritated by its failure to appreciate the depth of West Indian nationalism, the Foreign Office observed: "The truth is that we have to face a growing, touchy and not always well informed brand of nationalism moving fast towards the opinion that bases can only be accepted in the long run if their objectives and the conditions of their operation are mutually agreed. It would be quite wrong, we think, to regard the more extreme manifestations of this trend as mere political gambits."[91]

It was a sign of changing times that the Foreign Office recognized and accepted the legitimacy of West Indian nationalism. But many notable Trinidadians, such as Albert Gomes, were still not so similarly disposed. Although the Foreign Office noted that Eric Williams "has inflamed feeling and without him the issue might have remained quiescent for some time," it was unwilling to silence him, if that were even possible. As D. H. T. Hildyard wrote of Williams on August 10:

The fact is that in a democratic state he was free to express his opinions and persuade others to share them which he has done very successfully. We ourselves are entirely convinced that the campaign for revision of the agreement is now genuine and recognition of it inevitable. There may come a point at which we shall have to take action to ensure that the base is not prevented from operating efficiently. But until this point is reached, it is simply not possible to slap Dr. Williams down . . . all we can do is to try gradually to bring him, his supporters and the leaders of Trinidad opinion to realize where their best interests lie. In what seems to us the very unlikely case that he is merely indulging in demagoguery and that the support, which he has gained on this issue, is only superficial, this will eventually become apparent and we would hope that in time more responsible and realistic leaders would take his place.[92]

Williams, in the view of the Foreign Office, was being irresponsible and unrealistic in his campaign for the return of Chaguaramas. Such a characterization of the chief minister revealed an imperial optic that, despite its growing appreciation of West Indian nationalism, still had a long path to traverse. The radiation issue gave Williams another and very dramatic opportunity to assert his claim to Chaguaramas, and he seized it with considerable aggressiveness.

On July 31, while the British were making plans to send a radiation expert to Port of Spain, Eric Williams was telling the acting governor of Trinidad and Tobago that the prestige of his government was at stake and that he could no longer "refrain from taking action within our legal and moral rights" to resolve the problem. Williams condemned U.S. intransigence, which made it "impossible for the present situation to continue." The acting governor reported the chief minister as saying:

It is unreasonable for the Americans, in the position in which they find themselves today as persistent and contumacious violators of an agreement whose validity in the present altered circumstances is challenged by us, to continue after two years to refuse to get around a table to negotiate [the] issue. It is the Americans who have rejected our offer of a new site for the base. It is the Americans who have unilaterally decided they will be prepared to review the need for Chaguaramas after say ten years. It is the Americans who claim the privileges which lack the sanction of Trinidad law required by the Agreement. It is the Americans whose planes land at will in defiance of any agreement with Trinidad and in contravention of the informal arrangements with the United Kingdom. It is the Americans who use the leased areas for purposes for which they were never intended and contrary to the very specific conditions laid down by the Foreign Office as far as the tracking station is concerned. It is the Americans who may even now be using or be planning to use the base for the purposes and for weapons with respect to which the recent revelations have created the present state of grave uncertainty and even apprehension among the population which should be a matter concerning not only Trinidad Government but also H.M. Government and even to the Americans themselves.

It must be clearly understood by all parties concerned that a definitive agreement concerning the revision of the 1941 Agreement must now be reached. Failing such agreement it will not be possible for [me] to postpone further the necessary steps to maintain self-respect of [my] government and protect the rights of the Trinidad people. These steps will include, but will not necessarily be restricted to:

(a) a control point outside of Chaguaramas for checking of all vehicles and persons entering or leaving the base, including controls of immigration, health, currency, customs, fire-arms, narcotics, animal and plant quarantine, licenses of drivers and cars, registration of cars;

(b) the fencing of Piarco Airport with the necessary precautions against unauthorized entry or exit:

(c) the boarding and rummaging of all planes, without prejudice to Trinidad's protest against the practice whereby these planes have . . . arrogated to themselves the right to land at will and act as they please;

(d) the immediate resumption of Waller Field, Carsen Field and dock site, with implementation of the plans for their full and permanent incorporation in the development programme of the country;

(e) the immediate cessation of all duty-free imports into Chaguaramas and the institution of rigid customs inspection and examination of all materials consigned to the base;

(f) a ban on all non-licensed and non-registered vehicles on the roads of the country.[93]

From Williams's perspective, these were the grievances of his small and powerless island and the steps that it was prepared to take to regain its soil and its dignity. Essentially mere irritants or pinpricks, they constituted the only tangible weapons Williams had at his command. Frustration with his inability to get the Americans to the conference table accounted for the increasing bellicosity of his language. The radiation scare heightened his feeling of impotence, although he would use it to underscore the abuses his people had suffered at the hands of foreign powers.

♦ ♦ ♦ ♦ ♦ Technical expert D. R. Evans began his investigation of Chaguaramas on August 24, inspecting the site and holding discussions with key personnel. He completed his work on September 1 and left for home the next day. When he submitted his report two weeks later, the Colonial Office sent an advanced copy to the U.S. State Department in order to "obtain their urgent confirmation that they have no objection from the security point of view to its contents being made public." D. H. T. Hildyard of the Foreign Office instructed the British ambassador to the United States to impress upon the State Department "that it would be very embarrassing for us, and would almost certainly make the report suspect, were it to become known in Trinidad that it had been shown to the Americans before being transmitted to the Trinidad Government."[94]

This was, of course, another glaring example of British collusion with the Americans against Williams and his government. Such behavior was hardly necessary in this instance because Evans's report was most favorable to the Americans, the alleged security considerations notwithstanding. Evans dismissed the charge that the Americans had removed equipment to avoid their inspection; rather, some low-power klystron transmitting valves had been returned to the United States because they were damaged. In addition, he found that the nearest point to Chaguaramas that could be irradiated was Morne Pierre, an area that "is just within the hazard zone but the terrain is difficult and is covered with almost impenetrable jungle." Evans concluded that "the jungle would provide substantial attenuation of the field and therefore even this region must be considered safe." Overall, no radiation hazard existed on the island, and "on site" precautions "are more than adequate."[95]

The government of Trinidad and Tobago received the report with some skepticism. The ministers were not convinced that Morne Pierre was safe, and chief minister Williams sent a statement to the Colonial Office on January 7, 1958, rejecting Evans's findings. Williams declared that his government would take such precautions in the Morne Pierre area that it considered necessary "and reserves the right to seek expert advice in respect of possible effects on flora and fauna, the game and hunters from radiation hazard." He emphasized his concern about "the constant readiness of the United Kingdom to sacrifice Trinidad's interests to American susceptibilities."[96]

The secretary of state for the colonies was quick to respond to this charge even though Williams was obviously on solid ground. He took "grave exception" to the chief minister's statement of January 7, noting that the United Kingdom had "on every occasion strongly opposed the Americans when we felt that Trinidad's interests were at stake." Assuming an imperial stance, the secretary told Williams that if he issued a public statement on the Evans Report that was "at variance with expert opinion" and if this alarmed the citizenry unjustifiably, the United Kingdom "would be compelled to issue a statement designed to correct public misunderstandings."[97]

The governments of Trinidad and the United Kingdom also disagreed on whether to make the Evans Report public. Williams wanted to publish it, as well as all of his correspondence with the British on the radiation problem. The Colonial Office only agreed to release the report, probably to deny the chief minister any political capital that he would earn him from publication of the correspondence. The British, contrary to their protestations of being evenhanded, also wished to protect the United States from any embarrassment that might result from public exposure of the documents. On December 18 H. A. A. Hankey of the Colonial Office wrote to Ambassador Logan in Washington, enclosing a summary of a recent speech that Williams had given. Hankey thought that the speech gave "an indication of the odium we are incurring in our efforts to have the [Evans] report presented as favorably as possible to the Americans. . . . You may be able to use it to counter the unfortunate impression that we are not being helpful to them on this issue."[98]

Such an admission would have been exploited to great effect by Williams had he known of it. Failing to dissuade him from his intention to publish the Evans Report and the official correspondence associated with it, Colonial Office personnel speculated that Williams's attitude reflected his desire to "get even" with the Americans for rejecting his requests for bilateral talks, as well as other disappointments. Still, the Foreign Office wanted to take the wind out of his sails by extracting a promise from the Americans on their use of tracking equipment at Chaguaramas. As R. H. G. Edmonds noted in a communication to the Washington embassy: "It would considerably strengthen any statement we make if we could say that the Americans have already undertaken to modify their tracking equipment so as to avoid possible irradiation of the Morne Pierre area."[99]

The U.S. officials obliged. A week later they were able to assure their British counterparts that "the U.S. Air Force has not utilized and does not intend to utilize the radar station at Chaguaramas by emitting signals in the direction of Morne Pierre. Such use is not necessary to carry out the assigned functions of this equipment. Therefore no radiation hazard at all can have possibly existed in that area. However, in order to allay any possible concern in this respect the equipment will be so modified that no possible signals can be transmitted to that area."[100] There was, of course, no way for the government of Trinidad to determine whether the Americans kept their promise or whether this was just another act of deception carried out with British connivance.

Eric Williams was not privy to British-American collaboration in thwarting some of his government's initiatives. But he smarted over the disappointments he had experienced in the struggle for Chaguaramas and what he perceived as unsympathetic responses by the United Kingdom to his case. On January 15, 1960, he wrote another stinging letter to the secretary of state complaining that "we have been left alone to bear the full burden of our struggle to vindicate our rights. Never at any time has H.M.G. given the slightest indication that it considers the cause for which we are struggling a just one."

Williams went on to list a number of initiatives for which he had received no support from the Colonial Office. Consequently, he wrote: "We have . . . learnt, Government and population alike, to see in this matter of the return of Chaguaramas to us by America that H.M.G. is neither mentor, friend, nor ally, but sees our struggle in the light of considerations of its own, in which the wishes and aspirations of the people of Trinidad and Tobago and of the West Indies play an insignificant role."[101]

No doubt the accusatory tone of this letter further annoyed colonial officials even though Williams had chastised them on many other occasions. The chief minister, as he said in the letter, wanted the United Kingdom to recognize "the inherent justice of our stand." He was convinced that had Trinidad "been free to deal itself with what are its own problems, we could by now have achieved a satisfactory and honorable settlement." Finally, he condemned the British because "the pressures [to which] you have subjected

us have created [a] fertile basis for misunderstanding among the population, which view matters in much the same way as is expressed here."[102]

♦ ♦ ♦ ♦ ♦ Williams's pressure for a new conference, as well as his verbal
assaults on the Americans and the British, had begun to show some glim-
mers of success by mid-1959. On September 6 he reported to a special
Convention of the PNM that his struggle now had "some prospects of
success." He was referring to discussions that he had had with the other
interested governments on the question of separate representation for Trinidad and Tobago at the upcoming tripartite conference on the Leased Bases
Agreement. Williams had also met with the parliamentary under secretary of
state for the colonies and two other Colonial Office officials in July to discuss
the agenda for the conference. In August he had held talks with the American consul general and presented his proposals for a joint U.S.–West Indian
base and for the release of all unused leased areas.[103]

Recognizing the obstacles he confronted in his demand for separate
representation at the tripartite conference, Williams modified his stance. In
September 1959 he informed the Colonial Office that his government would
be prepared to form part of the Federal delegation to the conference provided that bilateral talks between the United States and Trinidad and Tobago
preceded the conference. The decisions that resulted from those discussions
should constitute the bases for the negotiations at the tripartite conference.
Williams received no immediate response to this offer of compromise, caus-
ing him to complain in December that there was "not one mumbling word"
from the Colonial Office about his proposals. "They will sell their souls, and
ours too if they could get hold of them," in order "to deprive us of the
political credit of settling the Chaguaramas issue," Williams lamented.[104]

There was positive movement on December 10, when Prime Minister
Grantley Adams announced that the United States, the United Kingdom, and
the West Indies would hold talks on the Leased Bases Agreement. Trinidad
would not be given separate representation but would be included in the
West Indies delegation. Williams, despite his stated willingness to be part of
the Federal delegation, was not pleased with the decision to deny his government separate representation and declined to say whether he would participate. At a press conference on December 12, he claimed ignorance of the
situation. Obviously peeved, Williams groused: "Nobody consulted us . . .

they can go and discuss what they want. . . . I am not prepared to waste my time on the matter. . . . As long as there is life, there is Chaguaramas. So let them go ahead."[105]

Williams was inclined to see the decision as the result of "intrigue" by the Federal government to reduce his authority and influence on the issue. "Whatever intrigues are going on," he said, "we have no part of it."[106] This apparent slight only made Williams more determined to press his case with greater energy and vituperative language. The massive demonstration and celebrated march in the rain on April 22, 1960, was the high-water mark of the battle for Chaguaramas that had begun in London in July 1957. Almost three years had passed, yet its élan had not diminished and Williams had not flinched, despite the withering criticism of his opponents, American intransigence, and British dissemblance.

Approximately six weeks after the spectacular April 22 show of strength, the British proposed a series of three conferences to settle the problem. The first, to be held in London, would engage the Americans and the British, with the West Indies Federation accorded observer status. The second conference would take place in Trinidad, with the Americans and the Trinidadians as the principal participants and the United Kingdom and the West Indies Federation as observers. The third conference would involve the signing of a new agreement by the Americans and the Trinidadians. This was acceptable to Williams and the PNM, so the stage was now set for serious negotiations by the various governments.

When the London parley began, Williams repeated his opposition to the terms of the 1941 agreement. He emphasized that a new one must have the approval of his people and recognize their "fundamental economic interests . . . [and] their efforts to utilize their limited resources, particularly their land, for the benefit of the population."[107] His meaning was unmistakable: Williams was now going to extract a price for the continued use of Trinidadian soil by the Americans. It represented a major shift in his stance, one that made practical sense but compromised the larger principles that the struggle represented. On their part, the Americans agreed to release those areas that were not needed for the operation of the naval base.

The long-awaited second conference was scheduled to take place in Tobago during November 28–December 9, 1960. In preparation for the meeting, the U.S. Department of the Navy sent a report entitled "Strategic Appraisal of Trinidad, B.W.I." to the Department of State. This very detailed study emphasized the importance of Trinidad and Tobago to protect the southern flank of the United States, essential air and strategic shipping routes, the Panama Canal, and logistic support for U.S. and Allied forces in the Caribbean area.

The navy recognized, however, that the agreement had to be renegotiated because the imminent independence of Trinidad and Tobago would render it obsolete. It is remarkable that even after three years of dispute, the navy did not understand its nationalist underpinnings and viewed it only as an expression of "resentment" against the United States. The navy's report accused "opportunistic politicians, such as Dr. Williams [of winning] popular support in 'Hate U.S. campaigns,'" and it blamed the British government for indirectly supporting Williams by advocating a revision of the base agreement. Characterizing Eric Williams as "basically anti-U.S." and "unscrupulous," the report found "it is most unlikely that any negotiations to which he is a party could produce any agreement satisfactory to both sides."[108]

The U.S. Navy's pessimism was unfounded. Eric Williams would later describe the atmosphere at the Tobago conference as "conspicuous for its harmony and good will."[109] The United States agreed to return about 21,000 acres of unused land at Chaguaramas and other sites to the people of Trinidad and Tobago. In the event of an outbreak of general hostilities, however, 1,400 acres at Waller Field and land at Monos Island, Scotland Bay, and Green Hill Harbour would be made available to the U.S. government. Lands in the Teteron Bay area could now be used jointly by the government of Trinidad and the Federal government to train and station Trinidadian and Federal naval units, marine police forces, and engineering construction units. The terms of the agreement would be reviewed in 1967. A second review would take place in 1973, at which time it would be decided whether the agreement should be terminated. Much would depend on whether there was any strategic need for the Americans to retain the base. Should both governments fail to reach an agreement by the end of 1973, the Americans would have four years to vacate the base.

Williams was able to extract from the Americans economic assistance amounting to US$30 million, spread over five years, for four major domestic projects. These included an arts and sciences college at the University of the West Indies, St. Augustine; the construction of additional roads linking Port of Spain to Chaguaramas; improvements to the government-run railways;

and port facilities in Port of Spain. At the end of the conference, an obviously delighted and relieved Eric Williams assured the delegates of his commitment to execute the letter of the agreement in a "spirit of friendliness and recognition of mutual needs."[110]

Understandably, Williams received much popular acclaim after the meeting. His ecstatic supporters greeted him as a hero and the PNM's General Council voted to place a plaque honoring him at the party's headquarters. A politically divided legislature eventually ratified the new agreement, but not before Williams was excoriated by members of the opposition. Displaying a shameless political volte-face, the DLP condemned the chief minister for signing an agreement that allowed the Americans to retain much of the base at Chaguaramas. Lionel Seukeran, the major opposition spokesperson in the debate, characterized Williams's action as "a gross betrayal of the people of Trinidad and the West Indies and a complete sell out to the Americans who will now determine how long they will want to stay on these shores." Williams had treated the Americans with "sarcastic rudeness" but had done "an acrobatic summersault" at the conference, selling out "Trinidad soil to the Americans as though he had a deed for all of it in his own right." Seukeran maintained that the "deal" involved "going down on our knees begging for American dollars."

According to Seukeran, the agreement itself represented "the worst contractual obligation that any country could have possibly entered into with any foreign country." He noted that other nations, such as Morocco and Panama, had received more favorable terms from the Americans for the use of their soil or water. Their leaders, he said, "were men of high caliber, sitting at [the] international level, dealing with problems like civilized people, demanding benefits for a country not like a mendicant but of right." Williams had been duped at the conference, Seukeran declared, and the result was "a damnable fraud, a wicked betrayal inflicted on the people of the country."[111]

The DLP was not alone in its censure of the agreement, but it had a political ax to grind as the major opposition party. Some people, such as C. L. R. James, opposed the continued American occupation of the island. Others were dissatisfied with the size of the economic package. Chastened by these criticisms, Williams complained to William Christensen of the U.S. mission that "you have no idea how vicious the Opposition is about the Chaguaramas Agreement." When Christensen advised Williams not to pay much attention to such invective because it was animated by domestic political considerations, the chief minister exclaimed, "It's the people, too," add-ing, "They are concerned because they feel we are letting them down."[112]

♦ ♦ ♦ ♦ ♦ The resolution of the Chaguaramas dispute helped to produce a dramatic change in the relationship between the United States and Trinidad. Although there were some prickly moments as the two governments dick-ered over the economic assistance package, by 1964 the U.S. embassy in Port of Spain was noting an improvement in bilateral relations. A 1965 embassy survey attributed this to the US$30 million grant-in-aid provided by the United States, which "has led the government to cease its attempt to manu-facture public agitation against the presence of the U.S. base in Trinidad." The American ambassador was obviously pleased with "the openly pro-Western policy by Trinidad on most matters, including Cuba and Guiana." Similarly, he was gratified by Trinidad's "cooperation on anti-subversive surveillance activities in the Caribbean."[113]

The impression that these comments may create, to be sure, is that Wil-liams's support of policies important to the United States had been pur-chased. Although it is certainly accurate to maintain that tensions had eased between the two nations, Trinidad's foreign policy was driven by an assess-ment of its own interests. Inasmuch as Williams was an ardent anticommu-nist who distrusted Fidel Castro's motives and personally disliked both Forbes Burnham and Cheddi Jagan of British Guiana as well as disagreed with their policies, it is not surprising that he did not support them on the international stage. Trinidad and Tobago had only become independent in August 1962, so its foreign policy was still taking shape in 1965. Conse-quently, it hardly made sense to imply, as the American ambassador did, that Williams had become more compliant and that his pro-Western stance was bought. The fact is that Eric Williams really had no extensive foreign policy record in 1965 to defend, modify, or change.

In an attempt to keep Williams as an ally in the Cold War, the Americans also made conciliatory gestures to him. The U.S. Department of State was concerned in 1965 when it appeared that Williams might establish diplo-matic relations with the Soviet Union. In a memorandum to U.S. national security adviser McGeorge Bundy on August 28, 1965, the State Department observed: "The Soviet Union is currently courting Prime Minister Williams with the probable intent of concluding arrangements for the establishment of a Soviet Mission in Trinidad. We are seeking means to strengthen Williams' normally pro-Western attitude and to discourage any Trinidad-USSR relationship."[114]

The rapprochement with the United States was further aided by Williams's break with his erstwhile mentor C. L. R. James. The "sometime Trotskeyist," as the American consul general described him, had been invited back to Trinidad from England in 1958. After his return, the chief minister appointed him managing editor of the Nation, a position he held until 1960, when he resigned after the paper was criticized at the PNM's Fourth Annual Convention. As managing editor of the Nation and a close adviser to Williams, James had played a major role in the formulation of policy on the Chaguaramas issue. In discussing his break with Williams, James accused the chief minister of being "callous" and denounced what he saw as a trend toward authoritarianism in the country. He was not pleased when Williams announced in mid-1960 that Trinidad was allied with the West, adding that such an alliance was not a subject for debate. Such a posture, James charged, was a "piece of political gangsterism." With a critic of such towering intellectual stature removed from his inner circle, and ultimately from the country, Williams's position on foreign policy issues, particularly Trinidad's relationship with the United States, and his fervent anticommunism gained an unquestioned ascendancy.[115]

Three years after the landmark Tobago Agreement had been hammered out, U.S. defense officials began to reconsider the strategic value of the Chaguaramas facilities. Consequently, for the first time they began to entertain the prospect of releasing the naval base to the government of Trinidad and Tobago. Writing to Edwin L. Sykes of the Commonwealth Relations Office on December 3, 1964, the British high commissioner in Port of Spain, Norman Costar, doubted that Williams "would want to see the U.S. Navy move from Trinidad," regarding the base as a source of stability for the country. Costar said that Williams had told him that if there was "army trouble" in Trinidad, he would not hesitate to seek help from the U.S. Marines at Chaguaramas. Since Trinidad "gets American money because of the base," Costar thought that that would be an important consideration. On the other hand, he observed, the value of the base would be "a windfall" to Trinidad.[116]

Understandably, Eric Williams kept a watchful eye on the ways in which the Americans were utilizing Chaguaramas. He told Costar on November 10,

1965, that since they were not using all of the land area at the base, they would have to release the land he needed to build a hotel, new houses of Parliament, or the supreme court. Two days later, Costar consulted with the American ambassador, who told him that the base was then, in the words of Costar, "of very little, if any value to the United States" except for its "navigational facilities" and its value as a missile tracking station. Although Costar did not believe that a U.S. withdrawal from the base was imminent, he got the "distinct feeling that the Americans had now reconciled themselves to giving up the bulk of the base if any pressure was brought to bear upon them by Dr. Williams to this end." Costar repeated his view that Williams would be disappointed if the Americans left, because that would mean the end of U.S. aid that was linked to the base agreement. Williams would, however, "nibble at specific areas of the base when he has a use for them."[117]

The end came rather quickly. By early 1966 the press in Trinidad had begun to report that the U.S. Navy planned to relinquish substantial areas of the base to Trinidad and Tobago. This was not denied in official circles. The announcement when it came on February 5 was not unexpected:

> The Government of the United States and the Government of Trinidad and Tobago have agreed that the United States will release a major portion of the Chaguaramas Defense Area to the Government of Trinidad and Tobago by July, 1967. The United States proposes to begin withdrawal in mid 1966 and to phase withdrawal so that the areas will be available to the Government of Trinidad and Tobago as they are vacated. Authorities of Trinidad and Tobago will be working together to provide for the orderly transfer of areas involved and hold necessary discussions.[118]

The Americans, however, continued to occupy the missile tracking station as well as a navigational station.

Throughout the prolonged struggle for Chaguaramas, Williams's main weapons were his sense of history, his harsh rhetoric, and his capacity to keep the dispute alive and his supporters engaged for so long a period. The conflict would have been less acrimonious, and may even have been of shorter duration, had it not become such a divisive issue in the domestic politics of Trinidad and Tobago. The Americans clung to the vain hope that Eric Williams would somehow lose his political base and would be defeated at the polls. They were convinced—and assured—by the DLP that it would be more accommodating to their position. But Williams's core supporters never lost confidence in him and never wavered in their embrace of the cause he promoted so vociferously and passionately.

The Americans were slow to understand the intensity of the feeling behind the Chaguaramas controversy and that the political mood of the West Indian people was changing. The struggle for Chaguaramas became part of a larger assault on colonialism, and the forces it unleashed could not be contained. In a speech at Arima on July 17, 1959, Williams had made a clear connection between the Chaguaramas dispute and the battle against colonialism:

> When we deal with Chaguaramas, we are not merely dealing with what has become today the symbol of self government and the symbol of independence for the Federation. What all this means, ladies and gentlemen, is that we in Trinidad and Tobago, you in the West Indies, have begun a long overdue attempt which India has started, which Ghana has started, which all the former colonial territories have already begun—we too in Trinidad and Tobago are well on the road—we who have been passive agents of a history made and written for us by other people, we in the PNM symbolize today the determination of Arima and Trinidad and Tobago to write their own history, and to keep it in the democratic tradition of which we are the proud standard bearers.[119]

Imperious refusals by the Americans to conduct direct talks with the West Indians only further inflamed passions. Williams skillfully played on these emotions, manipulating them to bring his mighty adversary to the conference table and to concede the legitimacy of his claims. America's intransigence was strengthened by the mixed messages it received from some of the other Caribbean leaders. Their private communications with U.S. officials and their public rhetoric often gave the impression that the Chaguaramas dispute was being driven by the need for U.S. funds and that their principles, to the degree that any existed, were for sale.

The Americans, and British officials as well, speculated that Williams would settle for an appropriate price. But there is no evidence that he made any such overtures. In fact, Williams insisted that Trinidad's national integrity had no price. His acceptance of a U.S. grant-in-aid of $30 million at the Tobago settlement was an act of pragmatism on the one hand and of real politik on the other. The Americans, if they wanted to remain at Chaguaramas, would have to pay Trinidad for the privilege. But there is no doubt that the acceptance of the money compromised the lofty moral legitimacy and idealism of Trinidad's very just claims.

Yet the Chaguaramas battle was hardly about a crass materialism. Eric Williams was on the right side of history when he demanded that his people's voice be heard on the important question of the alienation of their soil, their birthright. Those who opposed him so vociferously were clinging to a historical moment that was passing. By privileging U.S. claims over their own, these people were demonstrating a lingering affection for the Massa who Williams had declared dead in 1961. In the end, the Americans' abandonment of Chaguaramas in 1967 was anticlimactic, given the intensity of their struggle to keep it. After a prolonged and debilitating David and Goliath–like conflict, Eric Williams had achieved the greatest victory of his political career.

◆ ◆

CHAPTER 4

ERIC WILLIAMS AND
THE GOLDEN HANDSHAKE

◆ ◆ ◆ ◆ ◆ ◆ The letter was not entirely unexpected. Still, its arrival on Harold MacMillan's desk on that November day in 1962 created a high degree of annoyance. "Dear Prime Minister" the letter opened coldly, a pointed departure from the more fraternal salutation, "My dear Prime Minister," that had graced earlier communications. "I acknowledge with many thanks your letter of November 15 in which you replied to my observations on the aide memoire from the Commonwealth Relations Secretary in respect of economic aid to Trinidad and Tobago," the text began. "The Cabinet has endorsed my recommendation which I conveyed to you in my letter of November 5," it continued. Then came the bombshell. "In the circumstances I must, with regret, decline your government's offer for the reasons I have already indicated," the letter ended. It was signed simply, "Eric Williams, Prime Minister of Trinidad and Tobago."[1]

This extraordinary letter, unprecedented in the history of Britain's relationship with its colonies and former colonies, was a haughty rejection of the parting gift that newly independent countries received from the former mother country. Known as the "golden handshake," the gift was designed to be an expression of Britain's goodwill to the new nation as well as to help the former colony grapple with the economic problems it would now have to face on its own. Beginning in the 1950s, the United Kingdom had granted independence to Ghana, Nigeria, Cyprus, Sierra Leone, Uganda, Ceylon, and Tanganyika, and, except for Ceylon, all had accepted the golden handshake without disputing its nature and size. Nothing in Britain's experience with these territories had prepared it for Williams's rejection of the gift and the lengthy and bitter row that ensued.

Eric Williams had spent much of his adult life researching, writing, and speaking about the unequal relationships between imperial countries and their colonies. As a persistent foe of colonialism, he maintained that the imperial powers bore the principal responsibility for the economic conditions of their colonies. The nation of Trinidad and Tobago was, to be sure, not poor when its per capita income was measured against those of other developing countries at the time. Of the British colonies that received independence up to that time, Uganda had a per capita income of £24, Nigeria £30, Jamaica £157, and Trinidad and Tobago, £229.[2] But Williams was convinced that Britain should provide a generous golden handshake to his country since it had not been a major beneficiary of aid in the years prior to independence.

Williams had known, of course, that he had to make a convincing case to the British government if Trinidad was to receive a generous golden handshake. In a letter to the secretary of state for the colonies in March 1962, he exploited the fear generated by the Cold War by invoking the specter of communism as a basis for significant economic assistance. "Quite frankly, I see our role as an independent country in this light," Williams wrote. "The crucial issue is defence with Trinidad and Tobago sitting astride the triangle of pro-Soviet influence from Cuba to British Guiana and across to Venezuela with its communist minority." As Williams saw it, the primary challenge that the new nation would confront was how to "develop the expanding democracy of Trinidad and Tobago, both political and economic, as to make it an obvious and visible contrast to these three countries." He reminded the British secretary that there was already "enough inflammable material and sufficient arsonists all over the Caribbean, without necessarily adding to both in Trinidad and Tobago."[3]

To help meet governmental obligations in Trinidad and Tobago, Williams requested an Exchequer loan of £5 million "possibly in anticipation of United Kingdom economic aid on independence."[4] There was no immediate response to the request, but in an exchange of telegrams on April 26 and May 1, 1962, Williams and the secretary of state agreed that any discussion of economic and financial issues should occur after the Trinidad and Tobago independence conference scheduled to take place in June. In anticipation of that meeting, on June 18 Williams submitted a document, entitled "Equipment for Independence," to the United Kingdom outlining Trinidad's case for substantial British support on the occasion of its independence. This carefully prepared statement, the tenor of which was unusual in its stridency, declared: "The concept of a 'parting gift' to a 'departing colony' has no place in the thinking of the Government and people of Trinidad and Tobago in respect of economic assistance from the United Kingdom." Ominously, the document continued: "What we seek, and regard as not unreasonable to expect, is to be adequately equipped for the journey on which we embark when we join the Commonwealth Caravan." Williams deftly raised the issue of British economic negligence by acknowledging that "it is of little value . . . to question why we do not now possess all that we now require to play our part" in "ensuring the continuous progress of the Commonwealth," as "this is no time for recrimination over past neglect."

This reminder of "past neglect" must have stung colonial officials as much as similar sentiments articulated by Williams in the past had done. Reiterating his rejection of a "golden" or "any other kind of handshake," Williams asserted that his new nation had no desire to be "pensioned off" or "compensated for loss of office." He merely wished to be "equipped" with the material resources without which the "spirit" and the "determination" of his people could not reach their possibilities.[5]

The premier elaborated on the issue of imperial support for Trinidad and Tobago in a statement to the Colonial Office dated July 9, 1962. He began by expressing his "disappointment and concern" with Britain's tendency "to regard the efforts made during recent years by the people of Trinidad and Tobago to help themselves, as in some measure reducing their eligibility for United Kingdom assistance." Here, of course, he was referring to his achievements in office since 1956, when he became chief minister, and these were considerable. He went on to press his case for significant assistance by pointing out that "it would be unfortunate indeed if the view were to gain currency that, on independence when the responsibilities are greatly increased, a Commonwealth country could expect little assistance from the British people because, during the period of its colonial existence, it had achieved by its own efforts some success in providing necessary but hitherto neglected facilities."

This biting and accusatory document continued: "If the achievements of Trinidad and Tobago in the sphere of economic and social development during the past five years are to provide an argument for rejecting the new nation's request for reasonable assistance then, at least for the benefit of those territories still on the road to independence, it should be made abundantly clear that self-help is a disqualification and that the United Kingdom would prefer to help those who do not help themselves."

Williams then enjoined the British government to "recognize the need to assure Trinidad and Tobago of the means not merely of maintaining the level of development already achieved but of raising it to the point where self sustained growth becomes a real possibility." As he had emphasized in his June 18 statement, his government needed the resources:

To secure the safety of the nation.
To strengthen its social and economic foundations.
To speed the development of the skills and capacities of its people.

Trinidad's independence coincided with the end of a five-year development program initiated by the Williams government in 1958. As much as 98½ percent of the funds for this program had come from the resources of Trinidad and Tobago to construct new schools, hospitals, and a variety of capital works. Williams wanted to initiate a new five-year development program in 1962, but one that had fundamentally different sources of funding. First, the plan called for a greater recourse to external loan markets. Second, its implementation would create a large gap between needs and resources that could be satisfied only by external aid. Williams thought that independence afforded "a conventional opportunity for seeking some of the needed external aid from the former metropolitan country."

Under the circumstances, Williams provided the United Kingdom with a detailed plan outlining his country's specific needs and the amount of money required to fulfill each objective. This included the creation of a defense force for the new nation; the construction of houses for those who needed them; the development of the town of Scarborough in Tobago; aid for the national airlines, the British West Indian Airways (BWIA); support for the University of the West Indies; and funds for the expansion of telephone service in Trinidad and Tobago.

To meet his defense needs, Williams requested £750,000 in grants for four fully equipped coastal vessels and four light aircraft, as well as funds to train personnel. To finance the construction of six thousand houses, he asked for an interest-free loan of £3 million and an additional loan of £2 million at a rate not exceeding 2 percent per annun, with both loans repayable in twenty years. Williams noted that housing construction would have a "multiplier-effect" because of its "immediate impact" on the problem of unemployment and its stimulation of consumer demand—both resulting in economic expansion and growth.

In making his case for funds for the "redevelopment" of the town of Scarborough, the premier called attention to the "consequences of decades of neglect." Lower Scarborough was "unplanned, cramped and congested, badly drained in certain areas and totally incapable of accommodating satisfactorily the volume of pedestrian and vehicular traffic which flow daily into it." Williams believed that Scarborough, as a seaport town, had enormous tourist potential. To improve the town, therefore, he wanted to acquire "appropriate" areas and effect a "physical reconstruction." He estimated the development costs to be £1.3 million and the acquisition costs, £1.8 million. The United Kingdom would underwrite the development costs, and a long-term interest-free loan would fund the acquisition costs.

Williams also needed assistance for the regional carrier of the British territories in the Caribbean, the BWIA. When the carrier had fallen on hard times, the government of Trinidad and Tobago assumed responsibility for its operation. Williams emphasized the operational losses that the carrier had experienced and the apparent unwillingness of the other islands to share the financial burden. Accordingly, he requested that Britain arrange for the transfer to BWIA the aircraft that it held on loan from the British Overseas Airways Corporation (BOAC). Moreover, he urged that Barbados and the Leeward and Windward Islands be allowed to become partners with Trinidad and the BOAC in the "ownership and operation" of BWIA. Detailed estimates of the cost of his requests were being prepared, and he hoped that Britain would "bear a reasonable portion of the cost of such operations as a contribution to the economic development of the islands."

With the independence of Jamaica and Trinidad, unspent funds allocated to them under the Colonial Development and Welfare Program would have to be returned to the United Kingdom, since the two entities had graduated from colonial status. Williams was troubled that £133,000 allocated to the University of the West Indies on Trinidad's behalf would revert to Britain. In his June 18 statement, he had asked that those funds be credited to Trinidad and Tobago in addition to a grant of £100,000 to enable the university's Faculty of Agriculture, located in St. Augustine, to create a research farm. Finally, Williams maintained that an Exchequer loan from the United Kingdom of £2.5 million would permit the new nation to acquire the existing telephone system. This would expand telephone service to meet the needs of an independent country.

In submitting these requests for £2.283 million in grants and £9.3 million in loans (excluding the cost of support for BWIA), Williams indicated that Trinidad's new five-year development plan would cost £50 million, or £10 million per annum. His rough estimates for the major areas of expenditure were as follows:

Agriculture	£4,000,000
Industrial Development	8,000,000
Roads and Bridges	3,500,000
Electricity	10,000,000
Sewerage	4,500,000
Education	3,000,000
Water	3,000,000
Housing	4,000,000

Seen in the context of the overall cost of the development plan, Williams was only asking the United Kingdom to underwrite slightly more than one-fifth of the amount. His statement explained that the projects for which he needed support "represent a relatively small proportion of the program of activities which are not merely desirable in themselves but essential to the preservation of the new nation as, perhaps, the major stabilizing element in the Caribbean region." Speaking as a historian, Williams assured British officials that their assistance would enable his nation "to play with increased success the role which history, and its own efforts, seems to have determined for it." Sensing that his requests were probably extravagant in view of the modest support Trinidad and Tobago had previously received from the mother country, Williams urged the government to resist, "in its own interests, to apply to Trinidad and Tobago the same criteria of assistance it uses elsewhere." The ardent nationalist concluded: "It is no spirit of national conceit that Trinidad and Tobago claims for itself a unique position in the Commonwealth, . . . a unique position justifies unique treatment."[6]

Colonial officials must have experienced apoplectic fits on reading these detailed and often sharply worded documents. Although they had grown accustomed to Williams's caustic comments about imperial behavior and neglect, these documents were requesting the kind of financial assistance that they were unwilling to imagine, much less contemplate. Williams was mindful of the lukewarm response to his earlier request for financial support. The under secretary of state for the colonies, Hugh Fraser, had told him on July 10 that the golden handshake would be in the vicinity of £2 million. Two days later, Williams requested a short-term loan of £589,000 to repay a housing debt to the defunct West Indies Federation, but the decision on this loan had been shelved.[7] An angry and disappointed Eric Williams responded by telling the airport audience that welcomed him home on July 13 that "in the United Kingdom everybody was absolutely fed up with the West Indies." Indeed, the British had an "absolute contempt for the West Indies." He admonished his greeters to "start off your independence understanding Britain is not going to help you. They have no interest in the West Indies whatsoever."[8]

As usual, colonial officials were annoyed by such outbursts. Williams was reacting to the recognition that Britain was unlikely to provide the kind of financial support he was requesting for the new nation. His statement at the airport was an exaggeration, but it was not untrue. Edwin L. Sykes at the Colonial Office suggested that officials need not take Williams's comments "tragically." According to Sykes, there were even "some advantages in getting it made known to the people of Trinidad that independence does mean independence, and that independence means getting a certain amount of 'kicks' and not additional amounts of 'ha'pence.' "[9] Had he seen this memorandum, Eric Williams would no doubt have responded that the entire colonial experience had been characterized by "kicks." He would have reminded Sykes of the role that the colonies had played in the construction and growth of the British economy. Such reminders would not have served any purpose, however, as colonial officials had long since decided to be parsimonious in their dealings with Trinidad and Tobago.

♦ ♦ ♦ ♦ ♦ In preparation for the Independence Conference to be held in late May and early June 1962, colonial officials informed the British delegation that the criterion for assistance to Trinidad "is need and on this basis alone Trinidad, as the wealthiest per head of the West Indian islands, has little claim on Her Majesty's Government." The memorandum, which would become official policy, emphasized that "our object, therefore, will be to give the least we can," adding, "if Trinidad wants independence, especially in a hurry, our aim should be to let it be on our own financial terms." The officials admitted, however, that the government had not yet given any detailed consideration "to the sort of financial settlement which we would hope to get away with for Trinidad."[10] Clearly, there was an enormous gulf between Trinidad's expansive assessment of need and expectations, on the one hand, and the British government's desire to give the departing colony as little as possible, on the other.

The colonial officials could not, on their own, determine the size and composition of the golden handshake. The Department of the Treasury had to approve any grant, and it had its own ideas on the dimensions of the financial package. In early August, a few weeks before Trinidad formally received its independence, the Colonial Office submitted its proposals for a financial settlement to the Department of the Treasury. The proposals included a gift of £500,000 from unspent Colonial Development and Welfare funds, as well as a gift of four Viscount aircraft that were then on charter to BWIA, with an estimated value of £500,000.[11] In addition, Trinidad and Tobago would receive a development loan of £1 million. As paltry as this potential offer seemed, the even more parsimonious Treasury rejected it but endorsed the Colonial Development and Welfare Grant of £500,000 and a development loan of the same amount. Recognizing the political difficulties involved in making such a Scrooge-like offer to Williams, and fearful of his wrath, the Colonial Office demurred. J. D. Higman, one of the officials, called the Treasury's proposals "derisory" in a departmental minute.[12]

Duncan Sandys, the colonial secretary, was equally appalled. In a letter to John Boyd-Carpenter, secretary of the Treasury, he complained that the Treasury offer is "one that I cannot put to the Trinidad government. If I did, it would virtually certainly be rejected." Sandys noted that he was mindful of the fact that the country faced a development deficit of £5.6 million for the current year and £25 million over a five-year period. But although Trinidad was "imprudent" in its plans and spending decisions, he argued that "we must offer a sum which, while admittedly only going a small way towards bridging this year's deficit, will at least be regarded as a steadying hand to Trinidad in its descent to realism." He firmly believed that Eric Williams would consider £500,000 in "new money" as "little better than a calculated snub" and that Britain's relationship with the new nation would be seriously affected. To prevent Williams from viewing the offer to his country as "discriminatory" vis-à-vis the £1.25 million given to Jamaica, he urged the gift of the Viscount aircraft to enable Trinidad and Tobago and BWIA to continue service to the Little Eight islands. Sandys also supported a development loan of £1 million in addition to the Colonial Development and Welfare Grant balance of £500,000.[13]

The Treasury responded with a compromise. The new offer included the Colonial Development and Welfare Grant of £500,000 and the choice of either a £1 million loan—without the Viscount aircraft—or a £500,000 loan with the aircraft. Secretary Sandys made a counterproposal: a loan of £750,000, the Colonial Development and Welfare Grant, and the aircraft. He noted that Williams, who would be attending the Commonwealth Prime Ministers' Conference in September, "is coming over here in a difficult mood and I am naturally anxious to avoid superimposing a row with Trinidad on this issue on top of the difficult negotiations which will inevitably arise during the Prime Minister's meeting."[14]

As the internal discussions continued, the Treasury reported that the unspent portion of the Colonial Development Welfare Grant was likely to amount to £375,000, substantially lower than had been estimated earlier. In addition, the Colonial Office discovered that there were complications arising from Trinidad's debt to the defunct Federation of the West Indies. In the opinion of the Colonial officials, Trinidad owed £75,000 toward the defense expenditure of the federation, though Williams had declined to accept that figure. H. A. F. Rumbold of the Colonial Office held the view that if Trinidad refused to pay its share of the defense costs, Jamaica was likely to follow suit. If that happened, the total assets of the federation would be insufficient to meet its liabilities unless Britain met the deficit.

The second complicating factor was that Trinidad had obtained a short-term loan from the federation to construct houses for the Federal officials who resided on the island. These funds had to be repaid, but Williams lacked the resources to do so. Under the circumstances, he requested a short-term loan from the United Kingdom and, according to Rumbold, implied "that this should be additional to whatever items were included in the Independence Settlement."[15] Colonial officials recommended against granting a loan to defray the housing debt. Yet they wanted to make the golden handshake dependent on Trinidad's discharge of its obligations to the federation. Because Williams was contesting the Colonial Office's position on the extent of his government's obligations to the defunct federation, the matter was certain to exacerbate tensions and invite a great deal of acrimony.

When Williams attended his first Commonwealth Prime Ministers' Conference in mid-September, he still had no clear idea about the nature and size of the golden handshake. At the end of the conference, he met with Duncan Sandys on September 21, 1962. Although the parting gift was on the minds of both men, it was never discussed. Colonial officials would later complain that Williams had delivered a lengthy "monologue" on the Little Eight, preventing them from raising the issue. H. A. F. Rumbold recalled that the Commonwealth secretary "was going to raise this matter but could not get a word in edgeways."[16]

Williams was, nevertheless, very upset by the failure of the colonial officials to address the issues that he had raised in the detailed statements that he had submitted to them in June and July. His irritation with the officials showed when he declined their invitation to meet with them on his return to London from a trip to continental Europe after the Prime Ministers' Conference had concluded. Not until October 30, roughly eighteen weeks after Williams had submitted his "Equipment for Independence" statement on June 18, did colonial officials inform him about the nature of the golden handshake

In an aide-mémoire from the Colonial Office, Williams learned that Trinidad would receive a Commonwealth Assistance Loan of £1 million for the "purchase of British goods and services" required for development. The loan would be repayable over a period of twenty-five years and the interest rate would be adjustable; the amount of interest would depend on the existing rate at each drawing on the loan (according to the aide-mémoire, the current rate was $5\frac{7}{8}$ percent). In addition, Trinidad would pay a "management charge" of $\frac{1}{4}$ of 1 percent. In order to provide the loan, the British government "would wish to agree with the Government of Trinidad and Tobago the purposes to which the loan would be applied and the phasing of disbursements from it."

The United Kingdom would make a gift of the unspent portion of the Colonial Development and Welfare funds that had been allocated to Trinidad. The nation would also receive that proportion of the funds earmarked for regional services, such as the University of the West Indies and its teaching hospital, but Trinidad would have to contribute at least equal sums to these services. The total amount of the grant "on present information" was about £250,000, a far cry from the original estimate of £500,000. The aide-mémoire also provided for the gift of the four Viscount aircraft, now estimated to cost £800,000, a wildly inflated figure. These offers were made contingent on Trinidad's repayment of its debt to the former West Indies Federation. Finally, the United Kingdom rejected Trinidad's application for an Exchequer loan of £600,000 that Williams had submitted in March.[17]

♦ ♦ ♦ ♦ ♦ The very disappointing aide-mémoire dashed Williams's hope of significant economic aid. Two months earlier he had told the British High Commission that the United Kingdom should invest substantially in Trinidad to make it a showpiece for successful British decolonization. When he visited Williams on the night of November 1, 1962, Sir Stephen Luke, the Federal interim commissioner, found him "depressed, morose, and more critical than ever of what he considers our 'niggardliness' towards Trinidad on independence."[18]

Yet Williams lost no time in attacking the terms of the aide-mémoire, which obviously were considerably less than the proposals that he had made in June and July for millions of pounds in gifts and loans. In an angry letter of November 5 to Prime Minister Harold MacMillan, Williams asserted that, except for the aircraft "write off," the proposals in the aide-mémoire "appear to have been drawn up with little reference" to those that he had submitted. "You will readily understand, therefore," "my inability to give them serious consideration."

Williams rejected the "unfortunate implication" that the proposals were conditional on Trinidad's assumption of "certain outstanding obligations" relating to defense arrangements for the former Federation of the West Indies. He had already "firmly refuted" those claims, and he did not propose to "revive the discussions on this particular subject." But he was prepared to refund to the United Kingdom the amount that his government had borrowed for the construction of housing for the Federal officials, "including, of course, that portion that might ordinarily have been regarded as representing the share of Trinidad and Tobago."

Williams was especially distressed that the British government had not responded to his request for a £5 million Exchequer loan to tackle the growing problem of unemployment in his country "and to forestall the inevitable threat of political instability." He added: "If the Aide Memoire is the answer, it would then become a serious matter if the question of economic aid to a former colony should end merely in the old-fashioned colonial policy of providing a colonial market for British industry and employment for British workers." Thus, the author of *Capitalism and Slavery* linked the past to the present, invoking the specter of colonial exploitation and its relationship to the construction of the British economy. It was a calculated assault on the British government and its people for centuries of colonial oppression and a blunt reminder that those days were passing. Williams was advising his Cabinet to reject the aide-mémoire since it did not, in fact, offer "economic aid."[19]

Calling Williams's letter "discourteous," seasoned officials could not recall seeing anything like it emanating from a colonial or, in this case, postcolonial leader. On November 15, ten days after writing to MacMillan, Williams continued his attack at a press conference in London. He declared that "Trinidad and Tobago is the only country reaching independence without having Britain extend a hand with something in the palm. We are the only country attaining independence within the Commonwealth which has received no financial aid, in loans or grants from Britain." "But," he added, "we are quite happy to have it remain so." This, of course, was not entirely accurate. Neither India nor Ceylon had received a golden handshake, and Trinidad had just received an aide-mémoire, however unattractive and unacceptable the terms.

Williams reserved some of his most biting comments for the clause in the aide-mémoire that required Trinidad to purchase British goods with the funds it borrowed. He observed: "If aid fails to create employment in the country to which it is given, then it is a trap. . . . Economic aid limited to the purchase of the goods and services of other people is nothing more than a perpetuation of colonialism."[20]

Five days later, on November 20, Williams told an audience at the London School of Economics: "The West Indies are in the position of an orange. The British have sucked it dry and their sole concern today is that they should not slip and get damaged on the peel." Vituperative comments such as these, no matter how justified, did nothing to improve the atmosphere of the discussions on the golden handshake. But Williams was not likely to hold his tongue, especially where Trinidad's interests were concerned and when the metropolitan power appeared to be shirking its responsibilities as he saw them. Thus, on November 25, he informed West Indian students in London:

> The [British] offer is quite unacceptable and we would prefer not to have it. . . . The British offer was not worth the time and energy we spent on [the] preparation of Trinidad's case. . . . The aid offer which I have turned down amounted to aid to Britain rather than to Trinidad. . . . People talk to me of giving aid in the form of goods and services. Goods and services

for what? To keep people unemployed in Trinidad and Tobago? What is this? I do not propose to accept any concept of the Commonwealth which means common wealth for Britain and common poverty for us.

Williams was equally incensed by the stipulation that he submit his development plans to British officials for their examination before his government could qualify for a loan. Such a request was probably justified from the perspective of the lender. But it conveyed the wrong message to a sensitive new prime minister who had spent much of his life criticizing colonial rule. Speaking to the students on November 25, Williams asked: "Must we, in order to get economic aid, have to submit our affairs to the countries giving aid, when we have our own economists working out our plan? Is colonialism to continue? If so, on what terms?"[21]

The British government was in no mood to make any concessions to Trinidad, and Williams had gone too far out on a limb to retreat, even if he were so inclined. The two countries remained adamant, and the former colony was now set to reject the former mother country's gift publicly and ostentatiously. On November 26, with his Cabinet's approval, Williams formally declined to accept the golden handshake, initiating a bitter year-long dispute between Trinidad and the United Kingdom.

In a vain attempt to mollify Williams, Prime Minister MacMillan sent him a letter on December 2 explaining his government's inability to change the terms of the aide-mémoire. The United Kingdom had "many other commitments," and "in deciding what we can do for one country we need to bear in mind its relationship with what we do for others." MacMillan was satisfied that "the terms of the financial settlement offered to Trinidad are in line with those offered to, and accepted by other independent territories."[22]

Neither Williams nor British officials showed any sign of compromising in the aftermath of the rejection letter of November 26. Colonial officials were particularly displeased when Williams ignored their appeals and published the text of his letters to MacMillan. In doing so, they argued, he had violated the customary norms of conduct of Commonwealth prime ministers inasmuch as correspondence between them was never made public. The day before he rejected the golden handshake, Williams gave a speech at Woodford Square castigating the British for their treatment of his country. According to the Trinidad Guardian, Williams said that "he wanted everybody to understand that the Government never asked the United Kingdom for one single penny": 'We said, 'Loan us some money to start and we would pay back.' Your own money would be voted year after year by the Minister of Finance and approved by the Parliament to pay back that loan which would help us to build houses and rehabilitate the population. We are entitled to ask for that. And if they say 'no' then, after all, it is their money and they do not have to live in damn barrack yards."[23] Williams, to be sure, had requested grants, but if the newspaper report is accurate, this was an example of his rhetorical excess.

Both governments sought to embroider their respective positions. It was an extraordinary spectacle of the former mother country and its tiny former colony locked in a dispute, each trying to second-guess and outmaneuver the other. The personality of Eric Williams remained at center stage. British officials tried to develop a strategy for dealing with him, and members of his Cabinet sought in subtle ways to get him to embrace a more conciliatory stance. Although colonial officials had been dealing with Williams since 1956, they barely understood the intellectually pugnacious West Indian politician. They spent an inordinate amount of energy speculating on his motives and formulating strategies based on their frequently flawed conclusions. To these officials, Williams was an enigma, and they scrambled to make his character the central issue in the developing conflict, as opposed to the merits of his claims. Interestingly, Williams and his persona still invite the attention of scholars as they attempt to understand his behavior in political office and his practice of statecraft. Such a preoccupation, to be sure, is not unique to the study of Eric Williams. The difficulties occasioned by the golden handshake, coming as they did about seven years after Williams entered the political arena, provide us with an opportunity to make an informed but risky assessment of his persona and the ways in which it might have shaped his modus operandi.

♦ ♦ ♦ ♦ ♦ To understand Williams's intellectual positions, particularly as they related to colonialism, colonial officials read *Capitalism and Slavery* (1944), although their comprehension of its thesis was often in doubt. When Williams published *The History of the People of Trinidad and Tobago* (1962), just prior to Independence Day, in August 1962, Stanley J. G. Fingland of the British High Commissioner's Office in Trinidad and Tobago quickly dispatched two copies to Edwin Sykes, explaining that "we have naturally not had time to read the book yet, but at a quick glance, it seems to contain some fairly acid stuff on colonialism as we had feared."[24] Sykes read the book as soon as he received it. Relieved, he wrote to Fingland on September 11, saying that the "the book does not strike me as too bad. It is—as the old lady said about Shakespeare's plays—full of quotations, and many of the criticisms levelled against British policy were really made by other people before Dr. Williams." Sykes reported that he included references to the book in the "Country Brief" that he had prepared for the secretary of state and the visiting prime ministers from the Commonwealth nations. He thought that Williams "might be flattered if he found that ministers knew of his latest publication."[25]

Colonial officials frequently offered negative assessments of Williams's ideas and personal style. On April 16, 1958, from Port of Spain, R. L. Baxter wrote that he had had his first exposure to the chief minister's oratory at Woodford Square. He had found the speech "a queer mixture of scholarly exposition and demagogic invective, ending with a parody of the New Testament that smells unpleasantly of Africa." The reference to Africa had unmistakable racial overtones.[26] About three years later, Hugh Gaitskell, a senior British Labour Party official, described Williams as a "difficult" person to get on with, one who required "most careful handling." He thought that Williams manifested an "unusual combination of the political demagogue" with a "highly intelligent, almost academic mind."[27]

The most sustained attempt to understand Eric Williams and his psychology was undertaken by Sir Norman Costar, the first British high commissioner in Port of Spain. Costar was not an admirer of the new prime minister and was never on consistently good terms with him. Williams had made a point of receiving Costar's credentials shortly after Trinidad and Tobago became independent, thereby making him the dean of the Diplomatic Corps. Officials in London relied heavily on Costar's advice. The high commissioner seemed to have relished his job, writing lengthy descriptions of the political developments in Trinidad and Tobago, laced with unflattering comments about Prime Minister Williams. On May 8, 1963, barely nine months after his arrival in Port of Spain, Costar wrote a detailed assessment of Williams's character, one that helped to shape Whitehall's attitude toward the Caribbean leader.

Costar began his lengthy report by stating that Williams had "two faces": one external and the other internal. To outsiders, he "often appears as the far-sighted and patient, if somewhat schoolmasterly, statesman with solutions for most of the problems of the Caribbean . . . and has words of wisdom for all the smaller and less developed countries." At home, however, he was "the bad tempered bottleneck through which all the administration of Trinidad and Tobago has to pass. He is also for good measure incalculable and inaccessible, and unwilling even to listen to arguments with which he is not disposed in advance to agree. The result is that problems needing attention are frequently left unattended because Dr. Williams has not pronounced."

Costar was not impressed by Williams's administrative style, charging that he tended to deal with only one issue at a time. "With Dr. Williams," the high commissioner wrote, "the best is the enemy of the good, and one more or less proposal after another gets laid on one side while yet another which might be slightly better is investigated." The consequence of all of this was that there "are long delays," and the solution that eventually emerged "is generally too complicated to be administered by his civil servants."

"Tolerance is not Dr. Williams' strong suit, despite the lip service he pays to the word," Costar reported. He was equally contemptuous of Williams's speeches at Woodford Square, asserting that the prime minister's "public outbursts in Woodford Square arouse interest as theatrical performances. There is no live theatre in Port of Spain and Dr. Williams' speeches are rated high as entertainment by those for whose benefit they are uttered." This was an extraordinary observation given the role that Williams's speeches had played in the construction of Trinidad's nationalism. Costar said that members of the middle class and government officials attended these presentations "to find out what is to be their fate, if in business, or their policy, if in Government." Costar added, uncharitably:

> However statesmanlike his utterances at Prime Minister's meetings, [or] in the University of Woodford Square; Dr. Williams is essentially the grassroots demagogue. His speeches have been marked by memorable phrases, such as "Massa's day done" marking the triumph of colored over white, and "I'm the boss now," emphasising the same point with a more personal flavour. Nevertheless few people leave Woodford Square, his "Hyde Park Corner," fired to be beastly to the British even though Dr. Williams' constant theme is that all Trinidad's misfortunes stem from her colonial past.

Costar painted a picture of "a man who likes to be top," an ambition that undermined Williams's effectiveness, especially in his dealings with other

Caribbean leaders. He aspired to be "the leading figure in the Eastern Caribbean, indeed its Saviour." But Williams was not the man to forge a unity among these islands, since "in the past his periods of frantic courtship of this country or that person have ended in an unpleasant quarrel and a house of cards of his own creation has collapsed into nothing." Costar reported that "at the moment" Williams was "on good terms with hardly anyone who he cannot boss; yet he is aiming high and should not be underestimated."

Despite being "his own worst enemy," Costar found Williams to be "industrious, intelligent, has financial integrity (not universal in the West Indian politician), he espouses the democratic ideas and institutions of the West, and he can, on occasion, show great personal charm, which he uses to good persuasive effect." But such qualities were negated by his "vanity and conceit and contempt for most of his fellow men. In addition, for all of his ability, he lacks the skill to administer wisely and put first things first. There is also, I am afraid, a streak of would-be dictator in the man. Like Cromwell, he believes that people should have the freedom to make their own choice provided always that they choose wisely. If they do not agree with him, it is he suspects because of antagonism to him personally, and an element of personal animosity having crept in, Dr. Williams loses all sense of balance in argument."

Costar urged British officials to "stand firm" in whatever stance they embraced for Trinidad "and avoid public polemics" on matters of policy "with such a past master in the art as Dr. Williams." He recognized that nothing the British did or said could dissuade the prime minister from his activities, and however "sound" his "concept," "he will sooner or later almost certainly antagonize the other political figures whose cooperation he needs to achieve it."[28]

Norman Costar's critical view of Eric Williams was reinforced by the comments of others. On March 7, 1963, Costar reported that Sir Solomon Hochoy, the native-born governor general of Trinidad, had said that the British "were not dealing with a rational man"; the "madman," Hochoy allegedly continued, had been elected by the people and was likely to remain in power for some time. Williams had "removed elsewhere" anyone who exercised some influence over him. As matters stood, Hochoy knew no one in the Cabinet or outside of it who enjoyed the prime minister's confidence.[29]

Newspaper columnist Peter Farquhar, a member of the opposition party, was most vitriolic in his assessment of Williams's personality and leadership style. He accused Williams of lacking coherent government policies and of keeping members of the Cabinet in the dark. Ministers attended Cabinet meetings "not to take decisions but to be informed of decisions already taken, but they are only informed of matters of little consequence; of important matters, they are as ignorant as the average citizen." Members of the Cabinet were "merely spectators, subdued and silent spectators who cannot even applaud." Farquhar, however, said he did not believe that Williams was a dictator since "a dictator is a man who knows where he wants to go and is prepared to cut down anyone who stands in his path. Our Prime Minister is quite prepared to cut down anyone but he does not know where he wants to go and is, in fact, going nowhere. . . . [He] is the captain of a rudderless ship in the midst of a typhoon."[30]

A week later Farquhar described Williams as an "expert dribbler," the soccer player who plays to the spectators and is not interested in scoring a goal. "Expert dribblers," Farquhar observed, are "apt to fall so deeply in love with themselves and their own expertise that they ignore the objective of scoring goals and amuse themselves and their fans by monopolising the ball. Williams was such a footballer, and he is such a politician . . . in football Williams played to the gallery and in politics he does the same . . . in politics he does not care whether his country rises or falls so long as he occupies the centre of the stage."[31]

In many respects, the characterization of Eric Williams by Norman Costar and others represented a caricature of his complex personality. Throughout his long tenure in office, the educated elite in Trinidad and Tobago became amateur psychologists in their attempt to understand the personality of their head of government. The somewhat diminutive leader who hid behind dark glasses and wore a hearing aid fascinated the citizenry, captivating them with his brilliance and his remarkable command of the issues of the moment, but simultaneously infuriating some with his intellectual arrogance. In November 1964 Costar observed that Williams "is not popular with the wealthier classes whom he does not even try to conciliate, but he is respected by them for his intelligence, drive and honesty, and is feared by them for his unpredictable moods."[32]

It is difficult to provide a reasonably plausible assessment of the persona of any historical personage, and psychological determinism as a mode of historical analysis has enormous pitfalls. In the introduction to this work, I indicated that I would attempt to do this only after the reader had been exposed to a good deal of information about Eric Williams the man, the scholar, and the politician. His unusually long tenure in public life complicates the problem, since the person he was in 1956 was obviously not the one he would become in 1970 or the one he was in 1981, when he died. His experiences in political office and his life in a rapidly changing world affected him in significant ways. Thus, care must be taken not to present a static picture of the man in order to capture his complex development over time. There were, of course, certain ideological positions and personal characteristics that appear not to have changed at all.

Possessed of a caustic tongue, Williams was somewhat austere in demeanor, although he could be a doting father, a genial host, and a relaxed conversationalist in social settings. Idle chatter easily bored him, and ill-informed or critical speeches by the parliamentary opposition drove him to distraction. On such occasions he would deliver the ultimate insult to his colleagues by unplugging his hearing aid. As Williams noted in Inward Hunger, "a hearing aid is a powerful weapon against an Opposition in Parliament, one can always turn it off!"[33]

◆ ◆ ◆ ◆ ◆ Eric Williams was, ostensibly, not given to humility. In his published memoirs, he observed that "Greatness, Trinidadian style, was thrust upon me from the cradle."[34] In fact, young Eric, the oldest of twelve children, was told by his parents that great things were expected of him. As Williams recalled in his unpublished memoirs, "I was regarded, and not only in the family circle, as a boy with a bright future, from whom, publicly and privately, many people expected much." In retrospect, Williams took exception to such an obligation: "This burden of responsibility far beyond the weight of such young shoulders has been borne by many before and after me; it is being borne by many today, and will continue to be borne until that revolution takes place in West Indian public opinion and social attitudes, of which there is of yet no sign, and the extensive production of good citizens is given precedence over the intensive cultivation of distinguished individuals."[35]

His parents gave the boy an inordinate amount of responsibility, becoming, as he put it, their "principal assistant." He was "a valuable aide" to his father in his second job as auditor of the "books of Friendly Societies." As a result of his work on these books, Williams acquired "an abiding love of figures which leads me even today to make all sorts of intricate computations—multiplications, divisions, square roots, cube roots, in my head, whilst driving, sitting on a veranda or walking on the beach."

Eric was equally helpful to his mother. As the number of his siblings increased, at least every two years, the amount of work became "too much for my mother." Consequently, he was "drafted into the service on the domestic front to the point where for several years I was so integral and necessary a part of [it] . . . that I ranked next in importance to my mother." He helped to prepare Sunday dinners and became "an excellent cook in the process." Eric also played his part "valiantly" in "that most arduous of West Indian chores in those days, getting down on one's knees and scrubbing the floor, and [I also] became an expert dishwasher."

After school Williams washed the babies' diapers, then he was allowed to go out to play games. He also did the marketing and went to town on Saturday mornings at his mother's request "to buy stockings or lace for the petticoats or ribbon for the girls' hair or to trim their hats." Encumbered with all of these domestic tasks, Williams concluded that he was "almost a daughter to my mother." But such responsibilities inevitably took their toll, at least on one occasion. He related, obviously with a humorous intent, an incident involving the celebration of a new baby's arrival: "I was nine years old at the time. With my mother immobilized, and my father at work, I was obviously the man of the home. As the neighbours, relatives, and friends trooped in, one by one, I poured the rum and mixed the drinks, and, as a young gallant, kept them company. I doubt that any boy nine years old can equal my record that day. I woke up some hours later, to find myself ignominiously under the table, with someone pouring soda water over my face."

Williams did not regret these heavy childhood burdens. On the contrary, he acquired "a keen appreciation of domesticity, a strong sense of masculine responsibility for the home, an ability to take care of myself in my bachelor days, and a practical training which, coupled with my innate good taste, has reflected itself in competence in delicate lingerie and feminine accessories for my wife or daughter which has never failed to amuse my friends or to astonish the store clerks."

Young Eric enjoyed some benefits for discharging his numerous domestic chores. Since they were heavier than those of his siblings and because he was regarded "as the intellectual hope of the family," his diet was "somewhat better" than that of the other children. "Many an afternoon," Williams remembered, "instead of the bread and butter and tea which comprised the children's supper, I found a whole red fish with a large pot of soup, or tasty curried shrimps awaiting me, on the theory, firmly held by my mother, that fish was good for the brain." If the meal proved too much for him to consume, and in the absence of refrigeration, "the other children were able to participate in the feast" after he had finished. He was undoubtedly the favored and therefore privileged child.

Based on his account, Eric was an exemplary and dutiful youngster. But his father was a strict disciplinarian and was never reluctant to beat him severely. When his shoes became worn prematurely because he played football with them, his father "paid out of his pockets, and I out of my buttocks." Williams surmised that this pattern was "really false economy in both senses," since "my buttocks became inured to the payment; the cost of repairs eventually added up to more than the price of football boots."

Corporal punishment of the most severe kind was not unusual in the Trinidad and Tobago of Williams's youth. He observed that "the emblem of the paternal power" in Trinidad was the strap, "its exaltation was a matter of principle and its application was made into a fine art." He maintained that such violence "betokened the slave parentage of the society." While conducting research in the Public Record Office in London, he encountered a document with "a description of a slave punishment which I was able to appreciate fully, having undergone the same experience [because] on one occasion when I had 'kicked off my [shoe] soles'—made to lie on the floor, in the foetal position with a long black ruler between my knees, my bare buttocks exposed to the leather belt." Eric was not the only recipient of parental violence. One of his siblings, afflicted with bed-wetting, was "in Trinidad fashion, 'disciplined' by my father by burying the child's head in the mattress, not as a substitute for but as an addition to corporal punishment."

Williams emulated his father in the exercise of violence on his playmates. When his family lived in Diego Martin, then a working-class neighborhood in Port of Spain, his playmates were some German girls of his own age. The regular pastime "was playing school under their house." Not surprisingly, Eric was "always the teacher." When his playmates misbehaved, he "stressed corporal punishment" as the corrective. Eric was "barely six" at the time but was quite precocious. He remembered that "the freedom of women in those days was for the most part unhampered at least at home, by underclothing, and, whether it was innate delicacy or a daunting respect for women, I preferred the personal touch to the birch."

Young Williams exercised similar control over his siblings. With his father preoccupied with his work and the struggle to "keep our heads above water" and his mother suffering from "the strain of looking after an increasingly complicated household, the discipline of the younger children fell increasingly on my shoulders." Eric found the challenge "exasperating." The younger boys sometimes drove him to distraction. "Many a time," Williams recalled, "I was rash enough to follow them under the house to catch one culprit who had insisted on disobedience; their loud guffaws when I invariably bumped my head as they ran this way and that were not calculated to improve my temper."

Williams found the task of keeping his four younger brothers at their lessons "and inculcating in them some intellectual discipline was a whole-time one utterly beyond the capacities of a boy himself buried in studies who had his own friends and obligations." He worried that the "early habits of discipline" that "form the foundation of the character in later years became more and more tenuous in these younger children."

As he grew into adolescence, Williams continued and perhaps even expanded his role as disciplinarian in chief. The following account from his unpublished memoirs reveals the power he exercised over his siblings:

> One day, as I was walking through the savannah, I noticed the oldest of the four playing football. One of his friends shouted to him that I was passing, and I noticed how slyly he looked at me. He told my mother glibly in the evening that he had been to his private lessons. When I asked him if he had not been playing football at the time when he should have been attending the extra classes for which my father had to pay, he called me a liar. I gave him the best hiding he ever got in his life, but even whilst administering it, I could not but wonder as to whether it would be any use. I could understand truancy and lying to protect oneself—I had done both at his age—but to call the one who knew you were lying a liar himself, that was what is called Trinidad brazenness.[36]

Williams was shaped by these early experiences as well as by the ethos of colonial society and the "solidly English" content of his education. None of this was unique. Many of his peers could undoubtedly have recounted similar experiences, and girls in particular were not strangers to enormous domestic burdens. Nevertheless, Williams's obligations as a boy must have developed in him a heightened sense of discipline and responsibility, thereby helping to prepare the youngster for the public duties he would later exercise. This is entirely speculative, to be sure, since girls with similar childhood experiences were not likely to achieve the successes that Williams did on the larger public stage and occupy positions of leadership. Their gender was a definite liability in a male-dominated society, their exercise of early leadership roles in their families notwithstanding.

These observations aside, Eric Williams was unquestionably the most privileged of the twelve children in his family, and he knew it. He occupied first of place; he was the focus of his parents' devotion and the repository of their dreams for familial success. A mature Williams, not surprisingly, had to be the principal actor on the political stage, and had to be in command of any situation in which he found himself. He had not been raised to play a secondary role in any capacity, a fact that made it difficult if not impossible for him to take orders from anyone, especially those whom he considered his intellectual inferior. He expected his associates in government to accept his leadership uncritically, just as his siblings had done, usually associating criticism or dissent with disloyalty. Although he could not administer the whip to them as he had to his siblings, he could banish them to the doghouse or to the political wilderness. This was hardly an admirable quality, and it was certainly not a political asset. It deprived Williams of frank advice from colleagues, who feared his wrath and confinement to the icebox.

Williams treated the representatives of foreign governments accredited to Port of Spain in a similar manner. If he had differences of opinion with an official or his government, he would decline to conduct business as usual until his anger had abated. Norman Costar was himself the victim of such treatment. In November 1962, for example, Costar reported that if Britain stood firm on the terms of the golden handshake, "the result . . . will be that Britain, and I in particular, will be put in the dog house for the next six months or so."[37]

The roots of this behavior are not difficult to fathom. Some have said that Williams possessed an authoritarian personality, but this may well be a misreading of the inner makeup of this complex man. The clue to this aspect of his character is to be found, once again, in his early childhood experiences. The untrammeled power that he exercised over his siblings meant, inevitably, that he had to be distanced from them emotionally lest he compromise his position as surrogate parent, senior sibling, and role model. Although these awesome obligations helped to make him an unusually responsible young man, they robbed him of a carefree childhood, the intimacies, the give-and-take that normally characterize relationships among siblings, and the social and familial bonding that are at the heart of the human developmental process. Nowhere in his memoirs does Williams speak of childhood activities that he enjoyed with his siblings, of their play together, or of the secrets they shared. He refers to them in a detached way as "the children" or "the boys." Deprived of strong emotional bonds with his siblings and of the attendant socializing lubricants, Williams grew into manhood conditioned to always being the exemplar, the *primus inter pares*, or all too frequently the *jefe máximo* whose superior talents and position had to be acknowledged.

Similarly, Williams's early experiences may account for his emotional distance from most members of his political family and his inability to deal with dissent with equanimity. To them, he always had to be the confident, self-assured leader. But this public persona masked his inner tensions, storms, vulnerabilities, and insecurities. None of this was readily apparent, given the pugnacity of his language; his unparalleled ability to outsmart, confuse, and belittle his opponents; his widely acknowledged grasp of the issues; and the awe and adulation he inspired in numerous supporters. His many accomplishments, notwithstanding, he was never satisfied with them, at least not for very long.

♦ ♦ ♦ ♦ ♦ Eric Williams undoubtedly derived much psychic strength from the respect and adulation lavished upon him by his supporters and enjoyed his spectacular victories over his opponents. But this was a fleeting gratification; he needed the constant nourishment of success for his emotional sustenance, but success when achieved only provided the impetus for the next battle, the next struggle, the next mountain to be ascended. This restlessness, this desire to be in continuous motion was, in part, a function of his personality. As Williams acknowledged in his unpublished memoirs, he was "a man of action who lacked the patience to be a spectator at athletic and cycle sports or cricket."[38] This self-assessment could be extended to include his behavior as a politician. At another level, Williams's predilection for hard work was not only a result of the discipline he acquired during childhood, but it was also driven by a profound need to constantly prove himself and to keep faith with his father's high expectations. In the end, Trinidad had a political leader who was thoroughly committed to its best interests as he saw them, but one whose idiosyncrasies sometimes made the chances of success more difficult. Norman Costar was close to the mark when he observed that Williams "is interested first in Trinidad, and secondly in the Caribbean. His interest in the world beyond the Caribbean, whether it be in Africa or in the relationship among the Great Powers and between the rich north and the poor south, is all looked at from the point of Trinidad and the Caribbean."[39]

Williams could be a cold, hard, and brusque taskmaster, quick to scold and to withdraw his trust. Costar described him as a prime minister "who works in secret, through a band of select but obscure advisors, who change from time to time, but who also are rarely, if ever, his official advisors on any given subject."[40] The fact that Williams could often make and unmake careers at will was due less to his authoritarian personality and more to the weakness of his political associates who cowered before him, dwarfed by his intellect and intimidated by the firm exercise of the power at his command. Those who summoned the courage to challenge his authority either licked the wounds they received in return and departed or were unceremoniously cold-shouldered and abandoned.

This seemingly harsh treatment of some of his subordinates invited charges that Williams was ruthless. Patrick Solomon, the deputy prime minister who fell out of favor with his leader in 1966, later depicted him as "being more ruthless, perhaps than de Gaulle, whom he admired, or Churchill, whom he affected to despise." But Williams was a skilled practitioner of a real politik borrowed from its European masters, Metternich and Bismarck, and adapted to the political environment of Trinidad and Tobago. Just as these Europeans had displayed an unapologetic toughness and moral pragmatism as essential ingredients of their statecraft, Williams had no compunction about using similar approaches in his relationships with colleagues and others. Solomon observed that to Williams "all human beings are the same; they either want to buy or have something to sell; and he has a single formula for dealing with them all—if the price is right, he will do business." But, as Solomon also concluded, "in many respects" Williams was "no better and no worse than other great men of this or any other age."[41]

Ambitious and brilliant, Eric Williams was the professor who saw Trinidad and Tobago as his lecture hall writ large. Norman Costar thought that "Dr. Williams' attitude to Trinidad is that of a school master to his class. He administers nods of approval or frowns of rebuke according to the behaviour of his pupils. If their behaviour looks like [it is] getting beyond what he thinks is right then he is not averse to using the rod."[42] But Williams never condescended to his fellow citizens and tried valiantly to educate them about their history and contemporary domestic and international issues, all the while attempting to forge a national consciousness. When an interviewer from the British Broadcasting Corporation (BBC) told him that other West Indian leaders often accused him of "intellectual arrogance, of considering yourself to have a better analytical mind than the people that you deal with" and asked him whether he felt he was "in intellectual contact with the ordinary people in Trinidad" or whether he thought of himself "as a rather remote and fatherly leader," Williams responded:

> No, I don't see anything remote about it at all because, after all, we organise on the basis of a political party in the British sense, the party decided that the principal plank in its platform would be the education of the people in the country. I speak to them about economic matters or constitutional matters or the position of oil on which they depend in world economy and the thing is they understand. I once told your Prime Minister, who was out in Trinidad not so long ago, that if he were going to speak in our University [of Woodford Square], I would ask him to speak precisely as he spoke in the House of Commons and not talk down to them and he said he was quite astonished by that, it must mean that Trinidad is the Athens of the Caribbean, quite right.[43]

Although Williams spoke the language of the intellectual, he said that he drew his strength from ordinary citizens. When the BBC interviewer questioned why he based his faith on the "common people," he answered: "What else could you put it in, you'd have to put it in something, you couldn't put it in the autocratic government, you couldn't put it in the Crown Colony regime, you couldn't put it in any small group of people, intellectuals, you had no intellectuals . . . you had no university . . . the only people you could put faith in was the people of the country, they didn't know much, you had to take them along with you."[44]

As the architect of the new nation, Williams challenged his compatriots to reach their possibilities, frequently denouncing the civil servants for their shortcomings. He expected the best from his Cabinet ministers but seldom gave them the autonomy they needed to discharge their duties. Williams never knew how or perhaps never wanted to delegate much authority to his subordinates. The result was that he became mired in detail, sometimes to the detriment of administrative efficiency. Although critics accused him of harboring dictatorial ambitions, Williams was committed, with reservations, to the principles of parliamentary democracy, despite his cavalier treatment of the legislative assembly. In November 1964 Norman Costar, a Williams critic and at times an astute observer, reported:

> In conversation with me Dr. Williams . . . has expressed sympathy with these African Prime Ministers who, after independence, tear up the Constitutions with which they have been saddled so that they can get on with the real job of governing the country without factious Opposition. Dr. Williams has said to me that the British institutions do not really suit Trinidad. He has private leanings towards a presidential system and a one party State, and he told me recently that it was his deliberate policy not to waste his time by attending meetings of the House of Representatives to answer futile questions or attend stupid debates. He would only go for really important occasions. But . . . I do not believe that, at any rate for the present, Dr. Williams would go so far as to scrap the Constitution, if only because the Opposition by lying low have not provided him with adequate excuse. Despite some signs, and there are some, that Trinidad might move towards a *near dictatorship* run by Dr. Williams personally, I do not think that this will come about as long as the Opposition remains as dormant as it is and Dr. Williams can continue to control his Cabinet and to ignore Parliament as he does at present.

Volunteering his overall assessment of the political climate under Williams, Costar noted that Trinidad "is still a realm within the Commonwealth; it still operates the Westminster-type Constitution agreed upon by the political parties before independence; Parliament still meets, debates, and legislates; political parties still function unfettered and no political leader has been put in gaol; there is still a free press." Six years later, High Commissioner Richard Hunt voiced an essentially similar assessment of Williams's political modus operandi. He thought that Williams's "attitude towards opposition is ambivalent. On the one hand he is clearly tempted to regard all or any opposition as subversive. On the other, he is normally punctilious towards the official opposition—though in fact he does not let them into his confidence." Williams, Hunt said, "dislikes force" but "is capable of firm administrative and indeed legislative action when he thinks that security requires it." In general, the high commissioner maintained, Williams's "first ploy" in "dealing with opposition from any quarter" is "to ignore it, and the second [is] to get the issue shelved or sidetracked. Failing these, he is apt to buy people off: if a man is a nuisance, give him a job, or a trip abroad, or even an embassy."[45]

Although he continued to smart from the racial discrimination he experienced at Oxford, harbored doubts about the efficacy of British institutions in Trinidad, and criticized its colonial policy, Williams never lost his admiration for the United Kingdom. Familiar with this lingering affection for the former mother country, Lord Bukhurst, a prominent member of the West India Committee in London, recommended that Williams be awarded an honorary doctorate by Oxford University. He felt that such an award "would be likely to do far more than anything else to cement relations between the United Kingdom and Trinidad." Although Williams would undoubtedly have accepted such a degree had it been offered at the time, J. O'Neil Lewis, a senior member of the Trinidad civil service and a man who worked closely with the prime minister, said that Williams really wanted to be a Fellow of All Souls, Oxford. Lewis believed that nothing would give him greater pleasure than such an honor. Lewis noted that Williams cherished his ties with the United Kingdom and had a deep affection for British culture. He believed that his negative public comments were not an indication of his feelings toward Britain.[46] These observations were doubtlessly reassuring to British officials, but they hardly captured Williams's ambivalence to, and even resentment of, the metropolitan country. He was at once an Anglophile, an ardent nationalist, and an overly sensitive man who wore his emotions on his sleeve.

Eric Williams was easily the most academically distinguished and controversial politician of his day in the Anglophone Caribbean. But except for his devoted supporters in Trinidad and Tobago—and there were many—Williams inspired a profound respect elsewhere in the Caribbean but not a deep affection. He manifested, at times, the charismatic appeal of Alexander Bustamante of Jamaica and Cheddi Jagan of British Guiana, but he disdained the empty flamboyance of Eric Gairy, the Grenadian chief minister. Williams lacked the quiet and more controlled persona of the equally brilliant Norman Manley of Jamaica, and he had little in common with the seemingly passive, indecisive, and politically accommodating Grantley Adams of Barbados.

The dispute over the nature of the golden handshake gave Williams an opportunity to display his political skills, but his weaknesses were visible as well. In the difficult days following his rejection of the aide-mémoire, British officials vigorously debated his personality traits and plotted their course of action based on their conclusions. Norman Costar counseled the officials to remain firm, since any concessions would serve "to encourage Dr. Williams to think that by being intransigent and unpleasant he can extract further concessions from Britain." According to Costar, that was Williams's "regular technique, and one which he practices on the Americans also." Costar urged the officials to remind the prime minister that Trinidad was the beneficiary of other forms of aid, such as the preferential price that Britain paid for the sugar it produced under the terms of the Commonwealth Sugar Agreement. Aid also came from the Colonial Development and Welfare Fund. Costar also believed that the growing investment by British citizens in Trinidad and Tobago constituted a form of economic assistance. The high commissioner, however, was under no illusion that Williams would find such arguments persuasive.[47]

Anticipating the failure of such a "difficult" exercise, Costar urged his government to seize the offensive by publicizing the extent of its aid to Trinidad and Tobago.[48] Colonial officials were also anxious to demonstrate that the terms of the golden handshake offered to Trinidad and Tobago compared favorably with those offered to other recently independent countries. To support this contention, they prepared a table, replicated here as Table 1, outlining the assistance Britain gave them.

The figures demonstrated that Trinidad and Tobago was the wealthiest of the Commonwealth countries listed as measured by its per capita income of £229. They also revealed that Trinidad and Tobago ranked third after Cyprus and Sierra Leone in terms of British per capita support, expressed in shillings. Moreover, British officials maintained, when compared with other Western countries, the United Kingdom provided generous support to "underdeveloped" nations. Based on their statistics, in 1961 Britain contributed 1.32 percent of its gross national product to these countries, whereas France gave 2.41 percent, Germany 1.17 percent, and the United States 0.97 percent. Over the years 1956–60 the United Kingdom contributed US$4,006,000 to developing countries, compared with US$2,917,000 by Germany, US$6,113,000 by France, and US$17,843,000 by the United States.[49]

Williams, of course, was not interested in such comparisons. His primary concern was to maximize the amount of aid to his nation, hence his relent-

TABLE 1 ◆ British Financial Assistance to Various Commonwealth Countries

Country	Amount of Grant or Development Loan	Population in Thousands	Expressed as Shillings Per Head of Population	National Per Capita Income
Nigeria	£12m	35,000	6/10d.	£30
Cyprus*	£15m (Grant)	578	—	£139
Sierra Leone	£3.5m plus £3m (Grant)	2,400	29/2. plus 25/	£25
Tanganyika	£4m plus £4m (Grant)	8,788	9.1d. plus 9/	£21
Jamaica	£1.25m	1,613	15/7d.	£157
Uganda	£1.5 (Grant)	6,682	4/6d.	£24
Trinidad	£1m	819	25/	£229

Source: DO 200/86.
*The high figure for Cyprus took account of the fact [that] this territory had suffered from
something approaching civil war for several years.

less assaults on the British government. His anger did not abate in the
months after his rejection of the golden handshake. In an effort to reopen
discussions with Williams, John Profumo, secretary of state for the colonies,
decided to visit Trinidad and Tobago over the 1962 Christmas break. Demonstrating his ire at the British, Williams refused to meet with High Commissioner Costar to discuss the visit. The permanent secretary in the Ministry of
External Affairs, K. F. Sealey, told Costar that Williams would be spending
the holidays outside of Trinidad and Tobago. Incredulous, Costar asked
Sealey whether the government realized that such a gesture "could only have
unhappy repercussions in all spheres of British/Trinidad relations." In reporting this conversation to Whitehall, Costar opined: "It would be wrong to
attribute Dr. Williams' attitude merely to sulks. It is due to [a] combination
of wounded *amour-propre* and belief based on past successes that it is the best
tactic for securing what he wants on aid. His bad manners in present circumstances are quite in character." In fact, "Dr. Williams' very difficult
temperament is notorious and is something we shall have to be prepared to
deal with. When he is in these moods our best policy is to do nothing for
him and ask nothing of him." In light of the experiences of Governor General Hochoy and the Americans, there would be a thaw in several months,

with Williams making it known "indirectly when his mood has changed and he is looking for an excuse to bury the hatchet."[50]

Williams never met with Profumo when he visited Trinidad and Tobago. This deliberate insult exacerbated the tensions between the two nations, a blunder for which Williams would later make a veiled apology. Profumo, however, held a meeting in Barbados on January 1, 1963, to discuss relations between Britain and Trinidad Tobago. Present were Sir John Stow, the governor of Barbados; A. R. Thomas, the assistant under secretary of state; and Costar. According to the minutes of the meeting, Profumo outlined his government's policy on Trinidad and Tobago as follows:

1. To take no present initiative ourselves to reopen the financial settlement;
2. Meanwhile to withhold all the items covered by our offer whilst leaving the offer open;
3. For the rest, to behave as if there was no disturbance in Anglo/Trinidad relations.

Those in attendance, the minutes said, "agreed that Dr. Williams, though at times personally charming, was a most difficult man to deal with, and the Secretary of State expressed his sympathy with those who carried this task."[51]

In public, the British officials and Williams clung tenaciously to their respective positions during the winter months of 1963. In private, the British considered various approaches to resolve the conflict, all the while speculating about Williams's intentions and state of mind. On March 2 Costar reported that he had heard that Williams was "raving" about the "conspiracy" to refuse aid to Trinidad and Tobago. Williams "attributes the lack of success of his negotiating methods to personal animus against him." Costar thought that the government was short of cash but that it was likely to be rescued by the Americans and by British companies operating in the country. "The pinch," Costar surmised, was on Williams's "pride and not on his finances." He feared that the prime minister would indulge in an "outburst" against the United Kingdom in a future speech and put a "squeeze" on British interests. Williams was likely to do both, since he "is not by normal standards a rational man."[52]

It seemed that the favorite sport of some British officials, led by Costar and his poisonous pen, was to denigrate Eric Williams at every turn. Williams was the brash, independent ex-colonial who could not be influenced, much less controlled, by the former colonial bosses. They found this galling and were not prepared to show any weakness or willingness to compromise lest that be construed as "a policy of appeasement," in the words of Denis Williams of the Colonial Office. This official mused that Eric Williams would gloat if the United Kingdom compromised on the terms of the financial settlement. As he expressed it, "I wonder indeed whether, while we are congratulating ourselves on the success of our tactics in dealing with Dr. Williams, he may not equally well be congratulating himself on something like the following lines: 'My tactics are working nicely. I rejected the British offer, defaulted on my debts and abused them publicly. I have now ceased abusing them, and—if I hang on for a few weeks more—they will be so anxious to "restore good relations" that they will substantially increase their September offer and excuse me both my original debts and also my subsequent ones.' "[53] Observations such as these demonstrated the myopia of the British officials and the substitution of wild fantasies for rational thinking. Eric Williams and his personality had become the primary issue, the validity of his claims on behalf of his country notwithstanding. The conflict had become a contest of wills, and in any such confrontation the metropole had an advantage.

In the late winter of 1963 there were signs that Williams was becoming amenable to a resolution of the conflict. He needed money to finance his new five-year development program, and some members of his Cabinet and party were quietly beginning to question his handling of the dispute. The first sign of a thaw appeared in March 1963, when Williams met with Sir Stephen Luke, the British official charged with winding up matters relating to the defunct West Indies Federation. Luke had visited Port of Spain to discuss with local officials Trinidad and Tobago's defense and housing debts to the Federal government. After initially refusing to see him, Williams met with Luke on March 7.

During the course of the meeting, as reported by Luke, Williams denounced Britain's "gratuitous and insulting" insistence on linking the repayment of the loans to their "ungenerous" proposed financial settlement. In response to Luke's inquiry about how the impasse could be resolved, Williams indicated that he could not take the initiative to reopen discussions because of the domestic political implications. He wondered, however, whether the British would do so. From this exchange, Luke concluded that

Williams was expecting him to convey his sentiments to the British government, thereby paving the way for new negotiations.[54]

Norman Costar was quite pleased when he learned of Williams's tentative overture to the British government. He thought that the prime minister "is beginning to realize that his own policy of public blackmail has not this time so far paid and he may have become more anxious to settle with us now that he is in dispute also with the Americans." He viewed this development as a measure of the success of British policy, cautioning colonial officials not to make "any early move" to settle the disagreement. Costar could not resist returning to his earlier negative assessments of Williams's character and to urge the officials to be wary of him:

> One hears more and more talk here of Dr. Williams being paranoiac. The particular form which, according to past patterns, his paranoia takes is to regard any thwarting of his will as due to a desire to persecute him personally. After he has carried on his vendetta for what he regards as the appropriate period, his custom is to seek a settlement. His normal practice is then to try to re-open negotiations by hinting his readiness to do so indirectly through an intermediary. But though this is his normal pattern, you need to consider very carefully before you fall in with the idea that the approach now made through [Sir Stephen] Luke . . . constitutes a sufficient indication of a change of heart to provide a basis for a successful negotiation.[55]

Several members of Williams's Cabinet were also beginning to grumble about the stalemate with Britain. Three of them confided their concerns to High Commissioner Costar in March, a development that the high commissioner thought was "in marked contrast to the silence previously observed on the subject." John O'Halloran, the minister of agriculture, industry, and commerce, actually raised the matter with Costar on two occasions, once in March and then in April. O'Halloran, Costar reported, was "unsparing" in his criticism of Williams's handling of the problem. Although Costar believed that O'Halloran's "intellectual capacity" was not "high," he found him "sensible and right thinking."

Obviously unaware of Williams's meeting with Luke on March 7, O'Halloran proposed that a "neutral" third party should try to persuade Williams to reopen discussions with the British. But he acknowledged that it would be difficult to find such a person. Costar noted that the chief significance of

O'Halloran's admission "was the absence of any suggestion that anybody in the Cabinet could play this role of influencing Dr. Williams."[56]

By the summer it became increasingly clear that both sides were prepared to resolve their problems. Still, the matter of Trinidad's indebtedness to the defunct West Indies Federation had to be settled before the terms of the golden handshake could be revisited. Colonial officials were adamant on this issue, and Eric Williams was not prepared to abandon his position. The first of the two debts was a loan granted to Trinidad by the Federal government in 1957 to build houses for Federal officials in Port of Spain, the capital of the new Federation of the West Indies. The second debt represented Trinidad's unpaid portion of the cost of expanding the federation's defenses.

Of the two issues, the defense debt was the more difficult. Sir Stephen Luke, the interim commissioner for the West Indies, was charged with the task of negotiating a settlement with Trinidad. The defense debt had originated in mid-December 1960 at a meeting held in Jamaica attended by representatives of the British, Federal, and Jamaican governments, including Federal prime minister Grantley Adams. The meeting decided that since the defense needs of the federation were expanding for 1961, the additional costs would be shared by Jamaica, Trinidad, the Federal government, and possibly the United Kingdom. Subsequently, Chief Minister Williams was informed by Federal officials of the Jamaica decision and told that Jamaica and Trinidad would be asked to contribute TT$683,080 each to the defense fund. The Federal government would provide TT$60,000, and the United Kingdom was expected to give TT$623,080.

In responding to this request, Williams emphasized on December 29, 1960, that his government "is not disposed to object to the financial arrangements, but the basis of this allocation is not readily apparent."[57] This reply, although it did not reject the request for the defense funds, fell far short of an enthusiastic endorsement. Williams seemed to have been deliberately ambiguous so he would later have a safety valve should he decline to provide the funds.

The problem became more complicated when the United Kingdom declined to make the contribution requested of it on the grounds that the Federal government had sufficient reserves to meet the costs. This decision was revealed by the parliamentary under secretary of state to several Caribbean leaders who were attending a meeting in Port of Spain on February 11, 1961. Williams would later issue a white paper stating, among other things, that at the February 11 meeting "the Premier of Trinidad and Tobago made it clear, in most emphatic and unambiguous language, that Trinidad and Tobago would not agree to contribute one cent more to any expansion programme to make up for Britain's failure to support Britain's creation."[58]

Colonial officials disputed this claim, noting that there was no such statement in the records of the meeting. They wanted it known that the United Kingdom declined to make any contribution solely because the Federal government had adequate funds at its disposal. In addition, it had agreed to contribute up to £1.2 million for the construction of barracks for the soldiers. Accordingly, the British government considered the use of the phrase "Britain's failure to support Britain's creation" to be "gratuitously insulting."[59]

Obviously displeased by Britain's failure to make a contribution to the defense fund, Williams declined to attend a meeting with Jamaican and Federal government representatives to establish a new contribution formula. Rather, he proposed that the matter be considered by the Caribbean leaders at the forthcoming Intergovernmental Conference. There, the defense program "should be modified with a view to its accommodation within the scope of the contributions already agreed upon."[60] This comment, especially the phrase "already agreed upon," would be used by the Colonial Office to support its contention that Williams had endorsed the defense levy.

When the Intergovernmental Conference convened in May 1962, the leaders who attended agreed that Jamaica and Trinidad should each contribute TT$683,080 to the 1961 defense coffers and the Federal government, the balance of TT$746,000. Williams, however, reserved his government's position on that decision. Two months later, at a constitutional conference held in London, he suggested that the defense levy be examined in relation to the overall issue of British aid to the Federal government, a matter that was scheduled to be discussed at another meeting in the fall.

The fall meeting never took place because Jamaica voted to secede from the West Indies Federation on September 19. As Williams put it, the defense question "was thrown into the waste paper basket." But the first real indication that Trinidad would not pay its share of the 1961 defense expansion costs came at a Common Services meeting held in July 1962. This meeting had been called to determine ways to continue those common services that the islands needed in light of the breakup of the federation. Speaking for Trinidad, Ellis Clarke noted that his government "did not bind itself at any time" prior to the Intergovernmental Conference of May 1961 to contribute to the defense costs. Consequently, Trinidad "regrets that it cannot regard itself as either legally or morally bound to contribute to those costs." "Such costs," he added, "should be borne by the defunct Federation." Shocked by this declaration, Jamaican delegate Edgerton Richardson announced that if Trinidad declined to pay its share, his government would demand the return of the money it had already contributed.[61]

The position taken by Trinidad on the defense debt was neither strong, persuasive, nor politically astute. The government was right to question how the debt of £75,750 as stated in the aide-mémoire was determined and why the issue was linked to the golden handshake. On the other hand, although Williams's contention that the defense costs should have been tied to the overall question of British aid to the federation possessed merit, it flew in the face of the commitment he had made on December 29, 1960, to accept the levy. In the end, Williams would have to make a graceful retreat.

♦ ♦ ♦ ♦ ♦ The housing debt was not as contentious and helped to exacerbate the tensions between the two governments. In 1957, as plans began to take shape for the inauguration of the Federation of the West Indies, the committee charged with responsibility for making recommendations on matters relating to the Federal capital, had recognized the need for housing for the Federal ministers and other officials. Accordingly, the subcommittee asked Trinidad to purchase a number of properties and to construct new houses on them for the occupancy of the Federal officials. These houses would be leased to the Federal government at a "reasonable" cost. The committee estimated that sixty-seven houses would be needed by April 1958.

The chief minister and his colleagues responded favorably to the request. The estimates that were prepared indicated that capital expenditures would amount to TT$2.75 million. To meet these costs, the British government agreed to advance the amount in question to the Federal government, which then loaned it to Trinidad with interest rate at 5½ percent. The money advanced by Britain, it should be stressed, came from the £1 million that it had promised to contribute to the cost of the Federal capital.

Williams agreed to repay the loan in three years. During this period, Trinidad would receive the equivalent of 2 percent per annum of the capital cost to meet maintenance expenses and the Federal government would not be assessed taxes or insurance costs. After the loan was repaid, and if the houses remained occupied by Federal officials, Trinidad would be paid rental costs at a rate equivalent to the loan charges at the time the loan was effected, in addition to 2 percent per annum. According to British estimates, Trinidad received TT$2,786,868 (about £600,000) in housing loans before the federation collapsed.[62]

Williams acknowledged responsibility for these loans even though the federation had become defunct. In fact, in the months preceding independence, he sought a short-term loan from the United Kingdom to repay the debt. The request was rejected on the grounds that British loans were not normally granted to meet debt obligations. In a letter to Prime Minister MacMillan on December 5, 1962, Williams regretted the failure to approve the £600,000 loan, noting: "The refusal to grant our request is, in effect, a demand for the immediate refund to your government of money which, it had seemed, was originally intended as a gift to the people of the West Indies, including those of Trinidad and Tobago. My Government will naturally refund the entire sum now claimed, including, of course, that portion that might ordinarily have been regarded as representing the share of Trinidad and Tobago."[63]

This was, unquestionably, an admission of responsibility. But Williams lacked the cash to make good on his promise. In succeeding months he would begin to question the amount of the debt to be repaid and the terms of the proposed settlement. In a white paper that he presented to the Trinidadian Parliament, Williams argued that there was "no written agreement between the Government of Trinidad and Tobago and the Federal Government in respect of the transaction." Moreover, "the whole arrangement was clearly based on the premise of the continued existence of the Federal Government." Since the federation no longer existed, the "arrangements and understandings" must be reviewed "in the light of events." The document also insisted that any negotiations on the debt must be restricted to the government of Trinidad and Interim Commissioner Sir Stephen Luke, the successor in title to the Federal government.

Williams's white paper noted that Trinidad was now burdened with houses that it would never have built but for the arrangement with the federation. In addition, the land could have been devoted to other uses. In contesting the amount that the British said was owed, the paper included a list of charges that should be deducted from the original loan, including expenditures for repairs to the houses, taxes, maintenance fees, the cost of furniture, rental costs, and so on. The total amounted to TT$1,789,114. The white paper acknowledged the government's liability for "some repayment" but demanded "appropriate deductions" from the sums advanced. Since the advances were made in installments, "no instalment can become due before the end of three years from the time it was made." This was a plausible argument. But Williams advanced another line of reasoning that placed the moral responsibility for the housing expenditures with the United Kingdom. It was an argument that deserved the mother country's serious attention and ultimate acceptance. According to the white paper:

> Any negotiations which may take place must be based on the acceptance of the position that the expenditure was incurred in the promotion of a venture which has failed. This being so, . . . the United Kingdom cannot reasonably expect to realize out of the assets of the Federal Government the full value of any funds it may have put into the unsuccessful venture. So . . . [it is unacceptable] to place on the shoulders of the Government of Trinidad and Tobago full responsibility for a burden which morally falls on the shoulders of Her Majesty's Government in the United Kingdom.

Britain rejected the assertion that it had a moral responsibility for the housing expenditures. It maintained, self-servingly, that it sought the repayment of the loans to raise the funds to meet the federation's liabilities, "the vast majority of which will be to West Indians." It questioned, understandably, the white paper's statement that there had never been any negotiations regarding the terms of the loan. The United Kingdom also dismissed the paper's list of expenses, "since with the possible exception of the claim in respect of maintenance charges, none of these matters appear to have been covered in the arrangements originally made between the Federal Government and the Trinidadian Government." In addition, the United Kingdom maintained that "rates and taxes" were to be waived. Strictly speaking, the government was on solid ground, but the times called for an imperial magnanimity to the new nation that was conspicuously absent.[64]

The difficulties in the way of a settlement notwithstanding, Sir Stephen Luke doggedly pursued negotiations with Prime Minister Williams. In early March 1963 he met with representatives of Trinidad and resolved some minor issues in dispute. Soon afterward, when Luke reported to the Colonial Office that he had detected a thaw in Williams's attitude toward the United Kingdom, the officials thought that Luke's conversation with Williams "was intended, in Dr. Williams' usual devious way to reopen discussion with us about the financial settlement."[65]

Colonial officials were accurate in their assessment of Williams's intentions, but their continuing mistrust of him was not helpful. In the ensuing months, Stephen Luke worked tirelessly with Trinidad officials to resolve the disputes surrounding the defense and housing debts. Simultaneously, British officials wrestled with various alternative scenarios to settle them. By the summer time had brought its rewards, and the weary governments began to see the possibility of a rapprochement. Strapped for funds, Williams held his tongue and offered no public criticism of the United Kingdom. Sensing the changing mood, Norman Costar had urged British officials in early May to "do nothing to disturb this growth of harmony by unnecessarily rocking the boat over the financial settlement."[66]

High Commissioner Costar was delighted when Williams invited him for a "friendly" talk on June 7, 1963. He reported on July 7 that "the thaw is now in steady progress," relishing the thought that Williams "has swallowed his pride." Costar was pleased with the conciliatory tone of his communications with the Trinidad officials. Nevertheless, he cautioned that "it would be ingenuous to suppose that, if we take advantage of the present thaw in order to settle our main difficulties with Dr. Williams, we shall not find ourselves in his bad books again some time in the future." Williams was "the type of person who must at all times have some whipping boy and both we and the Americans have often served the purpose in the past." But Costar urged the colonial officials to reach some accommodation with him on the outstanding debts, since it was in the United Kingdom's interest to do so.[67]

Costar had warned that if Williams felt that "his overtures were rebuffed," British officials "must be prepared for him to really turn sour." He feared that Williams would "make moves" against British interests in Trinidad and Tobago since he was "irrational enough when roused to do so despite the damage to Trinidad which might also result." Williams might "encourage" or "at any rate not discourage" strikes against British firms, or he could make it difficult for expatriates to receive immigration permits. If the prime minister "put his mind to it, there are many other things of increasing seriousness which he would have no difficulty in thinking up." Costar pointedly reminded the officials that in 1962, British exports to Trinidad and Tobago amounted to £28 million. Under the circumstances, he encouraged the officials to make a change in the "old offer" and perhaps promise some future help to Williams, which he could "represent in Trinidad as justifying his acceptance of the settlement."[68]

Relieved by the conciliatory sounds emanating from Port of Spain, Edwin Sykes of the Commonwealth Relations Office thought that "they are now behaving in a proper manner." He was gratified that "our nine months stand has thus achieved one of its objectives by teaching Trinidad that rudeness does not pay." Sykes was also pleased that the Williams administration was now proposing "confidential negotiations." That was the course of action it should have originally pursued instead of "making public speeches in Kensington and publishing tendentious White Papers in Port of Spain." Clearly, British officials wanted to punish the new nation for what they considered to be the "rudeness" of its leader and his violation of diplomatic norms. Nevertheless, Sykes welcomed the new developments and expressed a willingness to compromise, particularly on the size of the housing debt. In addition, the United Kingdom was now prepared to approach the dispute on an issue-by-issue basis rather than as a complete package.[69]

By early fall, the dispute over the debts was settled, thereby paving the way for a resumption of the golden handshake negotiations. Sir Stephen Luke and officials of the Trinidad government agreed that the defense and housing debts amounted to £581,250, a considerable reduction from the almost £700,000 that the British had originally claimed the island owed. British officials gloated over their apparent victory, since Williams was now willing to settle on terms that were somewhat less satisfactory than those that had been included in the aide-mémoire of October 31, 1962. Trinidad received all of the gifts that had been promised originally except that instead of a loan of £1 million, it would receive one for £581,250, the exact amount that it needed to settle its debts to the defunct West Indies Federation. The British government received a promissory note from Trinidad to repay the loan no later than the December 9, 1965, with annual interest at 4½ percent.[70]

British officials were obviously elated when the negotiations were concluded, essentially on their own terms. Before the final negotiations began in early December, Edwin Sykes had admitted that "our position in the negotiations will be a strong one." When the relevant documents were finally signed on December 9, Sykes reported that "the whole business concluded with goodwill all round."[71] There was probably more restraint in Port of Spain, as the Williams government could hardly claim that its position had prevailed.

The end to the year-long dispute was anticlimactic. Williams had to settle on the United Kingdom's terms, as Norman Costar had long predicted he would do. There were large issues involved, to be sure. By using the most pejorative terms to describe Williams and reducing him to a caricature, British officials avoided granting his demands any legitimacy and believed them to be driven by other than economic and political considerations. To them, Eric Williams was a cantankerous, irrational, and paranoid leader who needed to be reduced to size. On the other hand, Williams had rejected the aide-mémoire precisely because he firmly believed that the imperial power had a responsibility to correct its history of exploitation by providing substantial economic assistance to colonies when they became independent. The British government contested such arguments and sought to abandon its colonies quickly with as little economic assistance as possible. The two positions were irreconcilable, and the imperial power never viewed Trinidad as its equal. Williams did not relish the role of a supplicant, hence the bellicosity of the language that usually accompanied his requests for aid. As a historian, he understood the power dynamics that governed the relationships between the colonized peoples and their colonizers. Consequently, the golden handshake imbroglio was not only about Trinidad and Tobago. It was a battle fought in the name of all colonized peoples. Its failure, if it can be so characterized, underscored the fact that independence did not transform the power relationships between the countries involved, and the new order that Williams sought would be long in coming.

Williams's struggle with the United Kingdom also had enormous psychological dimensions. He wanted the former mother country to recognize that a profound change was occurring in the attitudes of the formerly colonized peoples. As he had expressed it in 1960: "Those discussing with us economic, political, or strategic problems will commit gross blunders if they do not realize that, apart from the material questions being discussed, the state of mind of our people must be taken into consideration. It is our right and our duty to ensure that, as we seek to establish the material foundations of our society, we define our spiritual attitude, we reject outworn attitudes, and we substitute new ones suited to our time and place."[72] The golden handshake dispute, then, was as much about economic aid to Trinidad and Tobago as it was about a new nation's painful, complex, and often contradictory struggle to claim itself.

♦ ♦

CHAPTER 5

COURTING GRENADA

♦ ♦ ♦ ♦ ♦ "One from ten leaves nought," declared the premier of Trinidad and Tobago when the Jamaican electorate voted to secede from the West Indies Federation on September 19, 1961.[1] Eric Williams's command of arithmetic, at least in this instance, was questionable, but the political implications of his comment were unmistakable. Jamaica's impending withdrawal from the ten-member federation was its deathblow, and the remaining nine islands were compelled to reassess their political future. The dissolution of the federation was a setback to the regional unity that Williams had advocated so vigorously, and no one, not even he, could predict the consequences for the Caribbean area.

Williams had worked tirelessly to help bring the West Indies Federation into existence. But the leaders of the various islands had fundamental differences over the federation's structure, taxation policies, issues relating to freedom of movement, economic development, and so on. Such differences were exacerbated from time to time by personality clashes among the leaders and by an endemic insularity that proved impossible to surmount. The three principal federalists of the region—Grantley Adams of Barbados, Norman Manley of Jamaica, and Eric Williams of Trinidad and Tobago—were not always on the best of terms, making it more difficult to resolve policy issues. There was strong antifederation sentiment in Jamaica, a problem that often tied Manley's hands and prompted him to make ambivalent statements about the viability of the infant federation.

When Jamaica decided to secede, however, it was not entirely clear what course of action Trinidad would pursue. In the immediate aftermath, the colony had two principal political options: remain a member of the now nine-member federation, becoming the largest and most powerful territory, or follow Jamaica's lead and opt for independence. A third option, but one that seemed a political long shot, was for the eight other islands, or at least some of them, to join Trinidad in a unitary statehood. In the several months following Jamaica's vote, Williams gave no indication as to which alternative he preferred. His tantalizing diffidence on the matter created much speculation in the Caribbean as well as in London. After Jamaica's vote, Federal prime minister Grantley Adams repeatedly expressed his confidence in the viability of a federation of the remaining nine islands. At a meeting in London in December 1961, he told the British prime minister that a federation of the Leeward and Windward Islands and Barbados, but excluding Trinidad, would be "lamentable." Adams urged Harold MacMillan to delay introducing an independence bill for Jamaica at least until August or September 1962. An earlier bill, he surmised, would make it politically imperative for Williams to demand independence for Trinidad.[2]

The British, to be sure, preferred to see an Eastern Caribbean Federation consisting of the remaining nine territories. Colonial officials looked wistfully at the prospect of British Guiana joining the new federation, since it would exclude Jamaica's large and predominantly black population. Cheddi Jagan and his largely Indo-Guianese People's Progressive Party would no longer fear being swamped by the black population of the other islands, they reasoned. The officials also entertained the thought that British Honduras might "think more favorably of joining," as "the British Hondurans have for Jamaica a long standing antipathy not extending to the rest of the West Indies."[3]

Colonial authorities feared the worst for the Leeward and Windward Islands if Trinidad sought independent status. The secretary of state for the colonies, Iain McLeod, felt that if Trinidad wanted independence, "it is difficult to see a 'rump' federation of Barbados and the smaller islands surviving." He thought that Barbados would want to continue as a separate self-governing colony, probably in view of that island's historically close ties with the mother country. McLeod was alarmed at the "most dismal prospect" of Britain retaining control of the remaining seven small Windward and Leeward Islands. They had "no prospect of making independence alone and all but one . . . are budgetarily in the red and supported financially by the United Kingdom." A new federation led by Trinidad would relieve the United Kingdom "of the prospect of having the smaller islands indefinitely on our hands." McLeod feared that Eric Williams would "in that case make full use of his strong bargaining position and no doubt demand a handsome financial contribution over the early years from Her Majesty's Government."[4]

There was considerable support among the leaders of the Leeward and Windward Islands for an Eastern Caribbean Federation. The chief ministers of St. Kitts, Antigua, and Dominica were quick to urge the salvaging of the federation within days of the Jamaica vote. They all shared the view, however, that massive economic assistance from Great Britain would be needed to make the new entity viable.[5] But Britain wanted neither to provide such assistance nor to keep these islands as dependents. In a brief prepared for Harold MacMillan prior to Sir Grantley Adams's visit in December 1961, colonial officials advised the prime minister to disabuse Adams of the notion that any new federation that excluded Trinidad could count on "much financial aid." Rather, MacMillan should say that he hoped that the nine territories would retain their political links. He should put a palatable face on British policy by affirming his nation's wish that these islands, united in a federation, would soon become independent. He should also remind Adams that he was "sure the natural political aspirations of the West Indian people would grievously suffer should the failure of this hope mean a continuation of the colonial status from which they are clearly fitted to emerge."[6]

♦ ♦ ♦ ♦ ♦ When Williams announced in January 1962 that Trinidad would seek independence, the news could hardly have come as a surprise. Ideally, as a vigorous advocate of regional unity, Williams would have preferred another scenario. He would have welcomed an Eastern Caribbean Federation under his leadership if the United Kingdom had been willing to provide the requisite economic assistance. At the West Indies Intergovernmental Conference in May 1961, Williams had indicated that if Jamaica withdrew from the federation, Trinidad would not assume any additional financial burdens to save it. The West Indies Federation was then receiving approximately 87 percent of its locally raised revenue from Jamaica and Trinidad.

Although Williams opposed being part of a new Eastern Caribbean Federation without the appropriate financial support, he was not averse to having some of the other islands join his country in a unitary statehood. In April 1962, for example, he invited the Leeward and the Windward Islands to consider becoming part of Trinidad. This extraordinary invitation, if accepted, would have had profound implications for the political landscape of the region, for Trinidad and Tobago, and for Williams's leadership and stature in the area.

The Williams invitation had an immediate resonance on the neighboring island of Grenada. This island, of some 87,000 persons in 1962, enjoyed a special relationship with its larger and wealthier neighbor. Residents of the two islands traveled back and forth, and Grenadians migrated to Trinidad to seek employment. In 1962 there were forty thousand Grenadians living in Trinidad and working in a variety of occupations. Trinidadians provided them with a generally welcoming environment, and many Grenadians became integrated into the host society through their involvement in its cultural and social life. Grenada, to be sure, was the junior partner, but the two islands enjoyed a harmonious if unequal relationship.

Although emigration to Trinidad and England represented a safety valve for the Grenadian economy, the island was experiencing severe economic deprivation. In 1965 an economic survey found that "in common with other under-developed economies, Grenada shows unmistakable signs of high levels of unemployment and even higher levels of under-employment." During the period 1954–60, the island's economy grew at a rate slightly under 3 percent annually, compared to about 8.5 percent in Trinidad and Tobago. The survey concluded that Grenada's economy "fitted very closely the classical description of an underdeveloped country with low income levels resulting from low production and productivity, under-utilised labour and primitive methods of production."[7]

Williams raised the question of unitary statehood at a time when Grenada was preparing for new elections. The island's constitution had been suspended for three months in early 1962 after a Commission of Enquiry found that the government led by flamboyant trade unionist Eric Gairy was guilty of corruption and intimidation of civil servants. The restoration of the constitution required new elections, which were scheduled to take place in September.

The principal opposition to Gairy's return to office came from Herbert Blaize, the leader of the Grenada National Party. Blaize, in the initial stages of the campaign, identified "squandermania" as the main issue. Despite the widely acknowledged view that the previous Gairy government had been corrupt, the issue failed to stimulate any enthusiasm among the majority of voters. The question of unitary statehood with Trinidad, Blaize discovered, provided just the right galvanizing issue for his party. Grenada's business community, which had extensive trading links with Trinidad, members of the middle class seeking to escape from Gairy and what his return to power portended, and those who wanted the freedom to emigrate to Trinidad, found unitary statehood with Trinidad an attractive proposition. These voters gave Blaize a 6-to-4 win over Eric Gairy and his Grenada Labour Party.

Blaize's victory forced Williams's hand on the nature of Trinidad's relationship with the "Little Eight," as Barbados and the Leeward and Windward Islands were now called. It was, and would remain, a relationship in dynamic formation, subject to bewildering fits and starts. On September 21, 1962, barely three weeks after becoming prime minister of Trinidad and a few days after Blaize's electoral victory in Grenada, Williams met with the secretary of state for the colonies in London. According to the minutes of the meeting, he told the secretary that Trinidad had no desire to "absorb" any of the Little Eight islands. Williams also said:

> The Party which has just won the election [in Grenada] . . . pledged to explore a relationship with Trinidad and a similar movement might develop in St. Vincent. But Trinidad would definitely not wish to absorb more than these two during the next three or four years. She might be ready to take on Dominica and St. Lucia later on, despite the French influence in those islands. Trinidad would definitely not want to absorb St. Kitts or Antigua because of their distance away and the trade union element, which dominates their politics. She has associations with Montserrat but her ability to deal with that small island would depend on communications.[8]

Statements such as these revealed Williams's pan-Caribbean dreams. He noted that he had had an exploratory meeting on unitary statehood with Eric Gairy in February 1962, and that Gairy had proposed a separate Parliament in Grenada in addition to Grenadian representation in the Trinidad Legislature. Williams said that he had "torn this idea to bits." In any event, he continued, Trinidad and Tobago would not accept any of the islands with more than a county council status. This meant that any island that was absorbed by Trinidad and Tobago would be relegated to the status of a county in the new nation. But he was in no hurry to arrange a meeting with the newly elected government in Grenada. Moreover, he had promised the former colonial secretary, Hugh Fraser, to wait for two years before assimilating any of the Little Eight.

Williams stressed that Trinidad's absorption of the islands would depend on the extent of Britain's financial support to improve their economies. His country could not share its own limited development resources with the other islands. This insistence on a significant commitment of resources by the United Kingdom for the islands of the Little Eight as a prerequisite for unitary status with Trinidad remained Williams's consistent theme. The secretary of state for the colonies urged him to keep the Grenada initiative "uncrystallized" until he had a chance to visit the West Indies and determine whether six or seven islands in a federation would be less viable than eight.[9]

Blaize, of course, was not privy to these discussions between Williams and the secretary of state for the colonies. Armed with what he considered to be an electoral mandate for political union with Trinidad and Tobago, he lost no time in requesting the permission of the secretary of state to open discussions with Trinidad. In mid-October the secretary responded: "I have no objection to your government having talks direct with the Government of Trinidad and Tobago on this subject, on the understanding that they are purely exploratory at this stage, without commitment either to you or to the British Government. The question of the British Government's joining in any such talks can be considered later, in the light of the results of the initial talks."[10]

Chief Minister Blaize immediately contacted Patrick Solomon, the acting prime minister of Trinidad, to arrange for the first of their discussions. The two officials agreed to begin as soon as Eric Williams returned from a European trip. Based on the statements of Grenadian officials, it was clear that they underestimated the difficulties they would confront and the speed with which an agreement with Trinidad could be reached. Blaize thought that the negotiations could be completed in a year, although Williams had earlier predicted two years. Whereas Williams, as he had told the secretary of state, wanted Grenada to become a county of Trinidad, Jimmy Lloyd, the island's administrator, appeared not to envision such a sharp diminution in Grenada's status, noting on October 4: "We are not unmindful of the fact that the acceptance of Unitary Statehood within Trinidad and Tobago will mean diminishing some of the direct power and authority over our people but my government is convinced that this can be achieved without loss of dignity."[11]

Herbert Blaize made a similar point in a radio broadcast on October 17. He assured his listeners that "this business of Unitary State of Trinidad and Grenada and Tobago is not an association of states; it is not merely Grenada attempting to join with Trinidad and Tobago; it also means Trinidad and Tobago willing to join with Grenada." Blaize wanted to dispel any notion that Grenada was a mendicant. As he put it, "Grenada is not going cap in hand, or on bended knees, or begging for economic security. Both Trinidad and Tobago and Grenada are expected to enter into these discussions on a basis of mutual partnership."[12]

Eric Williams, on the other hand, never saw the potential marriage as being a contract between equals. He clung to the position that Grenada, without massive economic aid from Britain, would tax Trinidad's limited resources. Trinidad's per capita income was, after all, more than twice that of Grenada's, a fact not lost on colonial officials and Grenada alike. But Williams had no desire to expend his country's funds on Grenada, thereby risking economic stability at home. On October 31, 1962, an official at the Commonwealth Relations Office complained that Williams was likely "so to arrange things that the size of the dowry to be granted to Grenada becomes the determining factor in whether or not union will come off."[13] In November Williams told West Indian students in London that "the discussions that are impending in respect of the incorporation of Grenada into the state of Trinidad and Tobago would not in any circumstances involve Trinidad and Tobago carrying Britain's baby for her." He predicted: "I expect nothing to come out of the negotiations with Grenada."[14]

Colonial officials were always annoyed by Williams's frequent private and public insistence that political union carried an expensive price tag. Time and time again he asserted his nation's inability to assume Britain's financial obligations to Grenada. The British High Commissioner's Office reported on the following exchange between Williams and a journalist at a press conference in Port of Spain on November 25, 1962:

> [Question]: Did I understand you to say that you would have nothing to do with Grenada joining a unitary state if Britain did not make a substantial grant?
>
> [Answer]: Dr. Williams is reported to have replied to [the] following effect. Trinidad's ties with Grenada were close but what did the questioner want him to do. Since 1956 his Government had tried to repair generations of colonial neglect and 98½% of Trinidad's development had been paid for from local resources. In Grenada the neglect was worse. Was he to saddle the people of Trinidad and Tobago with yet another bill—and Grenada might not be the only bill. Not at all. He had to deal with realities and this time Britain was not going to get away with it.[15]

The United Kingdom's developing policy on political union was characterized by a lack of clarity and much ambivalence. British officials confronted two important issues: first, the need to develop a coherent policy on the potential federation of Barbados and the Leeward and Windward Islands, and second, the need for a policy on Grenada's desire to be integrated into Trinidad and Tobago. On the former, the United Kingdom had four options: (1) encourage federation of the eight territories, (2) try to establish a looser form of association such as the sharing of common services, (3) keep the territories as separate entities, or (4) effect their integration into Trinidad and Tobago.

◆ ◆ ◆ ◆ ◆ The government of Grenada stood alone in its enthusiastic endorsement of unitary status with Trinidad and Tobago. Although others such as Montserrat and St. Vincent did not oppose the prospect of doing so, the clear preference among them was for a federation of the "Little Eight"with Grenada or the "Little Seven" without Grenada. The Colonial Office, in a memorandum dated October 15, 1962, argued that federation offered the "best prospect of advancing all the islands to independence and of securing some measure of economic vitality for them." If they became independent as a federated unit, they would be eligible for aid from sources other than the United Kingdom, "thereby lessening the burden on us." In addition, provided that the central government was made strong enough, federation offered "the best prospect of cutting the small island political bosses down to size."

Federation, the memorandum suggested, had its disadvantages as well. The islands would continue to need substantial aid. "The smaller islands," it asserted, "have shown themselves to be financially irresponsible and administratively incompetent." That being the case, federation would mean that "we shall have even less control over the way they spend our money than we have now." There was not much to recommend a looser form of association. Political independence could hardly be granted to "a common services organization and . . . it would leave the small island political bosses dominant in their own territories." Keeping the islands separate was also not an inviting prospect for the United Kingdom. The islands would remain dependent on the mother country, which would be "stuck with them indefinitely and we could expect growing political frustration in the islands, which might lead to trouble."

The Colonial Office welcomed the idea of the islands' absorption by Trinidad, because "we thereby get rid of all responsibility." They would become part of a unitary independent state with responsibility for their welfare residing with the central government in Port of Spain. But the office feared that Williams would demand "very considerable sums" to assimilate any of the islands. Weighing the advantages and disadvantages of each option, the Colonial Office concluded that federation, "provided it can be brought about on suitable terms—particularly with a strong central Government—offers the best solution to the problems of the area."

But the United Kingdom should not place any obstacles in the way of the negotiations between Trinidad and Grenada. Still, the Colonial Office recognized that the "defection" of Grenada to Trinidad and Tobago "will diminish the already meager resources of the Eight—though not fatally." If some of the other islands followed Grenada's lead, this would jeopardize any prospect that the rest would federate, the memorandum surmised.[16]

The animating impulse behind British policy was to jettison the islands as quickly as possible and at the lowest possible cost. Britain was prepared to endorse any means to this end provided the initiative appeared to emanate from the islands themselves and not from London. But although Williams was never an ardent suitor, he would have become one if the dowry had been sufficiently attractive. With the exception of Grenada, the other islands were not committed to a marriage with Trinidad and Tobago, a match Britain would have welcomed but did not consistently encourage.

There was, understandably, some opposition in Trinidad to the prospect of integration with Grenada. The opposition Democratic Labour Party (DLP) voiced concern about its potentially negative impact on the economy and social services in Trinidad and Tobago. In the legislature on November 23, 1962, the deputy leader of the opposition, Ashford Sinanan, declared that Trinidad should reject this "dangerous experiment, which is likely to overburden further the people of this country." He thought that union would exacerbate the already high unemployment and underemployment problems and would place great pressures on schools, hospitals, and other public institutions. Sinanan also believed that the business community, in particular, would resist any additional taxation that might be needed to support the services provided by these institutions.[17]

In reporting Sinanan's observations to the Commonwealth Relations Office, the British High Commissioner's Office in Port of Spain noted the "mounting" public opposition to union. The official (presumably Norman Costar) commented on the prevailing "selfish, but natural feelings in all communities" that union would mean loss of jobs. There was, he said, "a longstanding genuine fear of Grenadians swamping the labour market." But the question of union also had "racial undertones." The "earlier rumblings" of the Indians "have now developed into a flat statement of opposition" to union. He believed that this was due to the pressure of the Indian Association, a powerful civic organization. "Indian feeling that union with Grenada is a move designed to prevent them catching up numerically with the Negro population in the country in fact lies at the root of the opposition." Assessing the overall situation, the official concluded that "it is fair to say that at the moment the wind of union seems to be blowing colder."[18] Sensing this internal dissent, Deputy Prime Minister Patrick Solomon said that union was "too big an issue" for the government to decide by itself, promising that citizens would be given a chance to express their views, presumably by means of a referendum. Such assurances notwithstanding, the DLP never wavered in its opposition to the projected union with Grenada. In July 1964, for example, DLP leader Rudranath Capildeo denounced unitary statehood as "dangerous political talk" and an effort to "play politics to upset the DLP vote." The government, he alleged, was "playing with fire" and "the DLP is not willing to burn."[19]

The primary legal obstacle to union was that it needed a constitutional amendment endorsed by three-fourths of the lower house of Parliament. Since the Williams government controlled only two-thirds of the seats, it was highly unlikely that political union would be approved, given the opposition of the DLP. The politics of the situation, to be sure, would become even more muddled if a referendum demonstrated majority support for union.

Williams and Blaize also had to contend with opposition to political union among some Grenadians. The administrator of Grenada reported to the Colonial Office in March 1964 that he sensed "a lingering but definite suspicion of Dr. Williams' intentions for this and the other small islands." Despite an early flirtation with the idea, Eric Gairy had become a vocal opponent. The opposition leader strongly supported Grenada's becoming a part of the proposed Little Eight Federation, arguing that "other countries were more likely to provide assistance to the small underdeveloped islands than they would to a wealthier Trinidad. He believed that the funds that unitary statehood would require should be used exclusively to enhance Grenada's development. Gairy feared that Trinidad would absorb Grenada's tourist trade and that its higher wage scale might upset the wage structure in Grenada. This, he predicted, would contribute to labor unrest. Gairy was also apprehensive that Grenada would lose its personality as a consequence of unitary statehood. He said that some Grenadians thought that Trinidad was "associated" with communism. This was an absurd allegation, given Williams's unwavering anticommunist stance.[20]

A petition from "women drawn from all classes and sections of the Grenada community" expressed fear of Trinidadian "contamination." The petitioners, characterized by the administrator of Grenada as Gairy supporters, were "horrified at the spectacle that Grenada is hardly likely to escape contamination in time in the face of the general and growing disregard for law and order in Trinidad." They also were alarmed by the inability of the police to control the "constantly mounting" incidence of violence and crime on the island, viewing with "special concern" the assaults on "women and young girls" by "vicious and unscrupulous males."[21] Gairy, the chief opponent of unitary statehood, had little credibility in official circles in London and Port of Spain. Indeed, Eric Williams ventured the opinion that he should be "in gaol."[22] British officials, on their part, could not understand Gairy's appeal to Grenada's working class. One Colonial Office memorandum described him as "a thug and a gangster [who] has an immense hold over the illiterate masses in Grenada who regard him as a kind of Messiah."[23]

Such uncomfortable realities posed serious difficulties for Williams, Blaize, and a British government that was anxious to dispose of Grenada either as part of a Little Eight Federation or as a territory of Trinidad and Tobago. The situation was complicated by British officials' distrust of Eric Williams: their attribution of the worst motives to him and their obsession with making him appear responsible for the failure of the discussions if they did fail. They were even prepared to play Grenada off against Trinidad if that would place Williams in a bad light.

Consequently, British policy on the issue of union had several dimensions. First, colonial officials did not wish to discourage the prospects of union, since a federation of the Leeward and Windward Islands—or the Little Seven—"might never come off and, if it did, would be slightly less expensive without Grenada." Clearly, the British wanted to be excessively parsimonious in their relationship with the seven small islands, which always teetered on the edge of bankruptcy. Second, Britain hoped that political union would succeed because its failure would result in Eric Gairy's return to office, a most worrisome prospect. Third, officials wanted "to ensure that in the event of failure the responsibility clearly lay with the Trinidad Government."[24]

Not surprisingly, Williams planned to blame the British if the negotiations failed. The principal issue was the size of the "dowry," as British officials characterized a potential financial settlement. On December 10, 1962, the British High Commission in Port of Spain predicted that Williams would present the United Kingdom with an "impossibly large bill as the price of take over." The two governments' division on this issue seemed to be irreconcilable.[25]

The United Kingdom, however, conceived a disingenuous policy in which Herbert Blaize was expected to play, unwittingly, a malevolent role. Colonial officials saw Blaize as an acceptable alternative to the unpredictable and corrupt Eric Gairy. But he did not inspire their deep respect. "He is a very good chap," one official wrote, "but needs help in clearing his mind."[26] In a December 1962 meeting, Blaize had assured the colonial secretary of state that the evidence would "prove that Grenada could hold her own without being a drag on any other territory." Seizing upon this comment, the secretary told Blaize that Grenada should be careful lest it kill the possibility of unitary statehood by requesting too much money from Britain.[27]

In an internal memorandum that referenced the December 1962 meeting, Denis Williams of the Colonial Office observed that the statements by Blaize and the colonial secretary "provide the way out of our difficulty," as far as financial support for political union was concerned. "While accepting that any proposals put forward must deal with the economic as well as the political aspects of union, what we need to ensure is that the proposals acceptable to Grenada are also acceptable to Her Majesty's Government. If such proposals are then not acceptable to Trinidad, then the onus for their rejection is on Trinidad and not on Her Majesty's Government."

In Machiavellian-like fashion, Denis Williams suggested how this travesty could be played out: "The ideal answer to our difficulty, therefore, lies in our persuading Grenada to put forward modest proposals to Trinidad and not simply to subscribe to exorbitant proposals put forward by Trinidad. If we have to face the situation that the initial offer must come from Trinidad, then I suggest if we can get the government of Grenada to reject the offer on the grounds that Trinidadian claims are exorbitant, we are still off the hook." He recommended that colonial officials in Grenada be enlisted to advise Blaize not to acquiesce to "an exorbitant demand from Trinidad for economic assistance."[28]

Blaize, to the extent that he was aware of these machinations, could hardly have been expected to sign his own death warrant. He had confided to the new Grenada administrator, L. A. Pinard, that if union failed, he would feel compelled to resign. Surely a disagreement with Eric Williams over the critical issue of the extent of British financial support would have invited the prime minister's wrath, guaranteed the failure of the project, and produced Blaize's resignation. Britain's bête noire, Eric Gairy, would undoubtedly have been returned to office.

Faced with this potential scenario, Ms. M. Z. Terry of the Colonial Office, in November 1963, complained that she saw "no way to get Blaize off the hook." She thought that "the best tactic is to take all possible steps to maintain the illusion that union with Trinidad is still a possibility and to keep the idea in play as long as may be necessary." The immediate challenge was to buy some time "during which external events and developments (and even possible internal developments in Grenada, such as an accident to Mr. Gairy) might come to the rescue." Comments such as these reflected the profound sterility of British policy with regard to the matter at hand.[29]

Eric Williams did little to move the discussions forward. As time wore on, he seemed to have realized that the obstacles to political union were insurmountable and wished to extricate himself. However, Stanley J. G. Fingland of the British High Commissioner's Office in Port of Spain was convinced that "Dr. Williams has never really been interested in Grenada for itself, but took up the question for a mixture of economic and political motives at a time when other avenues [federation] for increasing Trinidad's influence and safeguarding her interests seemed closed to him. His interest in Grenada was only a means to an end."[30]

This comment had some merit, but it gave short shrift to Williams's long-standing commitment to regional integration. Williams, in his turn, was getting ready to throw in the towel, informing the secretary of state in July 1963 that in order to discharge his obligation to Blaize, he would introduce the constitutional amendment in Parliament that was needed to facilitate union. Williams knew that this was an empty exercise, since there was little chance that the amendment would be adopted. The prime minister, however, never kept his word.[31]

Having staked his political life on effecting unitary statehood with Trinidad and Tobago, Herbert Blaize remained naively optimistic throughout 1963 that his goal would be accomplished. In December 1962 he had led a delegation of Grenadian officials to meet with Prime Minister Williams in Port of Spain to initiate talks on political union. Blaize returned from the talks, praising Williams, his government, and the people of Trinidad and Tobago "for creating the proper atmosphere in which delicate negotiations must take place." But, he cautioned, "a start is not necessarily the end."[32]

♦ ♦ ♦ ♦ ♦ ♦ The December talks resulted in an agreement to create five fact-finding commissions, comprised solely of officials from Trinidad and Tobago, to prepare reports on five major issues. The first and most important commission would prepare a development plan for Grenada. As Blaize explained in a radio broadcast on December 12: "In order to have constructive discussion on any subject so important as the joining together of two territories into one, a reasonably good idea of the development potential of both territories must be obtained."[33] Accordingly, the "Commission on the Development Program for Grenada" was to establish such a program, "taking into account the proposals prepared by the former Federal Government for the period 1959–1964, and to make recommendations for its financing."

The second commission, called the "Fact Finding Commission on Grenada Public Service," was to undertake a study of the Grenada civil service and recommend ways in which it could be reorganized and integrated into that of Trinidad and Tobago. The third commission, known as the "Economic Commission," was to examine "the implications" of assimilating the fiscal structure of Grenada into that of Trinidad and Tobago and the integration of the two economies. The fourth commission, the "Legal and Constitutional Commission," was to study the constitutional implications of integration, with a focus on citizenship, electoral law, judicial and legal organization, and so on. The fifth commission, the "Local Government Commission," was empowered to study the organization and operations of local government authorities in Grenada and to recommend how much local autonomy Grenada should possess in a unitary state. These five commissions began their work in December 1962 and January 1963.

As the civil servants continued their fact-finding studies, Eric Williams once again began to harbor dreams of absorbing some of the other islands as well. To maintain his credibility with these islands, he told Norman

Costar that he would "be obliged to attack Britain for providing insufficient aid to enable the federation of the Little Eight to get going." According to Costar, Williams predicted that the proposed federation would not occur and Barbados would seek its independence. Williams "looked forward ultimately to the day when Trinidad would pick up Grenada, St. Vincent and perhaps St. Lucia. Jamaica could take the Leeward Islands, and perhaps Barbados could take one or two islands." Costar added, cynically, that the ones that Barbados could potentially acquire were "presumably those not wanted by Dr. Williams." Williams stressed, however, that much would depend on the amount of aid the United Kingdom would be willing to commit to the development of the island economies.[34]

With the exception of Barbados, Williams was not certain that the islands deserved independence. In late 1963 he had told Costar that the British government should not succumb to pressure to grant them independence. Williams believed that if Jamaica, Trinidad, and an independent Barbados continued to develop closer ties among themselves, the smaller islands might be persuaded to join them, provided that they did not embrace individual courses of their own. Williams, in keeping with his Pan-Caribbean vision, thought that Cuba, the Dominican Republic, and Haiti should be invited to join any renewed effort at regional integration.[35]

Williams confided his fears about political union with Grenada to the Duke of Edinburgh when His Royal Highness visited Tobago in 1964. Williams had emphasized that he was not enthusiastic about unitary statehood but that it was politically advantageous for him to pursue it. Williams, the duke reported, was worried about Grenadians migrating to Trinidad as well as integrating Grenada's inefficient civil service into that of Trinidad and Tobago. Impatient with Williams because of such seeming vacillation and ambivalence on unitary statehood and other matters, British officials blasted him. When Williams wrote to the secretary of state in November 1964 on the Grenada issue, Denis Williams characterized the letter as "the kind of tissue of half and quarter truths one has come to expect in any communication from Dr. Williams. He always gives a highly selective version of events, convenient to his own thesis, which has little relation to facts." The colonial official added contemptuously, "That, after all, is the reason why he failed to get a fellowship at All Souls!"[36]

Not content with accusing Prime Minister Williams of mendacity, Denis Williams went on to blame him for the apparent failure of the attempts to create an Eastern Caribbean Federation and for demanding an exorbitant price to absorb Grenada. "Dr. Williams' blatant pan Caribbean ambitions are anathema to all the other territories in the Eastern Caribbean except Grenada," wrote the colonial official. "To them he is 'the threat from the South.' If we once provided extra money on this scale for Grenada, we should appear to the other territories to be providing financial encouragement to Trinidadian imperialism," he concluded.[37]

Such unhelpful statements by colonial officials reflected their inability to address the problems of the Eastern Caribbean islands with understanding, good judgment, and foresight. Eric Williams was not the stumbling block to the federation of the Little Eight or even to unitary statehood with Grenada. These islands stood no chance of achieving some degree of economic sufficiency without substantial British aid to compensate for centuries of neglect by the imperial government. Williams, more than anyone else, recognized that truth. Colonial officials knew it, too, hence their extreme sensitivity to Williams's demands and criticisms.

Williams's insistence on significant aid for Grenada as the sine qua non of unitary statehood received substantial support when the Commission on the Development Program for Grenada and Economic Commission presented their reports. The Development Program Commission recommended capital expenditures of approximately TT$32 million (£6.5 million) in Grenada for the years 1964–68; this represented "the minimum sum required to push the economy of Grenada forward." The commission urged that about TT$12 million be earmarked for agricultural development, TT$5 million for roads and bridges, and substantial sums for social services. For Grenada to become economically self-supporting, the commission recommended capital expenditures of TT$60 million (£12 million) on the island's infrastructure and agricultural base over a ten-year period.[38]

The Development Program Commission calculated that at least TT$29 million (£6 million) of the money needed for the first five-year plan would have to come from internal sources. Recognizing that Trinidad and Tobago could not provide those resources, it recommended that the funds be obtained in the form of soft loans rather than grants. Such loans were preferable to commercial loans at existing market rates, because Grenada would have difficulty repaying them. The soft loans should be for a longer term than the customary commercial loans and should carry interest rates from zero to 2½ percent. These loans should not be tied to the import content usually associated with development loans, whereby the recipient must use the money to purchase goods and services only from the creditor country. This was one of the requirements that had led Eric Williams to reject the golden handshake on the occasion of his nation's independence.

The Economic Commission's report presented a comprehensive survey of the economy of Grenada, as well as a detailed examination of the major implications of the assimilation of the fiscal structures by Trinidad and of the integration of the two nations' economies. The report also included a cost study of the proposed unitary state emphasizing aspects of public finance, namely capital receipts and expenditures, current receipts and expenditures, and the balance of payments.

After assessing the economic condition of Grenada and its long-term prospects, this commission noted that "the need to develop the economy of Grenada does not arise from the establishment of the unitary state." Rather, "some effort to promote the well being of the people of this colony would be necessary regardless of which of the various alternatives for political organization may be selected." The commission was convinced that "the integration of the economies of Trinidad and Tobago and Grenada hold out the enhanced prospects for economic development in both islands."[39] Accordingly, it recommended a program of phased implementation of five economic objectives, namely:

1. A unified tariff
2. A common tax rate and structure at the national level
3. Free movement of products between the two islands to create a larger market
4. Free movement of the factors of production with[in] the area, that is to say capital and labour
5. The greatest possible parity between the social services of the two countries in order to minimize the pressure for population movement from the more rural to the more urban areas.[40]

The program of phased economic integration, as well as the one for development, should be supervised jointly by officials from Grenada and Trinidad who, together, would constitute a mixed commission. But, the report cautioned, "firm commitments for a programme flow of capital funds from the United Kingdom for an agreed time period is a fundamental prerequisite, and so too is the commitment to assist in the financing of certain current expenditures." The first two commissions both recognized the centrality of significant British economic assistance for the success of unitary statehood. This, to be sure, was unwelcome news to colonial officials, but they could hardly have expected to have heard otherwise.[41]

The development and economic reports provided Eric Williams with additional ammunition for his case that massive economic aid was required for the potential unitary state. As usual, colonial officials demurred. His political future in grave peril if political union was stillborn, Herbert Blaize proposed a compromise. He asked the United Kingdom to foot one-third of the cost of the development program and support his island's request for loans elsewhere. The colonial secretary turned a deaf ear to this proposal, informing Blaize that his government's limited resources and competing overseas claims made it impossible to endorse his request.[42]

Eric Williams was never the compliant figure that Herbert Blaize was in his relationship with the Colonial Office. Whereas colonial officials smarted from Williams's verbal assaults and worried over his every move, they had little respect for Blaize because they knew that their support was crucial to his remaining in office. A memorandum from the West Indian Department at the Colonial Office, for example, described Blaize as "morally sound" but "politically ineffective." A personable, gullible, and compromising individual, Blaize became a tragic figure caught between the arrows emanating from London and Port of Spain.[43]

Throughout much of the lengthy period in which Blaize waited for the unitary statehood issue to be resolved, he never seemed to have lost confidence in Williams's intentions. In June 1964 Norman Costar observed that "Blaize still seems to be under Dr. Williams' spell, even though other West Indian leaders are perhaps becoming disenchanted."[44] After a visit to Port of Spain in November 1964, Blaize expressed satisfaction with the progress of the negotiations, although by then it should have been clear that unitary statehood was experiencing its last gasp.

By the spring of 1965, however, Blaize was beginning to doubt whether his dream of unitary statehood could be accomplished. A Colonial Office memorandum in April welcomed the seeming lack of movement on the issue. Such inactivity was desirable, it reasoned, "in light of our own policy of helping to keep alive the illusion of union so as to maintain Mr. Blaize in power in Grenada in the hope that something might happen to release him from his electoral commitments."[45]

♦ ♦ ♦ ♦ ♦ Despite his own doubts, Eric Williams never completely shut the door on unitary statehood. Had it been possible, he would have welcomed Grenada by itself, but his preference was for as many of the islands as appeared feasible. Norman Costar was close to the mark when he said: "My guess would be that his ambitions focus on the whole shoal in the Eastern Caribbean and not on a single sprat, even one as attractive as Grenada." Williams never cut bait even when he realized that unitary statehood was an exercise in futility. As Costar expressed it rather colorfully, Williams "wants to keep Blaize on a string. Everytime Blaize may feel tempted to write union off, Dr. Williams will give another pull to the string." Whenever Blaize demonstrated any interest in another regional grouping such as a federation of the Windward Islands, Williams felt that that was "the right moment for a tug."[46]

In the end, Williams neither hooked a sprat nor the whole shoal. Toward late 1965 the issue of political union disappeared from the consciousness of all the parties involved. By that time, Blaize, Williams, and colonial officials had begun to realize the futility of the project, an awareness that seems to have been unduly late in coming. The British government was left with Grenada on its hands. As the disappointed officials put it, "Our present policy is really one of keeping alive an illusion to maintain Mr. Blaize in office in the hope that something will turn up. But nothing seems very likely to turn up except—alas—Mr. Gairy."[47]

In retrospect, the realization of a unitary state of Trinidad and Grenada was illusory. The DLP in Trinidad opposed the plan, and without its support there was no chance that the requisite constitutional amendment would have passed. Williams did not pursue political union as aggressively as he could have, fearing that Trinidad and Tobago would have had to assume Grenada's considerable economic burdens. Williams was also torn between a policy of integration with Grenada and one that involved the absorption of several additional islands. The two policies were not necessarily contradictory, but he pursued both simultaneously, to the detriment of both. Britain wanted to be rid of Grenada at the lowest possible cost, a policy steeped in myopia, duplicity, and selfishness. It did not work because it was morally bankrupt, and the West Indian leaders knew it. The trusting and somewhat naive Herbert Blaize was the victim of forces he could neither shape nor control.

♦ ♦

CHAPTER 6

BLEEDING GUIANA

♦ ♦ ♦ ♦ ♦ ♦ Situated on the northeastern coast of South America, British Guiana was the largest of the Anglophone Caribbean colonies. Its area of 83,000 square miles made it slightly smaller than the British Isles. In 1965 its population numbered only 605,000 and was concentrated in Georgetown, the capital city, and on the coastal belt. British Guiana was home to many ethnic groups. Indo-Guianese, who were the descendants of indentured servants from South Asia, numbered 297,000, constituting about 50 percent of the population. The African Guianese, the descendants of enslaved Africans, comprised about 192,000 persons, or 32 percent of the inhabitants. Racially mixed groups, generally referred to as "coloureds," amounted to 74,000 people. The descendants of Portuguese immigrants from Madeira numbered 7,000, other Europeans 3,000, Amerindians 28,000, and the Chinese 4,000.

The modern political history of British Guiana began in 1950, when a young Indo-Guianese dentist, Dr. Cheddi Jagan, along with his American-born wife Janet, founded the People's Progressive Party (PPP). The new party received the support of Forbes Burnham, an African Guianese attorney, who became its deputy leader. Attracting the votes of Indo-Guianese and African Guianese, the PPP won the elections that were held in April 1953 and Jagan became the first premier. His government was short-lived, however, as the British government became alarmed at Jagan's public assertion of Marxism and the behavior of his administration. It suspended the constitution a bare six months after Jagan had assumed office, returning British Guiana to crown colony status, or direct rule.

The association between Cheddi Jagan and Forbes Burnham ended in 1955 after a series of disputes based mainly on their rivalry for the leadership of the PPP and to some extent ideological differences. Two years later Burnham founded the People's National Congress (PNC), which attracted substantial support from the African Guianese population, while most Indo-Guianese remained with the PPP. When the constitution was restored in 1957 with severe restrictions on the power of the elected legislature, the PPP won the new elections, and Jagan once again became the dominant political personage in the colony, although the office of premier no longer existed. The future did not augur well for British Guiana. Party alignment began to crystallize along racial lines, and Jagan's continued articulation of Marxist dogma earned him the antipathy of officials in the United Kingdom and the United States. This was the era of the Cold War and the political anxieties it engendered in the Americas. Fidel Castro's ascendancy to power in Cuba in 1959 and his alliance with the Soviet Union thereafter exacerbated American and British fears that British Guiana could become the second communist bastion in the hemisphere.

The colony, however, remained sufficiently stable for the British government to call a conference of its leaders in London in March 1960 to determine its future. Delegates at the conference endorsed the principle of independence for British Guiana. In July 1961 full internal self-government was introduced, although responsibility for defense and external affairs remained with the British governor. But there was trouble on the horizon. In the general election held in late 1961, the PPP received 43 percent of the votes but won 20 seats in the 35-member legislature. The PNC won only 11 seats but received 41 percent of the votes. A newly formed party, the United Force (UF), received 16 percent of the votes, winning 4 seats. Led by Peter D'Aguiar, a wealthy businessman of Portuguese descent, this conservative party won the support of white voters, coloureds, and members of the middle class in general.

Critics of Cheddi Jagan were disturbed by the fact that his was a minority government, having received only 43 percent of the votes cast. They were troubled by his pro-communist rhetoric and his attempts to seek closer relationships with Cuba and the Eastern Bloc countries. His wife Janet, a gifted organizer and Marxist theoretician, was his acknowledged ideological mentor and principal adviser. Jagan's opponents feared independence under his leadership and were worried that he would continue to remain in office indefinitely if the "first past the post" electoral system were not changed. Indians, who comprised the largest sector of the multiracial electorate, were expected to remain the basis of his support.

The period 1962–63 saw the country wracked by one crisis after another,

Cheddi Jagan, premier of British Guiana, greets Eric Williams at the airport on
Williams's arrival in the territory, March 1963. Photograph courtesy of Eric Williams
Memorial Collection, University of the West Indies (Trinidad and Tobago). © Eric
Williams Memorial Collection and used by permission.

stimulated in part by the U.S. Central Intelligence Agency. Unhappiness with
the budget that Jagan introduced in 1962 led to a major strike and social
disturbances mainly in Georgetown. British troops were hastily dispatched
to restore law and order. In 1963 Jagan introduced legislation to ensure that
the PPP-backed Guiana Sugar Workers Union (GSWU) would replace the
older and more independent Manpower Citizens Association (MPCA) as the
organized voice of the sugar workers. This precipitated a lengthy strike that
pitted Indians against blacks, especially in rural areas, again necessitating
the use of British troops to restore order.

In October 1963 the Guianese leaders met with British officials in London
to settle their constitutional differences. To resolve the crisis in their country,
the two opposition parties endorsed a system of proportional representation. Cheddi Jagan, recognizing that this could lead to his removal from
office, adamantly rejected the proposal. He also proposed reducing the vot-

ing age to eighteen, a change that would be to his advantage in view of the growing Indian population. Peter D'Aguiar and Forbes Burnham opposed this proposal. The three leaders also failed to agree on whether fresh elections should be held before independence.

Having failed to reach an agreement on these critical issues, Jagan, D'Aguiar, and Burnham invited the secretary of state for the colonies to resolve them on their behalf. "We are agreed to ask the British Government," their letter read, "to settle on their authority all outstanding constitutional issues and we undertake to accept their decisions."[1] Secretary of State Duncan Sandys welcomed this opportunity in view of Britain's support for proportional representation and its expressed desire to grant independence to the colony. Sandys announced his decision on October 31, endorsing proportional representation. He thought that British Guiana's problems could be attributed to the development of party politics along racial lines. Proportional representation, he predicted, would encourage coalitions between parties and would make it easier for multiracial groupings to develop. He gave his assurance that elections under the new system would be held expeditiously, to be followed by a conference to set a date for independence.

Jagan vociferously rejected proportional representation, as he was convinced that its objective was to defeat the PPP. Although he probably had no hard evidence that the British wanted to drive him from office, this was indeed the case. Not only did the imperial government see the removal of Jagan as a priority, it was anxious to jettison British Guiana altogether. In a brief prepared for Prime Minister Harold MacMillan in early July 1963, the Colonial Office admitted flatly that "we have no strategic interest in British Guiana and the sooner we can shed our obligations there the better from our point of view." After reviewing internal developments in British Guiana, the office noted that since 1960 "our aim in government had altered from "making the best of Jagan" to the achievement of independence under a government "not led by Jagan." This policy had been developed "in agreement with the Americans."[2]

The United States also strongly opposed granting British Guiana independence under Cheddi Jagan's leadership. U.S. officials dreaded the creation of a communist state after independence, a development that would have "profound and lasting effects on Anglo/US relations . . . and on the overall position of the West," a British top secret document revealed. The Americans "said that an independent British Guiana under Jagan was unacceptable to the U.S. They, therefore, believed that we should set as our immediate policy objective the removal of the Jagan government prior to independence. As a long run objective the US officials believed that we should work for an independent British Guiana with a government prepared to cooperate with the West and to govern the country in the interests of all races."[3]

The Americans urged the suspension of the British Guianese constitution and the assumption of direct rule by the British. But colonial officials tied such actions to a commitment by the United States to provide resources for Guiana's development. In addition, they thought it "essential for the Americans to give us full diplomatic support at the United Nations and elsewhere for the resumption of direct rule."[4] After reviewing all of the policy options, the Colonial Office held that proportional representation provided the most feasible means of achieving its objectives. But the officials were under no illusion that this constituted a long-term solution for British Guiana's ills. "At best," they concluded, "proportional representation might produce an electoral victory for Burnham and D'Aguiar at the first election only."[5]

Although the Colonial Office disliked Jagan, it was hardly enamored of Forbes Burnham or Peter D'Aguiar. In March 1960 colonial secretary Iain McLeod had dismissed Jagan as "of no great ability" and characterized Burnham as "being much more able" but "showed himself so incredibly conceited" that it was difficult to discuss issues with him. Other officials considered Burnham "unreliable" and predicted that a coalition government formed by D'Aguiar and Burnham "would be inefficient, [and] would be subject to severe internal strains."[6] Nevertheless, the introduction of proportional representation was a boon to opposition leaders.

The stage was set for a prolonged, acrimonious struggle by the three leaders for political ascendancy. British Guiana became a veritable battleground as its leaders fanned the flames of racial fears, mistrust, hatred, and discord. None of the leaders seemed capable of stanching the flow of blood from the wounds they had helped to inflict on their country. Worse, British Guiana's racial sparks threatened to ignite similar fires in other countries such as Trinidad, with its almost similar ethnic composition and uneasy relationships between African Trinidadians and Indo-Trinidadians. A communist-controlled British Guiana supported by Cuba and the Eastern Bloc was also deemed to threaten the stability of the Anglo-Caribbean area. Eric Williams, for one, understood that he could not remain a disinterested observer of British Guiana's descent into disorder, violence, and poisonous racial hatreds. Trinidad and Tobago had too much to lose if he did not act.

Thirteen hours after Trinidad and Tobago became an independent state and a member of the British Commonwealth, Eric Williams raised the subject of British Guiana with British High Commissioner Norman Costar. According to Costar, Williams said that he was going to devote his attention "to the problem of British Guiana where both Africans and Indians were acting foolishly." Costar reported that "I forbore to enquire more about this lest I should be taken as encouraging an interest or activity which might not be welcome to us."[7] In succeeding months Williams made good on his promise. But he did not develop a coherent policy on British Guiana, tending more to respond to the changing situation in the colony than to articulate a consistent course of action. The interests of Trinidad and Tobago were, understandably, paramount in all of his efforts, although he genuinely desired to play a useful role in British Guiana.

♦ ♦ ♦ ♦ ♦ Williams's attempts to resolve the crisis in British Guiana formally began in March 1963. While in Georgetown on an official visit, he conversed with many groups, individuals, and politicians on the political situation. According to Williams, this gave him an opportunity to emphasize his position "(1) for independence, (2) against proportional representation, (3) on adequate constitutional safeguards to protect the interests of the people, and (4) for, based on the experience of Trinidad and Tobago, the maximum possible community participation in the exercises preceding independence."[8]

During his visit in British Guiana, Williams said that he encountered an atmosphere of "fear, frustration, stagnation and a division in the country that could only be described as chaotic."[9] On his return to Port of Spain, he wrote to Prime Minister Alexander Bustamante of Jamaica, describing the "situation" he had found in British Guiana and suggesting that their two nations, as the only independent Commonwealth countries in the region, should consider "most seriously direct representation in British Guiana at the Commissioner level." It was his view that Jamaica and Trinidad should combine their efforts to resolve "the difficult situation" and that the self-governing territory of Barbados should also be involved.[10]

On April 24, 1963, he sent Bustamante and Errol Barrow, the premier of Barbados, a telegram expressing his deep concern about "the possible repercussions on all of us in the West Indies, Jamaica, Barbados, Trinidad and Tobago if we make no effort to mediate in the British Guiana difficulty." Williams urged the two leaders "in all sincerity" to join him in offering their services to Jagan and to endorse the following telegram to the Guianese premier:

> The Prime Minister of Jamaica, the Premier of Barbados and I are very deeply and sincerely perturbed about the recent developments in British Guiana and their possible effects, both short term and long term, on West Indian development and prospects and the reputation of our peoples. We appeal to you therefore in the interest of peace and stability to postpone further stages of the Labour [Relations] Bill. We would like to suggest that you give us the opportunity of face to face discussions with you and your advisers either in Georgetown or in any other place of your choice. We are satisfied that such action on your part will be widely acclaimed not only in your own country and in our countries, but in the world at large.

Williams hoped for an "urgent and sympathetic" reply, since "all three of us have a grave responsibility, moral and political, to do all in our power to avert what appears to be impending catastrophe as a result of a confrontation of legitimate government and the labour movement which sets a precedent that bodes no good for any one of us."[11]

It is noteworthy that Williams's potential involvement in British Guiana's internal affairs at this stage was narrowly conceived. He avoided any mention of the worsening racial climate, confining his concerns to the controversial Labour Relations Bill. But the impetus behind the bill and the firestorm it created reflected the deeper tensions in British Guianese society, its festering racial sores and systemic ills. Williams certainly realized this, and he probably knew that Jagan would not, at that point, look favorably on outsider mediation on the larger issues.

Bustamante responded with alacrity to Williams's appeal. "You have my full support," he telegraphed his Trinidadian counterpart on April 26.[12] According to the British High Commissioner in Kingston, the Jamaican prime minister acted without consulting his ministers. There was "no sympathy" for Jagan in Jamaica, nor was there any disposition there to become involved in British Guiana's affairs. Nonetheless, the high commissioner observed, "Bustamante seems to find it difficult to resist Williams' leads."[13]

The Barbadian premier also assented to Williams's request. The British high commissioner in Port of Spain was, however, restrained in his embrace of the prime minister's initiative. "I am sure that Dr. Williams' action," he reported to the Commonwealth Relations Office, "though perhaps a little precipitate, is well meant . . . he will handle matters in his own way."[14]

Nothing of consequence emerged from the overture to British Guiana from the three heads of government. Cheddi Jagan replied that he was prepared to send Ashton Chase, the president of the British Guiana Senate, to Port of Spain for talks with Williams. Finding this response somewhat insulting, Williams sent a telegram to Barrow and Bustamante stating: "While I understand the present circumstances make it impossible for Dr. Jagan to leave the territory at this time, I think you will agree that it would be preferable if the discussions took place on the basis of direct contact and not through an emissary. I therefore suggest that Dr. Jagan be informed that, in order to secure direct contact, the Premier of Barbados and Prime Ministers of Trinidad and Jamaica would be prepared at whatever inconvenience is involved to go to Georgetown for the purpose." Bustamante and Barrow quickly agreed with him.[15]

British officials were not enthusiastic about Eric Williams's potential involvement in the Guianese crisis. They distrusted him, and Williams had not helped matters when he said, in a speech on April 22, 1963, at the University of Woodford Square, that he feared British Guiana was not ready for independence. According to a report transmitted to the Colonial Office by Sir Ralph Grey, the governor of British Guiana, Williams stated that "the British could not be expected to hand over control of the territory at the present moment when there were insufficient safeguards against the abuse of minorities by the majorities and vice versa. This would create a dangerous precedent for other emerging territories." Grey thought that these statements were impolitic, commenting: "One would have supposed that Williams' speech . . . would disqualify him from effectively offering help. But things are different in the Caribbean."[16]

Williams was probably unaware of such criticisms, but if he had known about them, he would most likely have ignored them. Although he possessed a thin skin, he was markedly stubborn if convinced of the righteousness of his cause and if his nation's national interests were at stake. As Stanley J. G. Fingland, the acting British high commissioner, had telegraphed the Commonwealth Relations Office on April 21: "Dr. Williams' interest in British Guiana is based on (a) fear that increased Communist influence in British

Guiana presents a potential risk to Trinidad . . .; (b) desire to include British Guiana in his plans for closer economic and ultimately political association in the Caribbean (under his own aegis of course); (c) willingness to acquire prestige as an international figure if this can be achieved consistently with his own objectives." Fingland believed, however, that "Dr. Williams' offer of his good offices is well intentioned." But, he warned, Williams "will of course play the hand his own way, treating British Guiana as he has said he would, as independent, and the way may not be our way."[17]

All of these and other overtures to Cheddi Jagan received a lukewarm reception, even though British Guiana had become paralyzed by the strike provoked by the Labour Relations Bill. Jagan's seeming lack of interest in the tripartite offer of mediation annoyed Williams, who told High Commissioner Costar that he would not continue to press the offer and that he was "writing B. G. off." In view of his fear that Jagan would establish a one-party communist state in his country, Williams proposed that British Guiana be given a new constitution containing effective safeguards to protect the opposition. He recommended a constitution based on the Jamaican model, which enshrined the role of the opposition, in contrast to the one in Trinidad, which had weaker clauses for its protection. According to Costar, Williams also urged the creation of an "impartial commission to re-define electoral boundaries on the basis of voters and not of populations (thus reducing somewhat the Indian preponderance)." All constitutional guarantees would be ensured by a United Nations force.[18]

Suspicious of Williams's motives, British officials were quick to dismiss these proposals. Referring specifically to the prime minister's suggestion regarding electoral boundaries, Edwin L. Sykes in the Commonwealth Relations Office observed contemptuously that there "is nothing in this suggestion and it shows the shallowness of Dr. Williams' judgment if he believes that all which is required to solve the problem of British Guiana is now to endow that territory with a Constitution based on what Dr. Williams considers to be the 'Jamaican model' rather than the 'Trinidadian model.' "[19]

In a conversation with Costar on November 12, 1963, Williams returned to the subject of British Guiana. He voiced his concerns about the policy of proportional representation that the United Kingdom was preparing to implement. Not wanting to irritate the British, he assured Costar that he "would not oppose the Secretary of State's decision." He believed, however, that British Guiana was not ready for independence in view of the existing

circumstances. The African leaders with whom he had discussed this question supported his stance, he said, provided that he endorsed their position
on Southern Rhodesia—that is, that the British remove the white minority
government in that colony.[20]

Despite his frustrations with Jagan, Williams continued his efforts to find
an answer to the British Guianese problem. Above all, he sought a West
Indian solution. When a United Nations subcommittee dealing with British
Guiana decided to visit the country, he instructed Trinidad's representative
to the United Nations to seek a delay. In a letter of July 11, 1963, to his envoy,
Williams wrote: "You will suggest, therefore, that in the circumstances, any
intervention from outside the West Indies should be eschewed until the West
Indians have had an opportunity to make their further approach to the issue
and to assess the results of that approach."[21]

Williams had hoped that when Jagan, Barrow, and Bustamante visited
Trinidad and Tobago on July 22, 1963, to attend the first meeting of the
newly created Big Four Conference, the leaders would have an opportunity to
discuss the Guianese situation. The matter was indeed raised with Jagan at
the conference, and Williams reported that Bustamante said "something
like this" to Jagan: "Look here, Jagan, I do not want to get into any discussions on this matter; I do not want any argument. What we are asking for is
this: that Williams, Barrow, and Bustamante should meet in the same room
with Burnham, D'Aguiar, and Jagan and that we would try to work out a
constitution in that atmosphere."[22]

According to Williams, there was no response—"neither favorable nor
unfavorable"—by Jagan to the proposal on that occasion or later. Nevertheless, the three leaders insisted that "certain safeguards" be included in
British Guiana's constitution before it proceeded to independence. These
included a bill of rights, an independent judiciary, an auditor general, a
Public Services Commission, and the inclusion of a senate in the parliamentary system. The three leaders also wanted elections in British Guiana to be
supervised by the United Nations. Jagan declined to respond to any of these
proposals, leading a disappointed Williams to admit that the exercise had
been a complete failure.[23]

In spite of this setback, Williams retained a strong interest in the British Guianese situation. When colonial secretary Duncan Sandys decided to
introduce proportional representation in the colony in October 1963, he
was concerned that he would antagonize Williams. Apprehensive that Indo-

Trinidadians would follow the Guianese example and launch a campaign for proportional representation, Williams adamantly opposed this electoral strategy. Shortly after Sandys made his decision, Edwin Sykes recommended that officials begin "softening up" Williams for "proportional representation, which is a solution he will not like."[24] The secretary of state quickly dispatched conciliatory letters to Williams inviting his understanding of the reasons for introducing proportional representation in British Guiana. In response, Williams assured him that:

1. We would be most unwilling here in Trinidad to do or say anything that would impede a settlement, because we are satisfied that some settlement is absolutely necessary;
2. Equally we will be most unwilling, if and when a settlement is arrived at, to do or say anything that would make the implementation of such settlement more difficult than it could confidently be expected to be;
3. We would consider it our duty to give all possible support to any settlement which we might feel is a satisfactory one, given all the miserable circumstances and wretched difficulties involved.[25]

The secretary of state was delighted with Williams's assurances of his support. His response was immediate, informing Williams on November 1 that "I cannot tell you how much I appreciate your message . . . [and] I shall look forward to keeping in the closest touch with you throughout and continuing to exchange views as the situation develops."[26]

♦ ♦ ♦ ♦ ♦ British officials never abandoned their commitment to seek Williams's blessing of the new electoral system. But they also never lost their distrust of him, scrutinizing all of his actions for hidden motives. Williams was willing to mute his public criticisms of British policy if that helped to facilitate a cure for Guiana's pain, even if he disagreed with the medicine. He was no admirer of the Guianese premier and had no tears to shed if and when his political demise occurred. Referring to the new electoral system, Williams admitted to Stanley Fingland of the British High Commissioner's Office in Port of Spain that "this solution is very difficult but Jagan has brought it on himself." Fingland reported to the Commonwealth Relations Office that Williams spoke in "a very disparaging way" about Jagan, describing him as "a frightful, frightful man."[27]

Overall, Fingland was pleased by Williams's cooperative stance on the

Guianese question. He thought that the policy of including him in the picture "has been so far a successful one." But he cautioned that Williams's public "attitude" will "be very dependent on how things develop both in British Guiana and in relation to the Opposition here." Fingland predicted that "it will pay us to continue to keep Dr. Williams as closely informed as possible."[28]

British Guiana's agony was further discussed informally at the second Big Four Conference, held in Jamaica during January 13–17, 1964. As Williams noted in his opening address, the leaders were meeting "in response to a general recognition by the four countries participating in the conference of the urgent necessity for presenting as far as possible a united front of the Commonwealth Caribbean countries to the increasing pressures of an increasingly confused world."[29]

Although Eric Williams and Sir Alexander Bustamante wanted to place Guiana's problems on the meeting's formal agenda, Cheddi Jagan demurred but agreed to informal discussions. The British high commissioner in Jamaica, Alec Morley, said that Errol Barrow was also not particularly keen on discussing British Guiana. Bustamante, in Morley's opinion, "probably nursed a simple hope that it might be possible to change Dr. Jagan's ideology and external policy." The high commissioner thought that "possibly only Williams felt any strong direct interest in furthering the resolution of the internal tensions in British Guiana both on the merits (because of their implications for Trinidad and Tobago) and in order to further his own ambitions as regional leader."[30]

The private conversations between Jagan and the other leaders resolved nothing. In a characteristic fit of pique, Bustamante declared that he was "through with Jagan" and forbade any of his ministers to see him off at the airport. Bustamante had no patience with Jagan's Marxism and, according to Morley, "had little use" for him personally. The Jamaican prime minister told the press on January 17 that his country's support for British Guiana's independence "would depend on Dr. Jagan's attitude toward the West."[31]

Eric Williams was equally disappointed with the failure to reach any agreement with Jagan. He was incensed that Jagan "was not prepared to accept" a "general declaration of principle on British Guiana" that Williams had drafted. The declaration asserted that Guiana's problem should be settled in the Caribbean by Caribbean leaders. It alleged that "the Commonwealth Caribbean countries, including British Guiana, are feeling today the full effects of centuries of colonial control and the deficiencies inherited from that control." The external world "tends far too often to take them for granted and to regard their independence as purely nominal." The statement urged solidarity among the Commonwealth Caribbean countries in defense of their vital interests. Acknowledging that Williams, Bustamante, and Barrow had ideological differences with Jagan, the declaration affirmed: "Whatever the particular variations of constitutional forms or economic practices which they may each adopt, consistent with the accepted conventions of national sovereignty, the fact is that what the Commonwealth Caribbean have in common is more important than the incidental differences of emphasis or temperament which may occasionally divide them."

With British Guiana squarely on the minds of the Anglophone leaders, Williams's draft statement embraced the "overriding principle" of independence, for it as well as other territories, "just so soon as the inescapable constitutional and other procedures can be settled." It rejected the "imposition of a settlement by the United Kingdom," because this was incompatible with the spirit of independence. Instead, the four leaders would meet in Tobago on February 1 and 2, 1964, "to begin consideration of the details involved in its implementation."[32]

Jagan told the press that he was unable to endorse this "declaration of principle" because the different approaches to foreign policy prevented a unified stand by the four leaders on the British Guianese question. This assertion, though accurate in acknowledging the foreign policy disagreements between Williams, Barrow, and Bustamante, on the one hand, and Jagan, on the other, was not the complete story. Offended by Jagan's statement to the press, Williams obtained Bustamante and Barrow's agreement to release the "declaration of principle." In a conversation with Park Wollam, the interim American chargé d'affaires in Port of Spain, Williams explained that Jagan had declined to endorse the declaration because it was not sufficiently strong in its condemnation of a British-imposed electoral solution. In addition, Jagan looked askance at any suggestion in the document that the intervention of the West Indian leaders in the Guianese problem was in response to a request by him. According to Williams, if Jagan had accepted the declaration, all four leaders would have met in Tobago to draft changes in the Guianese constitution and then invite Peter D'Aguiar and Forbes Burnham to meet with them for talks.

During the same conversation, Williams acknowledged that his "principal fear" was the establishment of a second communist "center" in the Caribbean. He was, according to the American diplomat, "not particularly worried about Guianese subversives unless they had been trained abroad, for example in Cuba or in Communist Europe." Williams believed that Jagan "would never be able to establish a state organized along Marxist lines but it was indeed a worrying possibility that foreign trained subversives might make British Guiana their base."[33]

Another reason that Jagan rejected the declaration of principle was that the other leaders might try to propose a settlement of British Guiana's problems that was not in his own best interest or that of the PPP. The Big Four Conference had convinced Jagan that his point of view and ideological positions found little support among his colleagues. On the fourth day of the meeting Bustamante had made matters worse by attacking Jagan's association with Cuba and his claim of political neutrality. Although Williams would later say that he "washes his hands" of Jagan, he could hardly ignore Guiana's difficulties in view of their implications for Trinidad's internal harmony.[34]

When he visited Africa in February, March, and April 1964, Williams discussed the problems in British Guiana with African leaders and other officials with whom he met. President Kwame Nkrumah of Ghana and President Ben Bella of Algeria had developed a keen interest in developments in British Guiana. In February 1963 Nkrumah had sent a Ghanaian delegation to Guiana to try to resolve the crisis. Ben Bella and Jagan were ideologically similar and seemed to have developed a close friendship as well. Williams did not welcome any African involvement in British Guiana's affairs, preferring a Caribbean resolution of the conflict. Moreover, he questioned Nkrumah's sincerity, telling the British high commissioner in Monrovia, Liberia, that there was "the probability that Dr. Nkrumah had sent his mediators merely in order to be able to say that Her Majesty's Government had once more sabotaged an honest attempt to reconcile the parties."[35]

Williams lobbied extensively against African support for Jagan and his administration. As the acting British high commissioner in Tanganyika (later Tanzania) reported after conversing with the prime minister: "Williams had done his best to undermine any African support for Dr. Jagan. In the end, this did not prove difficult. He had found little regard for Jagan in Ghana. A member of the Ghanaian good will mission to British Guiana had commented to him in Accra that Jagan 'was not even a good Communist—he just spouted the language without understanding it; he was basically just an out-and-out racialist.'" The acting high commissioner also reported that Williams felt that "the East African Governments were not likely to cause us any trouble" over British Guiana. In particular, President Jomo Kenyatta of Kenya had "formed a poor impression of Jagan" when he attended his nation's independence celebrations.[36]

On returning home, Williams made a similar report to Norman Costar. According to Costar, "Dr. Williams believes that his tour of Africa, and especially his talks on British Guiana with Dr. Nkrumah and President Ben Bella (hitherto Dr. Jagan's friends) have undermined the position of the British Guiana Premier in the Afro-Asian group."[37]

During his African tour Williams had sought to assure U.S. officials that he could assist them on matters relating to Soviet influence in British Guiana and Cuba. He told the American ambassador in Cairo, for example, that he had advised the Soviet ambassador to the United Kingdom that his government should not involve itself so deeply in the internal affairs of Cuba and British Guiana. Obviously taking the side of the United States, Williams also said that he wanted the U.S. State Department to inform him about the extent of Soviet support for the Jagan government. He promised that he would use this information against Jagan, who was "playing the fool" in British Guiana. It is not clear whether the State Department acquiesced.[38] (In February 1962 it had denied Williams's request for information on communism in British Guiana and the Dominican Republic, stating rather incredibly that it had "no appropriate unclassified information on this subject.")[39]

♦ ♦ ♦ ♦ ♦ The worsening political climate in British Guiana during the spring of 1964 forced Cheddi Jagan to reconsider the offer of mediation by Barrow, Williams, and Bustamante. But, as his subsequent behavior would indicate, he never had much confidence in their ability to resolve the crisis. Of the three Caribbean leaders who were potential candidates to act as mediator, Eric Williams was the obvious choice, given the ethnic composition of his nation-state and his acknowledged interest in British Guiana's problems. On April 7, 1964, its deputy premier, Brindley Benn, requested that Trinidad raise the Guiana question at the Commonwealth Prime Ministers' Meeting scheduled that summer. A month later, Jagan formally asked Williams to mediate the dispute in his country. At Williams's invitation, Jagan and a number of his ministers were visiting Trinidad at the time to discuss matters arising from Williams's recent trip to Africa, Europe, Canada, and the United States.

Williams readily accepted Jagan's invitation. Evidently, he felt that his anti-Jagan stance in Africa would not compromise his ability to be an impartial mediator. On the other hand, the invitation provided him with an opportunity to resolve a burning dispute in the Caribbean, while simultaneously enhancing his stature at home and abroad. Williams indicated to Jagan that the Cabinet of Trinidad and Tobago would be asked to approve his role as mediator. As a condition of his acceptance, Williams required a free hand to summon to Port of Spain for talks all political party leaders in British Guiana, as well as others whose opinions and counsel might be useful. He also wanted the discretion to keep "other interested parties" advised of developments. Jagan assented to these provisions and agreed to return to Trinidad "as soon as possible."

According to Williams, the politically wily Jagan then asked that he propose that the United Kingdom defer the new electoral system while the talks in Trinidad were in progress. Jagan, Williams reported, attributed the political difficulties in British Guiana solely to the newly devised system of proportional representation. Williams said that he was unable to do this. Jagan then suggested that the talks in Trinidad be restricted to himself and Burnham and their parties, and that D'Aguiar be excluded. Williams also rejected this request, emphasizing that he needed "complete freedom" if he were to accept the assignment.

These issues evidently decided, Williams held lengthy talks with Jagan and his visiting team "to ascertain where, if anywhere, a wall had been set up by the ruling PPP that would make concessions difficult." In these discussions, which took place on Saturday, May 2, and Sunday, May 3, Williams explored such matters as:

1. [The nature of] consultation with the Opposition;
2. An upper chamber based on proportional representation and with revised powers;
3. A coalition government;
4. The removal of the police from Ministerial control;
5. International guarantees of the
     (i) neutrality and
     (ii) territorial integrity of British Guiana;

6. [The nature of] association with the West Indies;
7. Independence of the judiciary;
8. [A] Bill of Rights;
9. Appointments to the Public Service without political interference;
10. Special legislation in respect of racial difficulties;
11. Constitutional provision for the recognition of unions and collective bargaining;
12. Supervision of British Guiana for a prescribed period by either the United Nations or the Commonwealth;
13. Emergency regulations;
14. Special entrenchment of particular clauses of the constitution.

These informal discussions concluded, Williams wrote to Burnham and D'Aguiar to ask whether they would be prepared to participate in the effort to resolve the crisis and "to come to Trinidad, with such associates as you may consider necessary, within a few days." Meanwhile, the Trinidad Cabinet quickly authorized Williams to accept the mediation assignment on May 4. D'Aguiar readily accepted Williams's invitation and agreed to visit Trinidad on May 6. After some difficulty in reaching Burnham, he agreed to meet with Prime Minister Williams on May 10.[40]

Burnham's acceptance of Williams's invitation amounted to a remarkable exercise in dissemblance. The next day he visited the American consul general assigned to Georgetown to discuss the Williams initiative. Burnham wanted to know whether the United States was "privy to Williams' efforts and [to make] sure [the] U.S. [was] not backing these efforts." The consul general assured Burnham that Williams "was strictly on his own" and that he believed that "Williams['] mediation hinged essentially around [the] same old coalition idea already so familiar to Burnham." Acknowledging that that was "also his impression," Burnham said that he did not want to waste time going to Trinidad for "this exercise in futility." He planned to go only for "courtesy sake." Burnham asserted that insofar as Guiana's problems were concerned, Williams only wished to "pontificate." Burnham, according to the consul general, criticized D'Aguiar for going to Trinidad "so promptly" rather than waiting "to coordinate strategy with the PNC."[41]

As far as Jagan was concerned, Burnham admitted to the American consul general that he was not amenable to compromise. He preferred to confront more violence and "oppose [the] well armed PPP onslaught" with nothing but "grease guns" than agree to "any compromise which would keep Jagan in power."[42] Unaware that Burnham was not acting in good faith and sensitive to the need for secrecy in the talks, Williams requested the newspapers in Trinidad and Tobago to refrain from publishing any comments by the visiting politicians since they could exacerbate the Guianese situation.[43]

In his meeting with Williams, Peter D'Aguiar accused Jagan of having an ideological fixation because, D'Aguiar contended, his government received loans from Cuba and the Soviet Union. He thought that British Guiana must "either follow the path to Marxism or the path away from Marxism." D'Aguiar felt that Jagan was losing popular support and might incite a race war to remain in power. The U F leader supported a coalition government but only if elected; such a government could not be imposed on the country. He saw the partition of the colony as the only alternative to continuing rule by Jagan. As D'Aguiar put it, "If you want a guarantee, the only guarantee is partition." The leader of the U F also advocated the removal of the police from ministerial control and the establishment of a Commission of Enquiry into the recent and continuing disturbances in Guiana. The commission should be -empowered to ascertain responsibility and award compensation for damages. D'Aguiar affirmed his support for independence but said that it should not be granted for another five years. "We support independence but we are not supporting communism," he declared. "I would rather be a colony of the United Kingdom than a satellite of Russia."

Throughout his eight hours of talks with Williams, D'Aguiar expressed an implacable opposition to Jagan as a person and as the head of government. He believed that no "sane" man or party could collaborate with the premier. For a coalition government to be established, Jagan would have to disavow communism and the P P P could not be entrusted with the premiership, the Ministry of Home Affairs, the Ministry of Finance, and the Ministry of External Affairs. Clearly, if his proposals were adopted, Jagan and the P P P would have no meaningful role in the government of British Guiana.

Forbes Burnham met with Williams for seven hours. He supported holding new elections to resolve the crisis. Burnham affirmed the P N C's endorsement of a bill of rights and human freedoms similar to those enshrined in the constitutions of Jamaica and Trinidad. He proposed the creation of an independent Elections Commission and a Judicial Service Commission whose members would be nominated by the premier, the leader of the opposition, and the Bar Association. In addition, Burnham advocated the creation of a Police Service Commission composed of a representative of the Public Service Commission and a nominee of the premier and of the leader of the opposition. He wanted the nature and scope of consultation with the opposition clearly delineated in the colony's constitution.

To reduce tensions and to lead the colony to independence, Burnham expressed his support for a "national" or coalition government. He thought that this would also improve British Guiana's international image. He endorsed a "serious declaration of non-commitment to existing power blocs" and closer collaboration with the British Caribbean area on industrial development policy, foreign affairs, and economic cooperation particularly with regard to sugar and bauxite.

To stop the proliferation of weapons in his country, Burnham proposed that all arms be turned over to the military, and he supported police and military searches of houses or people without warrants. He wanted a general amnesty declared to allow all unlicensed arms and ammunition to be turned in during a two-week period; failure to do so would constitute a criminal offense for which the penalty would be imprisonment. Burnham stressed that unless the PPP accepted these conditions, there would be no basis for discussion. Should a national government be established, he said, his party would expect to be assigned the Ministries of Home Affairs, External Affairs, Education, Housing, and possibly Agriculture. A government formed by him would not expropriate property and would provide fair and adequate compensation in the event that nationalization occurred.

Although the talks with D'Aguiar and Burnham proceeded smoothly, difficulties soon arose. On May 8 Janet Jagan, the minister of home affairs, appeared before the United Nations Committee of Twenty-Four in New York to express her government's opposition to the United Kingdom's introduction of proportional representation in British Guiana. When he heard about her testimony, an angry Eric Williams telegraphed Premier Jagan: "Report has been received from our U.N. representative that your representative before Committee of Twenty Four has been authorized by your Government to put forward proposal to invite Commonwealth and non-Commonwealth team to discuss constitution for independence. Urgently request clarification of this position, which is difficult to reconcile with our request that Trinidad and Tobago should use its good offices to explore possibilities of a peaceful solution of present deadlock."

Prime Minister Williams also expressed displeasure at an alleged attack on D'Aguiar's property while he was in Trinidad. He seemed to attribute responsibility for this assault to Jagan and his supporters. "I must further deplore," Williams said in the telegram to Jagan, "the reported attack on the property of one of the parties in British Guiana at the very moment when he is in Trinidad at our express invitation . . . and I must formally request you to use publicly all your influence to put a stop to all activities calculated to render the present exploratory efforts abortive for such period at least as these exploratory efforts continue."

The premier was quick to respond by telegram. He did not find his wife's "representations" to the Committee of Twenty-Four to be "inconsistent" with Williams's assignment. As he explained:

> Our representative seeks to expose to United Nations American intervention and intrigue in British Guiana and American pressure on Britain to withhold independence. Committee of Twenty Four had on October 8, 1963, adopted resolution requesting appointment of constitutional experts to visit British Guiana and formulate acceptable constitution. Britain had rejected proposal on ground that Independence Conference was to be held in London later that month. The British imposition being unacceptable, my representative has now requested Committee to pursue resolution of October 8. This does not preclude your good offices to help achieve peaceful solution, which if successful, will indeed make United Nations intervention unnecessary.

Jagan was on secure ground when he charged British and American collusion in delaying independence for Guiana. Although he did not mention it in his telegram, he also knew that the two countries would welcome his removal from office as a prerequisite for awarding his country independence. On the other hand, the timing of Janet Jagan's appearance before the Committee of Twenty-Four was problematic and indicated a lack of confidence in Williams's capacity to resolve the deadlock in British Guiana. Jagan would later say that the decision to send her to New York had been made by his Cabinet before Williams agreed to mediate the conflict.The premier was incensed by Williams's remarks concerning the alleged attack on D'Aguiar's property. In his telegram to Williams, Jagan noted that he regarded "your reference to the reported attack on the property of one of the parties in British Guiana as unfortunate and reject its implications." In denying responsibility for any behavior that might compromise Williams's work, Jagan shifted the blame to the opposition. "As regards activities likely to jeopardize your efforts," he wrote, "you may be aware that sections of the press including a newspaper owned and controlled by one of the leaders of the Opposition [D'Aguiar] have been devoting their columns to rendering talks abortive."

Undeterred by these comments, Williams sent a terse cable to the premier on May 12: "Grateful if you would return to Trinidad tomorrow, Wednesday." Not surprisingly, Jagan denied the request. In a move calculated to annoy Williams, Jagan did not respond to him directly but sent his reply through the Trinidad high commissioner in Georgetown: "In view of statements made by Opposition leader, Premier would like to know whether Prime Minister considers his return at this time essential. Premier thinks that a proposal put forward by Opposition or any suggestions Prime Minister may have could be communicated to him for consideration by colleagues before his return to Trinidad if it is agreed that this is desirable."

Clearly, Jagan was being disingenuous. In the first instance, he was using an intemperate outburst by Forbes Burnham as an excuse not to return to Trinidad and participate in the talks. Addressing the students at the University of the West Indies, St. Augustine, on May 12, Burnham had declared: "I don't think that Dr. Williams can solve the problems of British Guiana. He has enough problems here in Trinidad and Tobago to solve." This comment, even if it contained some truth, was impolitic at best and insulting to the prime minister at worst.

Jagan's desire to be made privy to any proposals put forward by the opposition was unacceptable to Williams. If he had acquiesced to this unusual request, it would have compromised his role as mediator. Jagan could hardly have expected Williams to tell him what his political antagonists had said as a precondition for his return to Trinidad. On May 15 the prime minister formally responded to Jagan's cable:

> I had indicated to you that I should like to see others first before inviting you to return for general exploratory discussion, which would not necessarily be limited to the three political parties in the legislature. I consider this the appropriate stage for your return for continuation of these discussions in the context of discussions with the others. I do not consider it would be appropriate procedure to send something in writing for consid-

eration. Our exploration was not to be limited to proposals that any of the parties might or might not put forward. I therefore repeat my invitation to come to Trinidad at the earliest possible opportunity so that we can explore with you the assignment which you requested me to undertake.

Evidently Jagan found this appeal unconvincing, for on May 16 he cabled Williams his regret that "developments here preclude my return immediately." He repeated his request that he be informed about what had transpired between Williams, Burnham, and D'Aguiar in Port of Spain. "In view of urgency," Jagan wrote, "I wonder whether your Commissioner would come to Georgetown to brief me on developments or alternatively whether I might send representative to Port of Spain for same purpose." Williams's response was predictable. On May 19 he told Jagan that "briefing through an intermediary is wholly inconsistent" with his request that I "should use my good offices to explore possibilities of a settlement [and] the agreement of the leaders of the Opposition to take part." In view of these circumstances, Williams asked Jagan to give him a "firm date" so he could complete "with a minimum of delay an assignment I undertook in view of what you assured me on May 2 was the urgency of the situation in British Guiana."

But Jagan would not budge. On May 22 he informed Williams that he regretted that the "deteriorating domestic situation still prevents me from fixing a firm date for visit. I will communicate with you as soon as situation is sufficiently improved to admit of my leaving the country." Jagan was certainly correct that the domestic situation had worsened, given the marked increase in racial violence. But the violence gave him an excuse to sabotage the mediation efforts that Williams had undertaken at his behest. Jagan's absence from British Guiana for a day or two would not have exacerbated local tensions; indeed, it may well have served to ease them.

♦ ♦ ♦ ♦ ♦ The violence in British Guiana intensified throughout May. On the twenty-fourth an ugly racial clash occurred at Wismar, a rural community, leaving several people dead and their property destroyed. Still trying to keep mediation alive, Williams issued a new invitation to Jagan, Burnham, and D'Aguiar to return to Trinidad together for discussions. He asked the three leaders to issue a joint declaration calling for a truce and an end to the violence in Guiana for at least a week so that the talks could proceed in an atmosphere of calm.

Of the three leaders, D'Aguiar was the first to accept the new invitation. Burnham declined, urging Williams to visit British Guiana to observe the situation firsthand. He would only participate in joint talks if Williams went to Georgetown. Moreover, Burnham indicated that he would endorse a truce only if an amnesty were declared, allowing firearms and explosives to be turned in to the authorities, with prison sentences to follow for those who declined to do so. Jagan's response to the new Williams initiative was ambivalent. He neither accepted nor rejected the invitation but renewed his request that he be informed about the details of the discussions in Trinidad. He told Williams that because he had invited Burnham and D'Aguiar to a meeting on June 1 to explore possibilities for ending the crisis, he was unable to respond to Williams's invitation until after that date. In this instance, as in the case of Janet Jagan's appearance before the United Nations Committee of Twenty-Four, Premier Jagan was actively undermining the Williams initiative.

Rhetorically at least, Jagan still professed to support Williams's mediation efforts. But he took no responsibility for the stalemate in the discussions. On June 4 he told Williams that he still supported his initiative provided it could be shown that a continuation of the exercise was not futile. As he had done before, he blamed others for his own failure to return to Trinidad. Jagan said that Burnham's refusal to compromise on the issue of elections under proportional representation impeded his return to Trinidad. Burnham's insistence that the Guianese people should settle their own problems was yet another obstacle, as was his statement that Williams should focus on his own difficulties in Trinidad. But Jagan emphasized that if Williams related the nature of his discussions with the other leaders, he would consult with his colleagues, and, if they approved, he would return to Trinidad.

In an attempt to solicit opinions from others in Guianese society, Williams invited Richard Ishmael, the president of the Trade Union Council, and H. H. Pollydore, the general secretary, to visit Trinidad. In their meeting with Williams on May 25, the two men accused the ruling party of trying to split the unions and affirmed their support for proportional representation and a national or coalition government. They recommended the adoption of a new constitution before the elections, with provision for a president as well as a prime minister elected by the legislature who would both have seats in the Cabinet. Presumably, one of these persons would be of Indo-Guianese heritage and the other would be an African Guianese.[44]

These meetings behind him, Williams met with the American ambassador, R. G. Miner, on May 26 to discuss the state of his mediation initiative. Miner reported to the U.S. secretary of state that Williams found Pollydore and Ishmael "more realistic" than Burnham and D'Aguiar, although "they had little to offer concerning ways and means to improve public order and stability in British Guiana." Williams indicated that Jagan's failure to return to Port of Spain meant that his efforts to mediate the crisis had "probably come to an end." He believed the "plain fact was that British Guiana was not ready for independence but in [the] present world climate GOTT [the government of Trinidad and Tobago] certainly could not take such a position publicly." According to Miner, the "only hope" that Williams saw "for restricting British Guiana's capacity for making trouble in the area was [the] formation of some kind of Caribbean regional grouping to include or at least fence in British Guiana."[45]

On June 12, approximately six weeks after he had accepted Jagan's assignment, a frustrated Eric Williams submitted his report to the premier of British Guiana. Its caustic tone reflected Williams's profound disappointment in his inability to advance the peace process in the colony and his low regard for its leadership. Although he was "satisfied that the essential prerequisite for British Guiana's development is independence," he found that "independence is little more than a slogan or catch-word in British Guiana, and the political parties have failed to appreciate the necessity of achieving some broad general agreement among the majority of the population as to the conditions under which the country must proceed to Independence, both in order to promote internal stability and avoid internal strife, in order to satisfy world public opinion and not discredit the world movement against colonialism."

In Williams's opinion, Guiana was "far removed" from the "ideal basis of national independence." He based this assessment on the seemingly "permanent disorder" in the colony and the failure of efforts to achieve a coalition government and of outsiders' attempts to help settle the crisis. He had accepted Jagan's invitation to mediate because "the interests of developing nations all over the world required that yet another effort should be made to ensure the early independence of British Guiana, and therefore to find some rational and stable basis on which that independence could be built."

Williams blamed the "various parties" in British Guiana for the failure of his efforts. Forbes Burnham, he said, objected to the joint discussions being held in Trinidad instead of British Guiana. Premier Cheddi Jagan had contributed to the "lack of confidence" in his initiative by "seeking alternative mediation" while his own efforts were in progress. Here Williams was referring to Janet Jagan's appearance before the United Nations Committee of Twenty-Four and the premier's own attempts to initiate tripartite discussions in British Guiana while joint talks were taking place in Trinidad. He also believed that Peter D'Aguiar's appeal to the leader of the opposition in the United Kingdom to intervene in the Guiana dispute was unhelpful.

Williams questioned the statesmanship of British Guiana's leaders: they lacked a sustained "sense of gravity and urgency" to resolve their problems. "There was no readiness on any side," Williams asserted, "to subordinate sectional interests or personal antagonisms or ideological vagaries to the overriding national interest." The political leaders' proposed solutions to their country's predicament were "either meaningless or intransigent or not intended to be taken seriously," and their "intemperate remarks" compromised the search for answers. "Notwithstanding the grim and tragic precedents which are there today [in Guiana] for all to see," declared Williams, "the vital importance of appropriate constitutional provisions and safeguards in the Independence Constitution received perfunctory consideration." Under the circumstances, he concluded, "I find that there is no basis or reasonable hope for any accommodation between the political parties, for any resolution of the political deadlock, or for any agreement on the national and stable foundation on which the independence of British Guiana must necessarily be built."[46]

Predictably, Jagan was not pleased with the Williams report. In a letter to the Trinidadian prime minister on June 29, he expressed regret that "your efforts have not been successful." He acknowledged his disappointment with his own attempts to resolve his country's crisis, blaming Burnham's refusal to join him in a coalition government as the principal cause of his own failure. Quite correctly, Jagan blamed U.S. support of Burnham's stance: "I think that the fact is that Mr. Burnham is supported and influenced by the United States, who seem to want nothing less than the destruction of me and my Party. He increases his demands with every concession I make: proposals which he found favour with a few months ago are no longer acceptable to him. It is clear that he feels that the cards are stacked against the Government and so has hardened his attitude."

Jagan was upset that Williams had released his report to the press since it was "a Report addressed to me [and] produced as a result of my request to you." He noted that it contained "a number of inaccuracies" that "should be corrected for the records." Jagan took issue with Williams's claim that Jagan had agreed that "[the] discussions would not necessarily be limited to the leaders of the political parties in the British Guiana Legislature." His delegation "has no recollection of any such reservation being expressed, and indeed was surprised that Mr. R. A. Ishmael was summoned to Trinidad and Tobago for discussion."

Jagan also contested Williams's assertion that the premier had asked him to persuade the United Kingdom to delay the implementation of the new proportional representation electoral system "whilst exploratory efforts were in progress on the ground that the tension in British Guiana was to be ascribed solely to the new system of proportional representation." This was "not correct." On the contrary, "My Attorney General and I made it quite clear that the current disturbances had their origin in an industrial dispute in the sugar industry. The employment of scabs mainly of another race caused the struggle for union recognition to gather racial overtones. We added that existing tensions were also in part due to the feeling that the imposition of proportional representation by the British Government was aimed at destroying the People's Progressive Party and the Government."

Jagan defended his decision not to return to Trinidad for the talks, repeating his earlier contention that "events at home prevented me from leaving the country during this period." His request to be made privy to the proposals made by the opposition "was reasonable in the light of the situation in British Guiana at the time and of the pronouncements of the Opposition leaders." In addition, Jagan rejected Williams's conclusion that his government's representatives who appeared before the United Nations Committee of Twenty-Four interfered with the mediation process. These representatives, he explained, were "aimed to the United Nations foreign intervention and intrigue in British Guiana and foreign pressure on Britain to withhold independence." Jagan could also not agree with Williams's statement that "my efforts to discuss our problems with my colleagues in British Guiana" impeded the mediation. He reminded Williams "of the horror that news of the disturbances at Wismar evoked in this country." He did not think "that in such circumstances my efforts to secure a meeting with the leaders of the Opposition needed to be justified."

Premier Jagan recounted his various attempts to achieve a compromise with the opposition. "I have made every effort to work out some sort of accommodation with Mr. Burnham, not only now, but since 1957, without success." He feared that "interracial relations in British Guiana will be damaged beyond repair" if something was not done immediately to "restore normal relations." Accordingly, he asked Prime Minister Williams to place his country's problems on the agenda of the forthcoming Commonwealth Prime Ministers' Conference. He was certain, he concluded on a conciliatory note, that "there is room for the working out of a genuine constitutional compromise and settlement by a Commonwealth team."[47]

It is hardly surprising that Williams's attempts to mediate the crisis in Guiana had failed. To begin with, he did not inspire the confidence of the Guianese leaders. Jagan's invitation to mediate the conflict notwithstanding, the three major politicians in British Guiana looked askance at any interference in their internal affairs by outsiders. In addition, none of them wanted Williams to increase his stature in the Caribbean by success in Guiana. Such was the pernicious nature of the crippling rivalries and jealousies in the region's politics. Williams, on his part, was never a consistent admirer of the Guianese leaders, especially Jagan. As early as December 1, 1962, for example, he had told Ambassador Miner that "we in Trinidad know how to cut Jagan down to size, and will do so when the time is right." But, he added, he could not do so "when it would appear that we were acting simply as American agents." Six months later, Williams said that he had "written off the idea of preserving good relations with Dr. Jagan."[48] Williams's acknowledged personal, ideological, and political antipathy to Premier Jagan was not helpful and raises questions about the integrity of the mediation process over which he presided.

Forbes Burnham's disingenuous stance on Williams's mediating efforts was not constructive, either. Basking in the clandestine support of the Americans, Burnham was unwilling to reach any compromise with Jagan that would endanger his chances of becoming the head of government or undermine his support from his friends outside the country. Two weeks after Burnham visited Port of Spain to meet with Williams, Ambassador Miner reported that Burnham's behavior was allegedly based on his expectation of U.S. support. The Trinidadian commissioner in Georgetown had told him that "Williams' mediation efforts [were] stymied principally by attitude of Burnham who claims U.S. supports him and approves his refusal [to] consider joining coalition with Jagan."[49]

These personality issues, political jealousies, and intrigues aside, the Williams mediation initiative confronted insurmountable problems. Given the deteriorating political situation in British Guiana, the talks were doomed before they began. The strike in the sugar industry was a major impediment, producing much violence, unrest, and chaos. When Williams wrote his report to Premier Jagan on June 12, 1964, the strike was already 118 days old. During the three weeks that led up to June 5, 16 people had died, 243 had been wounded, and 315 had been arrested. During the eleven awful days that immediately preceded that date, 365 houses had been damaged or destroyed. By the time the strike ended in late July, 166 people had lost their lives and over 800 had been wounded; approximately 1,400 buildings, mostly houses, were razed. In addition, many cane fields were destroyed by arson.

As the situation worsened, Janet Jagan, as minister of home affairs and the official responsible for internal security, resigned on May 22. She charged that the police force was controlled by the government's opponents and rejected her authority. Premier Cheddi Jagan, seeking to exploit the situation politically, declined to name a successor to his wife. This forced the colonial governor to assume responsibility for internal security, a role he exercised until mid-December 1964. Employing his emergency powers, the governor on June 13 ordered the detention of 36 persons, including 34 members of the PPP and 2 members of the PNC, as well as the arrest of 6 PPP members of the legislature—among them, Deputy Premier Brindley Benn. The governor's dramatic action reduced the level of violence temporarily, only to have it reappear with increased vigor in July.

The violence began to abate in August, partly because the bitter and racially divisive strike in the sugar industry had ended. The governor had also used his powers to disarm the civilian population in the coastal areas, where violence had become almost endemic. Further, the creation of a multi-racial Home Guard eased tensions considerably. Above all, the people of British Guiana had grown tired of violence, arson, and murder and welcomed the uncertain truce.

♦ ♦ ♦ ♦ ♦ The difficult political climate that existed throughout the spring and summer months helps to explain Eric Williams's failure to mediate the Guianese crisis successfully. Williams, the anticolonialist, was highly critical of the governor's assumption of emergency powers in June, since "the control of the intensified lawlessness and disorder has now been transferred to the hands of the colonial power." But British Guianese leaders also guaranteed the failure of the Williams initiative by their political grandstanding and inability to place their country's interest above their narrow partisan concerns and their penchant for blaming others for its difficulties.

Peter D'Aguiar, for example, was not inclined to place the national interest above his own. In rejecting Burnham and Jagan's call for a coalition government, D'Aguiar admitted: "I am not desirous of pulling Dr. Jagan's chestnuts out of the fire. Dr. Jagan is sinking in the mud he himself created. To try and help him out only means getting dragged in the mud too." Never an enthusiastic supporter of the Williams initiative, Forbes Burnham also questioned the efficacy of his role, noting that "in this kind of atmosphere a negotiable solution is an absolute impossibility."[50] These leaders could summon neither the courage nor the statesmanship to address the serious problems that they had helped to create and that they continued to exploit for partisan ends.

Having made this direct, albeit unsuccessful, foray into the political quagmire in British Guiana, Eric Williams seemed unwilling and unable to extricate himself. In June 1964 he instructed Trinidad's permanent representative to the United Nations, Sir Ellis Clarke, to convey his proposals for a Guiana settlement to the British mission in New York. In his meeting with Sir Hilton Poynton, Britain's representative to the United Nations, Clarke noted that his government had concluded that Guiana's problems had to be solved expeditiously to avoid the risk of a major East-West confrontation. He said that Trinidad agreed with the United Kingdom that the political leaders in British Guiana had not shown the capacity to govern. Indeed, the country was not ready for and "did not deserve" independence.

Any grant of independence to Guiana, Clarke opined, would be disastrous, since there would be an inevitable breakdown of law and order. The Trinidadian government feared that if Cheddi Jagan were in control, he would seek assistance from "undesirable" quarters, meaning Cuba or the Soviet Union. Clarke believed that this would produce an immediate confrontation with the United States, a development that would be fraught with risks for the Caribbean area. Clarke was highly critical of the United Nations Committee of Twenty-Four, which he accused of making incessant accusations of "imperialism" and "divide and rule," thereby adding to the difficulty of Britain's task in Guiana. Any solution, he asserted, must meet the approval of the United States in view of its interest in the future of British Guiana.[51]

Under the circumstances, Ellis Clarke expressed the willingness of his government to help the British "get off the present hook" in British Guiana, where they had been "taking all the kicks" for a situation that they were powerless to control. Williams's desire to help the British, as articulated by Clarke, was not as altruistic as it appeared. Two months earlier, the prime minister had instructed John O'Halloran, Trinidad's minister of agriculture, industry, and trade, to tell British officials that since he, Williams, was being helpful to their government on the Guiana question, he hoped that they would be generous to him in return.[52]

Sir Ellis Clarke, acting on Williams's behalf, proposed that the United Kingdom set an early date for British Guiana's independence, perhaps October 1965 or January 1966. In the interim, the colony would become a trustee of the United Nations. His government believed that if Britain left the scene, most of the existing turmoil would dissipate. Under United Nations trusteeship, the secretary general would appoint a commissioner to replace the colonial governor and oversee government operations. Once "a suitable formula" had been worked out, the commissioner would arrange to hold national elections and prepare the colony for independence. The Trinidadian government believed that a New Zealander would be best suited to assume the duties of commissioner, as his country had had no prior association with British Guiana and he could be expected to be impartial. Efforts should be made, however, to appoint nationals of other Commonwealth countries to his staff. Eric Williams specifically excluded nationals of England, Australia, Canada, and the African and Asian nations, as well as communists, from consideration for the job of commissioner.[53]

This proposal received a cool reception in the Colonial Office. Britain had no intention of involving the United Nations in the internal affairs of its colonies, as this would have meant an admission of failure to solve an essentially imperial matter. In dismissing the plan, Sir Hilton Poynton said flatly that "it offers no solution for British Guiana." He thought that it would be irresponsible to fix a date for independence without first removing the obstacles to it. Poynton doubted very much that the United Nations would assume the financial burden—probably £3 million or more—attendant upon its assumption of the trusteeship. Moreover, he believed that the violence in Guiana would increase if Britain departed. In any event, the Williams plan "would involve the United Nations, but would do nothing to quiet American fears that an independent Guiana under Jagan would be a Communist satellite, or to keep out Cuban and other Communist influences."[54]

This rejection not withstanding, Williams presented a similar proposal at the Commonwealth Prime Ministers' Conference held in London later that summer. It failed to receive any support, not even from Donald Sangster, the acting prime minister of Jamaica. Opposition leader Norman Manley chastised Sangster for his failure to support Williams, but this was not representative of Jamaican opinion. The Jamaican daily tabloid, the *Star*, was closer to the nation's pulse when it attacked Manley for his "elite kinship with anti-Jamaican Eric," characterizing Williams's ideas as "impracticable." Jamaicans were incensed when Williams declared that the Commonwealth "has meant little in our part of the world," prompting Donald Sangster to assure the other prime ministers that Jamaica attached considerable importance to its Commonwealth ties.[55]

Betraying his frustration at the unfavorable reception of his proposals, Williams once again threatened to ignore developments in British Guiana. In September he told Norman Costar that Guiana no longer interested him, repeating his opposition to proportional representation and declaring that should Burnham win the upcoming elections, the British would find him as bad as, and possibly worse than, Jagan. The only solution would be to get rid of both Jagan and Burnham.[56]

But on December 7, 1964, Election Day, the Guianese people had other ideas. Held under the new and controversial system of proportional representation, the entire country formed one constituency and each of the parties submitted a list of candidates. Consequently, the electorate voted for parties and not for individuals. Under the system, the number of seats in the fifty-three-member legislature won by each party reflected the proportion of votes that it had received. When the votes were counted, the results were as shown in Table 2.

Had a system of proportional representation not been implemented, the PPP would have won 20 seats, with 45.8 percent of the votes; the PNC 13; and the UF 2. An extraordinarily high 96.3 percent of registered voters went to the polls. Had a "first past the post" system been in operation, the PPP with its projected 20 seats would have been a minority government, thereby guaranteeing the continuation of political chaos. Although Cheddi Jagan was unable to command majority support in the House of Assembly because

TABLE 2 ♦ Results of 1964 General Election in British Guiana

Party	Votes	Seats
People's Progressive Party	109,332	24
People's National Congress	96,657	22
United Force	29,612	7
Guiana United Muslims Party	1,334	—
Justice Party	1,194	—
National Labour Front	224	—
Peace and Equality Party	177	—

the PPP had only 24 seats and a coalition with the PNC or the UF was infeasible, he declined to resign as premier in protest against the new electoral system that had resulted in his impending removal from office. The colonial governor had no choice but to dismiss him and swear in Forbes Burnham as the new premier of a coalition government consisting of members of the PNC and the UF.

♦ ♦ ♦ ♦ ♦ The Burnham-D'Aguiar administration succeeded in restoring some modicum of stability to British Guiana during its first year in office. Relieved, the colonial authorities began to make preparations for independence, hoping that internal peace would prevail. At a conference held in the fall of 1965, the decision was made to grant independence to the colony in the following summer.

Burnham's assumption of the reins of government did not reduce Williams's concern about the fate of British Guiana. He distrusted Burnham, and that sentiment was amply reciprocated. During the early months of the Burnham administration, Williams kept his distance, watching developments largely from a posture of interested and often irritated silence. When the Big Four Conference was held in British Guiana in March 1965, Williams declined to attend—in part, because a strike of sugarcane workers in Trinidad required his attention. Still, the Nation, the PNM's news organ, implored Williams to boycott the meeting for other reasons. It is likely that he had inspired the article, given his antipathy to Burnham. In an open letter to Williams, the Nation related an encounter that "we" had with "four representatives" of the "ordinary man in the street." Concerned for Williams's safety in Guiana, the "ordinary men" urged him to stay in Trinidad. The men, the open letter continued, "were of the opinion that the prestige you acquired over the years as the strongest protagonist of independence in these parts and of the defunct West Indies Federation and as the arch enemy of colonialism, that this prestige was now to be used to bolster a government nurtured in the very bosom and tradition of colonialism. They meant, they said, no offence to the present government of Mr. Forbes Burnham because, as they said, 'Burnham was our boy; he is one of us.' What they did not like was the means whereby the government came into being."

The letter reminded the prime minister that "British Guiana is today what you deplore—a mess created by colonial powers, imperialists, governments who can see only 'red' and who must have around them only persons who would do their bidding or through whom they can carry out their wishes." There was no reason why Williams "should go getting your fingers burnt drawing out of the imperialist fire, colonial chestnuts." The letter went on to assure him that "the mess" was not of his creation, so he should not "wallow in it." Williams should allow all those who created "the mess" and "all those who created it who are sitting smiling by, manipulating the strings come out from behind the stage and mend the figures, change the scenery and fix everything before the world audience." The letter ended on a high Shakespearian note: "We appeal to you in the name of political decency, for your own political prestige which you have so painstakingly built up over the years since your student days to keep hands off. In the words of that popular hit parade song 'Please stay, don't go.' Or, if that is too modern, we appeal in the sober and respected language of Shakespeare: It is meet that noble minds shall keep ever with their likes."[57]

Whether Williams inspired this letter or not, there is no doubt that it reflected his view of Burnham and the government over which he presided. Williams's absence from the Big Four Conference exacerbated the tensions between the two men, and they continued to annoy one another over seemingly minor policy decisions. When Burnham signed a new trade agreement with Jamaica, for example, the British high commissioner said that an angry Eric Williams responded by banning the importation of British Guianese plantains. Reportedly, Burnham then threatened to purchase his country's main imports from Trinidad elsewhere. Williams was also displeased when British Guiana, Barbados, and Antigua created the short-lived Caribbean Free Trade Association (CARIFTA) at Burnham's initiative.[58]

Although Williams repeatedly said that British Guiana no longer concerned him, his public statements did not reflect his private anxieties. In fact, he confided to High Commissioner Costar his fear that if Guiana were granted independence under Burnham, Jagan's supporters would create turmoil that could spill over to Trinidad. Williams hoped that the British would keep his potential difficulties in mind when they acted. Costar did not believe that Williams's concerns should be allowed to determine British policy, but he felt that he should be kept fully informed of any developments. After all, Costar maintained, despite Williams's criticisms of the United Kingdom's policy toward British Guiana in private, he had been generally helpful in public. The perpetuation of this policy would continue to pay rich dividends, Costar believed.

The visit of Trinidad's deputy prime minister, Patrick Solomon, to British Guiana in March 1965, representing Williams at the Big Four Conference, seemingly offered the prospect of a thaw in the relations between the two countries. Although Solomon had a favorable impression of Burnham, he had his doubts about the wisdom of racial balance in the police force if that would reduce its efficiency. According to Norman Costar, Solomon, "who is inclined to be a negro racialist, or at any rate to have little patience with East Indian maneuverings, said that talk of racial balance in the police and security forces in British Guiana was not very sensible if the objective was the maintenance of an efficient police force." Solomon's generally favorable assessment of Burnham, Costar hoped, would have a positive impact on Williams's attitude toward independence for British Guiana. Costar noted that in the past, "Dr. Williams has had little time either for Burnham or Jagan and has said that British Guiana is unfit for independence. If he changes his mind, which now seems possible he may well urge early Guiana independence."[59]

Williams did not urge independence for British Guiana when the Commonwealth prime ministers met in London in June 1965. He was, however, sharply critical of British policy and repeated his proposal that the colony be placed under a United Nations trusteeship. He once again condemned the system of proportional representation and predicted that it would do nothing to improve the racial climate in Guiana. Trinidad, he threatened, would hold the United Kingdom responsible for the consequences of its actions in the colony. These criticisms having been articulated, Williams declined further participation in the discussion and requested that Trinidad be disassociated from any conference report on British Guiana.[60]

Williams continued to be troubled by developments in the colony and their implications for the political and racial health of his nation. On October 5, 1965, he told David Rose, the administrator of Antigua, that he could not endorse any American interference in the affairs of British Guiana. In addition, Williams maintained that there were sound reasons why he could not accept the legitimacy of the Burnham regime, which had come to power as a result of proportional representation. His critics did not realize that his good relations with Indians in Trinidad were held in a fine balance and that he could ill afford to jeopardize that rapport. If he supported Burnham and the means by which he came to power, Williams speculated, the Indians in Trinidad might demand proportional representation. This stance was consistent with his belief that proportional representation was a threat to national unity. Indeed, in an address to his nation on April 10, 1962, Williams rejected proportional representation because it would "emphasise and in fact establish sharp lines of division between the various social groups" and "in that way madness lies." Rose informed the Colonial Office that "the thread that ran through all our conversation was the thinly veiled suggestion that British Guiana had much to gain from cooperation with Trinidad, but that the initiative must come from British Guiana in order to prevent what Dr. Williams regards as his good relations with the Trinidad Indian community becoming soured."[61]

Administrator Rose also reported on his talks with other officials in Trinidad and Tobago. He said that the governor general, as well as opposition leader Ashford Sinanan, both believed that Williams wanted a thaw in his relations with Burnham and was under considerable pressure from politicians and from the business community to end the freeze. Both men believed that the initiative should come from Burnham, that he should make "a private and tactical approach" to Williams. Burnham, however, should demonstrate a willingness "to accept Dr. Williams informally as *Primus Inter Pares* in regional councils," and this would lead to "a very rapid development of good relations and economic cooperation." Although Norman Costar generally agreed with this approach, he thought that "the depth of Dr. Williams feeling about British Guiana is . . . ingrained . . . there is certainly a clash of personality between himself and Mr. Burnham. Dr. Williams wants to patronize Mr. Burnham and the latter has not played up to this wish. Mr. Burnham will not bow to Dr. Williams; not that I suggest he should consider doing so except as a calculated course to smooth his road; and Dr. Williams will not hold out his hand."[62]

There was, of course, no immediate thaw in the relations between Williams and Burnham. After visiting British Guiana in January 1966, High Commissioner Costar reported that Burnham expressed a desire for improved relations with Trinidad. But, according to Costar, he was aware that Williams "could be a very difficult man." Burnham expressed a willingness to welcome Trinidad into the recently established CARIFTA. As Costar reported, "contrary to the wishes of Mr. Barrow, who appeared to have the strongest possible dislike of Dr. Williams, he, Mr. Burnham, had insisted on postponing bringing the Free Trade Area into effective operation for some months in order to give Trinidad a chance to be a founding member." Andrew Rose, the Trinidad high commissioner to the United Kingdom, had an explanation for Williams's hostile reaction to the formation of CARIFTA, noted Costar. The attorney general of British Guiana, Shridath Ramphal, had told him that Rose "had inferred that Mr. Burnham could not seriously expect Dr. Williams to join an organization sponsored by anybody but himself."[63]

♦ ♦ ♦ ♦ ♦ As British Guiana took its first awkward steps toward independence in 1966, the relationship between Williams and Burnham remained cool and ambivalent. In an effort to promote a rapprochement, High Commissioner Costar recommended to the Commonwealth Relations Office that Williams be encouraged to make a statement supporting British Guiana in its continuing border dispute with Venezuela. In response, D. M. Cleary agreed that this support was desirable but emphasized that the idea should emanate from Williams himself. Echoing the long-standing official distrust of the prime minister of Trinidad and Tobago, Cleary added: "There is, I am sure you will agree, always the possibility that Dr. Williams might take a deliberately perverse position if he felt that we were attempting to influence him."[64]

Weary of the difficulties with Trinidad, Burnham told High Commissioner Costar in February 1966 of his desire to improve relations between the two countries. When Williams was apprised of this desire, he denied any responsibility for the tensions. He acknowledged, however, that Burnham resented his opposition to proportional representation.[65] Williams would make a major step toward a rapprochement with Burnham by appointing a high commissioner to British Guiana, though after some delay. This development led D. M. Cleary to hope that "with the advent of further independent neighbours, Dr. Williams can be brought to realize that it is to his advantage to be on good terms with them."[66]

As British Guiana's Independence Day approached in the summer of 1966, Eric Williams declined the invitation to participate in the celebrations in Georgetown, saying that it would be inappropriate for a head of government of an independent country to attend. His attendance, notwithstanding the protocol he invoked, would have gone a long way toward healing the breach with Burnham. Williams also made it known that he objected to the presence at the celebrations of C. L. R. James, his former mentor, political associate, writer, and later political antagonist. Costar reported Williams's objections to the Commonwealth Relations Office, characterizing James as "the elderly left wing Trinidad writer, whose distaste for Dr. Williams is more than balanced by Dr. Williams' own almost morbid hostility to, and suspicion of him. . . . To Dr. Williams, this is equivalent to Trinidad giving an honored position to Dr. Jagan."[67] Alarmed by this latest problem between the two leaders, the officials immediately investigated the reasons for the James invitation. The Guianese attorney general acknowledged that James had been invited as a representative of "literature" but denied that there had been any intention to irritate Williams or to embarrass the government of Trinidad and Tobago. The matter was thereby contained, but that it became an issue at all spoke volumes about the nature of Caribbean political life and its leadership.

Eric Williams's involvement in the British Guianese quagmire was an exercise in futility. He had a genuine desire to be of service to the people of that country, but he also understood that what was occurring in Guiana could be reproduced in Trinidad and Tobago. His involvement was, accordingly, an expression of enlightened self-interest. But Guiana's problems could not be solved in Port of Spain. The colony lacked mature leadership, and years of racial politics had scarred its fiber and its soul. While British Guiana bled from its internecine warfare, its leaders thought mainly in terms of their chances of retaining power or how to assume it. The country's agony was a Caribbean agony. Eric Williams looked into his crystal ball and saw a bleeding Trinidad and Tobago if he failed to provide leadership at home that transcended race. This was a daunting challenge, as the frustrations and the minefields tested his character and his skills.

♦ ♦

CHAPTER 7

ERIC WILLIAMS, AFRICA, AND AFRICANS

♦ ♦ ♦ ♦ ♦ Fresh from a six-week tour of eleven African states, Prime Minister Eric Williams addressed one of his favorite audiences on April 22, 1964. It consisted mainly of West Indian students at McGill and Sir George Williams Universities in Montreal who had gathered to hear the former professor discuss his tour, the historical connections between Africa and the West Indies, colonialism, and neocolonialism. Energized by his young audience, Williams said that "the historical connection between Africa, principally West Africa, is nothing to be ashamed about, though the West Indians don't like it and I get the feeling that the West Africans like it even less."[1]

This statement captured the historical ambivalences in the relationship between the peoples of Africa and of African descent in the Americas. Fifty years earlier (1914) Jamaican Marcus Garvey had founded the Universal Negro Improvement Association (UNIA) to promote racial pride and a back-to-Africa movement. Eric Williams was born three years before Garvey founded his organization and came to maturity at a time when peoples of African descent were beginning to struggle against colonialism. Intellectuals from Trinidad and Tobago played important roles in this campaign as well as in conceptualizing, fostering, and enhancing relationships among the peoples of African descent in the diaspora. Henry Sylvester Williams, for example, organized the first international gathering of Pan-Africanists in London in 1900. Attended by such African American luminaries as Anna Julia Cooper and W. E. B. DuBois, the congress was called to "bring into closer touch with each other the peoples of African descent throughout the world" and "to the securing to all African races living in civilized countries their full rights," among other goals. The conferees established the Pan-African Movement to give organizational expression to their objectives and to fight for self-government for colonized peoples in Africa and the Caribbean.[2]

The 1900 congress was held at a time when Liberia, Haiti, and Ethiopia were the only historically black countries that remained free from colonial rule. Finding this situation intolerable, the Pan-Africanists held congresses in 1921, 1923, 1927, and 1945 to raise the political consciousness of blacks in the diaspora and to contest European domination. Although the Pan-African Movement did not boast a large membership, the elites who comprised it were intellectually gifted, pugnacious, and eloquent in their condemnation of colonialism. Among the most prominent and influential voices were those of Trinidadians George Padmore, C. L. R. James, and Claudia Jones.

The fledgling Pan-African Movement did not stand alone, however. Proclaiming "Africa for the Africans at home and abroad," Marcus Garvey's Universal Negro Improvement Association advocated an end to European domination of Africa when it was founded. The UNIA drew its membership chiefly from the lower middle and working classes and from persons who were phenotypically black. Espousing a philosophy of "race first," the association promoted the interests of blacks worldwide, including the assumption of political power and the assertion of economic independence. Garveyism politicized millions of blacks in the diaspora, but the dream of an end to colonial rule was never achieved in its heyday. The Italian invasion of Ethiopia in 1935 dramatized the political weakness of blacks universally, although it elicited angry protests and demonstrations in the United States and elsewhere. Emperor Haile Selassie and Ethiopia came to represent the plight of blacks who were the victims of foreign domination, emphasizing the need to struggle against it and to command their own destinies.

The anticolonial struggle was only partially driven by such developments as the American occupation of Haiti, the Italian invasion of Ethiopia, and the racist ideology and its practice that caused World War II. Its major impetus came primarily from internal developments in the black colonial world. The Pan-African Movement and Garveyism had sensitized many people to fight for political independence. Colonized peoples and blacks in the United States were becoming increasingly literate, in many cases forming an expanding professional group and a growing middle class. Some of these highly skilled individuals were frozen out of jobs they deserved, as the colonial state and other employers preferred to hire whites. Such exclusionary practices based on race fed the demands for political change. Though it would be erroneous to maintain that the colonized peoples had never challenged their status, it is clear that new energies were unleashed during the

1940s and 1950s. Emboldened by the rhetoric that animated the struggle against fascism and the racist ideology espoused by Adolf Hitler and others, a new group of colonial leaders became uncompromising in their assaults on European rule.

Reflecting the change in the temper of the times, the Fifth Pan-African Congress, which met in Manchester, England, in 1945, was attended mainly by delegates from the colonized countries. W. E. B. DuBois was the lone delegate from the United States. The conference was dominated by anti-colonial issues, demonstrating a rising nationalism among African and Caribbean peoples that would culminate in political independence for many countries in the ensuing decades.

♦ ♦ ♦ ♦ ♦ The previous discussion—albeit brief—provides the context within which to situate Eric Williams and his positions on Africa. Williams grew up at a time when the challenges to colonial rule were acquiring a new fervor. Not surprisingly, the politically conscious historian could write in 1951 that "a governing principle of my life has always been that complete self-government is the first prerequisite to the unleashing of the dammed energies, productive and spiritual, of the people of the European territories."[3]

Williams became chief minister of Trinidad and Tobago in 1956, just before Ghana received its independence in 1957. By December 1963, thirty-two British, French, and Belgian colonies in Africa had also won their independence. Williams welcomed these developments. As the prime minister of a newly independent Trinidad and Tobago, however, he had to formulate his country's policy toward these nations, a challenge that the early advocates of Pan-Africanism did not have to confront.

Eric Williams, to be sure, had demonstrated a long-standing interest in Africa and its peoples. During his visit to Africa in 1964, he recalled that while working for "one of the small and new Research Foundations" in Washington, D.C., in 1947, he began doing some research on Kenya and Nigeria. The foundation, however, "could not understand why a West Indian should go meddling in African affairs." It declined to publish what Williams wrote about the two African colonies "and insisted that I write on some insipid metropolitan organization dealing with the West Indies."[4]

Although he never used the term, Williams would, in today's parlance, be characterized as a student of the African diaspora. He was an advocate of making the study of Africa and its peoples a fundamental part of the university curriculum in the Caribbean, as well as on the African continent and in the United States. As early as 1947, while a member of the Howard University faculty, he proposed that the university establish "an Institute of what necessarily had to be called in those days Colonial Studies, which had to deal with Africa and the West Indies."[5] Seventeen years later, on February 21, 1964, he told the students at Hansberry College at the University of Nigeria, Nsukka, that he wanted a Chair in African Studies created at the University of the West Indies. On that occasion, Williams also called for "a conference of West Indian and African specialists in the general field of African studies, using 'African' in the widest possible sense to include the Africans abroad wherever people of African origin and descent have settled and therefore have made some impact on societies in the world."[6]

Such views clearly suggest a diasporic vision. Approximately one month after his address in Nigeria, Williams told the students at Haile Selassie University, Addis Ababa, Ethiopia, that he wanted to see students and scholars from African universities and the University of the West Indies, as well as those in the United States, Europe, Brazil, and elsewhere, meet "to discuss this whole bag, this vast field of what, for want of a better phrase we might call Afro-American Studies."[7]

Williams also supported collaborative research in African studies by African and West Indian scholars. He viewed the field "as not only important in itself" but "as absolutely essential as an integral part of the process of decolonization which cannot be limited to the political and economic." In his opinion, African studies had "the equally important contribution to make of redefining the basis of our civilization, of our heritage, and giving to Africa and what Africa represents in the world a status and dignity which the imperialist historians have deliberately tried to take away from Africa over the centuries."[8]

By political conviction, as well as by the imperatives of racial heritage, Williams was most certainly a Pan-Africanist in the traditional sense. By 1962, however, when he became the leader of an independent Trinidad and Tobago, the political vocabulary insofar as Africans and the peoples of the diaspora were concerned, had changed. The desire for some link between Africa and its diaspora never waned, but the emphases in Africa became the construction of individual nation-states and the fostering of some degree of political unity among them. In May 1963, for instance, the leaders of the newly independent African states established the Organization of African

Unity (OAU) at a meeting held in Addis Ababa. The purpose of the OAU was to promote unity among the African nations, and it espoused such goals as a common defense, an African development plan, an African free trade area, an African university, an African news agency, and so on. The OAU also advocated an end to colonial rule on the continent, denounced the system of apartheid in South Africa, and wanted Africa to be declared a denuclearized zone. In a speech to the Trinidad Legislature on December 6, 1963, Prime Minister Williams welcomed the formation of the OAU and associated his government with its objectives. He announced that his minister of labor had recently walked out of a meeting of the International Labor Organization when South Africa's representative took the floor. Trinidad's representative at an international conference on tourism held in Rome was instructed to behave similarly.[9]

Although Williams identified his government with a variety of causes promoted by black Africans, he took pains to point out that it was part of both the Afro-Asian and European blocs. As he said three weeks after his nation received its independence: "We are naturally part of the Afro-Asian bloc and at the same time we are just as naturally a part of Europe. Our political traditions have come from Europe, our trade to a large extent is with Europe. . . . We are part of Europe and we are likely with independence to have that connection with Europe strengthened."[10]

Despite his anticolonial rhetoric and his assertion that the imperial powers were responsible for the ills of the West Indies, Williams could not sever his nation's ties with Europe. He manifested this ambivalence to Europe throughout his career, even as he became known as one of the most vociferous critics of colonialism and of Europeans by extrapolation.

Notwithstanding the black majority on the Anglophone islands, Williams contended that they were not "African communities." He emphasized, accurately, that the nation of Trinidad and Tobago was comprised of several ethnic groups. In an address to students at the University of Dakar, Senegal, in March 1964, Williams stressed that Trinidad "is Afro-Asian on a European base." Although recognizing that "West Africa was depopulated in order to populate the West Indies" and that there was "a powerful African influence in the West Indies," the prime minister argued that "this cultural contact does not mean, contrary to what so many Africans think, that the West Indies are African communities." He cautioned his audience that "whilst you emphasize the cultural link, you must not over emphasize the racial association." After four centuries of colonialism, the West Indian "is not an African, nor is he an Asian, nor is he a European. He is an African or Asian assimilated to the European."

Pleased with the reception to this speech, Williams sent a copy to his Cabinet, observing that the lecture "went down quite well, particularly because I spoke in French; you will see the line that was taken there, after being worked out by the ministers and diplomats." He reported that "we have been able to establish the realities as we see them" on "the other great danger": the "tendency to equate Trinidad and Tobago with the African states."[11]

Williams had little patience with those African diplomats at the United Nations who viewed Trinidad as an African state and courted its vote accordingly. Speaking at Oxford University in April 1964, he underscored this point: "It had emerged at the United Nations that the Africans were tending to take the view, a little too often for our comfort, that we were an African state and therefore must vote uncritically with the African bloc. Trinidad and Tobago is not an African state."[12]

Such a declaration, to be sure, did not mean a repudiation of an emotional connection with Africa or a denial of common political and economic interests as developing countries and former colonies. In explaining the reasons for his forthcoming visit to Africa, Williams had told his nation on February 7, 1964, that "I have a strong personal interest in this African tour. As you know, I have been working for many years on the History of the West Indies, and I have consciously sought to recover the roots of our nation. . . . The present tour, therefore, will embrace the sources of our African heritage."[13]

The prime minister gave a second reason for his visit. Noting that the trip "has wider significance" than a search for the nation's roots, he said: "The Organization of African Unity is one of the fundamental realities of the world today. The Arab League also has deep political significance. Both organizations are heavily involved in the world struggle against colonialism and both are particularly concerned with the problems of developing countries. Our brief experience of Independence has shown us that there is a great similarity of interests in many areas of international affairs between the Caribbean, Africa, and the Middle East, and that we have many economic and commercial problems in common."[14]

Williams had been less than candid about the primary reason for the trip. As he would later explain, his mission was intended to lobby the African nations to support Trinidad's request for preferential treatment in European markets. Williams had learned that some African countries, led by the United Arab Republic, were developing criteria that would have excluded Trinidad from such preferences if their proposals were endorsed by the forthcoming Geneva Trade Conference. These nations were taking the position that countries like Trinidad with petroleum resources and a relatively high per capita income should not receive preferential treatment in the European markets. Williams believed that this call for free trade would, if implemented, be a disaster for the small West Indian countries, since preferences amounted to "a form of reparation, inadequate and belated, for centuries of preferential arrangements imposed by the United Kingdom and in the interest of the United Kingdom investors in the West Indies."[15] Evidently fearing that the failure of his African mission in this regard might invite criticism at home, Williams chose not to bring the public into his confidence, although his Cabinet was fully aware of the nature of the negotiations he hoped to undertake.

♦ ♦ ♦ ♦ ♦ The prime minister's trip to Africa provides us with the most complete picture of his views on the continent and its peoples. He insisted on speaking to university students in most of the countries he visited and sent written reports to his Cabinet on his sojourn in seven countries. Williams had the trained optic of a scholar, the curiosity of a tourist, and the ear of a politician. His reports were thus laced with informed judgments, caustic comments, and humor.

Williams visited eleven countries: Sierra Leone, Liberia, Ghana, Nigeria, Uganda, Kenya, Algeria, Ethiopia, Senegal, the United Arab Republic, and Tanganyika. As a result of internal difficulties, his visit to Guinea had to be canceled at the request of the country's president. Williams's entourage included Cabinet ministers, civil servants, and Trinidad's ambassador to the United Nations. The prime minister had been to the African continent only once before, when he made a brief stop in the United Arab Republic. Consequently, his observations on the places he visited and their political leaders were fresh and candid.

Williams characterized Senegal as being "tied hand and foot to France, and nobody attempts to conceal it."[16] On the other hand, "the outstanding characteristic of Sierra Leone is the domination of Great Britain"; moreover, "there are expatriates everywhere, indicating the tremendous disadvantage the country faces in respect of technically qualified personnel to operate its Independence. The expatriate domination is to be seen both in the Police and in the Army, and in view of the spate of mutinies one has to keep one's fingers crossed."[17] The prime minister was quick to add—knowingly or perhaps tongue in cheek—that "the minister of Home Affairs in Trinidad ought not to exclude the possibility of the spread of the contagion."[18]

According to Williams: "The dominant feature of Liberia is the domination of the United States of America. One sees this at the Firestone Plantation, in the Peace Corp this is very much in evidence, in the composition of the University Faculty, and in the presence of the American Military Mission, and the American Aid Mission."[19] He was aware of the "many rumours of political repression, and brow beating of opposition elements." But it was his description of the ostentatious decor and trappings of Liberian official life that seemed devastating. He wrote:

> A special feature of Liberian life is the enormous waste of public funds by and on the President and his entourage. The most monstrous example of this is the Executive Mansion. It was almost an embarrassment to stay there. To put it simply it is "*Le roi soleil*" transferred from Versailles to Monrovia; Versailles is depicted on murals, and the mansion is all crystal and gold. The dining room where the President offered a State Banquet in our honour is a positive scandal. The expensive rugs, cutlery, plate, furnishings, air-conditioning, the troops that seemed to be on 24-hour duty merely to give a fanfare to the President or distinguished visitors on arrival or departure, apart from the general impression of indecency that all these convey, all suggest the positive danger of unrest and disturbance. The President's lavish Banquet for his wife's birthday, at which he presented her with a Lincoln Continental, is a positive invitation to disorder. One can only assume that his philosophy is *après moi le deluge.*[20]

Williams was appalled by the "*ancien regime* atmosphere" in the country. The "ridiculous protocol" was seen at its worst "at the Grand March with which the President and his wife opened the dancing at his wife's birthday party." The prime minister concluded that "not just a man but a dynasty" ruled Liberia: "the President's son is married to the Vice President's daughter; the Vice President's brother is also a member of the Cabinet; the President's brother formally [sic] held a high army rank and lives in the Executive Mansion." Williams formed a low opinion of President William Tubman. He thought that Tubman "was quite delighted, his vanity being what it is, at my invitation to him to visit Trinidad."[21]

Unlike his negative reaction to Liberia, Williams was favorably impressed by what he saw in Ghana. "The dominant note in Ghana," he reported, "is the domination of Nkrumah and the Peoples Convention Party." He described the country as being "predominantly African." Moreover, "If Senegal is predominantly French, if Sierra Leone is predominantly British, if Liberia is predominantly American, then Ghana is predominantly African." Ghana "is an African state, ready to oppose Britain, France, America, and all of these combined, and it is belligerently African. After Senegal, Sierra Leone, Liberia, one moves into a new world in Ghana."[22]

Williams was impressed by President Kwame Nkrumah's leadership and vision. He was very aware, however, of the rising sentiment against him in the country. The Trinidadian delegation "encountered more than one example of the jealousy and intrigue and struggle for position among the members of the presidential entourage." Such intrigue, Williams confessed, "is not strange to any member of the PNM." But he was certain that "nothing will come out of Africa without Nkrumah." "If Nkrumah goes," he predicted, "then Africa will be for several decades to come a battle ground of competing American, European, Russian, and Chinese interests."[23]

As in the case of Liberia, Williams was troubled by Nigeria's "tremendous expenditure of public funds on status symbols—magnificent Parliament buildings, gigantic Ministerial offices, Ministers' houses, quarters for Federal legislators in Lagos." In his opinion, "the dominant feature of Nigeria is suspicion of and dislike for Ghana."[24]

Williams noted striking differences between the West African and East African countries that he visited: "Where in West Africa the dominant note is the African personality—most pronounced in Ghana, suitably muted in French Senegal, British Sierra Leone, and American Liberia, the dominant note in East Africa if Uganda is taken as typical is that the African personality is very much in the background. The most obvious illustration of this is the general Westernization in terms of dress, both male and female. . . . Uganda gives the appearance of almost being [in] a different continent from Ghana or even Nigeria."[25]

In his report on Kenya, Williams elaborated on the differences between East Africa and West Africa. He found President Jomo Kenyatta's Cabinet "the best balanced that we have encountered in Africa and for competence is probably superior to all others." Furthermore, Kenya's "economic potential probably exceeds that of any other country." Williams was so impressed by what he saw that he concluded: "The way to the future of Africa in general and of East Africa in particular, is Kenya."[26]

Williams held very congenial and productive meetings with President Kenyatta. The visiting prime minister reported that "the dominant feature of Kenya is the personality and prestige of the Prime Minister, Kenyatta." He was struck, however, by the tension between the country's unique African cultural identity and its "general Westernization in dress." As he explained: "Apart from the personality of its Prime Minister, Kenya's importance lies in the fact that it is supremely African. This is not to say that it emphasizes the African personality of Nkrumah or the Negritude of Senghor. It is African in the sense that it remains predominantly tribal, it looks in every respect African, even to the length of the grandmothers' [dresses?] with cleanly shaven heads."[27]

Williams's impressions of the individual countries and their leaders undoubtedly shaped Trinidad's future foreign policy. He thought most highly of Presidents Nkrumah and Kenyatta and their respective countries and was obviously troubled by what he observed in Sierra Leone and especially Liberia. Williams was shocked by the low level of administrative competence he encountered, particularly in East Africa. "The general impression conveyed by Uganda," he concluded, "is one of inefficiency and confusion."[28] On leaving Africa, he told an audience at Oxford University that he found a "total absence in some places of anything that could be called an administrative apparatus."[29] Williams was surprised that the East African countries had such a paucity of teachers, doctors, lawyers, stenographers, and so on. "The problem," he noted, "is greater in a place like Tanganyika, where there is nothing at all . . . you look at Tanganyika and feel that the Europeans never intended to stay there, never expected that they would have to stay too long."[30]

In view of their urgent need for technical assistance, the East African countries requested Trinidadian aid. The Kenyans, for example, wanted teachers, lawyers, doctors, and help in training their students at the College of Agriculture at the University of the West Indies.[31] Uganda had an acute shortage of stenographers. When he met with the Ugandan Cabinet, Williams was surprised to find that the stenographer was "an English girl."[32] He was, understandably, sympathetic to the requests for assistance. After meeting with Kenyan officials, he reported to his Cabinet that "we MUST do whatever we can to assist."[33] But as the requests for aid multiplied, the prime minister told his audience at Oxford, he was unable to help them all, given his nation's own pressing needs.[34]

The West Indian prime minister was pleased to see the number of West Indians in important positions in the countries he visited. He did not believe, however, "that this is a case of West Indian superiority over [the] African." Rather, it was the consequence "of the longer colonial regime in the West Indies, which, in the field of education, has done more for assimilation to Europe than the shorter period has done in Africa."[35]

Williams was particularly interested in the question of African unity. In Ethiopia on March 16, he told the students at Haile Selassie University that "the reason why in fact we came to Africa apart from the fact that since Africa did not come to the Caribbean, the Caribbean thought it best to come to Africa—is the movement for African Unity which we regard down in the West Indies as one of the fundamental realities of the political world in which we live." He saw in African unity "a powerful political movement towards decolonization," as well as the "removal of colonialism and its attendant evil of racial discrimination and apartheid."[36]

But the West Indian prime minister was not oblivious to the internal as well as external obstacles that had to be surmounted. The external threat emanated from what he called the third "scramble" for Africa. The first scramble, in his view, was the Atlantic slave trade, and the second was the division of the African continent among the European countries in the 1880s. The third scramble was "for influence and control over the independent African states . . . as if the better way to control former colonial areas of the world of the 1960s is to declare them independent and to indulge in what the Ghanaians and others call neo-colonialism."[37] He was also suspicious of the role that the Chinese and Russian communists might play in exacerbating local tensions.[38]

Williams's visit to Nigeria exposed him to some of the internal problems that undermined the quest for African unity. Here he was briefed on the boundary disputes between Morocco and Mauritania, between Morocco and Algeria, between Ethiopia and Somalia, and between Kenya and Somalia. He was also apprised of the tension between African unity and Arab unity. This issue revolved around whether the United Arab Republic's primary loyalties resided with the Africans or with the Arab world. The same question arose in relationship to Algeria; but Algeria was thought to be more African in its allegiances, whereas the United Arab Republic was said to be more oriented to the Arab world. There was also the added complication, as Williams would later learn in Uganda, of "the contradictory Arab and African views on Israel."[39]

The African governments, as Williams was told in Nigeria, were divided on how the movement for further decolonization should be conducted. The problem was whether this should be done "on a continental basis through Governments, or by freedom fighters supported by one or more individual governments."[40] Williams also recognized the distrust with which some governments viewed others, creating further disunity. Nigeria, for instance, had such a great "suspicion and dislike" for Ghana that it "refused to bite at our suggestion for a Prime Ministers' conference to deal with Southern Rhodesia. It was quite obvious that the explanation is that Ghana had previously agreed to this."[41] Similarly, Williams observed, "The dominant note in Senegal is suspicion of Ghana, to the point of dislike. Senegal's friends in Africa, in Senegal's eyes, is [sic] non-French Africa, [especially] Nigeria and Liberia. Its particular bete noir after Ghana is Mali."[42]

He also came to understand that such practical complications as different currencies stood in the way of African unity. His visit to Sierra Leone dramatized this problem rather starkly: "The difficulties of African unity are very obvious in Sierra Leone. Sierra Leone, tied to Sterling, is surrounded by the Ivory Coast, part of the French Community, using a currency of its own which no one wants; Liberia using the American dollar. Trade relations are close with all these countries. It is obvious that Sierra Leone is not too optimistic about the African Common Market. It has a deep suspicion of Ghana, and a profound respect for Nigeria; what Nigeria does in Africa, Sierra Leone is likely to do."[43]

Williams saw additional obstacles to African unity. He was acutely conscious of the absence of effective networks of communication, the difficulty involved in traveling from one country to another. As he expressed it, "There is a lot to be done in the field of African communications before you make a reality of the African Unity in the political field."[44] In his address to the student body at Haile Selassie University, Williams elaborated on another problem that he identified: political unity could not be fully achieved until the "intellectual boundaries" that divided one nation from another were erased. He bemoaned the almost complete lack of cooperation between the various African universities. "Its worst example," he said, was "the important field of African Studies." The former professor warned the students: "If the institutes [of African Studies] are working in isolation one or the other possibly having some contact with the outside world but not with the world inside Africa, it would appear, ladies and gentlemen, as if in essence, the conception is as much colonial as the old colonial system which is being eroded and destroyed by The Organization of African Unity. . . . The movement for African Unity which has developed very powerfully in recent months has not yet extended to the intellectual field."[45]

Overall, Williams was only guardedly optimistic about the future of African unity. He expressed his concerns quite early on the tour, after visiting Senegal. "African Unity is likely to be a plant of very tender growth," he wrote, "if one accepts as a fundamental assumption the suitability of the soil."[46]

Williams's embrace of an African heritage and his unquestioned identification with the struggles of blacks on the continent for selfhood did not make him an uncritical admirer of the leaders and scholars he met. He was unimpressed by the justifications for the one-party systems he encountered and was profoundly skeptical of the constructs of African socialism, negritude, the African personality, and so on. Williams wondered, for example, how the African personality, "whatever it is," could withstand the consequences of the introduction of Western technology: "Wherever it is one finds this curious juxtaposition of the African values and the African personality in contradistinction to the European values and, let us say, the American personality, existing side by side with the conscious, deliberate and vociferous adaptation of Western technology in Africa, leading immediately at least to the intellectual dilemma as to whether the African personality and the African values could in fact survive the impact of Western technology."[47]

Eric Williams the academic criticized African scholars for not devoting adequate attention to the history of the slave trade, slavery, and the impact of Africans on the societies of the diaspora. Speaking to this point at Haile Selassie University, he said: "It is almost as if Africans have been upset by their previous history and seek by the simple formula of forgetting slavery to behave as if it didn't exist at all . . . you cannot remain satisfied by what has been done by European scholars, or American scholars or by West Indian scholars.[48] Williams would later articulate another reason for this seeming lack of interest in the history of the slave trade and slavery. "The African, I believe," he told the audience at Oxford University, "still suffers from that sense of inferiority, he doesn't want slavery recalled."[49]

Although very sympathetic to the desire of some African nations for technical assistance from the Caribbean, Williams thought that some reciprocity should be involved. When he spoke to students at the University of Ife, Nigeria, on March 4, 1964, he was particularly candid on this subject: "The problem is that you in West Africa have got a lot of help from the West Indies and we in the West Indies have got no help from you at all in West Africa. We haven't even got visits from your political leaders to us and it can't only be a one-way traffic. We in the West Indies have made significant contributions to you in West Africa for West Africa to begin to reciprocate."[50]

♦ ♦ ♦ ♦ ♦ Williams's speeches and written reports from Africa provide important insights into his image of that continent. But these should be weighed against the frequently uncharitable assessments of the trip by British officials. Their reports generally described the mixed reactions of African officials to the Williams visit. In addition, the officials listened carefully to any criticisms that the visiting prime minister made of colonialism and the British, reporting them faithfully. The British ambassador to Liberia observed that Williams gave a number of speeches in that country, speaking "with great fluency in a pleasing voice." He was relieved that Williams said "nothing very important or damaging . . . [since there] were no kicks at the colonialists." Williams, the ambassador wrote, admitted that he felt "at home" in Monrovia because of the "West Indianness" of the city.[51]

The ambassador in Dakar, Senegal, reported that Williams's visit coincided with the last two days of the "grand French Week of Art, Technology and Elegance," a celebration of French culture. He thought that the festivities "made a profound though distorted impression upon Dr. Williams and his party." The prime minister greeted with "acid remarks" his suggestion that "the celebrations and the city of Dakar" were not representative of Senegal as a whole. The ambassador noted that Williams compared the British unfavorably to the French, telling him not to make "derogatory remarks abut the French presence." In general, Williams's visit "gave him some useful ammunition for discrediting the British effort in the Caribbean, which he appeared to be by no means averse to doing." The British were not the only targets of Williams's criticism, however. He delivered a "vigorous onslaught" on the "personality and policies" of Cheddi Jagan of British

Guiana in a conversation with President Leopold Senghor and the minister of foreign affairs. Williams also made "a strong attack" on Fidel Castro in the speech he delivered at the University of Dakar, but his comments were "not well received" by the audience, the ambassador reported.[52]

D. J. C. Crawley, the British high commissioner in Freetown, Sierra Leone, thought that Williams made "his most waspish comments about the legacy of British colonialism" when he spoke to the students at Fourah Bay. "This was apparently heady stuff," Crawley wrote, "that was received with slightly self-conscious delight . . . even the Principal was licking his lips over it a little." At a state dinner given by the governor general, Williams "delivered himself of his, by then, customary polished and dryly humorous contributions," in contrast to Sir Milton Margai, the prime minister of Sierra Leone, who "was not having one of his most lucid days, but spoke volubly and impromptu." In his speech, Williams stressed the similarities between Trinidad and Sierra Leone, their common traditions and ancestry, and the role that West Indians had played in the building of the country. The high commissioner observed that "some of his hosts, I fear, demonstrated that these similarities did not extend to a common tradition of polished manners." He noted, with a hint of bemusement: "A few of the Ministers, centered as so often round Albert Margai, the Finance Minister [the prime minister's son], became somewhat rowdy towards the end of dinner, and the Trinidadian sitting next to my wife remarked that if Trinidadian ministers behaved like that in Trinidad their Prime Minister would have sent them out of the room."

Crawley thought that in "propaganda terms," Williams's visit would be represented as a success, although "the continual journeyings of ministers of minor countries which is so prevalent today, is admittedly extravagant." But he was uncertain how the Sierra Leoneans perceived the West Indian visitors, surmising that they may have thought of them as "a little too consciously brilliant and superior for comfort." According to the high commissioner, Williams was "an impressive emissary" but "he and the senior members of his delegation were demonstrably more civilized, poised, and urbane than their counterparts here." He speculated that the visitors considered the Sierra Leoneans "a fairly rough lot, however much they might feel curiously at home in a country where even the capital's architecture shows such a marked West Indian character."

The high commissioner reported that there was "a patronizing streak, hidden but undoubtedly present" in Williams's comments on his country's relations with Africa. Although the Sierra Leoneans had made much of Williams's African descent, Crawley thought that he "put this sentimentality" in its place "by declaring flatly (according to press headlines on the day he left) that Trinidad was not a part of the Negro world and that West Indians as a whole were not of African descent." This was obviously a misrepresentation of what Williams had said. Most likely, he was underscoring the multiracial composition of Trinidad and Tobago, a point that the news report missed. In any event, the high commissioner thought that Williams "rubbed the superiority" of his country in the field of education by drawing attention to its literacy rate of 90 percent. Williams added fuel to the fire by seeming to apologize for the rate not being higher, thereby making "an implicit comparison with the miserably low figure on this side of the Atlantic." High Commissioner Crawley wondered whether the Sierra Leoneans would "want to have much to do with Trinidadians, or even perhaps West Indians, if they are personified by the rather chill, touchy and superior Dr. Williams, who may have won respect but certainly no affection."[53]

The United Kingdom's ambassador to Ethiopia, John Russell, gave a more favorable assessment of Eric Williams's sojourn. "On balance," he wrote, "the visit was a success." The West Indian prime minister had made "an agreeable impression on his hosts, who are now aware that Trinidad exists newly independent and pursuing courses not widely different from those favored by Ethiopia." Russell thought that Ethiopians were "a little puzzled" that this "small country" should have spent so much money to visit so many African states. He doubted, however, that the Williams visit would alter the relations between East Africa and the West Indies, although he found Williams's "general attitude on African affairs shrewd and well informed."

Ambassador Russell reported that Williams was highly critical of President Nkrumah of Ghana, saying that he had "lost all his standing in Africa and was now a little mad." This surprising comment was at variance with the prime minister's written report to his Cabinet stressing his high regard for Nkrumah. Russell must have been aware of Williams's earlier positive assessments of the Ghanaian prime minister because he surmised that "it is possible he [Williams] suits his conversation to his audience." The ambassador described the author of *Capitalism and Slavery* and the recipient of a doctoral degree from Oxford University as "a relatively sophisticated West Indian" and a "mature product of the British colonial system." His observations constituted an extraordinary assertion of British official condescension. The "interest" in Williams's visit, Russell stated, "lies in the impact of Africa on a relatively sophisticated West Indian, with all the accumulation of British colonial heritage behind him, overlaid in recent years by the bright new varnish of the American connection. He was certainly impressed by what he saw here, both material and spiritual. It will, in turn, I think, have done his hosts good to see this mature product of the British colonial system as it was on the other side of the globe."[54]

F. S. Miles, the acting British high commissioner to Tanganyika, also stated that Williams's visit "appears to have been quite a success." Prime Minister Williams and President Julius Nyerere "seem to hit off well." Williams was able to brief Nyerere on "Cuban and Communist subversion in the Caribbean" and "probably had a beneficial effect" on Nyerere, who was becoming concerned at the prospect of "Communist infiltration" from Zanzibar into Tanganyika. In an hour's private conversation with the acting high commissioner, Williams said that he had told President Jomo Kenyatta of Kenya that if he feared subversion by the Chinese embassy in Nairobi, "the simple answer" was not to establish diplomatic relations with communist countries, a policy that he had pursued in Trinidad. Williams, Miles thought, felt more at home in East Africa than in West Africa because those countries had a racial mix similar to Trinidad's.[55]

Williams's tour was closely followed by the press in Trinidad and Tobago. He was roundly censured at the outset for saying in his radio broadcast to the nation that he was going to Africa to "embrace the sources of our African heritage." Obviously stung by the criticism, he retracted by saying that "Trinidad was not a negro country," a mantra he repeated on the tour. Williams was also reprimanded by the largely Indian opposition in the legislature for spending an estimated TT$500,000 on his African "safari." High Commissioner Norman Costar felt that the trip "has not been greatly resented by the non-Indian man on the street, who, if he thinks about the trip at all, sees it as more 'bigness' for Trinidad and a feather in the cap for the tough little terrier at the top." The Indians, he noted, "are less impressed."[56]

Williams's African tour strengthened the relations of his new nation with the eleven countries he visited. He developed a fresh understanding of their problems, established a warm rapport with leaders like Julius Nyerere, and acquired a deep respect for Kwame Nkrumah, Jomo Kenyatta, and especially

Ben Bella of Algeria. Williams saw Ben Bella, in the words of Norman Costar, as "an outstanding leader, the outstanding leader in Africa." He was able, Williams said, to undermine any support that existed in Africa for Cheddi Jagan.[57] He was also very outspoken in his criticism of Fidel Castro, but this was not always well received and probably had little effect.

There can be no doubt, however, that Williams's tour enhanced his stature among the African leaders. He received substantial support for his view that small developing nations should embrace common positions in their relationships with the wealthy industrial nations as well as the larger developing ones. The first test of this solidarity would be at the forthcoming World Conference on Trade and Development scheduled to take place in Geneva. Williams also wanted the Africans to recognize Trinidad as the leader of the West Indian islands in international affairs. After meeting with Williams on his return to Trinidad and Tobago, High Commissioner Costar reported that "rightly or wrongly (and he is not a modest man) Dr. Williams feels that he had made an impression in Africa, upon which he can build." He "believes that he has been recognized in Africa as a, indeed the, unifying leader in the Caribbean." Furthermore, Williams "sensed" that moderation toward Britain "earns no plaudits in Africa." Under the circumstances, Costar predicted that in the future Williams would "take a more publicly unfriendly view towards British policies, both in Africa and the Caribbean."[58]

Costar always expected the worst from Eric Williams. He never quite understood that the interests of Britain and Trinidad were not the same. Williams was the principal spokesperson for his new nation, and its interests, no matter how he defined them, were always paramount. This was seldom recognized by the former colonial masters, and it would take them some time to realize that the nation of Trinidad and Tobago had to chart—as best it could—its own destiny.

Williams's African tour obviously broadened his appreciation of the political pulse of the Africans. His visit to Ghana, for example, had made him understand the "economics of neo colonialism." He looked approvingly at the changes under way on the continent and the colonial world in general. Williams was not displeased that the map of the world was "completely torn up . . . there is still some tearing up to be done, I believe. They are about doing it in Nyasaland and in Rhodesia and so on." An unrepentant anticolonialist and opponent of apartheid, Eric Williams returned from Africa

convinced that Europeans "tend to underestimate the force of African opposition to South Africa, to colonialism, and to Apartheid."[59]

♦ ♦ ♦ ♦ ♦ Shortly after his return home, Williams discussed with Jamaica
the question of joint diplomatic relations overseas. Although the details
remain somewhat unclear, it appears that Trinidad had agreed to represent
Jamaica's interests in Africa and that Jamaica would reciprocate in Latin
America. But implementation of this understanding was stymied because of
poor personal relations between the leaders of the two countries. Perturbed
by the lack of movement, Williams attacked Jamaican officials at a public
meeting in Trinidad in late August 1964 for not taking steps "to put the plan
in operation." An angry Alexander Bustamante responded: "If Dr. Williams
has so much unused time on his hands, one would think he would use it
more profitably in the interest of his country. One thing I wish to make clear
is that the Jamaican government is not following Dr. Williams[,] as we are
too experienced and knowledgeable in West Indian and World Affairs to
follow those who know less than we do. When Jamaica decides how it wants
to be represented overseas, it will take appropriate action."[60]

These were harsh words, indeed, and an intemperate criticism of a fellow
Caribbean leader. In the months after it gained its independence, Jamaica
had accepted Trinidad's leadership in foreign affairs. The British high commissioner in Jamaica had considered this a period of Jamaica's "docile acceptance" of Trinidad's "tendency to speak for Jamaica . . . and in some
respects appear[s] to be running Jamaica's external policy." Soon, however,
the Jamaican leaders began to chafe under this situation, and, according to
the high commissioner, a "reluctance to continue to be led by the nose has
become explicit." Bustamante's outburst against Williams must be seen in
this light, although the personal animus between the two leaders exacerbated the political tension.[61]

Although the concept of shared overseas representation for these two
small, developing Caribbean nations made sense, it was never implemented.
Trinidad and Jamaica went their separate ways on the matter, although they
generally had similar views on anticolonial issues, apartheid in South Africa,
and black majority rule in the African countries. Williams was outspoken in
his rejection of white minority rule in Southern Rhodesia. His government
denounced Ian Smith, its white leader, when Smith declared the colony

independent rather than submit to black majority rule. Williams urged the United Kingdom to intervene in the former colony and accused British officials of racial prejudice when they declined to do so. He gave tacit approval to university students in Trinidad and Tobago when they protested against British policy in Southern Rhodesia and sought, unsuccessfully, to get the volatile issue discussed at the Commonwealth Prime Ministers' Conference in the summer of 1964.

A citizen of the African diaspora, Eric Williams was also a Caribbean man and a Trinidadian nationalist. His embrace of Africa was bereft of empty sentimentalism and romantic condescension. His opposition to colonialism and racism was strident and unwavering. As a scholar and the descendant of enslaved Africans, he wanted to emancipate black people everywhere from the political, economic, and intellectual fetters that circumscribed their human possibilities. Speaking of his work as a historian in February 1964, Williams told students at Fourah Bay College that "it is the slave-owners who have written the history of slavery and when I—I have spent my life writing the history of slavery—write the history of slavery I don't write like a slave-owner, I write like a slave who has been emancipated."[62] Williams kept faith with this imperative, one that defined his career as a scholar and as a politician.

Still, Eric Williams was from a small country that exerted little influence in the international arena. Any influence that he wielded outside of Trinidad's borders resulted from the power of his pen and his compelling rhetoric. As a descendant of Africa and as a scholar who wrote primarily about peoples of African descent, he had an emotional and an intellectual connection to the continent. As head of government of a multiracial Trinidad and Tobago, however, he had to perform a balancing act. He had to appear to transcend a narrow identification with the peoples of African descent in his political behavior, a goal that sometimes eluded him. Williams's trip to Africa in 1964 reflected the importance he placed on that continent in a changing world and his recognition that Trinidad and the West Indies as a whole had to develop and nurture ties with the various African peoples. A vigorous advocate of this vision, Williams realized its crucial role in the construction and shaping of a modern West Indian identity.

♦ ♦

CHAPTER 8

THE ECONOMICS AND
POLITICS OF RACE

♦ ♦ ♦ ♦ ♦ Eric Williams always boasted about Trinidad and Tobago's ethnic diversity. To him, the two islands comprised the most distinctive Caribbean peoples. Writing in 1964, he characterized the new nation as "the most cosmopolitan of all the West Indian territories—its African stock having been supplemented in the last century by large numbers of immigrants from India and lesser numbers from China and Syria, all superimposed on its diverse European base." He took pride in recognizing that the nation of Trinidad and Tobago had been able "to integrate its various stocks and strains into a multi-racial and multi-religious community." The historian, nationalist, and politician was also elated when Prime Minister Harold Mac-Millan described Trinidad and Tobago as "the Athens of the Caribbean." Such an accolade, Williams said, constituted a powerful tribute to the "political genius" of his country.[1]

Certainly Trinidad and Tobago constituted one of the most racially diverse and politically sophisticated countries in the Caribbean. In 1965, the year after Williams praised his nation for its apparent racial harmony, 43 percent of the people were predominantly of African descent, 36 percent Indo-Trinidadian or of South Asian provenance, and 16 percent mixed or white African; Europeans, Chinese, and Syrians together made up 3 percent. The population as a whole was increasing at an annual rate of 3.6 percent, with Indo-Trinidadians as a group showing the highest rate of growth. The population amounted to just over one million in 1970, with a density slightly above four hundred inhabitants per square mile. Unlike in the southern United States, residential segregation had no basis in law, though most Indians resided in rural areas and the majority of blacks lived in cities and towns. Regardless of their ethnicity, socioeconomic status, place of residence, religion, and so on, many people accepted the unofficial motto, "All ah we is one" as an ideal, if not quite a reality.

In many respects, the two principal racial groups—Africans and Indians—shared a similar but also a different historical trajectory. Their ancestors had been brought to Trinidad to work for the Europeans, who themselves were immigrants. The Africans had come as slaves and the Indians arrived as indentured servants, replacing the Africans in the cane fields after coerced African labor ended in 1838. Despite the cultural differences that existed between them, in time the Indo-Trinidadians and the African Trinidadians worked out a modus vivendi and lived, for the most part, without serious tension or conflict. In fact, during the labor unrest that marked the society before and after World War II, Indian and black workers cooperated in the struggle for social justice. Representatives of the two groups also worked together, if sometimes uneasily, to promote constitutional reform.

The interwar and postwar years of the twentieth century saw enormous political ferment in the Caribbean. The insistent demands by workers for their rights, the strikes that advanced their cause, the introduction of universal adult suffrage, and constitutional reform in some islands produced a heightened political consciousness everywhere. In 1947 Anglophone West Indian leaders met in Montego Bay to begin discussions on the creation of a West Indies Federation. An agreement to federate was hammered out a few years later, and some political leaders, intellectuals, and others began to imagine an end to colonialism and the achievement of independence for a federated West Indies.

In 1950 Trinidad and Tobago received a new constitution that introduced a modified ministerial system. The colonial governor, in whose hands ultimate power resided, chose five ministers from among the elected representatives of the people. Such tentative steps toward self-government produced anxiety among the white colonial elite and others who feared a diminution in their privileges. Indians, who were beginning to flex some political muscle, at first worried that, with federation, they would be smothered by the black majority. Although these concerns were deeply felt, they rested on the premise that blacks throughout the West Indies shared a similar political vision and spoke with one voice. West Indian politicians were nothing, if not a fractious group, characterized by ideological and personality differences. Nevertheless, Indo-Trinidadian fear of black domination presaged unhappy developments in the civic life of the colony. The problem eventually became one of competing racialized nationalisms, and this did not augur well for the health of the body politic.

The evolution of a racialized tone to the political culture of the country had deep historical, economic, and cultural roots and preceded Eric Williams's election to political office in 1956. British colonialism had fostered divisions among Indians and blacks, producing a situation where the two groups frequently took their cues from colonial authorities and shared a mutual distrust of each other. Such habits of mind were not easily exorcised, and the proverbial Massa remained imprinted on the psychology of many people. Not until 1946, however, did "race" become a very divisive factor at the electoral level. It was demonstrated most blatantly in the constituency of Victoria, setting an ugly precedent for the emerging nation.[2]

There were, to be sure, cultural differences among the various ethnic groups, notably between Indo-Trinidadians and blacks, but these should not be exaggerated historically. Indo-Trinidadians clung tenaciously to their cultural and religious traditions. The overwhelming majority of them were Hindus; Muslims comprised about 16 percent, and Christians formed an even smaller minority. Indians had, to some extent, resisted cultural assimilation, but this never meant that they lived in a world alien to other Trinidadians. In fact, they crossed cultural boundaries at will, and their claims to full participation in their country's life were as authentic as those of any other group.

The racial tensions that manifested themselves in political behavior, particularly after 1956, also had a profound economic basis. Although in 1962 Trinidad had a per capita income of £229, making it one of the wealthiest developing nations, the territory was characterized by severe inequities in access to resources,as well as large pockets of poverty and high rates of unemployment. Since poverty wore both black and brown faces, there were structural reasons for the economic disabilities of the people. The expectation that the majority black population would inherit the political power exercised by Great Britain in the wake of constitutional reform and use it to its advantage frightened the Indian minority. But since African Trinidadians as a group had never exercised political power in Trinidad and Tobago, such fears were misplaced. The major tensions were generated by the competition for the society's scarce resources and who would occupy the locus of governmental power. That this competition would, in time, become racialized, represented a failure of leadership and a disposition on the part of many politicians to exploit race to their party's advantage. Similarly, when Eric Williams later faced a Black Power–inspired revolt in 1970, the underlying problem was not the product of race although the language of race was used.

As damaging as the racial bogey was, and has been, to Trinidad and Tobago's civic life, it did not poison social relations between the two principal groups. Citizens of all racial groups interacted at various societal levels with ease and good humor, and without acrimony. Responding in 1962 to a question from a reporter for the British Broadcasting Corporation, Eric Williams admitted that, although there was not a great deal of intermarriage in Trinidad and Tobago, "there is a lot of social intercourse, one sees it in the clubs at night, one sees it at carnival, one sees it in the office, one sees it on the road work that is going on in the territory, at the professional level there is almost total Westernization, assimilation . . . the schools are the most interracial aspect of Trinidad."[3]

♦ ♦ ♦ ♦ ♦ Eric Williams was obviously familiar with the construction and operation of race in Trinidad and Tobago. He grew up in a family and in a society that were deeply conscious of the importance of skin color in a white-dominated society. Williams recalled that his parents "had all the complexes of the lower middle class and 'status' involved 'questions of colour and hair.' " In later years, he wrote: "Perhaps in no other respect is it possible to see more clearly the price that the West Indian society has paid for slavery than in the pathetic concern with the quality of one's hair. The phrases used to describe the bad variety speak for themselves: tic-tic, scroop-scroop (allegedly [an] expression of the task of counting out the knots), and a gang of us boys could think of no more adequate description of a certain local girl than to call her 'wirehead.' But, in the phrase 'goat dung' local contempt for the typical Negro hair reached its nadir."[4] Williams escaped such pernicious psychological onslaughts since he had "good" hair or "good grass." His parents took great pride in his "curls," which "were allowed to grow to a considerable length before it was agreed that my locks should be shorn."[5]

His siblings, Williams recalled, fell "broadly" into two categories. He belonged to the group that consisted of the "dark skinned ones with good black hair," whereas the second group comprised "the lighter skinned ones with bad lighter hair known locally as shabeens." Occasionally, a child did not fit into either category, with the lighter-skinned child having "good" hair and the darker-skinned one cursed with "bad" hair. According to Williams, the children were never discriminated against either inside or outside the family on the basis of their phenotype or hair. He thought this was due to the fact that "the lighter ones were obviously coloured" and because "I, one of the dark ones achieved [such] intellectual position in the face of which the conventional barrier among coloured people is lowered."[6]

Williams had a complex, although not necessarily unique, racial ancestry. He described his father as "dark brown." His father's mother was white, "the daughter of a local family of means" who was "disowned by them for eloping with and marrying a negro employed by them in a menial capacity." Williams's "light skinned" mother was "connected with an old French creole family." His parents, in common with many others, never embraced their African ancestry. "My parents were adamant in their philosophy that one might come from Africa—that was one's misfortune, but hardly one's fault," Williams recalled, "but there was no point in going back to Africa—that would be not only one's misfortune but one's fault." His parents disliked "the negro associations of some of my aunts" and "the illiberal occupations of these [men] only reinforcing the objections on grounds of colour." They wanted professional men—doctors and lawyers—for the women and "lighter skinned women for the boys." For the girls, his parents wanted educated men, and for the boys, "colour in the case of wives, or, in its unavoidable absence, education or a good family background."[7]

Williams's girlfriends did not always win the approval of his parents. "The satisfaction they showed with my choice of my first girl friend, shortly before my departure for England, the daughter of a prominent coloured professional family with important political status, was as great as their disappointment with her substitute, the daughter of a retired school teacher, without education herself and without means." His father forbade him to see the girl, but he continued to do so. Williams's parents were delighted with his eventual marriage "to a woman whose English education, personal means and fairly good hair compensated for her humble antecedents." He never knew what his father would have thought of his subsequent marriage "to a girl whose beauty of face and hair [was] combined with a lack of means and the absence of corruption by higher education," because he was already deceased. Williams admitted that he never sought his mother's opinion of his second bride. He knew, however, that his parents had disapproved "of the mulatto primary school teacher and the junior civil servant to whom other brothers and sisters subsequently became attached." They showed their "displeasure" by "their resort to one of the highest manifestations of the *patric potestas* in the Trinidad of those days, forbidding the *persona non grata* the house."[8]

The future prime minister was the product of a family that was racially heterogeneous. He characterized it as running "almost the entire gamut of race and colour in Trinidad." He had white relatives and "cousins with French and Spanish names." His first wife had a Portuguese father, and his second wife was Chinese. One of his sister's husbands, he wrote, "has Indian blood," three of his aunts and an uncle married mulattoes, and two other aunts chose "negroes" as their husbands.[9] This familial configuration made it easy for Williams to operate comfortably in diverse racial settings. Ashford Sinanan, a prominent opposition politician and himself an Indian, told David Rose, the administrator of Antigua, that Williams "was often more at home in Indian villages than he was in some of the Negro villages."[10]

His diverse family background hardly prepared Williams to deal with the racially inspired insults that he received as a student at Oxford University and later in the United States. As a youth in Trinidad and Tobago, he had witnessed racially based mistreatment of African Trinidadians and Indo-Trinidadians at his school, but he does not appear to have been a victim of it. Perhaps these early experiences help to explain his acute sensitivity to any slights from white Americans or Europeans, which he was inclined to interpret in racial terms. Norman Costar observed that Williams's skin "is so thin as to be almost non-existent."[11] To temper the pain of some of the racially motivated wounds inflicted on him in the United States, Williams had to "discipline" himself: "Yes, I met [racism] because I traveled about the US a great deal . . . but one knew what one was going into, one resented it but one learnt to discipline oneself. As individual protest was absolutely futile we learnt to keep one's temper."[12]

Probably because of his experiences, Williams developed a profound intellectual interest in the roots of racism and its expression historically. In *Capitalism and Slavery*, he maintained that "slavery was not born of racism, rather, racism was the consequence of slavery."[13] This assertion remains controversial, as some historians have questioned its validity. But whether his conclusion was valid is not the point. Williams's corpus of works emphasized the centrality of race, racism, and slavery to the construction of the Caribbean. To Williams, slavery and its progeny, racism, were responsible for the Caribbean's ills, which he described as "our urge to run away from agriculture, the domination of our society by racial and colour distinctions, the prevalence of crime and violence, the flimsiness of our family structure, our propensity for conspicuous consumption, our individualism, and political inexperience."[14] Slavery had corrupted the Caribbean, and "the minds of the West Indian people have been warped—in my more pessimistic moments I believe they have been permanently warped by slavery."[15]

Throughout his career Williams also emphasized the historical links between colonialism, imperialism, and racism. In a speech that he delivered at Woodford Square, he declared: "The root of this problem of race is imperialism, which has sought to justify its economic control by regarding the colonial peoples as inferior, despising their personal habits and social customs, denying their fitness to govern themselves, and describing them as a people without a history." Williams argued that the West Indies had served as the guinea pig for the expression of European forms of racism: "What has been done in Africa was first thought out in the West Indies, practiced in the West Indies, and then at its best, shall we say, it was transported to Africa and the Africans have some knowledge of what it was we West Indians went through over the centuries."[16] This was an overstatement, for the system of rigid racial segregation known as "apartheid" that South Africa was then experiencing had no precedent in the modern Caribbean. But there was no denying the fact that slavery in the Caribbean and elsewhere was legitimized by racism and its legacy remained, in varying degrees of intensity, in the islands. Williams the politician associated himself and his government with the struggle against apartheid in South Africa, assuring students at Montreal's McGill and Sir George Williams Universities in 1964 that Trinidad and Tobago "stand solidly with the Africans against racial discrimination."[17]

♦ ♦ ♦ ♦ ♦ Eric Williams's first extended public discussion of the contemporary racial climate in Trinidad and Tobago occurred in a lecture, entitled "Federation in the World Today," that he gave on February 25, 1955, before his formal entry into politics. But the ideas he espoused shaped his philosophy, if not always his behavior, once he assumed political office. Among other issues, he addressed whether cultural and other differences among the constituent units of a federation were sources of strength or weakness. His analysis of several federations and their constitutions, Williams said, "has not indicated that community of language or of race or of religion or of nationality is an essential prerequisite of federal government." Rather, he asserted, "in so far as the history of federal systems indicates anything at all, it suggests that differences of race, religion, language or nationality, far from encouraging hostility to federation, strengthen the sentiment for it, as the only means of securing the advantages of union whilst retaining separate allegiances."

Sensitive to the opposition of some Indians in Trinidad and Tobago to the prospective federation in the West Indies, Williams assured his audience that autonomy could exist within unity:

> Here in the British West Indies we have our insular differences and our racial distinctions. We are Barbadian and white, Trinidadian and Indian, Jamaican and Negro. We now face the problem of imposing a common nationality upon these differences. The very existence of the differences suggests the desire for separation within union. . . . The Indians, for example, might be as vociferous a minority as the French Canadians, but *demanding* federation. . . . They could be tenacious of their own identity as the Swiss cantons, as the majority group in British Guiana, as a powerful minority in Trinidad, they could be insistent on state's rights. The position in many respects suggests that they can be excellent federationists.

Williams was disappointed that this was not the case, however. He had the impression that there was opposition to federation from "a tiny minority of leaders whose nationalism, focused on India is potentially disruptive of West Indian nationalism." But he was certain that most Indians remained unaffected by such pulls. "One has only to recall," he said, "the recent carnival to appreciate the hollowness of the claim that the Indians were not good West Indians. Carnival, that great leveler in our community, is liberty, equality, above all fraternity, not as an empty slogan, but as a living and fascinating reality for two days in the year." In fact, "the Indian masses will really become a hostile minority in Trinidad only when they cease to jump up to the music of the steel band or when they propose the suppression of carnival." But "there is not the slightest prospect of either." To Williams, then, Indians were integrated into the political and cultural life of their native land. Yet he opposed the teaching of Hindi in the schools. He wondered whether the teaching of Hindi might not lead to requests for the introduction of African languages and "the allocation of each racial or religious group of a percentage of the educational revenues proportionate to their numerical strength in the population."

Eric Williams the historian noted that the Indians had been in the West Indies for over a century and had been "steadily assimilated." Thus, it was "hard to see how the further division of our already over-divided communities can help either the British West Indies as a whole or even the Indians themselves in their quite legitimate and understandable aspirations for integration into the civil service and the professions and employment generally." Saying that "this so called desire for cultural independence must end somewhere," Williams conjectured: "It was the denominational school yesterday, it is Indology today, what will it be tomorrow? The communal vote?"[18]

In this lecture Williams displayed empathy with the Indians, but he did not endorse any sentiment for cultural autonomy. He blamed the desire for the teaching of Hindi on "outside interference," and, as we shall see, this was not totally untrue.[19] Although his embrace of the teaching of Hindi would not, by itself, have led to his having a greater rapport with the Hindus, it certainly would have paid some political dividends. But Williams was probably not thinking of a political future when he delivered the lecture. On the other hand, he intimated that he would not support requests to teach African languages as well. He was more comfortable with "a basic curriculum built around West Indian history and the English language and literature."[20]

The state of race relations, particularly its black-white expressions, in Trinidad and Tobago was one of Williams's major concerns, but he saw racism as a legacy of slavery and colonialism so it was a global phenomenon. Unlike several of his contemporaries, Williams understood that racial diversity constituted one of the considerable strengths and appeal of the West Indies, but he also knew, as the racial blood bath in British Guiana would show, that unscrupulous politicians could stimulate and exploit racial tensions to their advantage. Williams had used his lectures at the University of Woodford Square to foster a nonracial nationalism in Trinidad and Tobago, but his message had a far greater resonance among African Trinidadians than Indo-Trinidadian and other groups. Blacks, particularly those who were young, working-class, urban, and literate, identified strongly and personally with the brilliant black historian to a degree that other ethnic groups never approximated.

His founding of the People's National Movement (PNM) in January 1956 gave institutional expression to Williams's vision of a nonracial nationalism. As such, the party promoted itself as multiracial in composition. Its charter endorsed the principle of interracial solidarity, and its leadership structure included representatives from the major ethnic groups, although Afro-Trinidadians predominated. Writing in the PNM's organ, the *Nation*, on August 30, 1956, Williams emphasized the party's multiracial commitment: "Recognizing and, indeed, welcoming cultural diversity, the PNM calls for unity among racial groups on one common platform—agreement on common economic, social and political objectives: utilization of all resources, human and physical, for the common good. . . . PNM proudly exhibits its banner on which are emblazoned the words revolutionary for Trinidad and Tobago—POLITICAL LIBERTY, SOCIAL EQUALITY, RACIAL FRATERNITY.[21]

Although the PNM was animated by a multiracial vision, its support came mainly from African Trinidadians. Few Hindus rallied to its banner, but it attracted a significant percentage of Indians who were Muslims and Christians. Their embrace of the PNM was due less to their being comfortable in that party and more to their tensions with the Hindus, who were beginning to constitute the party's principal opposition. The unfortunate reality was that political party alignment in Trinidad and Tobago was becoming more racialized precisely when the emerging nation's challenges were decidedly more complex, notably its entry into the West Indies Federation, the selection of a Federal capital site, the future of Chaguaramas, and a new five-year development plan. In contesting the general elections of September 1956, the PNM presented a racially diverse slate of candidates. Of its 25 candidates, 15 were African Trinidadians; 6 were Indians, comprising 3 Muslims, 2 Hindus, and 1 Presbyterian; and 1 each was European, Chinese Creole, and Spanish Creole.[22] The specter of race haunted the election campaign, an unhappy development that presaged the country's pain. Fearful that a PNM victory would undermine their privileges, the old established elite waged an unsuccessful campaign to thwart the PNM juggernaut.

The PNM's assumption of political power would, in time, produce a crystallization of its opposition and the politics of race. The Democratic Labour Party (DLP), when it was founded, consisted of a motley group of politicians united only by their opposition to the PNM and Eric Williams. Yet a substantial proportion of its support came from Indians. The DLP was established to contest the Federal elections that were held in March 1958. Its defeat of the PNM and its affiliated West Indies Federal Labour Party was a stunning blow to Williams and, according to some critics, a repudiation of his party and leadership. It was an ugly campaign at best, as supporters of both parties hurled racially charged abuse at one another. One scholar captured the essence of this developing cancer by concluding: "No party was blameless; there was instead a balance of blame. As the nationalist movement became more fully developed, the irresistible tendency was for race and nationhood to become interrelated. Both ethnic groups interpreted nationhood and emancipation in terms of their own communities and symbols. Even the party leaders, committed though they were to universalistic norms, could not resist the temptation to manipulate sectional symbols sometimes subtly, sometimes quite unashamedly, in their pursuit of political advantage."[23]

Such behavior, to be sure, wounded the nation's social fabric. A growing and increasingly confident Indian minority had emerged to challenge an uncomprehending black majority. A hemorrhaging of the nation's spirit was occurring, and the wounds inflicted by the politicians defied any simple treatment. The Federal elections of 1958 and the racially charged rhetoric that it engendered marked a nadir in Trinidad and Tobago's civic life.

Events that occurred in the election's aftermath only exacerbated racial tensions. On April 1, one week after the PNM experienced defeat, an angry and disappointed Eric Williams addressed his supporters at the University of Woodford Square. It was an unusual speech. The chief minister delivered what was essentially an academic paper presenting a statistical review of the voting patterns at various polling stations. He told his audience that his analysis was not an attempt "to juggle with election statistics." Rather, he was providing "a factual, cold blooded analysis of a situation which poses a dangerous threat to the stability of our country and new nation." He went on to demonstrate that Indians, in the polling divisions in which they predominated, had voted almost exclusively for the DLP. Williams claimed that "P.N.M's decimation in areas with an overwhelming preponderance of Indian votes reflects the D.L.P. campaign and the D.L.P.'s appeal that Indians should vote for D.L.P. so as to ensure an Indian Governor and an Indian Prime Minister." He also said that "religion figured heavily in their campaign." And then the chief minister charged: "By hook or by crook they brought out the Indian vote—the young and the old, the literate and the illiterate, the lame, the halt and the blind, men and women."

Williams accused his opponents of "distributing by the thousands . . . a letter addressed, 'My dear Indian Brother' and signed 'Yours truly, Indian.' " The letter was "seditious in intent, offensive, derogatory, an insult to the West Indian nation they claim the honour to represent." Williams was especially offended by a sentence that read: "If my dear brother you have realized these occurrences and the shaky position in which our people are placed, woe unto our Indian nation in the next ten years." An outraged Williams continued:

> Just think of that, Ladies and Gentlemen. An election to bring into being a West Indian nation is fought on one side on the issue of "our Indian nation." The Indian nation is in India. It is a responsible, reputable nation, respected the world over. It is the India of socialism, the India of Afro-Asian unity, the India of the Bandung Conference. It would repudiate any divisive attempts as are being made in Trinidad, as it has repudiated them in Kenya, South Africa, Ceylon and Malaya, in all of which countries the Indian nation and its representatives abroad are working with the movement for self-government and not against it.

After invoking the name of the distinguished prime minister of India, Jahawarlal Nehru, Williams went on to denounce the Trinidadian advocates of "an Indian nation" as "the recalcitrant and hostile minority of the West Indian nation masquerading as 'the Indian nation' and prostituting the name of India for its selfish, reactionary political ends." This was, arguably, the most controversial and criticized speech that Eric Williams delivered during his long political career. Its reference to a sector of the Indo-Trinidadian population in politically pejorative terms was the most memorable phrase in an otherwise dull and perhaps sleep-inducing address. The unfortunate language would come to be perceived by some, notably Indo-Trinidadians, as the signifier of Williams's attitude to the entire race. But it is unlikely that this was his intention, since the PNM included many pro-federation Indo-Trinidadians—as did the DLP—and the chief minister would not have included them in his strong and ill-chosen verbal denunciation.

The speech, entitled "The Danger Facing Trinidad and Tobago and the West Indian Nation," was well crafted. Williams had obviously spent a great deal of time gathering statistics and framing his arguments and conclusions. About twelve typewritten pages in length, this address lacked the spontaneity of the ones he customarily gave at the University of Woodford

Square. The fact that it was carefully researched was an indication of the seriousness of the occasion and the chief minister's intention to say exactly what he meant.[24]

Several observations can be made regarding the timing and nature of the chief minister's speech. Stung by an electoral defeat coming less than two years after he assumed office, Williams was unable to accept the people's apparent repudiation with equanimity. Although it was a Federal election, domestic issues and the young government's performance received disproportionate attention during the campaign. By emphasizing the race-based support for the DLP, Williams was trying to dilute the charge that the PNM's weak performance in office helped to account for its defeat.

An argument can also be made that Williams, despite his commitment to fostering a multiracial democracy, had not completely kept faith, at least rhetorically, with those high-minded principles. His speech could be read as a castigation of the African Trinidadians who had stayed away from the polls, believing that a PNM victory was inevitable. The presumption was that these people would have supported his party and, as Williams said, "Today they regret it bitterly, and they are already swearing that it must never happen again." In the context of the increasing racialization of the country's politics, this seemed to be a soft-core invocation of race. "We sympathize deeply with those misguided unfortunates who, having ears to hear, heard not, eyes to see, saw not, who were complacent . . . who had the DLP covered," Williams asserted.[25]

The chief minister's characterization of the Indo-Trinidadians whose propaganda and rhetoric he cited as "the recalcitrant and hostile minority of the West Indian nation masquerading as 'the Indian nation,' " appeared to be harsh and intemperate. It was a politically charged statement, and Williams was undoubtedly questioning the patriotism of those who were rejecting the Pan–West Indian nationalism that the federation represented and was helping to call into being. These people were the ones who constituted the "recalcitrant and hostile minority" of the emerging West Indian nation. It was first and foremost a political characterization, one that was unacceptably pejorative, sharp, and biting, coming from the head of government. But since it referred to a sector of another "race," it was almost inevitable that the political and the racial would be conflated by many. Yet, as we shall see, Williams was not alone in his concern, first expressed in 1955, about centrifugal forces in Trinidadian society. The chief minister, in an act of incredible political misjudgment and insensitivity, however, exacerbated the passions his speech had aroused by repeating it at San Fernando, a town with an Indo-Trinidadian majority.[26]

♦ ♦ ♦ ♦ ♦ In the immediate aftermath of Williams's speech, European Creole Albert Gomes and Indo-Trinidadian Ashford Sinanan—two prominent opposition politicians—met with British secretary of state John Profumo, Governor Edward B. Beetham, and colonial secretary Solomon Hochoy on April 22. Gomes and Sinanan accused the PNM of inflaming racial tensions with the connivance of the police and government authorities. According to the minutes of the meeting, they said that the PNM trained "gangs of negro roughs," called "marabuntas" or "hornets," to disrupt meetings held by the DLP. They made the startling allegation that these individuals were paid for their services from the public treasury. Governor Beetham contested their assertion that the police allowed heckling at DLP meetings but not at those held by the PNM.

Secretary Hochoy agreed that racial tensions in Trinidad and Tobago were cause for concern. He noted that some government ministers, especially Winston Mahabir and Gerard Montano, had voiced their apprehensions. The charges leveled by Gomes and Sinanan were endorsed by Indo-Trinidadian Bhadase Maraj, another well-known member of the opposition, when he met with Profumo on April 28. The British official who sent a report on the two meetings to London observed that "racial tension and threats are nothing new in the political life of Trinidad and . . . it is more a question of tacit connivance by the Chief Minister in the actions of his supporters than explicit direction by him of a full scale campaign." According to the report, Governor Beetham agreed with Profumo that the "situation was potentially extremely ugly, and that wherever the blame may have lain in the past, the Chief Minister was very seriously at fault for having made a most injudicious speech on racial lines earlier in April which brought strong reaction from the Opposition."[27]

The opposition's primary reaction to the Williams speech found expression in a motion in the Legislative Council on May 23, 1958, to censure him. Offered by Lionel Seukeran, the member for Naparima, the motion accused the chief minister of making a "derogatory attack" on Indo-Trinidadians. Prior to the start of the expected debate, Williams read a statement denying that his intention was to malign Indo-Trinidadians. "All of my public activities," he said, "indicate a complete negation of all forms of racial discussions, racial division, and racial discrimination." He went on to affirm that "my whole philosophy is based on racial integration, racial harmony, and on the policy that where there is a division on political issues, that division must be totally divorced from all considerations of race." He emphasized that both his government and the PNM were committed to "interracial solidarity." Some legislators believed that a debate on the motion to censure was certain to be racially divisive, thereby further inflaming societal tensions. Consequently, they persuaded Seukeran to withdraw it, and he did so, as he put it, "in the interest of this country and in the interest of better racial relationships." In withdrawing his motion, however, Seukeran said that the chief minister had "suddenly gone racial" by virtue of the controversial speech that he had delivered. This was an injudicious comment in light of the conciliatory statement that the chief minister had just read to the legislators and ultimately to the country.[28]

Williams's denunciation of a sector of the Indo-Trinidadian community for lacking in commitment to "the West Indian nation" probably had a favorable resonance in the Colonial Office. Beginning in the mid-1950s, colonial officials had become increasingly concerned about the antifederation stance embraced by some Indo-Trinidadians. Their position on the Federal issue, the officials maintained, was being stimulated by Shri Badir Nath Nanda, the Indian commissioner. The post of Indian commissioner to the West Indies, with headquarters in Trinidad, had been created in 1948. The jurisdiction of the post initially included Jamaica, Trinidad, and British Guiana, but it was later expanded to cover Barbados, St. Vincent, St. Lucia, and Grenada. As one draft of a document prepared for the Colonial Office in the fall of 1954 noted: "The activities in the cultural and social field of successive Commissioners have had the inevitable effect of building up a sense of Indian nationality among the East Indians. In addition to this, the Commissioners have tended, though not too obviously, to exceed their instructions both by the issue of controversial material likely to exacerbate racial tensions and by interesting themselves unduly in local politics."

The draft report, entitled "East Indians in the West Indies," was particularly critical of the conduct of Shri Badir Nath Nanda. It revealed that in September 1954 the acting governor of Trinidad, presumably the colonial secretary, "spoke informally" to him about his interference in local politics. Nanda, the report asserted, "has taken undue interest in the issue of Federation in Trinidad." It continued:

> He is known to have consulted with many of the East Indian politicians . . . and is believed to have spared no effort, unsuccessfully, towards the defeat of a recent motion passed in the Legislative Council. He was present during the first part of the debate both in the morning and the afternoon. He was obviously enthusiastic, smiling appreciatively and nodding his head, at any point scored by an Indian speaker. He listened seriously and with occasional fleeting distaste to other speakers. In the intervals he talked in animated fashion with all of the Indian members. The Trinidad Ministers and non Indian members of the Legislature are convinced that the Commissioner was behind and had organized Indian opposition to Federation. Not a single Indian voted for the government motion.

Moreover, the report contended, "there is not the slightest doubt that Indian party politics is now emerging into the open in Trinidad, that it is a stronger and better organized bloc than expected and that the Indian Commissioner is actively engaged in it all." The commissioner was so influential that "little of political importance now goes on in East Indian circles without his being consulted." And "for the first time in Trinidad there are real fears that the next elections, due in the summer of 1955, or perhaps the elections after that, may return an East Indian party to power." The report concluded on an alarmist note:

> The Indian Government maintains a Commissioner in the West Indies the result of whose activities, both innocent and otherwise is to accentuate the East Indian sense of separateness from the rest of the community and to encourage them to look forward to a position of political and economic domination. It may be that the Government of India cherishes the hope that if and when the East Indians secure control, these two territories [Trinidad and British Guiana], in the course of their constitutional progress, will turn towards India [rather] than the United Kingdom.[29]

Albert Gomes, the chief minister, was not pleased with Nanda's interference in Trinidad's domestic politics. In a private conversation with American consul general William Maddox in late November 1954, he charged

Nanda with "being the directing Indian politician in the Colony, and the spearhead of Indian Imperialism." "If I were a private member and not a Minister," Gomes reportedly said, "I would introduce a motion to have Nanda . . . thrown out of Trinidad." Two weeks later, Maddox reported to the U.S. Department of State on a legislative debate on federation that took place on Saturday, December 11. Titling his report "East Indian Racialism Dominates Legislative Debate on Federation," Maddox went on to observe that "the 18-hour debate which preceded this vote brought a latent but growing East Indian racialism out in the open as a major political factor in Trinidad. . . . The outcome of the debate, important as it is, has been completely overshadowed by the accompaniment of racialism, sinister intrigue, and reported venality . . . threatening to plunge this Colony into internecine politico-racial warfare which could be disastrous to federation as well as to domestic political stability and development."[30]

Troubled by these developments, the Colonial Office held a meeting on January 19, 1955, to develop a strategy to confront them. It was attended by the colonial secretary of Trinidad and seven other officials. According to the minutes of the meeting, Maurice Dorman, the colonial secretary, "explained that the appointment of an Indian Commissioner to the West Indies with headquarters in Trinidad had had the effect of coordinating the local East Indian community on a racial, cultural, and religious basis." Nanda "was a much pleasanter person than his predecessor and this was a factor in making him much more effective." Dorman stated that Nanda "had no love for some of the East Indians' [sic] leaders whom he considered his social inferiors but nevertheless they all found a focal point in him and this tended to strengthen the East Indian separatist movement." The commissioner's status was enhanced "in local Indian eyes" because he ranked higher than "any other representative of a foreign state or other Commonwealth country."

Those attending the meeting wrestled with the appropriate course of action based on the evidence presented against Nanda. One official, a Mr. Mathieson, was of the opinion that if it "could be clearly shown that the Indian Commissioner had infringed his Instructions in any matter or that serious embarrassment was being caused as a result of his activities, it would be possible to ask for his recall." Similarly, if it could be shown that Nanda's behavior "was such that his position had become compromised in the eyes of the Trinidad public as a whole to such an extent as to make it potentially embarrassing both for the Trinidad government and the Indian Government to continue him in office, in these circumstances the Government of India would have no answer to a request for his removal."

It was ultimately decided that there were adequate grounds to ask for Nanda's recall. The governor of Trinidad was to be informed that the secretary of state was prepared to make the request, "and it would greatly help if the request for his removal were to have the backing of the Trinidad Government, although this would presumably entail bringing the subject up in Executive Council." Accordingly, the minutes continued: "The Governor should be asked for his views on this point and in this connection it might be suggested that in order to shorten discussion in the Council the Governor might mention the matter privately to some members beforehand and perhaps arrange for the item to be taken late on the agenda. It should be made plain in any decision reached by the Executive Council that the damage already caused could not be rectified however the Commissioner behaved in the future."[31]

The decision to request Nanda's recall was not surprising in light of the serious allegations against him. Colonial officials seemed to have made up their minds to pursue that course of action before the January 19 meeting with Secretary Dorman. On January 3 N. L. Mayle had observed in a departmental minute that "the East Indian opposition to Federation undoubtedly adds to the difficulties inherent in the attempt to federate the West Indian territories and the possibility of the East Indians getting into power at the next election in Trinidad and reversing the decision in favor of Federation before the Government of Trinidad can be formally committed makes the situation very uncertain." Mayle thought that the problem could be mitigated to some extent if Nanda were withdrawn "and [by] deferring our consent to the appointment of a successor." Five days later, W. I. J. Wallace, another colonial official, stressed that "it is important to bring out that it is not merely the malevolent activities of the Indian Commissioner which are dangerous; even his innocent activities have the bad effect of building up an East Indian sense of separateness from the rest of the community."[32]

Nanda had not confined his activities to Trinidad. In fact, he was accused of "several misdemeanours" in British Guiana as well. A report prepared for the Colonial Office in February 1955 noted that his conduct in British Guiana "can only be regarded as an extension of his main field of action in Trinidad." But "the stimulation of Indian separatism in British Guiana is still in its very early stages." Desirous of containing what one functionary called "Indian Nationalism" in Guiana, the Colonial Office declined the request of the Indian government to open a "sub-office" of the commission in that colony. Nanda had become persona non grata in the two colonies, and his government quietly withdrew him in the fall of 1955, less than a year before Eric Williams became the head of government in Trinidad and Tobago.[33]

Nanda's recall did not ease the fears of the Colonial Office that Indo-Trinidadians would not support a West Indies Federation. Cognizant of the continuing opposition to the union, the Colonial Office and Chief Minister Albert Gomes wanted the British Parliament to quickly adopt an Enabling Act to create the federation. As Lord Lloyd of the Colonial Office explained to Sir Hugh Foot, the governor of Jamaica:

> The Trinidad problem is, I am sure, well known to you and it is a very real one. I am advised that the Indians may well win the Trinidadian elections next September [1956]. As long as they regard Federation as a foregone conclusion, they will probably accept it and an Enabling Act will, I hope, have the effect upon them. If, however, there were no Enabling Act they might well decide to withdraw from Federation which would mean the collapse of the whole scheme. It is therefore not merely a parochial Trinidad interest. On the contrary it involves the future of Federation itself and I am satisfied that if Federation is to come about an Enabling Act before the Trinidad elections is absolutely essential. . . . For all these reasons [Albert] Gomes' interest is to expedite Federation."[34]

The dire prediction by colonial officials that Indo-Trinidadians would constitute a majority in the legislature after the September 1956 elections never materialized. Eric Williams led the pro-federation P N M to victory, and African Trinidadians won most of the seats. As the new head of government, Williams was most likely briefed by the British colonial authorities in Port of Spain on the Nanda imbroglio and their profound unease about the implications of the Indo-Trinidadian opposition to federation. He may have had prior knowledge of Nanda's conduct and probably saw the relevant classified official records. Consequently, he would have been sworn to secrecy and so could not have mentioned Nanda and his behavior to buttress and justify his angry attack on a sector of the Indo-Trinidadian population at Woodford Square on the night of April 1. Since Nanda's indiscretions were not common knowledge, Williams's language appeared to some to be incomprehensibly strident, provocative, and racially insulting, even in a political culture where verbal abuse of opponents had been elevated to an art form and provided good theater. The ghost of the speech would continue to haunt Williams, but he never invoked the Nanda affair to help exorcise it. To do so would have embarrassed the Indian government, compromised official secrets, and further inflamed local tensions.

♦ ♦ ♦ ♦ ♦ In spite of what appeared to be a political misstep at the time, Eric Williams continued to affirm his commitment to a multiracial Trinidad and Tobago. He promoted "interracial solidarity," expressing the view that it should be "translated into practical terms." He was committed to "the equality, not only juridical and constitutional but also political and moral, of all, with reservations only in respect of merit and talent." Without identifying any individuals or groups, he rejected "the opposition which seeks to divide our inter-racial community and to substitute a new colonialism based on the aristocracy of race for the old colonialism based on the aristocracy of the skin." Affirming his identification with his native land, Williams denounced "the opposition which looks to Mother England, or Father India or Grandmother Africa." By 1960 he had begun to show a greater empathy for the cultural pulls of Indians by endorsing "such practical steps toward unity whether it is the teaching of Hindi or the attention to Indian culture." He also spoke approvingly of a proposal by his colleague, Winston Mahabir, that an Institute of Afro-Asian Studies be established at the University of the West Indies.[35]

As part of the process of effecting a modus vivendi with his opponents, Williams developed a very cordial relationship with the Indo-Trinidadian leader of the DLP, Rudranath Capildeo. In November 1964 Norman Costar informed the Commonwealth Relations Office that Capildeo spent most of the year in London teaching mathematics at the University of London, the result being "that many people suspect him of being in the pay of Dr. Williams, who has indeed told me himself that he has an understanding with him." As Costar did not elaborate on the nature of that "understanding," and if his report is accurate, this issue and its implications for the political ethics of the two men must remain tantalizingly speculative.

The high commissioner reported that since the Independence Conference of 1962, "there has been a tacit agreement recently made almost explicit between the Government and Opposition not to play on the underlying racial animosities which still exist below the surface in Trinidad." Costar maintained that "Dr. Capildeo's occasional racialist utterances contrast with his actual tameness in action." He noted that "in practice there is undoubtedly some degree of racial discrimination in the handing out of jobs and in determining how and where the Government spend their [sic] money." But "this discrimination . . . is not very serious and in the job sphere is more anti-white than anti-Indian." Embracing some of the stereotypes of whites about the incapacities of blacks, Costar held that any discrimination in their favor "is counter-balanced by the superior industry, ability and providence of the non-negro races in Trinidad."

Costar correctly observed that Trinidadians feared that "racial troubles in British Guiana will spread by example" to their nation. Consequently, "British Guiana is a useful object lesson to Trinidad on the awful consequences of the incitement of racial feelings by politicians." This had led the two principal parties in the country to refrain from pursuing "overt racialist policies."[36] Williams, as we have seen, was actively involved in the quest for a solution to British Guiana's problems. As head of government, particularly after the controversial speech of April 1, 1958, he was sensitive to the need to avoid exacerbating racial tensions in Trinidadian society and to spare his nation British Guiana's agony. Williams was undoubtedly pleased when Commonwealth secretary Duncan Sandys compared Guianese premier Cheddi Jagan unfavorably to him in October 1963. "The trouble with Jagan," Sandys wrote Williams, "is that he has failed to show your statesmanship in dealing with racial matters and merely pays lip service spasmodically to your example."[37]

The intractability of the racial problem in Trinidad could be observed in the personal anguish and disappointment of Victor Bryan, an African Trinidadian who served as minister of agriculture from 1950 to 1956. Bryan was elected to the Federal Parliament in 1958 as a candidate of the DLP but left the party to become an independent member. At a meeting with American consul general Edwin Moline in September 1960, Bryan said that he probably enjoyed greater respect among Indians than any other black person in Trinidad. Nevertheless, he, in Moline's words, "had been disappointed, and indeed exploited, by the East Indians in the past and that he can no longer do business with them." He had "been forced to swallow humiliation in the interests of party harmony." According to Moline, Bryan had concluded that "the East Indian community cannot be trusted and has no independent political future in Trinidad." The consul general continued:

He elaborated somewhat on his visit to East Africa in 1955, where he claims to have seen how Indian communities on that continent treated the Negro far worse than did the White man—and is convinced that the East Indian community of Trinidad is essentially no better. He suggested a visit to the shops owned by East Indians in downtown Port of Spain where one would observe that there are no Negroes in positions above that of janitor or lowliest clerk. The East Indians, he insisted, practiced widespread nepotism, and if they took control of the government would open the way to greater infiltration and domination of the business community by people of their own race. He added that even an educated and well-placed representative of the community such as Ashford Sinanan, Leader of the DLP Opposition in the Federal House, was not an exception to this generalization.[38]

Bryan's candid conversation with Moline points out the obstacles that stood in the path of racial understanding and healing. His comments, which were intended only for the ears of the American diplomat, revealed a distrust of the Indians as deep as that displayed of blacks by Indian leaders Rudranath Capildeo and Ashford Sinanan in similar conversations. Public remarks by the country's leaders, no matter how racially conciliatory, reassuring, or sugarcoated, must be weighed against this inner climate of mutually shared suspicion and mistrust.

Florence Daysh, another member of the Federal Parliament, who was described as a light-skinned Barbadian, was persuaded that the racial problem in the Caribbean resulted primarily from a failure of leadership. She maintained that Harold MacMillan's observation that "multi-races" were "living together in harmony in the West Indies" was "utterly ridiculous." In fact, "we loathe each other." Referring specifically to Trinidad and Tobago, Daysh, according to the American consul in Barbados, believed that Ashford Sinanan could be a real leader if "he would only admit that he is partly Negro, as she did several years ago. She said that she has talked to him at length about the advisability of doing this." Sinanan never made such an admission, and there is no independent corroboration of Daysh's claims about his racial background. Still, the notion that a leader's mixed racial ancestry was an asset in the Caribbean at the time was at best intriguing and may even have been a perspicacious observation.[39]

Racially intemperate remarks by politicians and others did not, however, lead to any serious disruption of the civic culture of Trinidad and Tobago. Despite being frayed, the bonds that united the various groups were stronger than those that divided them. The competition for political power at election time worsened the racial tensions, but some degree of normalcy was restored after the political wounds inflicted by the protagonists on one another and on the society as a whole had healed. Still, Eric Williams's policies such as the demand for Chaguaramas and his use of a virulent anticolonial rhetoric angered many, and the opposition to him did have a racial dimension. Some Europeans interpreted his attacks on colonialism as the product of racism and felt he was undermining the privileges they had acquired in society by virtue of colonial rule and their skin color.

♦ ♦ ♦ ♦ ♦ White business leaders feared and therefore generally opposed a government headed by Eric Williams. The term "white business community," of course, lends itself to diverse interpretations. One American diplomat, Harry M. Phelan, gave what appears to have been a valid definition of this group: "Since the adjective 'white' when applied to people in Trinidad is used rather loosely, we will define the 'white business community' as composed of those Trinidadians (they are mostly white) who own or otherwise control the large import agencies, wholesale and retail establishments and include other Trinidadian or foreign whites who manage foreign-owned investments in the banking, shipping, exporting and agricultural fields."[40] These enormously privileged people comprised a relatively small group, but they exerted an influence on the economic life of the society that far exceeded their numbers.

Many other Europeans, not just business leaders, also disliked the idea of a black head of government. Williams was aware of this opposition, once telling William H. Christensen of the U.S. mission that it consisted of "reactionary, fascist forces that live in the past." Writing to the State Department on November 24, 1961, Christensen observed that the "remark of Dr. Williams about certain people not liking the idea of having a black Premier was not without foundation." The previous day, a white businessman "with roots going back 100 years" had complained to him that Trinidad was a "police state," claiming that his mail was being opened and his telephone tapped. The businessman accused Williams of wanting to start "a black aristocracy." Fearful of developments, the businessman had sent his wife and children to England before the elections scheduled for December 4.

Christensen acknowledged that the views of "this white businessmen are not unique." The president of the federated Chamber of Commerce had told him that it would be in Trinidad's best interest if Williams were defeated. His informant "also felt that Williams was displaying excessive arrogance and crudity in his talks to the electorate that was 'not becoming.' " A third white man "with large agricultural interests" also expressed the hope that Williams would be defeated and accused members of his government of corruption. Christiansen believed that people such as his informants "represent a white element of Trinidad comprised of older and senior members of the Chamber of Commerce, but their views were not shared by "the younger, more progressive types."

The American envoy, like so many others before and after him, could not resist providing an assessment of Williams's character and personality, particularly as they related to his stance on race. Although he believed that the premier "has a great potential as a genuine leader who could accomplish much for Trinidad," he "is volatile and easily offended and he has a chip on his shoulder and a smoldering resentment in his heart against colonialism which, of course, means the whites." Christensen had known Williams for eighteen years, having worked with him on the Anglo-American Commission and the Caribbean Commission. Williams was now "a more outgoing and confident man" but "is capable of lapsing into irresponsible hate language, and dredging words like colonialism, slavery etc., into his conversation, which of course is calculated to impress those who have nothing to lose—and Trinidad has a disturbing number of these people." Clearly, Christensen wanted such unpalatable aspects of Trinidad's past forgotten, viewing any discussion of them as expressions of antiwhite sentiment. But he understood Williams's pugnacity: "He is a black premier and he will, he believes, be reelected and he will make them like it—and if they don't, they can lump it."

Christensen feared both Williams's reelection and his defeat. Since Williams "had drunk the heady wine of political leadership his re-election could make him into such a brash and arrogant semi-dictator that he would be difficult to deal with," the envoy predicted. On the other hand, defeat "would fill him with such dangerous frustration which, on top of the ones he has lived with all his life, could turn Trinidad into a dangerous racial cauldron that could well spill over and cause trouble." Yet, "with proper handling," Williams could use his talents for the benefit of Trinidad and the West Indies.[41]

Christensen correctly captured the fears of the white business community in his report, but he caricatured Williams, continuing a familiar practice by British and American diplomats. The December 1961 election campaign and its aftermath produced great unease among whites. The premier did nothing to lessen this anxiety as he singled out Europeans for sustained abuse during the campaign. "These vagabonds . . . these people whose hands are at your throats," he declared, "see your rising dignity and economic progress as something to be destroyed so that they may enter and rule." He denounced "the local business big-shot families, French creoles in particular, [who are] determined to control this country as they controlled it for several years, [and who] are going all about the place irritating PNM members, saying they don't want any black Premier."[42]

It was widely rumored during the election campaign that wealthy white businessman, J. B. Fernandes, had contributed $160,000 to the DLP for the avowed purpose of getting Williams "out." Ten days after Williams's electoral victory, prominent whites received an anonymous letter recommending that they leave the country. Two PNM functionaries also promised that the party would "take care" of its friends and its enemies, a declaration that Williams repudiated. Whites feared retribution, but, according to Harry Phelan, "very few of these fears have been specifically identified in the conversations" he held with them. However, whites thought that the Williams government lacked administrative talent and was given to "graft and corruption and they lacked confidence in the police and the courts." Despite the "scare talk," there was no "concrete evidence" of the export of capital from the island. But Phelan predicted that, given the "jittery nerves" of the white community, "further threats by PNM leaders or any overt discriminatory action on the part of the government prior to complete independence, could seriously affect the confidence of the business community in the future of the territory."[43]

Whites were not the only ones "jittery" about the future. The 1961 election campaign, as did the campaign of 1958, exposed the festering racial tensions in the country. The DLP, with its largely Indo-Trinidadian following, adamantly opposed the new system of voter registration and the use of voting machines, which, it argued, would intimidate "unsophisticated" Indo-Trinidadians and keep them from the polls. The DLP's passionate opposition to voting machines was matched by the PNM's equally strong defense of them. The rhetoric on both sides was harsh and irresponsible. DLP leader

Rudranath Capildeo urged his supporters to make bonfires of the voter registration cards that they would be issued before the election and "smash" the voting machines. Obviously annoyed by PNM hecklers when he addressed a meeting on October 15, Capildeo declared: "Arm yourselves with weapons in order to take over this country. I have stood as much of this nonsense as I can. We have to take measures in order to protect ourselves. We can no longer stand up and allow people to trample on us anymore. We are taking over this country whether they like it or not because for the past five years this country has noted a decline, which has never been witnessed before. Break up and destroy every PNM meeting; wherever Dr. Williams goes, run him out of town; wherever Dr. Solomon goes, run him out of town."[44]

The PNM spokespersons used similar inflammatory rhetoric. Minister of Home Affairs Patrick Solomon threatened: "If Capildeo incites violence, I will slap him in gaol fast . . . and he would not get out again. Nobody will be able to bail him out. . . . No tuppeny ha-penny dictator [is] going to walk through this country and tell people to take up arms."[45]

These and other bombasts by both sides were unworthy of the political leadership of Trinidad and Tobago. At another level, the DLP complained bitterly about hooligans who broke up its meetings at will. On November 27, 1961, Capildeo, accompanied by an unnamed "prominent white businessman," called at the U.S. mission to discuss the political situation with William Christensen. He was also hoping to meet with the American ambassador to the United Nations, Adlai Stevenson, who was then visiting Trinidad, to solicit his help in having a U.N. observer monitor the elections. Capildeo complained to Christensen about the violence against DLP supporters by "PNM hoodlums." He predicted that in a fairly contested election, the DLP would win, since the PNM's black support was concentrated in the urban areas, whereas Indians who supported the DLP were distributed throughout the country. "They can't beat us in the country," Capildeo boasted.

Capildeo said that he was exercising restraint over his "extremist" supporters who wanted to use violence against the PNM. But, he added, "if we lose the elections, Trinidad is going up in smoke." He would not be responsible for such a development, since "the decision would be forced" on his supporters. Indians, Capildeo said, were not easily intimidated, and the view among them as far as blacks were concerned was that "we can mash [match?] them [P N M] bullet for bullet and still have half to spare." Calling Eric Williams a congenital liar, Capildeo maintained that he, Capildeo, had no color or religious prejudices and that he was more at ease in the company of non–East Indians than with his own ethnic group.[46]

Christensen, in reporting the conversation to the State Department, noted that Capildeo spoke "lucidly," but he "gave the impression of being somewhat elusive and also displayed a penchant for exaggeration in order to drive his point home." Christensen believed that "the intense preoccupation of Dr. Capildeo with race, and the widespread talk on all sides of East Indians versus the blacks with the whites caught somewhere in between, has elements of explosive trouble."[47]

"Explosive trouble" did not occur, however. During the campaign Williams courted Indo-Trinidadians and openly asked for their support, telling them that they, like blacks, had been the victims of oppression.[48] This appeal, in effect, transcended race, but it met with little if any success. Williams also assured his supporters that "the new society of the P N M is a dramatic demonstration of the fact that we, all of us from Africa, from India, from China, and from Europe, all of us who now know the contributions which our respective ancestral home has made to the advancement of world civilization, all of us, the amalgam of all these separate and distinct strains of racial stocks, all of us, we too can take our place, our rightful place in the sun."[49] Such high-minded invocations of the virtues of Trinidad's multiracial society failed to ease the tensions, as the racial lines continued to harden. In an ugly but interesting twist, the D L P published court records relating to Eric Williams's alimony obligations in the United States, describing him as "recalcitrant, hostile, contemptuous and mutinous to law," words eerily reminiscent of Williams's 1958 "recalcitrant minority" speech.[50]

♦ ♦ ♦ ♦ ♦ Williams's spectacular electoral victory did not allay the fears of the growing Indian minority or those of the whites. Prior to the election Capildeo had told the U.S. mission that the partitioning of the island between Indians and blacks was a strong possibility. Eric Williams had indicated his opposition to such an action, but the issue did not disappear. This was an extreme proposal, but it reflected the festering racial tensions and fears. On January 16, 1962, Capildeo, Ashford Sinanan, and Burnley Jardine, a prominent businessman, presented William Christensen with a catalog of complaints. The men charged that the Williams government was tapping telephones and watching the houses of certain people, including Jardine's. Indians were experiencing discrimination, and the police had committed indecencies against Indian women during the recent election campaign. Sinanan contended that Williams was on the way to making Trinidad and Tobago a police state, and Castroism and communism were on the horizon, an extraordinary charge given Eric Williams's avowed anticommunism. Sinanan said that Spanish was being emphasized in the schools not because of Venezuela's proximity, since "Venezuela does not welcome Negroes from Trinidad." Rather, "it's all because of Cuba." He promised that he would "stay and fight it out," but he was making preparations to send his family out of the country. The men, according to Christensen, argued that Britain had "sold the West Indies down the river, and that the United States must stiffen the back of Britain."

The DLP delegation bemoaned the alleged emergence of a black aristocracy in Trinidad and Tobago, comprised of such people as Eric Williams, Patrick Solomon, and Ellis Clarke, the chief justice designate. The three men hinted that an association with the United States might be a way out for their nation. Capildeo assured Christensen that the vast majority of the people would vote for political integration with the United States. Sinanan was even more optimistic, predicting that "at least 90 percent of the voters would vote for association with the United States." "Make no mistake about that," the legislator emphasized.[51]

Their predictions did not materialize and the corrosive racial tensions eased somewhat after 1962, although race still remained central to Trinidad's political culture. Governor Solomon Hochoy remained pessimistic about the future of race relations in his native land. He feared what might happen when the Indo-Trinidadians achieved majority status and assumed power. As he lamented to American consul general R. G. Miner in March 1962, "I hope I am not around when the East Indians are in the saddle in Trinidad . . . this may sound far fetched but believe me I know my people." This was a tantalizing observation, subject to different interpretations. Hochoy may have been predicting a racial blood bath if the Indo-Trinidadians came to power, or he may have been suggesting that once in power, they would initiate reprisals against the blacks for allegedly discriminating against them. Only time would tell whether Hochoy's crystal ball was accurate.[52]

Although there was an apparent racial modus vivendi in the mid-1960s, the language of race was still used as the elastic signifier for the problems that bedeviled the young nation. African Trinidadians, especially those who remained at the bottom of the economic ladder, began to use a racialized language to articulate their grievances. Hoisting the banner of "Black Power," these people blamed the predominantly black Williams administration for their condition, further complicating Trinidad's racial climate. Their language was the language of race, but the roots of their problems were essentially economic.

On assuming the post of chief minister in 1956, Eric Williams had committed himself to an aggressive program of economic development. His first five-year development plan, which was financed largely by the country's own revenues, represented a shift from concentration in agriculture to the establishment of an infrastructure to provide a hospitable environment for foreign capital. This meant, in practice, allocating funds to the repair and construction of roads, an emphasis on education, the improvement of health care, and so on. In many respects, the development plan was based on the "industrialization by invitation" principle borrowed from Puerto Rico and initiated by the previous administration. The results of this program were impressive: between 1951 and 1961 the country's GDP experienced an annual growth of 8.5 percent.[53]

Trinidad's economic growth was enhanced by its oil resources. Texaco and Royal Dutch Shell contributed substantially to the development of the oil industry by building sizable refineries. The economy also benefited from the Commonwealth Sugar Agreement that the government signed with the United Kingdom, guaranteeing it a market on favorable terms. In 1966, for example, the raw sugar that Trinidad and Tobago exported to Britain, the United States, and the other West Indian Islands averaged TT$227.72 per ton, compared to the world prices of TT$62.00 to TT$76 per ton. The production cost per ton was estimated at an alarming TT$200 per ton, a clear indication that the Commonwealth subsidies were crucial for the health of the sugar industry. Significantly, foreigners controlled the oil and sugar industries.

Much of the white businessman's suspicion of the Williams government waned after the nation achieved its independence in 1962 and Williams toned down his verbal assaults on white privilege. In fact, the new prime minister developed a rather cozy relationship with the big companies. He embraced "free enterprise," an aggressive anticommunist stance, and passed the controversial management-friendly Industrial Stabilization Act in March 1965, creating an industrial court system that had the power to render binding decisions in labor disputes.

The political stability of Trinidad and Tobago and an industrialization-friendly government proved attractive to foreign investors. In 1965 American citizens had about US$350 million invested in the island; by 1970 the amount had climbed to US$500 million, distributed among roughly forty firms.[54] Similarly, British investment amounted to £150 million in 1970. Despite these expressions of confidence in the Williams regime, there were some very disquieting signs of potential trouble. Per capita income, for instance, had averaged an astonishing growth of 7.9 percent annually between 1956 and 1961, due mainly to an expansion in oil production. Such growth could hardly be sustained indefinitely, and it fell markedly after 1963 to an annual average of about 2 percent. The unemployment rate for much of the 1960s and in 1970 ranged between 14 and 20 percent, and the young graduates of the schools felt its impact most keenly. A maldistribution of wealth, a rather limited domestic market, an economic dependence on oil and sugar, and their vicissitudes on the world market, in addition to an annual population increase of 3 percent, exacerbated the nation's economic and social problems. In 1964 Norman Costar observed that Trinidad "was apparently politically stable and economically prosperous and welcoming overseas capital," but it had "real problems in the field of unemployment and labour-employer relations which need careful handling if disaster is not to come."[55]

Solomon Hochoy, who later became the governor general of an independent Trinidad and Tobago, recalled that he had told Eric Williams in 1956 that he had fifteen years (or three terms in office) to make fundamental changes in the country or he would face "rejection." Fourteen years later, on April 17, 1970, just three days before Williams requested a declaration of a state of emergency in the nation, Hochoy "hinted broadly" to the acting British high commissioner that "he was not himself satisfied with Williams' achievements and that unless clear signs of progress became evident during the next twelve months, senior civil service disenchantment would lead to the withdrawal of their support from Williams."[56]

Hochoy was not alone in expressing some disenchantment with Williams's stewardship of the government. The ascendancy to power of the Williams-led PNM in 1956 had created enormous expectations that the emerging nation would be radically transformed. The P N M was a nationalist party par excellence led by a man who was intellectually gifted, who understood the world and its power relationships, and who recognized the necessity to educate his people politically and to shape their national consciousness. Williams's lectures at the University of Woodford Square were unparalleled as the former professor imparted his understanding of history to the people, enjoining them to command their destinies. This experiment in the political education of a people reflected Williams's view that a literate and politically conscious citizenry constituted the foundations of the new Trinidad and Tobago and the bedrock of the democracy that he envisioned.

His lectures, speeches, and other public statements helped to create, arguably, the most politically informed and sophisticated citizenry in the Anglophone Caribbean. Those Trinidadians who were in their teens in the 1950s and who came of age in the 1960s were socialized into an intellectual climate of repeated condemnation of colonialism, human oppression, and racism. Williams's speeches of the 1950s and after independence promoted the gospel of self-determination, sacrifice, and nation building. His "Massa Day Done" speech of March 1961 is the best known, but it was one of scores he delivered in Trinidad and abroad. His Independence Day broadcast to the nation on August 31, 1962, invoked similar themes. When he pugnaciously rejected the paltry sum that the British offered his new nation on the occasion of its independence, the new leader spoke for much of the colonial world, although no one followed his example. His challenge to the Americans over Chaguaramas was another bold exercise in anticolonialism and an assertion of the right of all nations, even one as small as Trinidad and Tobago, to chart their own destiny.[57]

By word and action, Williams not only produced an informed citizenry but also, by so doing, unleashed certain forces that he could not control and that ultimately threatened to overwhelm him. The Trinidad and Tobago of 1970 was not the Trinidad and Tobago that Williams inherited in 1956. There were fundamental differences in political consciousness, and many of those who had been socialized by Williams into the need for change had become impatient with the pace of that change. It is important to underscore the fact that Williams's most vociferous critics in 1970 were in their twenties and thirties, and, in some cases, in their teens. This included people like James Millette, Geddes Granger, Carl Blackwood, and Dave Darbeau. Even A. N. R. Robinson, who would play a seemingly ambiguous role in the events of April 1970, had been a disciple of Eric Williams and was widely seen as his heir apparent.

Lloyd Best, a university-based intellectual who became a caustic critic, praised Williams for shaping the consciousness of his generation. When Williams offered himself to lead the country in 1956, Best wrote, "it touched a chord in the Anglo-Saxon personality. The time at last had come. Here was a leader with technical command, with abundant energy and with roots among the people. What mountains could not now be moved? Williams evoked the whole past of Negro struggle not only in Trinidad and Tobago but in the wider West Indies as well. The Negro population, moved to tears that this, their most distinguished son, had come back to lead, gave him all the trust they had. They trusted him blind; they trusted him almost without question."[58]

Best showed himself to be a good student of *Capitalism and Slavery* by noting that Williams's assumption of political power provided Trinidad with "the long awaited chance to take the economy in its charge, to redress for once and all the historical balance which had from the start been so heavily weighted against the men from across the Middle Passage." Best admitted that the Williams administration had made significant contributions to the welfare of the country: "They have raised levels of material welfare for the Negro as for everybody else; yes, they have wrought all manner of changes across the face of the land." In this rendering, Eric Williams and the PNM had produced major transformations in the texture of the nation's life, but, according to Best, "The one thing that the PNM has not done is to redress the historical balance and to give the Negro a sense of being master in the castle of his skin." Yet the fault did not lie entirely with Williams. As Best put it, "We have found it easier to rely on a Doctor than to take up our own beds and walk."[59] The kind of psychological remaking that Best and other critics desired could not, of course, have been accomplished in eight years. Williams himself had repeatedly emphasized this imperative. But the prime minister had other problems to confront, including the continuing task of improving the standard of living for the citizens of a nation with limited resources.

Critics of Williams's economic policy said that its reliance on foreign capital constituted a form of neocolonialism. Lloyd Best maintained that this dependence promoted "obsequiousness, servility, and in the last resort [represented] a shattering vote of no-confidence in the population of Trinidad and Tobago."[60] Others complained that a white-dominated economy was reminiscent of the days of slavery. George Weekes, the outspoken president of the Oilfield Workers Trade Union, expressed this point of view at a speech in Woodford Square on May 12, 1966:

> I am a man of color. I am a black man. This is a black man's country. We have shed our blood for independence. Some of us have traveled thousands of miles to fight imperialism. The people of Trinidad and Tobago are determined to be free. . . . It is a struggle of the people of Africa, Asia, and Latin America against white imperialism. Today as I stand here, I am looking not at Dr. Williams' government. They are the visible government. But what I look at is beyond that. There is an invisible government of the country: the same people who are responsible for us being here as slaves, who gave us the whip. . . . The invisible government of Trinidad and Tobago is the Chamber of Commerce, the US and the UK.[61]

These were harsh words, indeed. But they reflected an emerging disenchantment with Williams, particularly among the young black youth who previously had been his ardent supporters. Many of them had been influenced by the ideology of Black Power, then being promoted by some African Americans. To those who subscribed to its promise, Black Power meant the control by blacks of their institutions, as well as political and economic autonomy. As an ideology, it rejected white control and asserted the right of peoples of African descent to chart their own destinies.

♦ ♦ ♦ ♦ ♦ The ideology of Black Power resonated among blacks in various parts of the diaspora. Although conditions in Trinidad and Tobago were not an exact replica of those that existed in the United States, some of Black Power's principles applied. The dispossessed groups in the nation were black and brown, and economic power, in large measure, continued to wear a white face. This was not new in a country that had seen slavery, indentured servitude, and colonialism. But Williams had assaulted white power and privilege, proclaiming an end to "Massa Day." To those who were still economically deprived even as they watched the growing foreign economic presence, Black Power had an immediacy that could hardly be restrained. The proponents of Black Power, therefore, framed a large proportion of their criticism of Williams in economic terms. Theirs was the language of economic nationalism, the language of the poor who did not share fully, if at all, in the economy over which Williams presided.

Eric Williams was not insensitive to the plight of the poor. In 1955, after a visit to John John, a notoriously depressed area in Port of Spain, he had recorded the following reactions:

> John John is incredible . . . the conditions are incredible; among the worst I have ever seen. After an hour, I could not distinguish between house and privy in many cases. A house in John John can be a wooden crate no bigger than the one in which I moved some of my books from the Caribbean Commission, or it is something at the angle of a hospital bed, one has to walk gently beside it for fear that it will tumble down; or if it is a building—the size of a two bedroom house but containing 25 "apartments," and if this does not tear you apart, then there is the pitiful shed with inhuman benches and a man's trousers hanging out to dry where Sunday School is kept. The flies, the garbage, the "drain" which will overflow even in an ordinary shower and flood all the houses around, the dirt tracks with boulders so slippery that even in a mild shower, I had to be assisted or I would have fallen; the distance that water has to be carried in these conditions: all that is John John. Heaven help its inhabitants if ever there is a serious fire, for no man can. . . . The clearing of John John is simple justice to the suffering people of John John, our own people, who like those of us do not live there, vote, work and pay taxes. John John must go, now.

In view of such economic hardship and deprivation, he urged in the mid-1950s the development of a welfare state. But "the social welfare state," he cautioned, "cannot be kind only to be cruel. It cannot encourage birth only to produce full unemployment from cradle to grave." Williams argued that "welfare automatically demands production [and] amenities automatically presuppose jobs." His prescient conclusion would return to haunt him in 1970: "A population which increases out of proportion to the exploitation of economic resources is a standing invitation to revolution, disorder, or at least, antisocial behaviour. The democratic right of life cannot be divorced from the complementary right of the pursuit of happiness, that is to say, the right to work."[62]

Williams never lost his deep concern for dispossessed people like the residents of John John. He continued to use his considerable rhetorical skills to shape their political consciousness: "Hold up your heads high, all of you, the disinherited and dispossessed, brought here in the lowest states of degradation to work on a sugar plantation or a cocoa estate for Massa. All of you, don't hang your heads in shame. You are today taking over this country from the Massa's hand."[63] Such exhortations were important for the mental regeneration of a people, but there were structural problems that impeded rapid and substantial change in their economic condition. Economic growth, at least in the 1960s, had not kept abreast of demographic increase, producing demands for radical transformations of the economy and admonitions to Williams to fulfill his promise to create a new order.

Trinidad did not stand alone as far as Black Power–inspired assaults on its economic structure were concerned. In October 1968, for example, Black Power advocates rioted in Kingston, Jamaica, forcing a frightened government to declare a state of emergency. Officials blamed Walter Rodney, a young Guyanese lecturer in history at the University of the West Indies, Mona, for stimulating the revolt. Rodney had given a series of lectures in the ghettos of West Kingston advocating the "assumption of power by the black masses of the islands." Misunderstanding the demands by Black Power advocates for an end to imperialism and for economic power to be concentrated in black hands, Prime Minister Hugh Shearer dismissed them as "irrelevant." He condemned "Black Power radicals" for "pushing causes and voicing slogans that they have adopted from elsewhere. We have a black government, we have votes for everyone, we have got rid of colour discrimination," the black prime minister asserted.[64]

The unhappy truth was that leaders like Hugh Shearer, and to some extent the Eric Williams of the late 1960s, were not fully attuned to the strivings of those at the societal margins and the young intellectuals who helped to give them voice. On the other hand, the accumulated problems caused by centuries of neglect could not be solved in a few years, despite governmental will and the best of intentions. Williams, for one, never doubted his own commitment to social transformation. This led him, at first, to ignore the criticisms of Black Power advocates. He viewed the leaders of the movement as "subversive" but not really dangerous, thinking that the public would eventually become repulsed by their methods and deny them legitimacy. The British high commissioner reported that "the Negro middle class (not to speak of the East Indians) did quickly become disgusted, but they became frightened by the violence and threats, and dismayed by Williams' inactivity and failure to give a lead."[65]

That some Black Power activists in Trinidad and Tobago would resort to violence in 1970 was neither anticipated nor predictable. In the preceding years there had been considerable intellectual ferment led largely by members of the New World Group, composed of intellectuals at the University of the West Indies. Their critiques of various aspects of Caribbean life were both trenchant and provocative. Founded in February 1969, the National Joint Action Committee (NJAC) became the organizational expression of the Black Power movement. Its membership consisted of university students, graduates, trade unionists, various youth groups, and so on. This amorphous collection of individuals was united by its passionate demand for a restructuring of Trinidadian society. Its members—articulate, energetic, and noisy—exerted an influence on black urban youth, in particular, that far exceeded their number.

Not all the leaders and supporters of the Black Power movement, to be sure, were inspired by high-minded principles of social justice. Some were motivated by a deep anti-Williams animus, others were political opportunists, and still others were ideologically barren hangers-on attracted by a chance to create mayhem in the society. British high commissioner Richard Hunt would later report that "early on in the troubles, one of the NJAC leaders was asked by a member of my American colleague's staff what he really wanted, and he replied, 'I want to see the white man crawl.'" Hunt added that "killing was a commonplace theme of speeches in Woodford Square. . . . The NJAC leaders would, I imagine, like to frighten away the white community—if necessary, or indeed for preference, by killing some of them."[66] This was undoubtedly an exaggeration and, to some extent, more a reflection of white fears than an informed assessment of the intentions of the principal leaders of the movement and their animating ideology.

There is no evidence that NJAC was planning to launch a frontal challenge to the Williams government, at least not so soon as early 1970. Its leadership of what would come to be called the "February Revolution" was a historical accident. On February 26, 1970, some NJAC supporters met in Port of Spain to demonstrate in support of students from Trinidad and Tobago who were on trial in Canada. The students had been accused of damaging the computer center at the Sir George Williams University to protest the alleged racism of some professors. With its vast investments in

Trinidad and Tobago, Canada became, in the eyes of Black Power proponents, a major example of white, foreign domination of the economy.

The demonstration was rather small, attracting about two hundred to
three hundred persons. Led by NJAC leaders Clive Nunez, head of the Transport and Industrial Workers Union, Geddes Granger, a former president of
the Guild of Undergraduates at the University of the West Indies, and Dave
Darbeau, an undergraduate at the university, the demonstrators damaged
some Canadian-owned banks. They entered the Roman Catholic cathedral
and, according to one newspaper, "staged a sit-in which lasted just under
an hour. Chanting 'Power, Power,' and other revolutionary slogans, the
marchers swarmed into the Independence Square Cathedral, occupied the
pews, the pulpit and other chairs near and around the altar."[67]

The government apprehended nine demonstrators, charging them with
disorderly conduct in a place of worship, unlawful assembly, and conspiracy
to disturb the peace. Their arrest inflamed tensions, and on March 4 ten
thousand people demonstrated in Port of Spain to protest their detention.
Over the next several days sporadic acts of violence continued, as Port of
Spain descended into disorder. Matters took an ominous turn when six
thousand supporters of NJAC marched to Caroni, a sugar-producing belt, to
make common cause with Indian workers. Although Bhadase Maraj, the
Indian head of the All Trinidad Sugar Workers Union, opposed this invasion
of his terrain, his people gave the marchers a generally polite reception.
The bond that NJAC wanted to forge with the sugar belt workers did not
materialize, for years of suspicion between African Trinidadians and Indo-
Trinidadians could not be erased overnight. Racial divisions trumped an in-
cipient class consciousness. The tensions had been exacerbated by sporadic
acts of arson targeting Indo-Trinidadian stores and houses in such places as
San Juan. Most Indo-Trinidadians were convinced by actions such as these,
as well as by attacks on businesses owned by whites, Chinese, and Syrians,
that Black Power was inimical to their interests, despite NJAC's rhetoric to
the contrary and the movement's efforts to enlist their active support.

Eric Williams responded to the developing threat to his administration by
addressing the nation on March 23. He admitted a failure in communication
between the government and the people and regretted that his administration had been tardy in implementing plans for economic reform. The prime
minister announced a number of new initiatives such as new taxes on banks,
industry, and higher incomes that would be earmarked to provide jobs and

technical training for the unemployed. He sought to assure the citizens of Trinidad and Tobago that he understood the imperative behind the protests: "The fundamental feature of the demonstrators was the insistence on black dignity, the manifestation of black consciousness and the demand for black economic power. The entire population must understand that these demands are perfectly legitimate and are entirely in the interest of the community as a whole. If this is Black Power then I am for Black Power."[68]

Williams's speech failed to satisfy the protesters and to restore order. Perceiving his plans as inadequate to meet the problems that they were highlighting, NJAC and its allies continued their efforts to destabilize the regime. The weeks of protest had produced a heightened sense of political consciousness among the dissidents, and their support was increasing. On April 9, for instance, some thirty thousand mourners attended the funeral of Basil Davis, who had been killed in a skirmish with the police. George Weekes of the Oilfield Workers Trade Union told his members on April 13 that the union was "in the ranks of revolution." Geddes Granger urged his supporters to cease paying their bills, purchase only the bare necessities, and prepare to be soldiers. He asked the military to withdraw its support for the government, a request that would take on a larger meaning as the crisis intensified. "This is war," Granger declared.[69]

The leaders of the Black Power movement underestimated Williams's developing resolve to restore law and order and to defend his administration. One anecdote provides a few clues to his subsequent response. During his visit to Tanganyika in 1964, Williams had been surprised to learn that President Julius Nyerere had shown signs of weakness when he faced a coup. As the acting British high commissioner there reported, Williams "asked me incredulously whether it was really true Nyerere had run away during the army mutiny, and I could only confirm that this was so. I said that anything he could do to put some stiffening into Nyerere would be of value. Williams expressed amusement at the thought of "little Trinidad" stiffening anyone, but said he would try."[70] According to the British ambassador to Ethiopia, Prime Minister Williams had told him that if he encountered a similar situation in Trinidad and Tobago, namely "a threat to the welfare and integrity of Trinidad from an unrepresentative and determined minority group, he himself would not have the slightest hesitation to follow the same course, in his case to call in the U.S. troops based in Trinidad. Why for a paper scruple and his personal face, should he hand over his country

to foreign subversion? He had offered President Nyerere the equation—
Zanzibar is to Tanganyika as Cuba is to Trinidad."[71] Communists in Zanzibar had been accused of subversive activities in Tanganyika, and Williams
feared that Cuba posed a similar threat to Trinidad. He undoubtedly learned
some enduring lessons from Nyerere's behavior.

As the crisis in his nation deepened, Williams not only had to pay more
sustained attention to the demonstrators who were growing in number and
gaining confidence, but he also faced threats to his leadership within his
administration and party. A. N. R. Robinson, the young, talented, restless,
and ambitious deputy leader of the PNM, enjoyed a certain degree of popularity within the Black Power movement and, to some, appeared ready to
participate in an effort to depose the prime minister. The acting British high
commissioner reported that Eric Williams was aware that Robinson "was
plotting some kind of mischief against him." This suspicion had persuaded
him not to leave the country on April 12 to attend a meeting of Caribbean
heads of government in Kingston. He had not revealed his intention to skip
the conference and even went to the airport. Williams "spoke of unusual
telephone calls which suggested that Robinson was surprised to find that he
had not left." The acting high commissioner, who reported that "Dr. Williams did not elaborate," admitted that "I may have read more into his words
than was really there." But, the British official continued, "it is widely believed that he [Robinson] was engaged in a plot to oust Dr. Williams and
rumour, picturesquely, has Robinson sitting behind the Prime Minister's
desk when Dr. Williams came back from seeing the Trinidad delegation off
to the Kingston meeting."[72]

Six weeks later Richard Hunt, the new British high commissioner, seemed
more certain that Robinson was implicated in a plot to remove Williams from
office. Writing to T. R. M. Sewell of the Foreign and Commonwealth Office
(formerly the Colonial Office) on May 29, he conjectured that Robinson
"having, it seems, failed in an attempted coup on April 12 . . . will probably
aim to sap Williams' strength within the party [PNM] as a whole rather than
aim for another coup." Robinson, however, had resigned his ministerial post
on April 13, adding further fuel to the rumors. He later explained that he had
stepped down because he was concerned that Trinidad and Tobago should
not "move into a situation where political activity would be virtually suspended and we would then rely on [a] naked police force . . . a grave danger to
all newly independent countries."[73]

Williams was not unduly worried by Robinson's defection from the Cabinet. In a letter to his daughter and close confidante, Erica, on April 13, he admitted that "it is a little too early to get the feel of the new situation, but the first reactions from [the] party and [the] country are favourable." Williams, in this very private letter, did not directly accuse Robinson of being involved in a plot against him, but he noted: "It turns out to be a good thing that I did not leave for Jamaica yesterday." He surmised that Robinson left the Cabinet "because of our weekend action to call out the Special Reserve Police and the Regiment Volunteers." Robinson, Williams speculated, "sees a confrontation looming ahead and wants to be no part of it." The prime minister was relieved that Robinson had resigned his Cabinet post. "People just cannot see that Robinson's move strengthens me rather than weakens," he asserted, adding: "I won't fall into the trap he has set of getting me to dismiss him as Deputy Political Leader. Leave him there where I tell him nothing, ask his advice on nothing, and everyone knows I have no confidence in him. He is just another George Brown. If the Party wishes him to be removed, that is another matter. But I shall not initiate it, especially on the advice of two-timers who were formerly his warmest supporters."[74] Williams's contemptuous reference to Robinson as "another George Brown" evoked memories of the man who served in various capacities in the British Labour Party, engaged in efforts to undermine its leadership, particularly in 1947, and became ineffective by the time his active political career ended in 1970.[75]

Meanwhile, Williams reported to Erica on April 18 that the PNM's Legislative Group had met to "discuss the general situation" and those in attendance had affirmed their loyalty to him and to the PNM. A. N. R. Robinson spoke at the end of the meeting, but Williams characterized his remarks as "unimpressive and [he] seems to have had no impact." He, however, awaited a clearer assessment by the party's General Council. Williams stressed the likelihood there of both an attack on certain ministers by supporters of Robinson, as well as "demands for [Robinson's] ouster" by his own. "I am trying to counter both," he asserted, assuring Erica: "In terms of strategy we should not at this stage give Ray [Robinson] an opportunity or an alibi to move [from the PNM]. He must make the jump himself." The party's view, however, "was that we should resist all demands for resignation of other Ministers."[76]

Although Williams thought that "the public seems reasonably satisfied" with his "call up of reinforcements," he had written to Erica on April 14 complaining that "the heaviest cross I have had to bear is the panic among the Ministers, especially after Robinson's resignation and the call up of the reservists." "[They] can't see," Williams continued, "that it is just a *show* of force, to let Black Power know what they are up against and to reassure the general population."[77] The prime minister was gratified that "there has not been a single incident since the calling up of the reserves," reassuring his daughter that "whoever is losing his head, I am not one of them."[78]

Betraying the human side concealed by his confident, tough, and inscrutable exterior, Williams confessed: "The only physical effect I can see of the strain is a bad night on Wednesday. I had had a piece of bad news before going to bed. I woke up at 3 and had trouble to get back to sleep. When I took my pressure on Thursday morning it had dropped to 110 [Williams suffered from low blood pressure all of his life]. But it may be a loss of weight. I was down below 140 this morning. I have to step up on what I eat."[79]

Williams himself would not be forced into taking any precipitous action. In his note to Erica on April 14, he had told her that he continued to "play it cool." He reported that his calling up of the reservists "has put the Black Power boys in a dither." He was of the opinion that many "are breathing fire and brimstone but are probably as afraid as hell." Williams also indicated that he was engaged in long-term planning to address the unemployment situation and that he was implementing some short-term measures. Moreover, he was "moving in to take control of the party" by meeting with the Youth League, the Legislative Group, the Chairmen and Secretaries of Constituencies, and so on. He was, he added, "working now on a statement of absolute priorities aimed at the unrest." But Williams recognized that there were "clouds on the horizon," such as the impending trial of those who had been arrested on February 26, the forthcoming May Day parade, whose leaders were predicting the participation of 100,000 workers and Black Power supporters, as well as the expected visit of Stokeley Carmichael, the influential American-based but Trinidadian-born Black Power leader, to Guyana. An incendiary speaker, Carmichael had the potential to inflame tensions in Trinidad, and Williams remained concerned about the possible disruptive effects of such a visit. The prime minister predicted, however, that "with God's help we shall overcome."[80]

In spite of possessing overwhelming confidence in his ability to control and defeat the developing challenge to his administration, Williams took no chances. He did not feel particularly threatened by the "Black Power Boys," assuring Erica that "I feel they are slowly losing ground, public resentment is rising, and we are in control of the situation." In his judgment, a far more serious threat was posed by "a deterioration of industrial relations." He informed Erica that there had been "several stoppages and strikes."[81] Although the labor unrest had different imperatives from the Black Power movement, the two forces fed off one another and were mutually reinforcing. The strikes that were occurring, as well as the ones that were being planned, threatened to paralyze the country, exacerbate tensions, and enhance the efforts of those who wanted to remove the Williams government from office.

The prime minister recognized the serious implications of the work stoppages and understood the need to calm a jittery public. "The place as you can expect is full of rumours," he told Erica on April 18. "As Trinidadians panic easily, you can imagine the position," he confided. But Williams continued: "More and more people are demanding that we call out the Regiment. The present position . . . is that the police are in full control of the situation."

Williams saw the hand of George Weekes behind the labor unrest. He informed Erica of Weekes's "growing influence," adding that he "has long been aspiring to take over all unions." Although the prime minister believed that "the police can handle the situation," by April 18 he was beginning to think about a firmer response to the labor- and Black Power–generated unrest. He indicated to Erica that a declaration of a State of Emergency would mean control by the army, and that would have two advantages. First, "it would allow us to detain all the leaders, including Weekes," and second, "it would assist in creating a climate of order and quiet in which one could pass essential legislation, including a Public Order Act to control demonstrations and an amendment to the Trade Union Act, limiting any union to one particular industry," a move that would have been clearly aimed at Weekes.[82]

Confirming the prime minister's resolve, the acting governor general informed the British High Commission on April 17 that Williams would not ask for a "proclamation of a state of emergency until he is surer than he is now that the mass of the people had lost patience with the NJAC." Williams did not wish to make martyrs of the Black Power leaders while they retained the loyalty of their supporters. He also did not want to produce a "confrontation between their supporters and the security forces, many of whose 'kith and kin' would be on the other side."[83]

But as Williams discovered, time was not on his side. On April 19 about three hundred factory workers at Caroni's main sugar refinery went on strike, and the next day NJAC marshaled two thousand sugarcane workers, mostly Indians, to join them in a six-mile march. The situation intensified when George Weekes and the NJAC leaders threatened to organize widespread strikes affecting utilities. Irked by the Weekes–NJAC alliance, the Trinidad and Tobago Labour Congress, an association of what its president called "responsible unions," threatened, according to Williams, "to take matters into their own hands" unless a state of emergency was declared.[84]

Williams was also beginning to fear the consequences of a march into Port of Spain, planned for Tuesday, April 21. This demonstration, organized by NJAC, was to be joined by some dissident sugar workers under Weekes's direction. Bhadase Maraj, the leader of the cane field workers, publicly supported the actions of the sugar workers, but, the British acting high commissioner noted, "privately he let it be known to Dr. Williams that Weekes would be unstoppable unless a State of Emergency was imposed."[85] Aware of the worsening situation, the beleaguered prime minister asked the acting governor general to declare a state of emergency, effective April 21. The police quickly rounded up the leaders of the Black Power movement and imposed a curfew.

♦ ♦ ♦ ♦ ♦ The state of emergency was essentially a vulnerable government's response to threats to its survival by civilians, not the military. Its declaration, however, became the catalyst for a mutiny by about eighty soldiers at the Teteron Bay barracks. Some loyal officers, soldiers, and civilians were held as hostages. The mutineers seized the armory, but quick action by Captain David Bloom, the English-born commander of the Coast Guard, prevented them from escaping, thereby containing the situation. Bloom would later describe the mutiny as "a close run thing for the country."[86]

Williams responded to these developments by turning his official residence into his command headquarters. Acting British high commissioner Charles Thompson described him as being "more animated than usual" on April 20, in "bounding good spirits in fact overconfident" on the twenty-second, but "preoccupied" on the twenty-third. American ambassador J. Fife Symington told Thompson "that at no time during the several visits which he paid to Dr. Williams was the latter anything but his usual self." Yet Symington later informed the State Department that Carlos Irazabal, the

Venezuelan ambassador to Trinidad and Tobago, said that during the crisis "he thought Williams was completely out of his head (loco) and that he had acted in a most irrational manner. He referred to frequent direct phone calls during the day and nights of April 21 and April 22."[87]

When new British high commissioner Richard Hunt presented his credentials to Williams on April 29, eight days after the emergency had been declared, he found him to be "very cordial and seemed wholly relaxed." He reported that "when I commented on his untroubled appearance he remarked with a laugh that somebody or other, and preferably the Prime Minister, should remain calm in the present circumstances." At the end of their meeting, "he observed jocularly that I should look after myself since it would be unfortunate if 'they' captured the new British High Commissioner."[88]

Understandably, Williams's mood varied in accordance with his assessment of the crisis and his chances of prevailing. The American ambassador, despite his observation that Williams was his "usual self" during the early days of the crisis, also noted the "tendency of [the] Prime Minister and [Cabinet minister] Gerard Montano to fluctuate between war panic and optimism." But the ambassador added: "We cannot overlook [the] possibility that Williams in normal times a very moody person, may have been pushed by tension which he is under dangerously close to irrationality." The prime minister "does not seem to grasp the basic fact that there can be no compromise with the rebels if his government is to survive for long." Williams had not appealed for public support on television and radio but "instead he has holed himself up in his residence."[89]

Confronting a major extralegal challenge to his administration for the first time, Williams must have experienced moments of confidence as well as deep concern. But there is no consensus among those who saw him in action that he lost his nerve. He realized, however, that he needed external help if he were to get control of the situation. The American ambassador, among others, "urged him to take forceful action against the mutineers, even at some risk to the hostages, since in his view, the situation demanded action and the majority of the country would support it." The acting British high commissioner believed that Williams was not receiving good professional advice "on what reliable forces were available to the government and how they could be effectively deployed against the mutineers."[90] Based on his assessment of the military needs, Williams urgently requested assistance from five countries: the United States, the United Kingdom, Venezuela, Jamaica, and Guyana. Each country would respond according to its own interests.

Once he received word of the mutiny, Williams asked the United Kingdom for 12 light machine guns, mortars, 300–400 rifles, hand grenades, and 6 scout cars.[91] Her Majesty's government was somewhat disposed to provide help, although members of the Cabinet wrestled with the propriety of intervening in the internal affairs of an independent Commonwealth nation. The government was willing to send weapons but not soldiers, even if requested to do so. The Cabinet was mindful of the sizable British investment in Trinidad and Tobago and of the two thousand British citizens who resided there. The chancellor of the Duchy of Lancaster, a Cabinet member, reminded his colleagues that Williams was a "strong and effective leader, who had considerable influence in the African Commonwealth countries, and it was therefore important that we should do what we could to maintain our relationships with him and avoid giving him any grounds of complaint as regards our response to his appeal."[92] National self-interest carried the day, and the British government dispatched two frigates to Trinidadian waters, the HMS Jupiter and the HMS Sirius. They were both ordered to stay safely out of sight, thirty miles off shore. The Sirius carried a detachment of Royal Marines, ostensibly to protect British citizens and property. Williams withdrew his request for weapons support a day after he made it, telling the high commissioner that he was expecting an adequate supply of weapons to arrive "very shortly," presumably from the United States.[93]

Williams also sought assistance from British prime minister Harold Wilson in conveying a request to the leaders of Nigeria and Tanzania to have one thousand soldiers and their equipment standing by in case they were needed to restore order in Trinidad. Wilson was somewhat disposed to intercede on Williams's behalf but saw some potential difficulties if he did. He assured the embattled prime minister of his concern "that you are faced with these difficult problems." Wilson asserted that "no one is better qualified than you to handle the situation," adding: "I am sure that your wise statesmanship will enable you to overcome successfully this emergency."[94] The British prime minister informed Williams that he had instructed his high commissioners in Lagos and Dar Es Salaam to stand by to convey his request for armed support to their respective governments. He thought, however, that "judging by our recent experience of a similar problem elsewhere in Africa, it might be that the chances of getting an early and favourable reply to your requests would be enhanced if your messages were transmitted by your High Commissioner in London to the Nigerian and Tanzanian High Commissioners." Wilson observed that the Nigerians were "very conscious of their reputation as an independent African state" and were likely to be more receptive to a request "that did not pass through our channels."

In asking for troops from the African countries (and from other Caribbean nations), Williams emphasized to the acting British high commissioner that the help he needed could not come from white soldiers. Nor did he want such assistance to fall under the auspices of the Organization of American States, since that alliance was dominated by the United States. Rather, the aid should come from the Commonwealth nations and might best be offered by Nigeria or Tanzania or Zambia, in that order. In reporting these views to his government, the acting high commissioner noted that Trinidad had pursued "an absolutely correct attitude" over Biafra and maintained close relations with Nigeria at the United Nations; it was expected to establish diplomatic relations with Nigeria shortly. He also indicated that Williams hoped that the British government would provide the air transport that would be needed, as the African nations were not equipped to do so.[95]

Williams's appeal to the United States received a rapid and to some extent positive response. The American ambassador reported that the prime minister had telephoned him repeatedly on the afternoon of April 21 pressing for any kind of assistance. Specifically, he requested troops, a warship, and weapons. The Americans denied the request for troops and the warship but quickly dispatched 50 general-purpose machine guns with 75,000 rounds of 9-mm ammunition, 10 81-mm mortars with 200 rounds of ammunition, 100 two-inch mortar smoke bombs, and 50 81-mm smoke bombs. They did not provide the 8 scout cars and 10 antitank weapons that Williams also wanted.[96]

Acting quickly, the Americans sent the helicopter carrier Guadalcanal to the area and ordered five other vessels to stand by. These vessels were sent to the territorial waters of Trinidad and Tobago "strictly as a precautionary measure for the safety of US nationals," according to the British high commissioner. The Americans would justify their provision of arms "if necessary, as a commercial sale to a constitutional government whose arsenal has been captured by mutineers." Williams would later report to the nation that Trinidad and Tobago had paid for those weapons.[97]

Venezuela also supported the Williams government. The prime minister had asked his neighbor for two warships, one to be sent to Port of Spain and the other to the army barracks at Teteron Bay, as well as soldiers and ammunition. In response to these requests, Venezuela sent a naval vessel to Chaguaramas and flew twenty armed men to Trinidad to protect Williams. The prime minister, however, rejected the "guards" that Venezuela was willing to assign to his residence. Although Venezuela had had an uneasy relationship with Williams, its government, according to the British embassy in Caracas, wanted Williams's "kind of government" to survive "against the subversive threat of a Black Power kind."[98]

In contrast to the positive responses of the United Kingdom, the United States, and Venezuela, the governments of Guyana and Jamaica were ambivalent. Forbes Burnham, never on consistently good terms with Williams, quickly decided against sending troops to Trinidad. Keenly aware of the presence of Black Power advocates in Guyana, he did not wish to exacerbate the tensions in his country. Meeting with the British high commissioner in Guyana on April 22, 1970, Burnham "made clear his deep anxiety about the situation in Trinidad and the effects it may have on Guyana." He also had to consider "whether he would be justified in backing a loser."[99]

The Jamaican reaction was similar. Prime Minister Hugh Shearer had confronted disturbances inspired by Black Power advocates in 1968 and had no desire to further alienate them. Accordingly, he sought to buy some time when Williams made his request by dispatching his security chief to Port of Spain to determine whether Jamaican aid was actually necessary. Shearer's emissary reported that Williams had the situation well under control, thereby relieving the Jamaicans of the need to make any decisions on the matter.

As it turned out, Eric Williams did not need the assistance of the Commonwealth governments to resolve his nation's crisis. The quick action by his Coast Guard in containing the mutineers was of critical importance. The appointment of the experienced Brigadier Joffre Serette to replace the incompetent Colonel Stanley Johnson was a masterstroke: Serette brought a fine reputation and energy to the tasks at hand, and he proved to be a skillful negotiator. In explaining his success, Brigadier Serette noted that the rebel leaders had proved unequal to the situation. He thought that their plans had been "shaky," as was evident from the maps that had been discovered. The heavy arms, he said, had been stacked in trucks on April 21 to be transported to Port of Spain before the rebels were ready for action. None of them, for instance, even knew how to use an 8-mm mortar.[100]

◆ ◆ ◆ ◆ ◆ The events of February to April 1970 represented a watershed in the political career of Eric Williams. The prime minister confronted a serious extralegal challenge to his administration, one that he could hardly have anticipated. Williams had predicted that Jamaica stood a better chance of experiencing racial unrest than did Trinidad and Tobago.[101] When compared to the February Revolution, however, the disturbances in October 1968 in Jamaica constituted an insignificant skirmish. For a leader who had spent much of his political career condemning colonialism and affirming the dignity of the peoples of African descent, the challenge from the Black Power advocates must have been a psychological blow of inestimable proportions.

To the proponents of Black Power, Williams had become the enabler of the imperial economic presence that he had denounced so persistently and vehemently. Dismissing Eric Williams as "that bitch," Geddes Granger said, "In Trinidad we have a black puppet in office presiding over the white exploitation of the island."[102] Such a pejorative comment must have been a bitter pill for Williams to swallow. After all, he was largely responsible for the high degree of political consciousness in Trinidad and Tobago, and those who denounced him and sought his removal from office were his progeny.

To end the crisis, Williams introduced a plan for national reconstruction to increase "the degree of national control over the national economy." The plan was also intended to expand "popular participation in all sectors of the economy," permit its diversification, and achieve "full employment." In addition, Williams accepted the resignation of two members of the Cabinet described as "white." The business community did not greet this development with any enthusiasm. Nor was Kamaluddin Mohammed, an Indian member of the Cabinet, pleased, leaving High Commissioner Hunt to report that he disliked "this concession to Black Power demands." Mohammed indicated that "he might have to reconsider his own position in the Cabinet." He admitted, according to Hunt, that "the gap between the youth, which had grown up since the PNM came to power . . . and the middle aged establishment—black, brown, and white—was very deep and the youth had been heavily indoctrinated with racial hatred." This was certainly a judicious observation on the political mood of some of the young, but Mohammed's comments also showed that to the degree that Williams assented to some demands of the Black Power advocates, he ran the risk of losing support from other quarters.[103]

The Foreign and Commonwealth Office watched the emergence of Black Power demands in the Caribbean with some trepidation. In the immediate aftermath of the February Revolution, an internal memorandum grudgingly acknowledged that "Black Power could be an overdue and welcome sign of a sense of national identity in the Caribbean." It speculated that Black Power could bring about a measure of unity among the states and could contribute to a "reduction of privilege." But, the memorandum cautioned, Black Power's "racist bias is sinister and in its more extreme manifestations its aims are inimical to our interests." The office feared that the spread of the ideology either "as a destructive force overthrowing constitutional governments or in terms of political movement in favor of nationalization of foreign enterprises . . . is bound at least to affect our commercial relations within the region." Quite clearly, the representatives of foreign economic privilege recognized the threat that Black Power posed to their interests in Trinidad and elsewhere in the Caribbean.[104]

The ideology of Black Power notwithstanding, successive administrations in Trinidad and Tobago pursued, with varying degrees of fervor, the economic policy of industrialization by invitation. Much of the capital needed for development continued to emanate from foreign sources and, in the language of Black Power, remained white. That said, the term "Black Power" was in many respects a misnomer in the Trinidad and Tobago of 1970. The language of race was employed, but the power that its proponents sought was one that would produce a restructuring of the economic arrangements of the society. The beneficiaries, it was hoped, would be a racially amorphous group of dispossessed peoples. Proponents of these changes used the language of race to legitimize their claims, but the demon was a structural oppression that knew no racial boundaries. Race, for some, became the grammar of the competition between blacks and Indians for political power and the spoils of office, simultaneously creating and exacerbating societal tensions. Generally speaking, neither the PNM nor the DLP resisted the temptation to exploit race to its advantage, and both parties were ultimately diminished by their behavior. The racial specter continues to haunt the nation, inflaming its tensions, heightening its fears, and corroding its soul.

◆ ◆

EPILOGUE

◆ ◆ ◆ ◆ ◆ Brilliant, brash, confident, buoyant and energetic, Eric Eustace Williams burst into the political arena of Trinidad and Tobago in 1956. He was fresh and idealistic when many other contestants, such as Tubal Uriah Butler and Albert Gomes, had seen better years and were visibly tired. The historian-scholar dominated that difficult arena for twenty-five years, and over the long haul he, too, would become exhausted. But the years 1956–70 saw him at the peak of his vitality as he displayed both his considerable talents and his limitations. For many, Williams the charismatic leader was the unquestioned messiah—the relentless foe of colonialism, the harbinger and enabler of change, and the architect of his country's independence. To others, he was an enigmatic leader who was cantankerous and divisive, contemptuous of opponents, and a harborer of dictatorial tendencies.

Williams was nothing if not a controversial figure throughout his long tenure in office. Unaccustomed to dealing with a pugnacious West Indian leader who was obviously their intellectual superior, colonial officials condemned him in the most pejorative terms. But Williams the historian knew all too well that rebellious slaves and those who sought to claim their freedom throughout the Americas were also the objects of contempt by slaveowners and the authorities. Those who challenged the status quo, and who imagined and struggled to attain more equitable power arrangements, could count on the opposition of the powerful and the privileged. The colonial authorities' opposition to Williams and to his policies that were anathema to them only fortified his sense of the righteousness of his cause. When Williams launched his campaign to reclaim Chaguaramas, an uncomprehending American counsel general recommended to the U.S. State Department that steps be taken to remove him from office. The British and Americans collaborated to contain an unyielding Williams, the British all the while maintaining a public posture of principled neutrality.

The struggle for Chaguaramas provided Williams with his most dramatic and significant political triumph. He had forced the Americans to abandon their intransigence and their disdain for negotiating with West Indians and to approach the conference table. Williams did not obtain all that he wanted at the Tobago conference in 1960, but the Americans agreed to release significant parts of the land occupied by the U.S. base to Trinidad and Tobago and to pay US$30 million for the privilege of occupying the island's soil. A small West Indian colony had contested American might and had come away from the struggle, if not completely victorious, at least having delivered some effective blows.

There were some obvious similarities between the Chaguaramas struggle and the imbroglio with the United Kingdom over the size of the golden handshake, or the parting independence gift. Williams, the leader of a small territory, had engaged in a David and Goliath–like contest with two powerful adversaries. But though he forced the Americans to concede the justice of his demands, the British, for the most part, remained imperiously stubborn. Williams settled the dispute largely on the United Kingdom's terms, providing him with a grim lesson in the continued efficacy of imperial might.

The contests with the United States and the United Kingdom were both symbolic and practical. It was not solely about the return of Trinidadian soil or the size of the parting gift. Williams had served notice that the old international order was crumbling and that even small colonies and fledgling new nations were claiming themselves both physically and psychologically. They would not remain passive when their perceived rights were being threatened or violated, regardless of the might of the perpetrator.

Williams's vituperative assaults on the colonial authorities and the Americans gained him few admirers among their ranks. But the bitter and accusatory language of protest was the only effective weapon he had at his command. Its tone frightened some of his countrymen and other West Indian leaders who feared retribution from the objects of Williams's criticism and ire. His language was acerbic, unrelenting, and devastatingly sharp. To Williams, colonialism was the source of the ills in the Caribbean, and the language he used befitted the enormity of the crime. He had proclaimed an end to "Massa Day" and enjoined Massa's victims to command their future, embrace a new definition of themselves, and act accordingly.

But this was easier said than done. While Williams lambasted the evils of colonialism, he could be the aggressive supplicant for imperial favors. The "golden handshake" imbroglio was one dramatic manifestation of this approach. The author of *Capitalism and Slavery* never saw Trinidad and Tobago as a supplicant, however. To him, slavery and the slave trade had constituted the foundations of Britain's wealth, and the colonies had a moral claim on the imperial treasury. Williams made this argument with persistence and intellectual vigor, but seldom to great effect. The imperial authorities were as adamant in their resistance to it as Williams was in the consistency of its articulation.

Eric Williams was, on the larger West Indian stage, the dogged proponent of political federation and economic integration. He did not stand alone in his advocacy of them, but he took second place to no one in the power and urgency of his arguments. The failure to save the West Indies Federation from its early death was a function of the triumph of a debilitating insularity over the interests of the common weal. Williams's insistence on a strong Federal center was farsighted, rational, and entirely feasible. Its adoption was the only way in which an effective union of the disparate islands could be forged, their centrifugal tendencies curbed, and a coherent, viable developmental policy implemented. His vision fell victim to the groundless fears of the Jamaicans that a strong Federal center posed a threat to the island's industrial development. Norman Manley's indecisive leadership on the Federal question and Alexander Bustamante's myopia also guaranteed its failure. The Jamaicans never made a credible argument that the Federal government wanted to stymie their island's economic growth or stood to gain anything by doing so. The referendum that resulted in Jamaica's withdrawal from the federation and its collapse was fought more on domestic issues and less on the advantages of federation to the polity and the sister islands.

By advocating a strong Federal center, Williams stoked the fires of Jamaican secessionism. His eventual willingness to compromise on the issue was an act of statesmanship, but as events unfolded it came to nought. That Williams chose independence for Trinidad and Tobago over a new Eastern Caribbean Federation should have been predictable. He had made it clear that his country would not assume the economic burdens such a union engendered absent substantial economic aid from Great Britain. It was more an expression of national self-interest than a rejection of an association with his neighbors.

The offer of unitary statehood to some of the other islands had little resonance, except in Grenada. The islands feared the loss of their individual identities, and there was a strong distaste for Eric Williams and his political style. Unitary statehood required even more planning and psychological preparation than a federation commanded; it could not be brought into existence by the stroke of a pen. The ill-fated West Indies Federation was a stark reminder of the centrifugal forces at work in the region and the inability of the leaders to contain them. Williams also knew that unitary statehood had no prospect of survival without the injection of considerable economic aid from a mother country anxious to abandon its impoverished children.

The racial bogey provided yet another challenge for Williams at home and elsewhere. Worried that British Guiana's racial virus would spread to Trinidad and Tobago and worsen its societal woes, the doctor offered his services as mediator. It did not take him long to recognize the futility of his efforts and that the country's leaders—Forbes Burnham, Cheddi Jagan, and Peter D'Aguiar—were not genuinely interested in healing its wounds. Back home, Williams as an African Trinidadian had an emotional connection with blacks, one that deepened as a result of his immersion in their history. His extended state visit to Africa in 1964 gave practical expression to his realization that a positive embrace of Africa was an essential ingredient for the development of a Trinidadian and West Indian consciousness and identity. Ironically, the fundamental role that Williams played in raising the racial consciousness of his people and proclaiming the death of Massa almost became his political undoing. In 1970 a young, impatient, and racially conscious group of Black Power advocates defined him as the enemy and sought his removal from office. His intellectual children, at least some of them, were repudiating their father. It was a case of attempted patricide.

William's relationships with the growing Indo-Trinidadian minority were equally complex. His description of the antifederation sector of that population as a hostile and recalcitrant minority in 1958 became, for many, the signifier of his attitude toward all Indians. But, as indicated in Chapter 8, the colonial authorities were also alarmed by the opposition of some Indians to the proposed federation and in 1955 asked for the recall of the commissioner from India, a man charged with encouraging such a divisive stance. Williams had made a colossal blunder, or so it seemed at the time, and though he would later speak eloquently and passionately of a racially blind nationalism, the damage had been done. Still, racial tensions ebbed and flowed and the society functioned normally except during the heat of election campaigns, when racialized passions were unleashed. On their part, the people of European descent had an uneasy relationship with the black leader, and the harsh invective he directed at them, at times, did little to alleviate mutual suspicions. Inevitably, the colonial past remained a part of the present, inflaming emotions and proving itself frustratingly tenacious to Williams, who was imagining a new order and calling it into being.

Eric Williams, more than any other Anglophone politician of his time, addressed the issues that were fundamental to the making of the modern Caribbean in greater depth and with admirable consistency and passion. But his success on the larger Caribbean stage was limited by the endemic insularity of many of the region's leaders and weaknesses in his character and political style that interfered with his ability to achieve his vision and to work productively with others to realize those possibilities. Williams, then, was unquestionably more effective in articulating a larger vision than in realizing its actualization in a Caribbean-wide context. His personal limitations notwithstanding, Eric Williams was the greatest leader his people produced in the twentieth century. His domination of the political arena, though at times halting and unsteady, was no historical accident.

A quarter century after his death, Williams continues to be a dominant figure in the political culture of Trinidad and Tobago but much less so in the West Indies as a whole. His imprint still remains on the societal landscape, and his successors have struggled to escape his shadow and to establish their own political identities. But the domestic issues he championed and the larger Caribbean causes he advocated—with the possible exception of a political federation—remain the essential concerns of the contemporary administrations. The measure of a political leader should not be his or her personal idiosyncrasies but rather the capacity to imagine a different and better future for a people and the possession of the will to challenge and lead them to achieve their possibilities. Seen in this light, Eric Williams's central place in the history of the modern Caribbean is secure.

ABBREVIATIONS

CO   Records of the Colonial Office, Commonwealth and Foreign and
        Commonwealth Offices, Public Record Office, London
CRO   Commonwealth Relations Office
DO   Records of the Dominions Office and of the Commonwealth Relations
        and Foreign and Commonwealth Offices, Public Record Office, London
EW   Eric Williams
EWMC   Eric Williams Memorial Collection, University of the West Indies, St.
        Augustine, Trinidad
FCO   Records of the Foreign and Commonwealth Office and Predecessors,
        Public Record Office, London
FO   General Political Correspondence of the Foreign Office, Public Record
        Office, London
NA-DS   National Archives, U.S. Department of State, Record Group 59, College
        Park, Maryland
PREM   Records of the Prime Minister's Office, Public Record Office, London
Report Report (Nos. 1-7) on African Tour, February 14-20, 1964, EWMC, vol. 008.
RG   Record Group

INTRODUCTION

1   EW, unpublished version of memoirs, EWMC, vol. 139. The information about
    Williams and his childhood years comes from drafts of his memoirs (referred
    to in this book as his "unpublished version of memoirs"), located in the
    EWMC. These scattered nuggets, which are both typed and handwritten, and
    sometimes unpaginated, do not appear in the published version. For the pub-
    lished memoir, see EW, *Inward Hunger: The Education of a Prime Minister* (London:
    Andre Deutsch, 1969).

2   EW, unpublished version of memoirs, EWMC, vol. 139.

3   Ibid.

4   Ibid.

5   Ibid.

6   Kelvin Singh, *Race and Class Struggles in a Colonial State: Trinidad, 1917–1945* (Cal-
    gary, Canada: University of Calgary Press, 1994), 13.

7   EW, "Life with Father," manuscript, EWMC, vol. 139.

8   EW, *Inward Hunger*, 113–14.

9   Ivar Oxaal, *Black Intellectuals and the Dilemmas of Race and Class in Trinidad* (Cambridge, Mass: Schenkman, 1982), 113.

10 Among those removed from the PNM were C. L. R. James, Williams's mentor and at one time editor of the *Nation*, the party's official organ. Patrick Solomon, Winston Mahabir, Elton Richardson, and Learie Constantine—all founding members of the PNM—also fell out of favor with Williams.

11 Edwin Moline to U.S. Department of State, July 12, 1961, Central Decimal File, Trinidad, NA-DS, box 1670, folder 741F.00/6-261.

12 Sir Stephen Luke to Philip Rogers, January 1, 1957, CO 1031/2573.

13 Ibid.

14 R. C. C. Hunt to Foreign and Commonwealth Office, July 29, 1970, FCO 63/594.

15 See Selwyn D. Ryan, *Race and Nationalism in Trinidad and Tobago: A Study of Decolonisation in a Multiracial Society* (Toronto: University of Toronto Press, 1972).

CHAPTER 1

1   EW, lecture on "The British West Indies in World History," Trinidad Public Library, April 19, 1944, EWMC, vol. 743.

2   EW, *Inward Hunger: The Education of a Prime Minister* (London: Andre Deutsch, 1969), 33.

3   Ibid., 35.

4   Ibid., 41.

5   Ibid., 33–34, 45–48.

6   EW, *British Historians and the West Indies* (New York: Charles Scribner's Sons, 1966), 37–58. For a discussion of these historians' views, as well as extensive quotations from their works, see ibid.

7   Ibid., 233.

8   EW, lecture on "Intellectual Decolonisation," Howard University, Washington, D.C., April 29, 1964, 13, EWMC, vol. 638.

9   Ibid., 17.

10 EW, *British Historians*, 13.

11 Ibid.

12 Quoted in EW, *British Historians*, 166–211.

13 EW, lecture on "The British West Indies in World History," 10.

14 Ibid., 10–11.

15 EW, lecture on "Intellectual Decolonisation," 13.

16 Ibid., 8.

17 Ibid., 11.

18 Ibid., 13.

19 EW, "My Relations with the Caribbean Commission," in Selwyn Cudjoe, ed.,

Eric E. Williams Speaks: Essays on Colonialism and Independence (Wellesley, Mass.: Calaloux Publications, Amherst, distributed by University of Massachusetts Press, 1993), 125.

20 Ibid., 116.

21 Ibid., 120.

22 Ibid., 121.

23 Ibid., 160. See also "Notes on a Conference of West Indian Writers," EWMC, vol. 812.

24 EW, "My Relations with the Caribbean Commission," 164–65.

25 Ibid., 165.

26 William P. Maddox to U.S. Department of State, June 22, 1955, Central Decimal File, Trinidad, NA-DS, box 3201, folder 741B.00/6-1655.

27 Cudjoe, Eric E. Williams Speaks, 238.

28 Ibid., 239.

29 Ibid.

30 Ibid., 240.

31 Ibid., 254.

32 Ibid., 255.

33 Ibid., 247.

34 Ibid., 254.

35 U.S. Consul General, Port of Spain, to U.S. Department of State, March 24, 1961, Central Decimal File, Trinidad, NA-DS, box 1670, folder 741F.00/ 1-561.

36 Gerald Horne, Ferdinand Smith, the National Maritime Union, and Jamaican Labor Radicalism (New York: New York University Press, forthcoming), 405.

37 Alain Locke, Foreword to EW, The Negro in the Caribbean (1942; repr., Brooklyn, N.Y.: A&B Books Publishers, 1994). For Williams's years at Howard, see Heather Cateau and S. H. H. Carrington, eds., Capitalism and Slavery Fifty Years Later: Eric Eustace Williams: A Reassessment of the Man and His Work (New York: Peter Lang, 2000).

38 EW, Inward Hunger, 62.

39 Locke, Foreword to EW, The Negro in the Caribbean.

40 EW, The Negro in the Caribbean, 104.

41 Ibid.

42 EW, Capitalism and Slavery (1944; repr., Chapel Hill: University of North Carolina Press, 1994), ix.

43 Ibid.

44 Ibid.

45 Ibid., 210.

46 See Reginald Coupland, The British Anti-Slavery Movement, 2nd ed. (London: F. Cass, 1964).

47 EW, Capitalism and Slavery, 178.

48 Ibid., 169.

49 EW to W. T. Couch, March 14, 1945, University of North Carolina Press Records, subgroup 4, Southern Historical Collection, University of North Carolina, Chapel Hill.

50 D. A. Farnie, "The Commercial Empire of the Atlantic, 1607–1783," *Economic History Review*, 2nd ser., 15 (1962): 212.

51 Frank Tannenbaum, book review, *Political Science Quarterly* 61 (1946): 247–53.

52 Carter J, Woodson, book review, *Journal of Negro History* 30 (1945): 93–95.

53 Lorenzo Greene, book review, *Negro College Quarterly* 3, no. 1 (March 1945): 46–48.

54 It is not my intention to offer a critique of *Capitalism and Slavery* here, but rather to provide only a brief synopsis of Williams's arguments.

55 EW, lecture, University of the West Indies, St. Augustine, June 17, 1964, EWMC, vol. 007.

56 EW, lecture, Montreal, April 22, 1964, EWMC, vol. 638.

57 Ibid.

58 Ibid.

59 EW, lecture, University of the West Indies, St. Augustine, June 17, 1964.

60 Ibid.

61 EW, lecture, Montreal, April 22, 1964.

62 Ibid.

63 EW, *Education in the British West Indies* (1950; repr., Brooklyn, N.Y.: A&B Books Publishers, 1994), 10.

64 Ibid., 60.

65 Ibid., 61.

66 Ibid.

67 Ibid., 87.

68 Ibid., 107.

69 EW, lecture on "Intellectual Decolonisation."

70 Press release, CO 1031/4281; also printed in *Trinidad Guardian*, July 15, 1961, 9, 11.

71 EW interviews, PREM 13/2433 and *Sunday Telegraph*, October 19, 1964, 32.

72 EW to Harold Wilson, November 28, 1964, PREM 90/531.

73 Ibid.

74 Ibid.

75 N. E. Costar to Sir Arthur Snelling, September 1, 1962, DO 227/2.

76 Ibid.

77 R. G. Menzies to Harold MacMillan, January 16, 1962, PREM 11/3653.

78 C. L. R. James, *A Convention Appraisal: Dr. Eric Williams: A Biographical Sketch* (Port of Spain: PNM Publishing Co., 1960), 5.

79 EW, excerpts from a speech to Trinidad Legislature, January 5, 1962, Central Decimal File, Trinidad, NA-DS, box 1671, folder 741F.00/11-161.

CHAPTER 2

1 *Trinidad Guardian*, June 18, 1960.
2 The preceding remarks by Bustamante and Manley are from the *Daily Gleaner*, January 8, 1955, 15, which reported the speeches made in Montego Bay on September 11, 1947.
3 John Mordecai, *The West Indies: The Federal Negotiations* (London: Allen and Unwin, 1968), 39.
4 Ibid., 46–47.
5 Williams's quotations are from a summary of his views on the West Indies Federation that he prepared for publication. See EW, "My Federation Record," EWMC, vol. 660.
6 Ibid.
7 EW, "Federation in the World Today," February 25, 1955, EWMC, vol. 813; EW, "The Proposed Federal Constitution for the British Caribbean," April 18, 1955, EWMC, vol. 635.
8 "Report of the British Caribbean Federal Capital Commission" (Mudie Report), September 25, 1956, Central Decimal File, Trinidad, NA-DS, box 3202, folder 741B.00/1-357.
9 Mordecai, *The West Indies*, 93.
10 Lord Hailes to Alan Lennox-Boyd, January 10, 1959, CO 1031/2573.
11 Colonial Office to Alan Lennox-Boyd, "Progress and Present Position of the Federation," November 1959, CO 1031/2574.
12 Sir Kenneth Blackburne to Philip Rogers, December 5, 1958, CO 1031/2573.
13 *Daily Gleaner*, editorial, November 10, 1960.
14 Sir Kenneth Blackburne to Philip Rogers, December 5, 1958, CO 1031/2573; British High Commissioner, Ottawa, Canada, to Lord Hailes, November 13, 1959, and Lord Hailes to British High Commissioner, Ottawa, November 30, 1959, CO 1031/2574.
15 Philip Rogers to Sir Hilton Poynton, October 20, 1959, CO 1031/2574.
16 J. O. Moreton, memorandum, March 9, 1959, and Iain McLeod, memorandum, March 17, 1961, PREM 11/3653.
17 Colonial Office, Note on Sir Grantley Adams, n.d., PREM 11/3635.
18 *Daily Gleaner*, editorial, October 11, 1960.
19 Ibid., November 5, 1958.
20 Mordecai, *The West Indies*, 255–57.
21 Philip Rogers, minute, February 7, 1959, CO 1031/2574.
22 *Daily Gleaner*, November 5, 1958.
23 Mordecai, *The West Indies*, 127–41.
24 Ibid., 124–27, 149–50. See EW, *The Economics of Nationhood* (Port of Spain: PNM Publishing Co., 1959), 69. I wish to thank Selwyn Carrington and Reginald Dumas for helping to procure a copy of this publication for me.

25 Mordecai, *The West Indies*, 161–65; EW, *Economics of Nationhood*, 11.

26 Ibid., 138–39.

27 EW, untitled manuscript, EWMC, vol. 736.

28 Mordecai, *The West Indies*, 173–80, 197–98.

29 Ibid., 130.

30 Lord Hailes to Alan Lennox-Boyd, January 10, 1959, CO 1031/2573; Sir Kenneth Blackburne to Philip Rogers, November 30, 1959, CO 1031/2574.

31 Note of a meeting with representatives of the JLP, June 4, 1960, during the secretary of state's visit to Jamaica, CO 1031/4269.

32 Extract from Address of the Honorable Norman Manley, Annual Conference of the People's National Party, October 25, 1959, CO 1031/2574.

33 *Daily Gleaner*, November 10, 1960.

34 Philip Rogers to Sir Hilton Poynton, October 20, 1959, CO 1031/2574, and Sir Kenneth Blackburne to Philip Rogers, October 30, 1959.

35 Lord Hailes to Sir Saville Garner, November 30, 1959, CO 1031/2574.

36 *Daily Gleaner*, December 17, 1955, p. 9, in EWMC, vol. 736.

37 EW, untitled speech, 1959, EWMC, vol. 736.

38 Sir Kenneth Blackburne to Philip Rogers, September 15, 1959, CO 1031/2574.

39 Ibid.

40 Douglas Williams to J. E. Marnham, August 26, 1959, and Lord Hailes to Philip Rogers, August 11, 1959, CO 1031/2574.

41 Joint memorandum by the Colonial Office and the Jamaican delegation summarizing talks on Federal matters in London, January 1960, CO 1031/4269. See also Mordecai, *The West Indies*, 201.

42 Mordecai, *The West Indies*, 232.

43 Ibid.

44 Ibid., 273–74.

45 Ibid., 341.

46 Lancaster House Conference on West Indies Independence, May 31–June 16, 1961, Central Decimal File, Trinidad, NA-DS, box 1669, folder 741F.00/11-161.

47 The statistics in this and the preceding paragraph are from the text of a lengthy speech that Williams gave prior to his departure for the Lancaster House Conference. All amounts are expressed in West Indian dollars. See EWMC, vol. 739.

48 Lancaster House Conference; U.S. Embassy, London, to U.S. Department of State, June 23, 1961, Central Decimal File, Trinidad, NA-DS, box 1670, folder 741F.00/6-261.

49 Sir Solomon Hochoy to Hugh Fraser, July 15, 1961, CO 1031/4281; Memorandum of Conversation between EW and William Christensen, September 29, 1961, Central Decimal File, Trinidad, NA-DS, box 1671, folder 741F.00/1-462.

50 William Christensen, U.S. Mission, Port of Spain, to U.S. Department of State, November 9, 1961, Central Decimal File, Trinidad, NA-DS, box 1671, folder 741F.00/11-161.

51 EW, excerpts from a speech to Trinidad Legislature, January 5, 1962, ibid.

52 William Christensen, U.S. Mission, Port of Spain, to U.S. Department of State, November 3, 1961, ibid.

53 Mordecai, *The West Indies*, 442.

54 R. B. Manderson-Jones, *Jamaican Foreign Policy in the Caribbean, 1962–1988* (Kingston: Caricom Publishers, Ltd., 1990), 4.

55 EW, BBC interview, August 9, 1962, DO 200/95.

56 "Note of a Meeting in Mr. Fisher's Room," July 23, 1964, CO 1031/5003. See also "Personal for Sykes," July 22, 1964, ibid.

57 "Dr. Williams' Proposal for the West Indies," n.d., ibid.

58 For an extended account of these discussions, see N. E. Costar to E. L. Sykes, July 27, 1964, ibid. See also Costar to Secretary of State for the Colonies, March 3, 1964, ibid.

59 Costar to Sykes, July 27, 1964, David Rose to W. I. G. Wallace, July 31, 1964, and Costar to CRO, September 1, 1964, ibid.

60 J. D. Murray to N. E. Costar, August 23, 1965, and Costar to Murray, August 30, 1965, DO 200/171.

61 Manderson-Jones, *Jamaican Foreign Policy*, 17.

62 Sir Grantley Adams, radio address, March 13, 1960, Central Decimal File, Trinidad, NA-DS, box 1669, folder 741F.00/1-660.

CHAPTER 3

1 These and subsequent descriptions of the march are from the *Trinidad Guardian*, April 23, 1960, 1–2. For the full text of Williams's speech, see EWMC, vol. 767.

2 *Trinidad Guardian*, April 23, 1960. The Mudie Report disparaged Trinidad and awarded the capital site to Barbados. Passed in 1939, the telephone ordinance gave monopoly rights to a French creole–dominated company.

3 EWMC, vol. 767.

4 Governor Edward B. Beetham to EW, April 9, 1960, and Williams to Beetham, [April 10?], in EW, *Inward Hunger: The Education of a Prime Minister* (London: Andre Deutsch, 1969), 227–30; Beetham to Secretary of State for the Colonies, April 14, 1960, CO 1031/3058.

5 U.K. Colonial Attaché, Washington, D.C., to Secretary of State for the Colonies, May 9, 1957, CO 1031/3058.

6 Secretary of State for the Colonies to Governor of Trinidad and to U.K. Colonial Attaché, Washington, D.C., May 13, 1957, ibid.

7 Sir Edward Beetham to Secretary of State for the Colonies, May 11, 1957, ibid.

8 U.S. Consul General, Port of Spain, to U.S. Department of State, March 25, 1957, Central Decimal File, Trinidad, NA-DS, box 3302, folder 741B.00/1-359.

9 U.K. Colonial Attaché, Washington, D.C., to Secretary of State for the Colonies, May 14, 1957, CO 1031/3058. See also Colonial Office memorandum, May 18, 1957, ibid.

10 Mr. W. J. Alexander was the other delegate from Trinidad and Tobago.

11 U.S. Consul General, Port of Spain, to U.S. Department of State, June 3, 1957, Central Decimal File, Trinidad, NA-DS, box 3202, folder 741B.00/1-357. See also Governor of Trinidad to Secretary of State for the Colonies, May 16, 1957, CO 1031/3058. The members of the SFC delegation included the chief ministers of Jamaica and Trinidad; the premier of Barbados; Robert Bradshaw, the minister of trade and production in St. Kitts–Nevis-Anguilla; and F. A. Baron, the minister of trade and production in Dominica.

12 Sir Edward Beetham to Secretary of State for the Colonies, May 22, 1957, and U.K. Colonial Attaché to Secretary of State for the Colonies, May 23, 1957, FO 371/126085.

13 U.K. Colonial Attaché, Washington, D.C., to Secretary of State for the Colonies, June 21, 1957, FO 371/26083.

14 "United States Memorandum on U.S. Naval Base, Chaguaramas, Trinidad, BWI," July 6, 1957, FO 371/126083.

15 F. Cooper to Under Secretary of State, Foreign Office, July 10, 1957, FO 371/126084.

16 U.S. Embassy, London, to U.S. Department of State, July 15 1957, Central Decimal File, Trinidad, NA-DS, box 2895, folder 711.56341B/1557.

17 John Whitney to U.S. Secretary of State, July 13, 1957, ibid., box 3895, folder 711.56341B/1159.

18 "Opening Statement by Mr. Manley," July 16, 1957, Chaguaramas Conference, Foreign Office, London, July 16–23, 1957, FO 371/126085.

19 Record of Meeting to Discuss Federal Capital Site, July 16, 1957, ibid.

20 Alan Lennox-Boyd to Philip Rogers, July 17, 1957, CO 1031/2024.

21 EW, "The Memorandum by the Chief Minister of Trinidad and Tobago Submitted to the Conference on the Federal Capital Site," FO 371/126083.

22 Secretary of State for the Colonies, memorandum on "United States Activities in the West Indies and Other British Dependencies," FO 371/26152.

23 Foreign Office to Mr. Butler, January 2, 1941, FO 371/27152.

24 EW, Proposal by the Trinidad Delegation, FO 371/126085.

25 U.S. Ambassador, Statement at the First Meeting of the Chaguaramas Conference, Foreign Office, London, July 16–23, 1957, Annex D, ibid.

26 EW, Report on the Chaguaramas Conference Held at the Foreign Office, London, July 16–23, 1957, FO 371/126086.

27 Ibid.

28 Daily Gleaner, August 14, 1957, in FO 371/126085.

29 Government of Trinidad, Statement on Construction of Missile Tracking Station at Chaguaramas, CO 1031/2025.

30 F. J. Leishman to E. G. Andrews, January 22, 1958, ibid.

31 U.S. Statement on the Tracking Station, FO 371/126085.

32 U.S. Consul General, Port of Spain, to U.S. Department of State, October 11,

1957, Central Decimal File, Trinidad, NA-DS, box 2892, folder 711.56341B/1557.

33 EW, "My Federal Record," EWMC, vol. 660.

34 U.S. Consul General, Port of Spain, to U.S. Department of State, August 15, 1957, Central Decimal File, Trinidad, NA-DS, box 2891, folder 711.56341B/1557.

35 U.S. Consul General, Port of Spain, to U.S. Department of State, August 15, 1957, ibid., box 3892, folder 711.56341B/1557.

36 Ibid., August 27, 1957.

37 U.S. Consul General, Kingston, to U.S. Department of State, November 4, 1957, ibid., box 2892, folder 711.56341B/1557.

38 U.S. Consul General, Port of Spain, to U.S. Department of State, November 4, 1957, ibid., box 2891, folder 711.56341B/1557.

39 U.S. Consul General, Barbados, to U.S. Department of State, August 29, 1957, ibid.

40 EW, statement, July 5, 1959, quoted from ibid., box 2894, folder 711.56341B/1557.

41 U.S. Consul General, Port of Spain, to U.S. Department of State, December 30, 1957, Central Decimal File, Trinidad, NA-DS, box 2892, folder 711.56341B/1557.

42 R. W. Jackling to H. A. A. Hankey, April 30, 1958, FO 371/131855.

43 H. A. A. Hankey, "The Chaguaramas Dispute," March 17, 25, 1958, FO 371/131854.

44 Foreign Office to Sir Harold Caccia, March 21, 1958, ibid.

45 British Embassy, Washington, D.C., to Foreign Office, March 29, 1958, ibid.

46 Foreign Office to Sir Harold Caccia, April 3, 1958, ibid.

47 Walworth Barbour to Selwyn Lloyd, April 3, 1958, ibid.

48 Memorandum by P. Dean, April 5, 1958, ibid..

49 Selwyn Lloyd to John Jay Whitney, April 7, 1958, ibid.

50 Report of the Chaguaramas Joint Commission, March 25, 1958, 6, Central Decimal File, Trinidad, NA-DS, box 2893, folder 711.56341B/1557.

51 Ibid., 11.

52 Ibid., 18.

53 Ibid., 32.

54 See various letters by colonial authorities, FO 371/131855.

55 Ibid.

56 Ibid.; United Kingdom Information Office, Port of Spain, to Secretary of State for the Colonies, May 15, 1958, FO 371/131855; U.S. Consul General, Port of Spain, to U.S. Department of State, May 15, 1958, Central Decimal File, Trinidad, NA-DS, box 2893, folder 711.56341B/1557; *Daily Gleaner*, May 27, 1958.

57 John Foster Dulles to Selwyn Lloyd, June 14, 1958, FO 371/131856.

58 Philip Rogers to H. A. A. Hankey, October 17, 1958, FO 371/131858.

59 *Speech Made by the Honourable Chief Minister during the Debate on the Chaguaramas Joint Commission Report*, June 6, 1958 (Trinidad: Government Printing Office, 1958), 1.

60 Ibid., 2–7.

61 Ibid., 9, 13–14, 16–17.

62 Ibid., 24.

63 Ibid., 29.

64 *Statement by the Honourable Chief Minister on the United States Leased Areas in Trinidad and Tobago*, June 20, 1958 (Port of Spain: Government Printing Office, 1958), 2.

65 Ibid., 3–4.

66 Ibid., 4.

67 Ibid., 8.

68 Sir Edward Beetham to Secretary of State for the Colonies, June 20, 1958, and Colonial Office to Governor of Trinidad, June 1958, FO 371/131856.

69 D. H. T. Hildyard, memorandum, August 25, 1958, FO 371/131857. Williams's Legal Commission never submitted its report.

70 Sir Edward Beetham to Philip Rogers, January 18, 1958, CO 1031/2060.

71 Sir Edward Beetham to Secretary of State for the Colonies, February 13, 1958, ibid.

72 Alan Lennox-Boyd to Sir Edward Beetham, n.d., ibid.

73 W. I. J. Wallace to Sir Edward Beetham, February 22, 1958, ibid.

74 Colonial Office, departmental minute, June 26, 1958, ibid.

75 U.S. Consul General, Port of Spain, to U.S. Secretary of State, July 14, 1958, Central Decimal File, Trinidad, NA-DS, box 2893, folder 711.56341B/1557.

76 U.S. Consul General, Port of Spain, to U.S. Secretary of State, March 12, 1958, ibid., folder 711.56341B/1557.

77 Walter Orebaugh to Willoughby, Dale, Swihart, and Burn, July 1959, ibid., box 3202, folder 741B.00/1-357.

78 U.S. Consul General, Port of Spain, to U.S. Department of State, May 29, 1958, ibid., box 2893, folder 711.56341B/1557.

79 U.S. Consul General, Port of Spain, to U.S. Department of State, October 7, 1958, ibid., folder 711.56341B/1557.

80 Douglas Williams to J. E. Marnham, August 6, 1958, CO 1031/2028.

81 U.S. Consul General, Port of Spain, to U.S. Department of State, October 29, 1958, Central Decimal File, Trinidad, NA-DS, box 2893, folders 711.56341B/1358 and 711.56341B/2159.

82 U,S. Consul General, Port of Spain, to U.S. Department of State, July 14, 1959, ibid., box 2894, folder 711.56341B/1259.

83 U.S. Consul General, Port of Spain, to U.S. Department of State, June 14, 1960, box 1670, folder 741F.00/6-1760.

84 See the charges and countercharges in Central Decimal File, Trinidad, NA-DS, box 1669, folder 741F.00/1-660.

85 EW, speech on "Perspectives for the West Indies," San Fernando, May 30, 1960, EWMC, vol. 643.

86 U.S. Consul General, Port of Spain, to U.S. Department of State, December 23, 1960, Central Decimal File, Trinidad, NA-DS, box 2894, folder 711.56341B/1259.

87 On the dispute, see ibid., box 2892, folder 711.56341B/1457, and box 2894, folder 711.56341B/1295.

88 See ibid., box 3892, folder 711.56341B/1457.

89 Extract from Trinidad Monthly Intelligence Report for Late June and Early July 1959, CO 1031/3060.

90 Winston Mahabir, *In and Out of Politics: Tales of the Government of Dr. Eric Williams from the Notebooks of a Former Minister* (Trinidad: Inprint Caribbean Ltd., 1975), 83. In this volume, Mahabir ridicules Williams's claim that a radiation threat existed. He notes that when Williams made the charge at the University of Woodford Square, he "did not know whether to laugh at him or cry for the gullible crowd that was being ultraviolated."

91 D. H. T. Hildyard to D. A. Logan, August 10, 1959, FO 371/139791.

92 Ibid.

93 Acting Governor of Trinidad and Tobago to Secretary of State for the Colonies, July 31, 1959, CO 1031/2069.

94 D. H. T. Hildyard to D. A. Logan, September 17, 1959, FO 1031/2069.

95 For Evans's "Report of Chaguaramas Visit," n.d. (but stamped as received in the Archives on September 19, 1959), see FO 371/139791.

96 Sir Edward Beetham to Secretary of State for the Colonies, January 7, 1960, CO 1031/3060.

97 Secretary of State for the Colonies to Governor of Trinidad and Tobago, January 8, 1960, ibid.

98 H. A. A. Hankey to D. A. Logan, December 18, 1959, FO 371/131855.

99 R. H. G. Edmonds to D. A. Greenhill, January 12, 1960, CO 1031/3060.

100 Secretary of State for the Colonies to Governor of Trinidad and Tobago, January 19, 1960, ibid.

101 Governor of Trinidad to Secretary of State for the Colonies, January 16, 1960, ibid.

102 Ibid.

103 *Nation*, December 11, 1959, in CO 1031/2069.

104 Ibid.

105 U.S. Consul General, Port of Spain, to U.S. Department of State, December 12, 1959, Central Decimal File, Trinidad, NA-DS, box 2895, folder 711.56341B/1159.

106 Ibid.

107 EW, *Inward Hunger*, 238.

108 U.S. Department of the Navy, "Strategic Appraisal of Trinidad, B.W.I., October 19, 1960," Central Decimal File, Trinidad, NA-DS, box 1674, folder 741J.00/3-860.

109 EW, *Inward Hunger*, 239.

110 Ibid., 239–40; Annex E, Trinidad and Tobago, DO 200/263.

111 U.S. Mission, Port of Spain, to U.S. Department of State, January 18, 1962, Central Decimal File, Trinidad, NA-DS, box 1671, folder 741F.00/1-462.

112 Memorandum of Conversation between EW and William Christensen, January 25, 1962, ibid.

113 Trinidad and Tobago Political and Economic Assessment, Subject Decimal File, 1964–66, NA-DS, box 2744.

114 U.S. Department of State to McGeorge Bundy, memorandum, August 28, 1965, Central Foreign Policy Files, Trinidad and Tobago, Political, NA-DS, box 2745.

115 For a summary of James's dispute with Williams, see "C. L. R. James Critical of Eric Williams and Peoples National Movement," U.S. Consul General, Port of Spain, to U.S. Department of State, August 10, 1960, Central Decimal File, Trinidad, NA-DS, box 1670, folder 741F.00/1-561.

116 E. B. Ashmore to Commander, British Navy Staff, Washington, D.C., November 18, 1964, DO 200/263.

117 N. E. Costar to D. M. Cleary, November 16, 1965, ibid.

118 British High Commissioner, Port of Spain, to CRO, February 11, 1966, ibid.

119 EW, speech on "From Slavery to Chaguaramas," Arima, Trinidad, July 17, 1959, EWMC, vol. 008.

CHAPTER 4

1 EW to Harold MacMillan, November 26, 1962, DO 200/86; United Kingdom Office of Financial Assistance to Trinidad and Tobago, DO 200/19.

2 "Financial Assistance to Various Commonwealth Countries," n.d., DO 200/86.

3 EW to Secretary of State for the Colonies, March 22, 1962, DO 200/85.

4 Ibid. An Exchequer loan was to be used solely for development purposes.

5 EW, "Equipment for Independence," June 18, 1962, DO 200/86.

6 EW to Colonial Office, July 9, 1962, ibid.

7 E. L. Sykes to Deputy High Commissioner, Trinidad and Tobago, July 12, 1962, ibid.

8 *Trinidad Guardian*, July 14, 1962.

9 E. L. Sykes to L. B. Walsh Atkins, July 26, 1962, DO 200/85.

10 Memorandum: Brief no. 12, United Kingdom Delegation Only, Trinidad Independence Conference, May 1962, DO 200/85.

11 The Colonial Development Welfare Fund provided grants to the colonies for development projects.

12 J. D. Higman, departmental minute, DO 200/85.

13 Duncan Sandys to John-Boyd Carpenter, August 22, 1962, DO 200/85.

14 John-Boyd Carpenter to Duncan Sandys, n.d., DO 200/85.

15 H. A. F. Rumbold to Duncan Sandys, September 5, 1962, DO 200/85.

16 H. A. F. Rumbold to N. E. Costar, December 10, 1962, DO 200/86. The "Little Eight" referred to the potential federation of the eight Windward and Leeward Islands.

17 Colonial Office to EW, aide-mémoire, November 30, 1962, DO 200/86.

18 British High Commission to CRO, January 9, 1962, DO 200/85; E. L. Sykes to Secretary of State for the Colonies, November 2, 1962, DO 200/86.

19 EW to Harold MacMillan, November 5, 1962, DO 200/86.

20 E. L. Sykes to H. A. F. Rumbold, November 13, 1962, ibid.

21 EW, excerpts from speeches on November 20 and 25, *London Times*, November 26, 1962.

22 Harold MacMillan to EW, December 2, 1962, DO 200/86.

23 *Trinidad Guardian*, December 6, 1962.

24 S. J. G. Fingland to E. L. Sykes, April 31, 1962, DO 200/95.

25 Sykes to Fingland, September 11, 1962, ibid.

26 R. L. Baxter to J. E. Marnham, April 16, 1958, CO 1031/2490.

27 U.S. Embassy, London, to U.S. Department of State, January 20, 1960, Central Decimal File, Trinidad, NA-DS, box 1669, folder 741F.00/1-660.

28 N. E. Costar, "Trinidad and Tobago: Dr. Williams and His Policies," May 8, 1963, DO 200/95.

29 N. E. Costar to L. B. Walsh Atkins, March 7, 1963, DO 200/87.

30 P. Farquhar, "All Fall Down," *Statesman*, April 26, 1963.

31 P. Farquhar, "Selling the Dummy," *Statesman*, May 3, 1963, in CO 1031/4438.

32 N. E. Costar to Secretary of State for Commonwealth Relations, "Trinidad and Tobago, after Two Years of Independence," November 22, 1964, CO 1031/5003.

33 EW, *Inward Hunger: The Education of a Prime Minister* (London: Andre Deutsch, 1969), 29.

34 Ibid.

35 EW, "Life with Father," unpublished version of memoirs, chap. 3, EWMC, vol. 139.

36 EW, unpublished version of memoirs, chap. 2, 1911–32, ibid.

37 N. E. Costar to H. A. F. Rumbold, November 10, 1962, DO 200/86.

38 EW, unpublished version of memoirs, chap. 2, EWMC, vol. 139.

39 N. E. Costar to H. A. F. Rumbold, November 10, 1962, DO 200/86.

40 Ibid.

41 Patrick Solomon, *An Autobiography* (Port of Spain: Imprint Caribbean, 1981), 151.

42 N. E. Costar to H. A. F. Rumbold, November 10, 1962, DO 200/86.

43 EW, BBC interview, August 9, 1962, DO 200/95.

44 Ibid.

45 N. E. Costar, memorandum to CRO, November 22, 1964, CO 1031/5003; Richard Hunt to T. R. M. Sewell, May 29, 1970, FCO 63/594; Costar, "Trinidad and Tobago: Dr. Williams and His Policies," May 8, 1963, DO 200/86.

46 L. B. Walsh Atkins to Minister of State, May 3, 1963, departmental minute, DO 200/95 (Bukhurst); J. A. Murray to Duke of Devonshire, September 19, 1963, DO 200/15 (Lewis).

47 Costar made the suggestion repeatedly to colonial officials. See, e.g., "Note of Discussion on Relations between Britain and Trinidad and Tobago Held at Government House, Barbados, Tuesday, January 1, 1963," DO 200/86.

48 N. E. Costar to CRO, ibid.

49 "Financial Assistance to Various Countries," n.d., ibid.

50 N. E. Costar to CRO, December 10, 1962, ibid.

51 "Note of Discussion on Relations between Britain and Trinidad and Tobago Held at Government House, Barbados, Tuesday, January 1, 1963," ibid. In his letter to Profumo regarding his failure to meet with him, Williams offered what could be taken as a weak apology. "The circumstances surrounding your visit," he said, "were unfortunate. But that is behind us now. . . . I look forward to seeing you again soon." EW to Secretary of State for the Colonies, May 7, 1963, DO 200/87.

52 N. E. Costar to L. B. Walsh Atkins, March 2, 1963, DO 200/86.

53 Denis Williams to N. E. Costar, May 13, 1963, DO 200/87.

54 Note of a meeting held in CRO, March 12, 1963; S. E. Luke, Note for the Record, March 9, 1963, DO 200/4.

55 N. E. Costar to L. B. Walsh Atkins, March 19, 1963, DO 200/87.

56 Costar to Walsh Atkins, March 28, April 19, 1963, ibid.

57 "Suggested Approach by the U.K. High Commissioner to the Government of Trinidad and Tobago," memorandum, DO 200/19.

58 EW, "United Kingdom Offer of Financial Assistance to Independent Trinidad and Tobago, 1962," white paper, ibid.

59 Ibid.; "Suggested Approach by the U.K. High Commissioner to the Government of Trinidad and Tobago."

60 EW, "United Kingdom Offer of Financial Assistance to Independent Trinidad and Tobago, 1962," white paper, DO 200/19.

61 Internal memorandum, DO 200/89.

62 Colonial Office to Sir Stephen Luke, December 7, 1962, ibid.

63 EW to Harold MacMillan, December 5, 1962, DO 200/19.

64 Colonial Office to British High Commissioner of Trinidad and Tobago, n.d., ibid.

65 "Trinidad Finance," internal memorandum, March 26, 1963, DO 200/89.

66 N. E. Costar to E. L. Sykes, May 4, 1963, DO 200/87.

67 Costar to L. B. Walsh Atkins, June 25, 1963, ibid.

68 Costar to Sykes, May 18, 1963, ibid.

69 E. L. Sykes to Mr. Lynch, Department of the Treasury, August 14, 1963, ibid.

70 E. L. Sykes to L. B. Walsh Atkins, December 9, 1963, DO 200/88.

71 Sykes to Walsh Atkins, November 27, December 9, 1963, ibid.

72 EW, "Perspectives for the West Indies," May 30, 1960, EWMC, vol. 007.

CHAPTER 5

1 EW, *History of the Peoples of Trinidad and Tobago*, 256.
2 Report of Meeting between Grantley Adams and Harold MacMillan, December 4, 1961, PREM 11/4074.
3 Memorandum for the Prime Minister, September 27, 1961, PREM 13/2999.
4 Ian McLeod to Harold MacMillan, September 22, 1961, PREM 11/4074.
5 Acting Administrator of St. Kitts to Secretary of State for the Colonies, September 24, 1961, Administrator of Dominica to Secretary of State for the Colonies, September 22, 1961, and Administrator of Antigua to Secretary of State for the Colonies, September 25, 1961, PREM 11/4074.
6 Colonial Office Brief to Harold MacMillan on the Occasion of Grantley Adams's Visit, December 1, 1961, PREM 11/3653.
7 "Report of the Economic Commission," January 1965, 1–2, CO 1031/4440. This survey was commissioned by the leaders of Grenada and Trinidad.
8 Record of Discussion between Duncan Sandys and EW, September 21, 1962, CO 1031/3242.
9 Ibid.
10 Secretary of State for the Colonies to Herbert Blaize, ca. October 19, 1962, reprinted in "Keeping the Faith: A Record of Progress towards Union of Grenada with Trinidad and Tobago" (a publication of the Chief Minister's Office, St. George's, Grenada), CO 1031/4439. As late as November 1964, the secretary of state told the administrator of Grenada: "I should like to assure you that if union with Trinidad remains the wish of your government, and if satisfactory terms acceptable to all three governments can be worked out, the British government would hope to facilitate it." Secretary of State Anthony Greenwood to Administrator of Grenada, November 24, 1964, CO 1031/4440.
11 "Keeping the Faith," 3.
12 Ibid.
13 CRO to S. J. G. Fingland, October 31, 1962, CO 1031/3242.
14 Report on EW's Address to West Indian Students in London, November 28, 1962, ibid.
15 British High Commission, Port of Spain, to CRO, November 26, December 14, 1962, ibid.
16 Colonial Office, "U.K. Policy towards a Federation of the Eight and Grenada's Proposal to Enter into Negotiations for a Unitary State with Trinidad," memorandum, October 15, 1962, ibid.
17 British High Commission, Port of Spain, to CRO, November 24, 1962, ibid.
18 Ibid.
19 Ibid., November 21, 1962; Edward B. Rosenthal to Department of State, July 15, 1964, Central Foreign Policy Files, Trinidad and Tobago, Political, NA-DS, box 2745.
20 Administrator of Grenada to Secretary of State for the Colonies, March 17,

1964, CO 1031/4438; Extract from Notes of Discussion between Secretary of State for the Colonies and Members of the Opposition of Grenada Legislature, December 31, 1962, CO 1031/3242; Departmental minute, CO 1031/4440.

21 Petition to Secretary of State, February 3, 1965, CO 1031/4440.

22 Record of Discussion between Secretary of State and EW, September 1, 1962, CO 1031/3242.

23 Note for Secretary of State on Trinidad/Grenada Union, November 11, 1964, CO 1031/4439.

24 Brief no. 52, Secretary of State's Visit to West Indies, January–February 1965, CO 1031/4440.

25 British High Commission, Port of Spain, to CRO, December 10, 1962, CO 1031/3242.

26 "T" to Secretary of State, April 4, 1965, CO 1031/4439.

27 D. Williams to Mr. Thomas, internal memorandum, January 22, 1963, CO 1031/3242.

28 Ibid.

29 M. Z. Terry to D. Williams, November 12, 1963, CO 1031/4438.

30 S. J. G. Fingland to E. L. Sykes, June 26, 1963, ibid.

31 D. Williams to L. A. Pinard, July 2, 1963, ibid.

32 "Keeping the Faith," 6.

33 Ibid.

34 N. E. Costar to CRO, May 4, 1964, DO 227/2.

35 Costar to CRO, November 13, 1963, ibid.

36 D. Williams to Sir Hilton Poynton, November 11, 1964, CO 1031/4439.

37 Ibid.

38 Reports of Commission on the Development Program for Grenada and Economic Commission, Unitary Statehood for Trinidad and Tobago and Grenada, CO 1031/4440.

39 Ibid., 34–35.

40 Ibid., 34.

41 Ibid.

42 Secretary of State to Administrator of Grenada, December 21, 1965, CO 1031/4440.

43 "The Secretary of State's Visit to the West Indies, January/February 1965," ibid.

44 N. E. Costar to Administrator of Grenada, June 3, 1964, CO 1031/4439.

45 Brief for Secretary of State, April 22, 1964, CO 1031/4440.

46 N. E. Costar to Administrator of Grenada, August 17, 1965, ibid.

47 Departmental minute, January 1965, ibid.

CHAPTER 6

1 Cheddi Jagan, Forbes Burnham, and Peter D'Aguiar to Secretary of State for the Colonies, October 25, 1963, FO 371/173552.

2 Brief for Prime Minister Harold MacMillan's Talks with President John F. Kennedy, July 4, 1963, CO 1031/4402.

3 Joint Assessment by U.S. and British Officials [on Guiana], June 25, 1963, ibid.

4 Brief for Prime Minister MacMillan's Talks with President Kennedy.

5 Joint Assessment by U.S. and British Officials [on Guiana], June 27, 1963, CO 1031/4402.

6 U.S. Embassy, London, to U.S. Department of State, March 19, 1960, Central Decimal File, Trinidad, NA-DS, box 1669, folder 741D.00/9-2861.

7 N. E. Costar to CRO, September 1, 1962, DO 227/2.

8 EW, Trinidad and Tobago and the British Guiana Question, (Trinidad and Tobago: Government Printers, n.d.), pamphlet, 5 (speech in House of Representatives, November 22, 27, 1963).

9 Ibid., 6.

10 Ibid.

11 EW to Errol Barrow and Alexander Bustamante, telegram, April 24, 1963, CO 1031/4402.

12 Alexander Bustamante to EW, telegram, April 26, 1963, ibid.

13 British High Commissioner, Kingston, to CRO, April 26, 1963, ibid.

14 N. E. Costar to CRO, April 24, 1963, ibid.

15 "Trinidad and Tobago and the British Guiana Question," 7–8.

16 Sir Ralph Grey to Secretary of State for the Colonies, April 26, 1963, CO 1031/4877.

17 S. J. G. Fingland to CRO, April 21, 1963, ibid.

18 N. E. Costar to CRO, June 7, 1963, DO 227/2.

19 E. L. Sykes to L. B. Walsh Atkins, June 13, 1963, DO 200/85.

20 N. E. Costar to CRO, November 12, 1963, DO 227/2.

21 EW, Trinidad and Tobago and the British Guiana Question, 10.

22 Ibid., 11. The Big Four Conference was established to permit the leaders of the four major Anglophone countries—Trinidad, Jamaica, Barbados, and British Guiana—to discuss common concerns.

23 Ibid., 10–13.

24 E. L. Sykes to Mr. Huijsman, October 23, 1963, CO 1031/4877.

25 EW to Secretary of State, ibid.

26 Secretary of State to EW, November 1, 1963, ibid.

27 S. J. G. Fingland to CRO, November 2, 1963, ibid.

28 Ibid.

29 Daily Gleaner, January 14, 1964, 14.

30 Alec Morley to CRO, February 6, 1964, DO 200/141.

31 Ibid.; Report of Press Conference, January 17, 1964, CO 1031/4405.

32 "Statement on British Guiana," n.d., DO 200/142.

33 Park F. Wollam to U.S. Department of State, February 12, 1964, Central Foreign Policy Files, Trinidad and Tobago, Political, NA-DS, box 1947, 1964–66.

34 Ibid.

35 British Embassy, Monrovia, to Foreign Office, March 6, 1964, FO 371/173668.

36 Acting British High Commissioner, Tanganyika, to Secretary of State for Commonwealth Relations, April 7, 1964, ibid.

37 N. E. Costar to Secretary of State for Commonwealth Relations, May 6, 1964, DO 200/248.

38 U.S. Embassy, Cairo, to U.S. Department of State, March 23, 1964, Central Foreign Policy Files, Trinidad and Tobago, Political, NA-DS, box 2745.

39 U.S. Department of State to EW, February 27, 1962, Central Decimal File, Trinidad, NA-DS, box 1669, folder 741D.00/9-2861.

40 "Eric Williams Report on Mediation in Guiana," n.d., CO 1031/4408.

41 U.S. Consul General, Georgetown, to U.S. Secretary of State, May 7, 1963, Central Foreign Policy Files, British Guiana, Political, NA-DS, box 1949.

42 Ibid.

43 "Eric Williams Report on Mediation in Guiana."

44 Ibid.

45 U.S. Ambassador, Port of Spain, to U.S. Secretary of State, May 27, 1964, Central Foreign Policy Files, Trinidad and Tobago, Political, NA-DS, box 1948.

46 The preceding discussion is based on Williams's written report to Jagan on his assessment of the crisis in British Guiana. See "Eric Williams Report on Mediation in Guiana." In those instances where Williams provides no documentation, the discussion is his recollection of his conversations with Jagan and others.

47 Cheddi Jagan to EW, June 29, 1964, CO 1031/4818.

48 R. G. Miner, Port of Spain, to U.S. Department of State, December 1, 1962, Central Decimal File, Trinidad, NA-DS, box 1668, folder 741D.00/1562; E. L. Sykes to L. B. Walsh Atkins, June 13, 1963, DO 200/87.

49 R. G. Miner, Port of Spain, to U.S. Secretary of State, May 25, 1964, Central Foreign Policy Files, Trinidad and Tobago, Political, NA-DS, box 1949.

50 "Eric Williams Report on Mediation in Guiana."

51 Sir Hilton Poynton to Secretary of State for the Colonies, July 7, 1964, FO 371/173553; Secretary of State for the Colonies to Richard Luyt, July 9, 1964, DO 200/199.

52 British High Commission, Port of Spain, to CRO, May 9, 1963, DO 200/87.

53 Secretary of State for the Colonies to Richard Luyt, July 9, 1964, DO 209/199.

54 Sir Hilton Poynton to Secretary of State for the Colonies, July 7, 1964, FO 371/173553.

55 British High Commissioner, Kingston, to CRO, July 23, 1964, DO 200/171.

56 N. E. Costar to CRO, September 23, 1964, DO 200/199.

57 Nation, March 5, 1964.

58 British High Commission, Port of Spain, to CRO, June 30, 1965, DO 200/199.

59 N. E. Costar to Governor of British Guiana, March 12, 1965, DO 200/199.

60 "Report by the Prime Minister on the Commonwealth Prime Ministers' Conference, July 23, 1965," EWMC. See also CO 1031/4409.

61 David Rose to Colonial Office, October 16, 1965, DO 200/199; U.S. Consul General, Port of Spain, to Secretary of State, April 10, 1962, Central Decimal File, Trinidad, box 1672, folder 741F.00/1-1162.

62 David Rose to Colonial Office, October 16, 1965, DO 200/199; N. E. Costar to Richard Luyt, August 20, 1965, ibid.

63 N. E. Costar to CRO, January 26, 1966, ibid.

64 D. M. Cleary to N. E. Costar, January 11, 1966, ibid.

65 N. E. Costar to CRO, February 4, 1966, ibid.

66 D. M. Cleary to N. E. Costar, February 14, 1966, ibid.

67 N. E. Costar to CRO, April 22, 1966, ibid.

CHAPTER 7

1 EW, speech at McGill and Sir George Williams Universities, Montreal, April 22, 1964, EWMC, vol. 007.

2 P. Olisanwuche Esedebe, Pan Africanism: The Idea and Movement, 1776–1963 (Washington, D.C.: Howard University Press, 1982), 45–49.

3 EW to Governor Muñoz Marín, November 8, 1951, EWMC, uncataloged.

4 EW, lecture at Hansberry College, University of Nigeria, Nsukka, February 21, 1964, EWMC, vol. 008.

5 Ibid.

6 Ibid.

7 EW, address at Haile Selassie University, Addis Ababa, Ethiopia, March 16, 1964, EWMC, vol. 008.

8 EW, lecture at Hansberry College.

9 Trinidad and Tobago Debates of the House of Representatives, vol. 3, 1963 (Trinidad: Government Printery, 1969), 558.

10 EW, speech at Woodford Square, Port of Spain, September 5, 1962, EWMC, vol. 0005.

11 EW, address at University of Dakar, Senegal, March 16, 1964, in Paul K. Sutton, ed., Forged from the Love of Liberty: Selected Speeches of Dr. Eric Williams (Port of Spain: Longman's Caribbean, 1981), 224–25; Report No. 1-7.

12 EW, address on "Impressions of Africa," Oxford University, April 13, 1964, EWMC, vol. 162.

13 EW, radio broadcast to Trinidad and Tobago, February 7, 1964, EWMC, vol. 809.

14 Ibid.

15 EW, private address at Oxford University, April 13, 1964, EWMC, vol. 162.

16 Report No. 1.

17 Report No. 2.

18 Ibid.

19 Report No. 3.

20 Ibid.

21 Ibid.

22 Report No. 4.

23 Ibid.

24 Report No. 5.

25 Report No. 6.

26 Report No. 7.

27 Ibid.

28 Report No. 6.

29 EW, private address at Oxford University.

30 Ibid.

31 Report No. 7.

32 Report No. 6.

33 Report No. 7.

34 EW, private address at Oxford University.

35 Ibid.

36 EW, address at Haile Selassie University.

37 EW, private address at Oxford University.

38 Ibid.

39 Report Nos. 5 and 6.

40 Report No. 5.

41 Ibid.

42 Report No. 1.

43 Report No. 2.

44 EW, private address at Oxford University.

45 EW, address at Haile Selassie University.

46 Report No. 1.

47 EW, private address at Oxford University.

48 EW, address at Haile Selassie University.

49 EW, private address at Oxford University.

50 EW, lecture at University of Ife, Nigeria, March 4, 1964, EWMC, vol. 008.

51 British Embassy, Monrovia, Liberia, to R. A. Butler, Foreign Office, March 6, 1964, FO 371/173688.

52 British Embassy, Dakar, Senegal, to R. A. Butler, March 9, 1964, FO 371/173688.

53 D. J. C. Crawley, Freetown, Sierra Leone, to R. A. Butler, February 27, 1964, ibid.

54 John Russell, Addis Ababa, Ethiopia, to Secretary of State, March 29, 1964, FO 371/178524.

55 F. S. Miles, Tanganyika, to Secretary of State, April 7, 1964, FO 371/173688.

56 N. E. Costar to Duncan Sandys, May 6, 1964, DO 200/248.

57 Ibid.

58 Ibid.

59 EW, speech at McGill and Sir George Williams Universities.

60 *Daily Gleaner*, September 1, 1964.

61 British High Commissioner, Kingston, to E. L. Sykes, CRO, November 11, 1964, DO 200/171.

62 EW, lecture at Fourah Bay College.

CHAPTER 8

1 EW, *International Perspectives for Trinidad and Tobago*, pamphlet, Office of the Prime Minister (Port of Spain, 1964), 7–8.

2 Patrick Solomon, *An Autobiography* (Port of Spain: Imprint Caribbean, Ltd., 1981), 73–77.

3 EW, BBC interview, August 9, 1962, DO 200/95.

4 EW, manuscript, EWMC, vol. 139.

5 Ibid.

6 Ibid.

7 Ibid.

8 Ibid.

9 Ibid.

10 D. G. Rose to W. I. J. Wallace, October 16, 1965, DO 200/199.

11 N. E. Costar to Duncan Sandys, August 9, 1962, DO 200/86.

12 EW, BBC interview, August 9, 1962.

13 EW, *Capitalism and Slavery* (1944; repr., Chapel Hill: University of North Carolina Press, 1994), 5.

14 EW, "The West Indian National Character and the Problems of Today," 19, n.d., EWMC, vol. 643.

15 Ibid.

16 Brinsley Samaroo, "The Race Factor in the Independence Discussions at Marlborough House, 1962," *Caribbean Issues* 8, no. 1 (March 1998): 119–35 (speech at Woodford Square); EW, "The West Indian National Character."

17 EW, speech at McGill and Sir George Williams, Montreal, April 22, 1964, EWMC, vol. 007.

18 EW, lecture on "Federation in the World Today," February 25, 1955, EWMC, vol. 813.

19 Ibid. See the later discussion in this chapter of the activities of the Indian commissioner.

20 Ibid

21 EW, *Inward Hunger: The Education of a Prime Minister* (London: Andre Deutsch, 1969), 154–55.

22 Selwyn D. Ryan, *Race and Nationalism in Trinidad and Tobago: A Study of Decolonisation in a Multiracial Society* (Toronto: University of Toronto Press, 1972), 161.

23 Ibid., 185

24 EW, speech on "The Danger Facing Trinidad and Tobago and the West Indian Nation," April 1, 1958, CO 1031/2490.

25 Ibid.

26 Winston Mahabir, an Indian and the minister of health in Williams's administration, later wrote that when he visited Williams after his address at Woodford Square, he found him "in an exuberant, gloating, hypomania mood of triumph. He had obviously gained exquisite emotional satisfaction from his
diatribe against the Indians." Mahabir contemplated resigning from the government. Mahabir, *In and Out of Politics: Tales of the Government of Dr. Eric Williams
from the Notebooks of a Former Minister* (Port of Spain: Imprint Caribbean, Ltd.,
1975), 79–80.

27 "Meeting with the Secretary of State Profumo and Gomes and Sinanan,"
22 April 1958, CO 1031/2490.

28 *Legislative Council Debates: Trinidad and Tobago, Vol. 8, October 25, 1957 to June 24,
1958* (Trinidad: Government Printing Office, 1959), 1787–90.

29 Draft report on "East Indians in the West Indies," December 30, 1955, CO
1031/1954.

30 This account is taken from Fitzroy Andre Baptiste, "The Emergence of Eric
Williams and the People's National Movement [PNM] in Trinidad and Tobago
Politics as Gleaned from U.S. State Department Records, 1952–56," unpublished paper. The comment by Gomes is found in RG 59, folio 741F.00/
12-3054, and that by Maddox on the federation debate in RG 59, folio 741F.00/
12-1554, both located in Central Decimal File, Trinidad, NA-DS.

31 "Note of a Meeting in Mr. Rogers' Room on 19/1/55 to Discuss the Activities of
the Indian Commissioner to the West Indies," ibid. Two days after this meeting, R. C. Ormeond of the Colonial Office informed a colleague that the
seriousness of Nanda's activities resided in the fact that he had "intervened
directly and effectively against a major matter of British policy—the encouragement of the West Indian territories to federate." Office correspondence, DO
35/5226.

32 Departmental minute, CO 1031/1954.

33 Report on "Activities of the Commissioner for the Government of India in British Guiana," February 1955, DO 35/5226.

34 Lord Lloyd to Sir Hugh Foot, November 17, 1955, CO 1031/1703.

35 EW, speech on "Perspectives for the West Indies," San Fernando, May 30, 1960,
EWMC, vol. 643.

36 N. E. Costar to Secretary of State for the Colonies, "Trinidad and Tobago after
Two Years of Independence," November 12, 1964, CO 1031/5003.

37 Duncan Sandys to EW, October 29, 1963, DO 200/62.

38 Edwin Moline to U.S. Department of State, September 14, 1960, Central Decimal File, Trinidad, NA-DS, box 1670, folder 741F.00/6-160.

39 U.S. Consul General, Barbados, Political Notes from Conversations with Barbadian Political Leaders, April 7, 1967, ibid., folder 741F.00/1-561.

40 U.S. Mission, Port of Spain, to U.S. Department of State, January 10, 1962,
ibid., box 1671, folder 741F.00/1-462.

41 U.S. Mission, Port of Spain, to U.S. Department of State, November 24, 1961, ibid., folder 741F.00/11-161.

42 Ryan, *Race and Nationalism*, 272–73.

43 Harry M. Phelan to U.S. Department of State, January 10, 1962, "Malaise in the White Community," Central Decimal File, Trinidad, NA-DS, box 1671, folder 741F.00/1-461.

44 U.S. Mission to Department of State, October 24, 1961, ibid., folder 741F.00/9-561.

45 Ryan, *Race and Nationalism*, 269.

46 William H. Christensen to U.S. Secretary of State, November 27, 1961, Central Decimal File, Trinidad, NA-DS, box 1671, folder 741F.00/11-161.

47 Ibid., December 1, 1961.

48 Ryan, *Race and Nationalism*, 275.

49 EW, "Address to Party Supporters before the December 1961 Elections," EWMC, vol. 005.

50 U.S. Mission, Port of Spain, to U.S. Department of State, January 6, 1962, Central Decimal File, Trinidad, NA-DS, box 1671, folder 741F.00/1-142.

51 Ibid., January 16, 1962.

52 R. G. Miner to U.S. Secretary of State, March 25, 1962, ibid., box 1668, folder 741D.00/3-162.

53 Ryan, *Race and Nationalism*, 385.

54 Central Foreign Policy Files, Trinidad and Tobago, Political 23-9, NA-DS, box 2631.

55 Political 2-3, box 2744, ibid.; N. E. Costar to CRO, October 19, 1964, DO 200/248.

56 British High Commissioner, Trinidad and Tobago, Colonial Office, April 17, 1970, CO 63/590.

57 Selwyn Cudjoe, ed., *Eric E. Williams Speaks: Essays on Colonialism and Independence* (Wellesley, Mass.: Calaloux Publications, Amherst, distributed by University of Massachusetts Press, 1993), 265–69.

58 Lloyd Best, *Black Power and National Reconstruction* (San Fernando, Trinidad and Tobago: Tapia Pamphlet, n.d.), 4, in CO 63/594.

59 Best, *Black Power and National Reconstruction*, 4.

60 Ibid.

61 U.S. Embassy, Port of Spain, to U.S. Department of State, May 24, 1966, Central Foreign Policy Files, Political Parties, Trinidad and Tobago, NA-DS, box 2744.

62 EW, "Impressions of John John," June 27, 1955, EWMC, vol. 812, and "An Economic Blueprint for Trinidad and Tobago," [ca. 1955], EWMC, vol. 766.

63 Ryan, *Race and Nationalism*, 280.

64 Colin Palmer, "Identity, Race, and Black Power in Independent Jamaica," in Franklin Knight and Colin Palmer, eds., *The Modern Caribbean* (Chapel Hill: University of North Carolina Press, 1989), 119.

65 British High Commissioner to Foreign and Commonwealth Office, May 29, 1970, FCO 63/594.

66 British High Commissioner, Port of Spain, to Foreign and Commonwealth Office, May 29, 1970, FCO 63/594.

67 Brian Meeks, "The 1970 Revolution: Chronology and Documentation," in Selwyn Ryan and Taimoon Stewart, eds., *The Black Power Revolution of 1970: A Retrospective* (St. Augustine, Trinidad: I.S.E.R., 1995), 140.

68 Ibid., 159.

69 "Black Power in Trinidad and Elsewhere in the Caribbean," April 27, 1970, FCO 63/593.

70 British High Commissioner, Tanganyika, to Foreign Office, March 16, 1964, FO 371/173688.

71 British Ambassador, Ethiopia, to Foreign Office, March 29, 1964, FO 31/178524.

72 British High Commissioner to Foreign and Commonwealth Office, June 26, 1970, FCO 63/594. Robinson never admitted to any involvement in a conspiracy to remove Williams from office, and there was no smoking gun. On June 26 the high commissioner reported that an informant had told him that had the military coup succeeded, Stokely Carmichael was to be the new prime minister and Cabinet posts would be offered to A. N. R. Robinson, Geddes Granger, and George Weekes. This may have been a wild fantasy.

73 In a report to the Foreign and Commonwealth Office that he wrote on May 29, 1970, the high commissioner speculated that the "mutineers of 21 April would "very likely" have installed Robinson as prime minister. He was worried, however, that if Robinson became prime minister, "we [whites?] should all need to watch out, though if he did so constitutionally, the transition would not necessarily be an occasion for violence." Richard Hunt to T. R. M.. Sewell, May 29, 1970, FCO 63/594.

74 EW to Erica Williams, April 13–14, 1970, in the author's possession.

75 I thank Clare Newstead for helping me understand the allusion to George Brown. I am also very indebted to Erica Williams Connel for allowing me to use selected excerpts from her father's letters, which remain a part of her private collection.

76 EW to Erica Williams, April 18, 1970, in the author's possession.

77 Ibid., April 13–14, 1970.

78 Ibid., April 18, 1970.

79 Ibid.

80 Ibid., April 14, 1970.

81 Ibid., April 18, 1970.

82 Ibid.

83 British High Commissioner to Foreign and Commonwealth Office, April 17, 1970, FCO 63/594.

84 "Acute Emergency in Trinidad," R. C. C. Hunt to Foreign and Commonwealth Office, July 27, 1970, FCO 63/594.

85 British High Commissioner to Foreign and Commonwealth Office, April 29, 1970, FCO 63/594.

86 "Black Power Disturbances," British High Commissioner to Foreign and Commonwealth Office, April 25, 1970, FCO 63/593; Record of call by Brigadier Serrette on the British High Commissioner, June 5, 1970, FCO 63/594.

87 U.S. Embassy, Port of Spain, to U.S. Department of State, July 31, 1970, Central Foreign Policy Files, Trinidad and Tobago, Political 23-9, NA-DS, box 2631.

88 R. C. C. Hunt to Foreign and Commonwealth Office, April 29, 1970, FCO 63/594.

89 U.S. Embassy, Port of Spain, to U.S. Department of State, April 30, 1970, Central Foreign Policy Files, Trinidad and Tobago, Political 23-9, NA-DS, box 2631.

90 British High Commissioner to Foreign and Commonwealth Office, April 26, 1970, FCO 63/593.

91 British High Commissioner to Foreign and Commonwealth Office, April 22, 1970, FCO 63/591.

92 "Extract from Cabinet Minutes, Held 23/4/1970," FCO 63/593.

93 Ibid.

94 Harold Wilson to EW, April 21, 1970, FCO 63/591.

95 Acting British High Commissioner, Port of Spain, to Foreign and Commonwealth Office, April 20, 1970, PREM 13/3530. In the 1960s Williams had opposed Biafra's secession from Nigeria, a position the British government welcomed.

96 British Ambassador, Washington, D.C., to Foreign and Commonwealth Office, April 22, 1970, FCO 63/591.

97 Ibid.; Central Foreign Policy Files, Trinidad and Tobago, Political 23-9, Intelligence Note, April 22, 1970, NA-DS, box 2631.

98 British Embassy, Caracas, to Foreign and Commonwealth Office, August 28, 1970, FCO 63/594; U.S. Embassy, Port of Spain, to U.S. Department of State, July 31, 1970, Central Foreign Policy Files, Trinidad and Tobago, Political 23-9, NA-DS, box 2631.

99 British High Commissioner, Guyana, to Colonial Office, April 22, 1970, CO 1031/2580.

100 Acting British High Commissioner, Port of Spain, to Foreign and Commonwealth Office, April 22, 1970, FCO 63/591.

101 M. J. Moynihan to E. L. Sykes, August 29, 1964, DO 200/171.

102 Michael Field, "Black Power Turns on Negro Rulers," *Daily Telegraph*, March 3, 1970.

103 Prime Minister's Broadcast on National Reconstruction, June 30, 1970, FCO 63/600; R. C. C. Hunt to T. R. M. Sewell, May 15, 1970, FCO 63/594.

104 "Black Power in Trinidad and Elsewhere in the Caribbean," April 27, 1970, FCO 63/593.

PRIMARY SOURCES

This study is based almost entirely on manuscript sources located in St. Augustine, Trinidad; London; and College Park, Maryland. I consulted the papers housed in the Eric Williams Memorial Collection at the University of the West Indies, St. Augustine, Trinidad. The manuscripts found in the Public Record Office, London, were particularly valuable since they contain the reports from the High Commission in Port of Spain and Eric Williams's communications with British officials. The National Archives in Maryland provided important sources on the relationships between the government of Trinidad and Tobago and the United States.

Manuscript and Archival Material
Eric Williams Memorial Collection, University of the West Indies, St. Augustine, Trinidad
    Volumes 005, 007, 008, 015, 016, 028, 123, 139, 451, 550, 635, 637, 638, 644, 648, 663, 668, 671, 736, 739, 740, 741, 783, 813, 1339, 1380, and 1636
National Archives of the United States, College Park, Maryland
    Department of State, Record Group 59, Decimal File, and Intelligence Reports
Public Record Office, London
    General Political Correspondence of the Foreign Office
    Records of the Colonial Office, Commonwealth and Foreign and Commonwealth Offices
    Records of the Dominions Office and of the Commonwealth Relations and Foreign and Commonwealth Offices
    Records of the Foreign and Commonwealth Office and Predecessors
    Records of the Prime Minister's Office
Southern Historical Collection, University of North Carolina, Chapel Hill

Newspapers
Caribbean Issues   Nation
Daily Gleaner (Jamaica)   Star
Daily Telegraph   Statesman
London Times   Trinidad Guardian

Published Sources

Cudjoe, Selwyn, ed. *Eric E. Williams Speaks: Essays on Colonialism and Independence.*
Wellesley, Mass.: Calaloux Publications, Amherst, distributed by University of
Massachusetts Press, 1993.

Legislative Council Debates: Trinidad and Tobago, Vol. 8, October 25, 1957 to June 24, 1958.
Trinidad: Government Printing Office, 1959.

Sutton, Paul. *Forged from the Love of Liberty: Selected Speeches of Dr. Eric Williams.* Port of
Spain: Longman Caribbean, 1981.

Trinidad and Tobago Debates of the House of Representatives. Vol. 3, 1963. Trinidad:
Government Printery, 1969.

Williams, Eric. *British Historians and the West Indies.* 1964. New York: Charles
Scribner's Sons, 1966.

———. *Capitalism and Slavery.* 1944. Reprint, Chapel Hill: University of North Carolina
Press, 1994.

———. *The Economics of Nationhood.* Port of Spain: PNM Publishing Co., 1959.

———. *Education in the British West Indies.* 1950. Reprint, Brooklyn, N.Y.: A&B Books
Publishers, 1994.

———. *From Columbus to Castro: The History of the Caribbean, 1492–1969.* London: Andre
Deutsch, 1970.

———. *The History of the Peoples of Trinidad and Tobago.* London: Andre Deutsch, 1962.

———. *International Perspectives for Trinidad and Tobago.* Pamphlet. Office of the Prime
Minister, Port of Spain, 1964.

———. *Inward Hunger: The Education of a Prime Minister.* London: Andre Deutsch, 1969.

———. *The Negro in the Caribbean.* 1942. Reprint, Brooklyn, N.Y.: A&B Books
Publishers, 1994.

———, ed. *Documents of West Indian History, Vol. 1, 1492–1655: From the Spanish Discovery
to the British Conquest of Jamaica.* Port of Spain: PNM Publishing Co., 1963.

Williams, Eric, and E. Franklin Frazier, eds., *The Economic Future of the Caribbean.*
Dover, Mass.: Majority Press, 2004.

SELECTED SECONDARY SOURCES

Ayearst, Morley. *The British West Indies: The Search for Self-Government.* New York: New
York University Press, 1960.

Baldwin, David A. *Economic Development and American Foreign Policy, 1943–1962.*
Chicago: University of Chicago Press, 1966.

Boodhoo, Ken. *The Elusive Eric Williams.* Kingston: Ian Randle Publishers, 2002.

———. *Eric Williams: The Man and the Leader.* Lanham, Md.: University Press of
America, 1986.

Brereton, Bridget. *A History of Modern Trinidad, 1783–1962.* Kingston: Heinemann,
1981.

———. *Race Relations in Colonial Trinidad, 1870–1900.* Cambridge: Cambridge
University Press, 1979.

Carrington, Selwyn H. H. "Capitalism and Slavery and Caribbean Historiography: An Evaluation." *Journal of African American History* 88, no. 3 (Summer 2003): 304–12.

Cateau, Heather, and S. H. H. Carrington, eds. *Capitalism and Slavery Fifty Years Later: Eric Eustace Williams: A Reassessment of the Man and His Work.* New York: Peter Lang, 2000.

Coupland, Reginald. *The British Anti-Slavery Movement.* 2nd ed. London: F. Cass, 1964.

Desoran, Ramesh. *Eric Williams: The Man, His Ideas, and His Politics: A Study of Political Power.* Port of Spain: Signum Publishing Co., Ltd., 1981.

Drescher, Seymour. "Eric Williams: British Capitalism and British Slavery." *History and Theory* 26, no. 2 (1987): 179–96.

Esedebe, P. Olisanwuche. *Pan Africanism: The Idea and Movement, 1776–1963.* Washington, D.C.: Howard University Press, 1982.

Farnie, D. A. "The Commercial Empire of the Atlantic, 1607–1783." *Economic History Review,* 2nd ser., 15 (1962): 205–18.

Fraser, Cary. *Ambivalent Anti-Colonialism: The United States and the Genesis of West Indian Independence, 1940–1964.* Westport, Conn.: Greenwood Press, 1994.

Gaspar, David. "They 'Could Never Have Too Much of My Work': Eric Williams and the Journal of Negro History, 1940–1945." *Journal of African American History* 88, no. 3 (Summer 2003): 291–303.

Gosine, Mahin. *East Indians and Black Power in the Caribbean: The Case of Trinidad.* New York: Africana Research Publications, 1986.

Greene, Lorenzo. Book review. *Negro College Quarterly* 3, no. 1 (March 1945): 46–48.

Horne, Gerald. *Ferdinand Smith, the National Maritime Union, and Jamaican Labor Radicalism.* New York: New York University Press, forthcoming.

Jagan, Cheddi. *The West on Trial: My Fight for Guyana's Freedom.* London: Michael Joseph, 1966.

James, C. L. R. *Beyond a Boundary.* New York: Pantheon Books, 1983.

———. *A Convention Appraisal, Dr. Eric Williams: A Biographical Sketch.* Port of Spain: PNM Publishing Co., 1960.

Knight, Franklin W., and Colin A. Palmer, eds. *The Modern Caribbean.* Chapel Hill: University of North Carolina Press, 1989.

Locke, Alain. Foreword to Eric Williams, *The Negro in the Caribbean.* 1942. Reprint, Brooklyn, N.Y.: A&B Books Publishers, 1994.

Mahabir, Winston. *In and Out of Politics: Tales of the Government of Dr. Eric Williams from the Notebooks of a Former Minister.* Port of Spain: Imprint Caribbean, Ltd., 1975.

Manderson-Jones, R. B. *Jamaican Foreign Policy in the Caribbean, 1962–1988.* Kingston: Caricom Publishers, Ltd., 1990.

Martin, Tony. "Eric Williams and the Anglo-American Caribbean Commission: Trinidad's Future Nationalist Leader as Aspiring Imperial Bureaucrat, 1942–1944." *Journal of African American History* 88, no. 3 (Summer 2003): 274–90.

———. *Race First: The Ideological and Organizational Struggles of Marcus Garvey and the Universal Negro Improvement Association.* Westport, Conn.: Greenwood Press, 1976.

Meeks, Brian. "The 1970 Revolution: Chronology and Documentation." In Selwyn

Ryan and Taimoon Stewart, eds., *The Black Power Revolution of 1970*, 135–75. St. Augustine: Multimedia Production Centre, 1995.

Millette, James. *The Genesis of Crown Colony Government: Trinidad, 1783–1810*. Curepe, Trinidad: Moko Enterprises, 1970.

Mordecai, John. *The West Indies: The Federal Negotiations*. London: Allen and Unwin, 1968.

Monroe, Trevor. *The Politics of Constitutional Decolonisation: Jamaica, 1944–1962*. Jamaica: University of the West Indies, 1984.

Oxaal, Ivar. *Black Intellectuals Come to Power: The Rise of Creole Nationalism in Trinidad and Tobago*. Cambridge, Mass.: Schenkman, 1968.

———. *Black Intellectuals and the Dilemmas of Race and Class in Trinidad*. Cambridge, Mass: Schenkman, 1982.

Pemberton, Rita, and Brinsley Samaroo, eds. *Eric Williams: Images of His Life, Volumes 1 and 2, Journal of Caribbean Issues*. Special ed. St. Augustine, Trinidad: School of Continuing Education, University of the West Indies, March 1998, March 1999.

Ryan, Selwyn D. *Race and Nationalism in Trinidad and Tobago: A Study of Decolonisation in a Multiracial Society*. Toronto: University of Toronto Press, 1972.

Ryan, Selwyn, and Taimoon Stewart, eds. *The Black Power Revolution of 1970: A Retrospective*. St. Augustine, Trinidad: Institute of Social and Economic Research, University of the West Indies, 1995.

Samaroo, Brinsley. "The Race Factor in the Independence Discussions at Marlborough House, 1962." *Caribbean Issues* 8, no. 1 (March 1998): 119–35.

Singh, Kelvin. *Race and Class Struggles in a Colonial State: Trinidad, 1917–1945*. Calgary, Canada: University of Calgary Press, 1994.

Solomon, Patrick. *An Autobiography*. Port of Spain: Imprint Caribbean, 1981.

Solow, Barbara L., and Stanley L. Engerman, eds. *British Capitalism and Caribbean Slavery: The Legacy of Eric Williams*. Cambridge: Cambridge University Press, 1987.

Tannenbaum, Frank. Book review. *Political Science Quarterly* 61 (1946): 247–53.

Woodson, Carter J. Book review. *Journal of Negro History* 30 (1945): 93–95.